# PRAISE FOR CARLTON STOWERS'

## *OPEN SECRETS*

"OPEN SECRETS is one of the most remarkable true crime books I've ever read. Every answer leads to a question; this is murder in the house of mirrors. Carlton Stowers is brilliant as he peels away the layers of a truly fascinating killer—and of the dedicated detective who finally discovered the 'mirror' with the real reflection. . . . It held me captive to the last page!"

—Ann Rule

"Treading in the footsteps of Texas crime writers Tommy Thompson and Mike Cochran . . . Carlton Stowers uses Morris McGowan as the steady eye in an ever-faster-spinning vortex of greed, crime, sex, and attempted suicide. Stowers draws chilling profiles . . . takes us on a nerve-racking police stakeout and a flight across the United States, into Canada, Mexico and finally to France. . . . OPEN SECRETS gives us the perfect opportunity to see a fine crime writer at his work."

—William D. Benge, *Fort Worth Star-Telegram*

"Filled with more twists, surprises, and suspicious characters than even the most fertile imaginations could concoct. . . . This is a difficult book to put down. . . . For true crime aficionados, OPEN SECRETS is a must read."

—Glenda Eckert, *Tulsa World*

**Books by Carlton Stowers**

Careless Whispers
Innocence Lost
Open Secrets

Published by POCKET BOOKS

# OPEN Secrets

## A TRUE STORY OF LOVE, JEALOUSY AND MURDER

# Carlton Stowers

**POCKET BOOKS**

New York   London   Toronto   Sydney   Tokyo   Singapore

POCKET BOOKS, a division of Simon & Schuster Inc.
1230 Avenue of the Americas, New York, NY 10020

ISBN: 0-671-70997-6

First Pocket Books paperback printing October 1995

10  9  8  7  6  5  4  3  2  1

POCKET and colophon are registered trademarks of
Simon & Schuster Inc.

Cover art by Tristan Elwell

Printed in the U.S.A.

*For Pat,*

*who insisted there was a light at
the end of this long, dark tunnel*

# Acknowledgments

IN KINDER MOMENTS during the three years of writing this book, I came to refer to it as my "Tour of the World's Legal Systems." Never, in my wildest dreams, did it occur to me when I decided to undertake the telling of a story that began less than an hour's drive from my front door that I would become a world traveler and struggling student of every branch of law enforcement this side of Scotland Yard before the task was completed.

Tracking the story from its beginning to end placed me in contact with the Richardson (Tex.) Police Department, sheriff's departments in Dallas and Kaufman counties, the Dallas County district attorney's office, U.S. marshals, FBI, State Department, Border Patrol, Royal Canadian Mounted Police, U.S. Customs, the Justice Department, Interpol, the Nice (France) Police Department, state and federal judges, and legal attachés in Mexico and France. I sat in on criminal trials and civil hearings, dug through records in courthouses on two continents, and became acquainted with enough attorneys, investigators, judges, justices of the peace, jailers, bailiffs, and court reporters to cast a big-screen movie.

If ever we should decide to hold a reunion, it will require hiring of a hall something along the size of the Astrodome.

That everyone is not specifically mentioned by name does not make my gratitude any less nor their input of smaller value. In fact, a number of helpful people asked that their names be kept private. I've honored that request but wish to thank them just the same.

Still, I would be woefully remiss if I did not specifically mention the assistance, interest, and kindness of certain indi-

# Acknowledgments

viduals—people who shared private agonies and frustrations, anger and hope, insight and expertise—who not only made my task easier but, quite honestly, possible.

Since the case began with the Richardson Police Department, so shall this catalog of salutes.

During my research, I watched Morris McGowan advance from the rank of sergeant to lieutenant and, most recently, to captain. The advancements are but small measure of the dedication he brought to his quest to solve the murder of Rozanne Gailiunas. Very honestly, without his willingness to help, this book would never have been written. That his wife, Sandy, warmly welcomed an intruding journalist is also appreciated more than she likely knows.

It is noteworthy, I think, that during our discussions, McGowan was always quick to give credit to those fellow officers who played roles, large and small, in the investigation. And just as they made his job easier, so did these make mine: Chief Kenneth Yarbrough, Deputy Chief Mike Leyman, Detectives Ken MacKenzie and Brent Tourangeau, Lt. Mike Corley, Capt. D. E. Golden, Investigators Ken Roberts and Wayne Dobbs, Detention Officer Alicia Sheppard, Investigator Ron Graham, Sergeants Glenn Hindman, Mike Sandlin, Melody Acord, and Rhonda Bonner, and Officers Richard Gross, J. E. Jackson, Jonathan May, Cynthia Percival, and Randy Smith.

And a special debt is owed Detective Huy Decloedt of the Nice Police Department, who took the time to lead a stranger by the hand.

Thanks, also, to Matt Chapman and Allen Ringgold of the FBI and Mike Johnson, Everett Kelly, Barry Moore, and Nyda Budig of the State Department.

Kevin Chapman, Dan Hagood, and Jim Oatman of the district attorney's office and U.S. Attorneys Candina Heath, Rose Romero, and Randy Fluke found time in their hectic schedules to answer just one more question.

And while this is the story of a police investigation, a marathon search for truth and justice, it is also one of people whose lives were forever altered by one brutal, senseless act commit-

# Acknowledgments

viduals—people who shared private agonies and frustrations, anger and hope, insight and expertise—who not only made my task easier but, quite honestly, possible.

Since the case began with the Richardson Police Department, so shall this catalog of salutes.

During my research, I watched Morris McGowan advance from the rank of sergeant to lieutenant and, most recently, to captain. The advancements are but small measure of the dedication he brought to his quest to solve the murder of Rozanne Gailiunas. Very honestly, without his willingness to help, this book would never have been written. That his wife, Sandy, warmly welcomed an intruding journalist is also appreciated more than she likely knows.

It is noteworthy, I think, that during our discussions, McGowan was always quick to give credit to those fellow officers who played roles, large and small, in the investigation. And just as they made his job easier, so did these make mine: Chief Kenneth Yarbrough, Deputy Chief Mike Leyman, Detectives Ken MacKenzie and Brent Tourangeau, Lt. Mike Corley, Capt. D. E. Golden, Investigators Ken Roberts and Wayne Dobbs, Detention Officer Alicia Sheppard, Investigator Ron Graham, Sergeants Glenn Hindman, Mike Sandlin, Melody Acord, and Rhonda Bonner, and Officers Richard Gross, J. E. Jackson, Jonathan May, Cynthia Percival, and Randy Smith.

And a special debt is owed Detective Huy Decloedt of the Nice Police Department, who took the time to lead a stranger by the hand.

Thanks, also, to Matt Chapman and Allen Ringgold of the FBI and Mike Johnson, Everett Kelly, Barry Moore, and Nyda Budig of the State Department.

Kevin Chapman, Dan Hagood, and Jim Oatman of the district attorney's office and U.S. Attorneys Candina Heath, Rose Romero, and Randy Fluke found time in their hectic schedules to answer just one more question.

And while this is the story of a police investigation, a marathon search for truth and justice, it is also one of people whose lives were forever altered by one brutal, senseless act commit-

# Acknowledgments

IN KINDER MOMENTS during the three years of writing this book, I came to refer to it as my "Tour of the World's Legal Systems." Never, in my wildest dreams, did it occur to me when I decided to undertake the telling of a story that began less than an hour's drive from my front door that I would become a world traveler and struggling student of every branch of law enforcement this side of Scotland Yard before the task was completed.

Tracking the story from its beginning to end placed me in contact with the Richardson (Tex.) Police Department, sheriff's departments in Dallas and Kaufman counties, the Dallas County district attorney's office, U.S. marshals, FBI, State Department, Border Patrol, Royal Canadian Mounted Police, U.S. Customs, the Justice Department, Interpol, the Nice (France) Police Department, state and federal judges, and legal attachés in Mexico and France. I sat in on criminal trials and civil hearings, dug through records in courthouses on two continents, and became acquainted with enough attorneys, investigators, judges, justices of the peace, jailers, bailiffs, and court reporters to cast a big-screen movie.

If ever we should decide to hold a reunion, it will require hiring of a hall something along the size of the Astrodome.

That everyone is not specifically mentioned by name does not make my gratitude any less nor their input of smaller value. In fact, a number of helpful people asked that their names be kept private. I've honored that request but wish to thank them just the same.

Still, I would be woefully remiss if I did not specifically mention the assistance, interest, and kindness of certain indi-

# Acknowledgments

ted on an October afternoon a decade ago. For many, the story is still not over. In truth, it is not likely ever to be.

For their time and candor, I am particularly indebted to Mike Wilson and to Dr. Peter Gailiunas, Jr., his wife, Pat, son, Peter III, and his mother, Kay. Henry and Angela Agostinelli, Steve and Paula Donahue, Frank Joyce, Carol Garland, Don and Maggie Kennedy, George and JoAnn Hopper, Doris Wilson, Victoria Wilson, and Joe Sylvan were most helpful, as were lawyers Peter Lesser, Lawrence Mitchell, Jean Bauer, Tom Mills, Chris Milner, Carl Gaines, Brett Stalcup, Doug Mulder, Curtis Glover, Brad Lollar, Bill Neal, John Barr, King Solomon, Michael Byck, Jim Moore, and Russ Hendricks.

It is always helpful having fellow journalists with whom to compare notes. Pete Slover and Tracy Everbach of the *Dallas Morning News* were good courtroom companions, and Howard Swindle and Anne Belli of the *News* were generous with their willingness to lend a hand when needed. The hospitality of *Paris Match*'s Chris Laffaille and Arnaud Bizot as well as that of *France-Soir* reporter William Assayag was most welcomed. A long-distance thanks also goes to Jerry Prillaman, press attaché at the U.S. embassy in Paris and *Los Angeles Times* Paris bureau chief Rhone Tempest. Jack Breslin of "America's Most Wanted" patiently answered questions, and Steve Pate pointed the way to valuable information.

An appreciative nod is also due those photographers whose names accompany the pictures inside.

The insight of Dr. Robert Powitzky was especially beneficial as was the help of Gray Cardinale of the Mansfield Jail, Sgt. Howard Taylor and Deputy Max Chester of the Dallas County Sheriff's Department, paramedic Bill Dugan, and former U.S. marshal Don Thompson.

State district judges Pat McDowell and Jan Hemphill, and U.S. district judge A. Joe Fish kindly lent understanding to the workings of the judicial system. Court reporter Pam Smith was also most helpful.

And Ann Harper of Presbyterian Hospital helped track down needed information.

For well-timed words of encouragement during the oft-rocky

# Acknowledgments

road this project traveled, special and sincere thanks are also due Jane Chelius, Dudley Frasier, Jennifer Miller, and Dan Witt.

And no book can boast a greater champion than Janet Wilkens Manus, a magnificent lady who goes far beyond the duties of literary agent. The counsel of her husband, Justin Manus, also proved invaluable.

Finally, a word of explanation. All occurrences and conversations in the book are based on court and police records, personal observations, and the recollection of parties involved. In some instances, dialogue has been re-created but is as close to exact as the memories of my sources permit.

In the interest of fairness, the names and occupations of certain minor characters—people in no way directly involved in any of the crimes—have been changed. They are: Darla Green, Lonnie Fielding, Lydia Montoya, Dominique Margot, Deena Lampley, Blythe Dobbins, Morgan Holmes, Billy Ray Newsome, Danny and Janie Colson, Calvin (Cal) Hobson, Don and Wanda Price, and Lynda Whittaker. Any similarity between the fictitious names used and those of living persons is entirely coincidental.

Throughout my information gathering, there was always but one goal: the true telling of the story.

—Carlton Stowers

xii

# PART ONE

---

# Murder

Death cancels everything but truth.
　　　　　　　　—Anonymous

# 1

Fall had begrudgingly begun to make its presence felt on that late Tuesday afternoon of October 4, 1983. Though the day-time temperatures remained almost summerlike, the lawns in the Dallas suburb of Richardson had turned to rust brown and the trees were bare, their naked branches now casting only tangled shadows where once they had provided a canopy of shade.

Along Loganwood Drive, a short street of small, modest homes, most of them at least a quarter century old, the rainbow of flowers that had brightened the neighborhood yards in previous months bloomed no more, a sure signal that winter was on its way.

For Detective Morris McGowan and his partner Mike Corley, assigned to the three-P.M.-to-midnight shift, the fast-cooling evenings were a welcome respite from the ninety-degree temperatures that traditionally lingered late into the north-Texas summer nights.

Each working separate robbery cases, they had been en route to conduct follow-up interviews with witnesses when the dispatcher's voice crackled from the car radio. Fire department paramedics were on their way to 804 Loganwood Drive. "We have an injured-person report," the dispatcher said, "circumstances unknown. No need to respond at this time."

McGowan, at the wheel of the unmarked Richardson Police Department car, glanced over at his partner. "Maybe we ought to check it out," he said. Corley argued briefly, suggesting they continue on to their planned destination, until a second dispatch came over the radio: "Gunshot victim at Loganwood address."

It was a few minutes past six as they sped through the remnants of northbound rush-hour traffic. Having once lived in that section of Richardson, McGowan knew the less-traveled short-

3

cuts and in fifteen minutes was turning onto tree-lined Logan-wood Drive.

Neither officer was prepared for the scene that awaited.

Already the narrow residential street was virtually blocked with emergency vehicles and passersby who had stopped to see what the sudden flurry of activity was about. People stood in their yards, hands shading their eyes from the flashing lights of the ambulance, their silent attention focused on the small frame and brown-brick house. White-clad paramedics, life-saving equipment in hand, raced in and out the front door, and residents were running back and forth across the street, carrying bits of information about what was taking place.

McGowan managed to drive only a short way down the street before pulling to the curb. For a split second he sat behind the steering wheel, taking in the circus-like atmosphere of the scene in front of him. ''Jesus,'' he whispered as he climbed from the car and began walking hurriedly in the direction of the ambulance, his partner quickstepping at his side.

Seeing that no victim had yet been placed into the ambulance, McGowan was walking up the driveway when the screen door of the house burst open and paramedics emerged, steering a gurney.

Walking ahead of the stretcher was Richardson police officer John May, who had been patrolling in the area and had arrived at the scene just minutes after the fire department paramedics. Seeing McGowan, he hurried to him. ''We've got a woman who's been shot. Rozanne Gailiunas. White. Probably in her early thirties. It looks pretty bad.''

McGowan walked toward the gurney, signaling the paramedics to stop. ''I want to see her,'' he said.

Lying beneath a sheet was a dark-haired woman, her once-pretty face badly swollen, dark eyes glazed and lifeless, her black hair matted with blood. The officer did not need to be told that she had suffered a gunshot wound to the head.

As he stood by the gurney, McGowan's attention was drawn to movement near the front door. A young boy, crying and screaming, ran across the front yard in the direction of a man who stood near the curb.

4

Turning to May, McGowan did not even get the question out before it was answered. "That's the lady's son," the officer said. "He was apparently here when it happened."

McGowan said nothing as he watched the child all but disappear into the arms of the tall, lanky man to whom he'd run. Despite the cool evening breeze that had suddenly swept across the neighborhood, McGowan realized that he was sweating profusely. Glancing first in the direction of the ambulance where the gurney was being loaded, then back toward the fragile, crying child, McGowan, taking charge of the scene, issued his first orders. He instructed John May to get into the ambulance and accompany the victim to the nearby Presbyterian Hospital emergency room: "Don't leave her side. If she comes to and has something to say, I want you to be there to hear it."

Then, in a voice filled with a sudden rage, he yelled out to several officers who had just arrived, "Let's get the kid out of here . . . now."

Already, Morris McGowan, a man who had been visiting the scenes of violent crime much of his adult life, had violated one of the cardinal rules of homicide investigations. The image of the frightened young boy, all but overlooked as he trailed his wounded mother's body from the house, had stirred a racing mixture of emotions unlike any he'd ever felt before.

As he watched the man walk quickly toward him, carrying the sobbing boy, McGowan felt his body stiffen and his jaws tighten.

"What's happening here?" the man yelled.

McGowan studied the bespectacled figure as he approached, waiting until he was just a few feet away before replying. "Sir, who are you?"

"I'm Dr. Peter Gailiunas, her husband." He glanced in the direction of the ambulance. "I'd like to get my son, Peter, away from all this. My mother is sitting over there in my car and can take him home with her."

In time, McGowan knew, the youngster would have to be questioned, but not until other more pressing matters were attended to. "Fine," he said, "but we'll need for you to stay around."

The doctor nodded, turning to take his son to the car as McGowan nodded to his partner. "Talk to the guy," he told Corley.

As the ambulance pulled away, the high-pitched whine of its siren drowning all other sounds on the block, McGowan turned toward the house and walked in the direction of grim-faced Officer Wayne Dobbs, who stood guarding the doorway.

"The back bedroom," Dobbs said, shaking his head. His terse message was clear: what awaited McGowan inside was something cruel and ugly.

As was his practice, he wanted to enter the crime scene alone.

Slowly, methodically, he walked through the house, moving from the small living room into the dining room, then to the kitchen. Entering the hallway, he stopped briefly to look in on what was obviously the child's room, then continued toward the master bedroom at the back of the house.

At the open doorway he stopped, arms folded, and let his eyes roam the crime scene. Blood stained the pillows and bed-sheets. On three of the cornerposts hung lengths of the cotton rope that had been cut away from the victim's wrist and ankles. Stained yellow tissue lay near a pillow through which two shots had been fired. A stocking was draped across one of the pillows and a blue robe lay across the foot of the bed. On the floor, near a pair of sandals, was a pool of vomit. Nearby was a multicolored belt that no doubt matched one of the dresses hanging in the open closet. The residue of violence was almost tangible, its cloying smells invading the officer's nostrils. Several minutes passed before he stepped into the room.

Throughout the room, evidence of a normal, routine life provided a bizarre contrast to the scene that had been played out here. An ironing board was set up in one corner, the iron plugged in and ready for use. On one corner of the vanity, clothing—jeans, bra, panties, and a plaid, long-sleeved shirt—had been neatly rolled into a bundle. There was an open jewelry box, a purse, a stack of papers, a pack of cigarettes, and an ashtray. On a small nightstand was a framed photograph of a lovely, smiling woman, a happy-looking young boy posing with her.

McGowan studied the picture for several seconds, mentally comparing the faces to those he had seen minutes earlier, one grotesquely misshaped by a gunman's handiwork, the other frightened and lost.

Burying his hands in the pockets of his pants, he turned and walked quickly out of the house. This, he instinctively knew, would be no ordinary investigation. Already, questions were forming within questions.

Outside, Richard Gross, a crime-scene technician, stood waiting, ready to begin his collection of evidence. "Bad, huh?" he said as he saw McGowan appear on the front porch.

"You're going to need some help with this one," the detective replied.

This, he knew, was something totally foreign to the community in which he'd been raised. It would trigger a new kind of fear that was certain to spread rapidly through the streets, violating forever the sense of safety and innocence that had made it such an enviable place to live.

Many of the seventy-five thousand people who called Richardson home had arrived from the North during the rust-belt exodus. Though it would be in Dallas that they earned their paychecks, they had chosen to live here, lured by the outstanding reputation of the public schools, the low crime rate, and the quality of life the suburb offered.

And, it wasn't just the Northerners who had contributed to the community's recent growth. Just a few miles down North Central Expressway, the robbers and rapists, killers and con men, had caused residents of Dallas to retreat to a safer, saner place. Many had chosen Richardson for their escape.

In effect, then, the community was now divided into two parts. Old Richardson was populated by those who had lived there since it was just a country town, not yet part of the population boom along what the real estate phrase-makers had begun referring to as The Golden Corridor.

Then there was the New Richardson, home of the relocated corporate executives and laborers whose jobs in the steel mills, auto plants, and factories had ceased to exist. Joining the Easterners, who were routinely surprised to find modern shopping malls, a symphony orchestra, and a community college instead of cowboys and cattle drives, there were those who had made the short move from Dallas's upper-middle-class neighborhoods to escape the evil ways of the big city.

All—the longtime residents and the newcomers—had one thing in common: they enjoyed the comforting knowledge that they shared a safe environment.

Now, in the wake of this senseless horror and violence, that was certain to change.

Standing in the front yard, McGowan breathed in the fresh night air, his mind racing as he contemplated the myriad tasks to be accomplished: canvasing of the neighborhood, interviews, dusting for fingerprints, collection of evidence, contact with the hospital.

A patrolman soon interrupted his thoughts. "Corley says he needs to see you."

McGowan found his partner near the street, standing next to the doctor. "He wants his lawyer," Corley said, motioning toward Gailiunas.

"What's the problem?" McGowan said, turning to the doctor.

"I just think it best that I have my attorney here before I say anything."

"Fine," McGowan said. "If that's what you want, get on the phone—right now—and get him here."

The detectives watched in silence as Gailiunas, his shoulders slumped and weary, walked toward a house across the street. Though neither mentioned it, they were looking at their first suspect.

Like others in the neighborhood, teenager Paige Billings had been standing, with her mother, watching the growing swirl of activity across the street. Though neither had really gotten to know Rozanne Gailiunas or her son, they had, in recent months, developed a smile-and-wave relationship. Rarely did they see the boy when his mother was not at his side. They had, in fact, agreed that she was clearly a loving, caring, perhaps a bit too cautious, mother.

For that reason, Paige had found it unusual when, arriving home from school shortly after five that afternoon, she had seen the little boy playing by himself in the front yard. She could not remember another time when the child had been allowed outside alone. But when she saw him go back into the house, she had given the matter no additional thought.

Both she and her mother had long since assumed that their neighbor was very likely newly divorced. They had, on several occasions, seen a man—the father, no doubt—stop by to either pick the child up or return him to his mother. It had been just a few weeks earlier, in fact, when Paige had watched the boy run from the man, refusing to get into the car. He had been forced to chase the child to the end of the block.

Now, as the two women stood inside their front door, that same man was walking in their direction.

Stepping up on the porch, the grim-faced doctor did not bother to introduce himself, only stating that there was an emergency and he needed to use their telephone.

"Would you mind," he asked, "leaving the house for a minute while I make a call?"

Shocked by the strange request, the women, sensing the urgency of the situation, nonetheless walked into their front yard, yielding their home to a stranger.

Minutes later, the doctor emerged from the house and walked over to Paige. "I saw you talking with a police officer earlier," he said, an accusing tone to his voice. "You didn't see me here today, did you?"

Scared, the young girl assured him she hadn't.

The doctor nodded and began walking away. Stopping after a few steps, he again turned to the girl. "Whatever you know," he said, "you should probably just keep to yourself."

Moving back across the street, Dr. Gailiunas informed Officer Corley that his attorney, Bill Neal, was on his way.

"When he gets here," Corley said, "we're going to the station."

\* \* \*

With almost thirty officers now on the scene, McGowan was making assignments in rapid-fire fashion. Teams were going door-to-door, in hopes someone might have seen a visitor to the Loganwood address. A search of the backyard and alley was under way. Inside, the evidence technician was at work.

When members of the media began arriving, McGowan huddled briefly with Joe Hanna, the department's public information officer. "The woman's still alive," McGowan said, "and for now I want to keep it that way. Tell them she's under police protection at the hospital." Though he feared it was unlikely the victim would survive to give a statement, he wanted someone, somewhere, to worry that she was at that moment giving details of the attack and a description of her assailant.

As McGowan completed his instructions to Hanna, newly arrived officers David Mankin and Cynthia Percival approached.

"The woman's boyfriend is here," Mankin said.

McGowan made no attempt to hide his surprise.

"His name's Larry Aylor," Mankin added, motioning in the direction of two men, one who appeared to be in his forties, the other considerably older, standing on the far edge of the front yard. "That's his father with him."

Christ, McGowan thought to himself, what the hell is everyone doing bringing momma and daddy with them? And why hadn't someone told him there was a husband *and* a boyfriend?

"He said he'd been trying to call her for several hours, and when he couldn't reach her, he decided he'd better come over and check on her," Officer Percival said.

As she spoke, Detective Ken MacKenzie stood nearby. Balding and bookish-looking, he had long since earned a reputation as one of the department's premier investigators and an excellent interrogator. McGowan turned to him: "You've got the boyfriend. Take him to the station and see what he has to say."

MacKenzie was moving in Aylor's direction even before McGowan completed his sentence.

For the next several hours, McGowan juggled the numerous responsibilities of coordinating the crime-scene investigation, checking with the hospital every half hour for updates on the condition of the victim, and contacting the station to see what, if any, progress was being made in the interview rooms.

It was almost one in the morning when he finally left the darkened neighborhood, posting two officers to stand guard at the front and rear entrances of the house for the remainder of the night.

As he made his way onto North Central Expressway, pleased by the lack of late-night traffic, he was surprised that six hours had passed since he and Corley had responded to the dispatcher's call. And as was always the case in the first lull that comes in the initial stages of an investigation, McGowan began replaying the event in his mind. Like a football coach reviewing videotapes of a game always in search of mistakes and poor execution, he had earned a reputation for grading himself harshly. A self-admitted perfectionist, he favored devoting what some of his fellow officers judged an inordinate amount of time to the most minute details of a case. There was always one more question that should have been asked, one more lead, however obscure, that needed to be checked out.

In such investigations, experience had taught him, time was the greatest enemy, forcing a delicate balance of speed and care. Statistics had proved, he knew, that most homicides were solved within forty-eight hours of their occurrence, or not at all.

And despite the fact the woman he'd seen wheeled from the house remained alive, McGowan was already viewing the case as a homicide.

Then, in the final miles before reaching the police station, his mind turned to the little he had learned about the victim. Rozanne Gailiunas was thirty-three years old, a registered nurse, and had lived at the Loganwood address since her June separation from her husband. And she was the mother of a four-year-old son.

Of all the disturbing aspects of the case, the images of the child being in the house as the brutal crime was committed and the look of terror and confusion as he followed the gurney bearing his unconscious mother into the front yard weighed heaviest on the officer.

As if attempting to wipe the scenes from his mind, McGowan pushed his boot to the accelerator, anxious to get to his office, where work could resume.

Inside the Richardson Police Department, officers sat at their desks, styrofoam cups of coffee at hand, compiling reports on their activities.

McGowan did not even make it to his office before the dispatcher called out to him, "I just took a call from the fire station, and they say there's some guy over there who's telling them he knows who shot the lady."

"Who is it?"

"They didn't say."

McGowan looked quickly around the squad room, then sent Detective Dennis Moeller next door to the fire station.

In just a few minutes he had an explanation: Larry Aylor's father, having accompanied his son to the station, had grown restless waiting for the interview to end and had gone outside for some fresh air. Seeing one of the paramedics who had been at the scene, he had walked over to the adjacent fire station and struck up a conversation.

He was, he told the paramedic, sure that the doctor was responsible for the shooting.

"Where'd he get that idea?" McGowan asked.

"From his son."

The detective smiled for the first time in hours, shook his head, and dialed the number of Presbyterian Hospital. Rozanne Gailiunas was out of surgery, Richardson P.D. investigator Ken Roberts reported, but there appeared to be little chance of her regaining consciousness. Though doctors refused to provide him with much information, he had overheard one of the nurses explaining to a caller that the patient had been placed on a life-support system.

The call, the nurse confided, had come from a woman who had identified herself as Mrs. Gailiunas's sister.

Among the messages piling up on McGowan's desk were notes that Rozanne's father and sister in Massachusetts had phoned the station several times, seeking information. As

McGowan prepared to dial their number, Detective Corley, having left the interview room where he had been talking with Dr. Gailiunas, entered the office and shut the door.

Though tired, he had a look of excitement on his face. "I've got the guy who did this," he said. "I'm sure of it. He and the woman have been separated for a while, and I don't think he's been too happy about it."

"Does he say what he was doing this afternoon?" McGowan asked.

"Some meetings, a seminar or something. Then, late in the afternoon he shuts his door and takes a forty-five-minute nap . . . at his desk."

McGowan leaned back in his chair, wearily rubbing his face. "Shit, I've fallen asleep at my desk before . . . I could probably do it right now . . . but damn sure not for any forty-five minutes."

Corley nodded his agreement, then continued. Earlier in the evening, the detective said, he'd had the doctor's son brought to the station. "We tried to talk to him, see what he might have seen or heard, but he was so damn hyperactive, bouncing around like a Ping-Pong ball, that we weren't getting anywhere. When he did talk, he was stuttering so badly it was difficult to understand him. All he'd say was that 'the Cookie Monster' did it."

It was a moment before McGowan, his own children now grown, recalled that "Sesame Street," the children's show popular with youngsters the age of the Gailiunas boy, featured a character by that name.

"So finally I took him into the room with his father, hoping he could settle him down and help us out," Corley continued. "The first thing the doctor does is ask the kid if there had been anyone else at the house during the afternoon. The little boy looks at him kinda funny and says, 'You were.' I'm telling you, this is our guy."

Even as the detective spoke, McGowan was mentally adding another item to his list of things that had to be done. "Get in touch with someone in the DA's office and Child Welfare," he said. If, in fact, the doctor was responsible for what had taken place, it would be necessary to place the child in protective custody immediately.

As soon as Corley left, Detective MacKenzie appeared in the doorway.

"How are you and the boyfriend getting along?" McGowan asked.

"I think this Aylor guy did it."

"Why?"

"The first thing he does when we get here is call his attorney. Then, when I try to pin him down about where he was at the time we figure the shooting took place, he starts telling me this wild story about how he was out in his neighborhood, riding a bike, when some old lady—or, he says, maybe it was a man dressed like an old lady—tries to run him off the road and kill him.

"And, another thing."

"What's that?"

"He admits that he owns a .25 semiautomatic."

MacKenzie didn't need to remind McGowan that the shell casings, one found at the crime scene, the other in the ambulance after it had fallen from Rozanne's hair en route to the hospital, were that caliber.

McGowan nodded. "You feel pretty strongly about him?"

"I sure do."

"Then stay with him," McGowan said, making no mention of his earlier conversation with Detective Corley.

It was past midnight when a strange gathering assembled in the parking lot outside the Richardson Police Department. Their interviews over, Larry Aylor and Dr. Gailiunas, each accompanied by his lawyer, had finally been released and emerged from the building simultaneously. For a moment the two men, both obviously drained by their interrogations, stood just a few feet apart, looking at each other. The doctor finally said in a breaking, pleading voice, "I swear to God I had nothing to do with this." Larry Aylor, his lips pursed tightly, had no response before his attorney urged him in the direction of his car.

His arm draped over the shoulder of his son, Gailiunas was halfway across the parking lot before he heard Detective Corley call his name.

"Doctor, I'm afraid your son will have to stay with us," the officer explained.

"I don't think so," Gailiunas replied in a voice whose calmness surprised him.

"Sir, we've received an order from the district attorney's office . . ."

"Fuck your order," Dr. Gailiunas replied.

Bill Neal, Gailiunas's attorney, took his client by the arm. "Peter," he said in a calming voice, "leave it alone. We'll take care of it tomorrow."

Holding tightly to his son, the doctor again refused.

"I expected they might do something like this," the lawyer said. "There's nothing we can do about it right now." He explained that young Peter would be placed in the custody of Child Welfare and that legally they could keep him for as long as ten days while the investigation continued. "But we'll start working on it in the morning. I promise you."

With his son at his side, once again crying, the doctor refused to release his grip. A hysterical look twisted across his face. "Fuck it. Nobody's taking this kid away from me."

To gain his client's attention, Bill Neal stood directly in front of Gailiunas, his hands gripping his client's shoulders, and spoke in a firm voice. "We're lucky that they aren't keeping you here. You give them much more of a reason and they're going to throw your ass in jail. So, dammit, shut up and let's leave here while you still can."

Reluctantly, Gailiunas released his son to the detective.

As his attorney drove him toward his home, the doctor fell silent, staring out into the dark night as tears blurred his tired vision. Though fully awake, he was already having nightmares about the trauma awaiting his frightened son at the Dallas Children's Shelter.

From his office, McGowan looked out on a dim, empty squad room. After all the other investigators were gone, he had sat drinking coffee and reading the reports handed over to him until well past three in the morning. Now, with his feet propped on his desk, he was beginning to feel the first wave of exhaustion sweep over him.

His sharpness dulled, he had put the reports aside and tried to reflect on what had happened during the frantic preceding hours.

Paramedic Bill Dugan had said that when he and partner Glenn Moore responded to the call, they had found the front door slightly ajar. After there had been no response to their knocking, they had opened the door to find the four-year-old sitting on the living room sofa, eating a bowl of cereal and watching "Sesame Street" on TV. As they entered the house, the youngster had immediately become upset, insisting they leave. "My daddy doesn't want you here," he had yelled. "He'll beat you up."

When the paramedics asked where his mother was, the boy had only glanced in the direction of the hallway. Even before Dugan and Moore reached the bedroom they had heard the chilling guttural sound of Rozanne Gailiunas's choking.

Finding the victim lying facedown, her head off the edge of the bed, Dugan had cut the bindings from her arm and legs while Moore started an IV and used forceps to remove the tissue lodged in her throat. As the men worked frantically, they realized her chances of survival were not good.

The crime scene, McGowan thought to himself, simply had not made sense. There had been no evidence of a break-in or a burglary. On one hand, the classic elements of a passion crime, a love triangle gone crazy, were in place. But the fact the victim had been bound and gagged suggested the kind of planning that seldom accompanied a scorned lover's sudden rage. Then, there was the cruel fact that the child had been present in the house during the attack. Now the horror had been compounded by his being removed from his father as well.

Too, the actions of Dr. Gailiunas had been troubling. Upon arriving at the scene, his initial concern had been only for his son. According to the report of John May, the first officer Gailiunas had spoken with, he had been extremely anxious to get the boy away from the scene. Only after his son was safely in the company of his grandmother had the doctor asked about his wife. When told she had been shot, the doctor's entire body had begun to shake, and his face contorted in what May had described as a mixture of anger and fear.

What, McGowan wondered, would have prompted that fear? And why the immediate call to an attorney? And the strange remarks made to the young woman across the street?

Then, there was the boyfriend. Larry Aylor, during his interview with MacKenzie, had been quick to point an accusing finger at the doctor. Across the hall, the doctor was suggesting that it was Aylor who was to blame.

With the case only hours old, McGowan already had a discomforting feeling that it was going to be hell to solve if the doctor and boyfriend were, as each insisted, not involved.

Draining the last of the cold coffee from his cup, McGowan wearily got to his feet. It was time to go home, to the warmth and comfort of a world that made sense.

Tomorrow, after he'd had some rest, there would be a great deal to do.

# 2

THERE ARE, IN the investigative process, unwritten rules that most police officers religiously attempt to follow: Distance yourself from the horrors you see, carefully maintaining an almost omnipotent attitude toward the event. By whatever means necessary, do not allow yourself to become emotionally involved.

By remaining separated from the impact of the disquieting violence, it is easier to remain focused, to concentrate on the task at hand. Once personal feelings get in the way, mistakes are invariably made.

It was a philosophy Morris McGowan knew well. And one

he had never been able to embrace. To completely block out the emotions felt at a crime scene such as that he had walked into on Loganwood Drive was at best impossible, at worst the act of a person grown far too callous, too jaded, to still be carrying a badge. A degree of personal involvement, he had long since decided, provided valuable incentive, the special fuel necessary for the long hours and concentrated efforts required to solve crimes.

It was part of the standard speech the forty-two-year-old detective gave to younger officers newly arrived in the Criminal Investigation Division: *When you get into a murder case, there's only one way to work it. The victim isn't someone you don't know or care about. The victim becomes your mother, your sister, your wife, your kid. If you don't believe that, you're never going to really put your heart into your job. You'll never care enough to find out who did it. The secret is to get to know the victim. As you do, you'll learn that they had good traits and bad. They might have been someone you could never have gotten along with. But, goddammit, they counted. Somebody's got to remember that, and that somebody is you. Your job is to befriend the victim, make him proud of the way you do your work.*

*You don't do it so people will think you're a hero. You don't do it because it is fun. You do it because the victim was someone who counted.*

McGowan knew there were old-timers in the department who did not share his feelings. Such intensity, they warned, was a sure ticket to big problems. Get too personally involved in your cases and eventually you're looking for a nice nine-to-five job in the private sector, nursing an ulcer, and wondering why your marriage went sour.

To the few who had voiced such an opinion to the detective, his reply had been quick and standard: the day a police officer quit caring, quit trying, was the day he should turn in his badge.

This attitude assured him an occasional enemy within the department, but also earned him a quiet, genuine respect from all who worked under him.

\*     \*     \*

Sitting on the front porch, her hands wrapped around the warmth of a coffee mug, Sandy McGowan listened intently as her husband recounted the previous night's events. This scene had been played out often during their marriage. Unlike some officers who steadfastly adhered to a rule of leaving their work at the office, Morris regularly discussed his cases with his wife, receptive to her genuine interest and any observations she might have to offer.

He felt sure, he told her, that the shots had been fired by either the woman's husband or her boyfriend. Already, however, he had a strong feeling that developing proof enough for an indictment was going to be difficult. "There are a lot of things about this case that make absolutely no sense," he said. "Unless someone decides to confess, this one's not going to be easy."

It was her husband's description of Rozanne Gailiunas's son that touched Sandy. As Morris spoke of the frail, terrified youngster he'd seen trailing his wounded mother's body from the house, she moved closer to him, gently placing a hand on his shoulder.

The decision to put the boy in the custody of child services, sending him away to a strange, no doubt frightening environment in the middle of the night, he admitted, troubled him.

"You did the right thing," Sandy offered.

"I hope so," Morris replied as he rose.

Watching him walk toward his car, Sandy took a final sip from her coffee cup, marveling at the eagerness in his step. With only three hours sleep he was rejuvenated and anxious to get back to work.

A wife who had seen countless dinners grow cold, movie dates canceled at the last minute, and who had even sat alone one Christmas eve after her husband's beeper had summoned him to the scene of yet another homicide, Sandy McGowan instinctively knew she would see little of him in the days and nights to come.

As the commercial flight from Boston prepared to land at Dallas–Fort Worth International, Paula Donahue was staring blankly out the window of the plane, her mind numbed by a sleepless night. Looking down on the unfamiliar city below, its buildings and roadways still miniature, toylike, she gripped the hand of her father, seated next to her, and stole a quick glance over at her distraught mother, who had hardly spoken during the three-hour flight.

Rozanne Gailiunas's sister and parents were, in effect, flying into a dark, dreaded unknown, their minds overloaded with fear and terrible, imagined images of what awaited them. They had been able to gather by long distance little more than the nightmarish fact that Rozanne had been shot and was in the intensive care unit of Presbyterian Hospital. What little they had been told had given rise to an avalanche of unanswered questions.

How? Who? And, Lord God, why?

It had been just after ten P.M. when Steve Donahue answered the phone at his Framingham, Massachusetts, home and listened as a stranger—a woman named Sandy Miller, identifying herself as the secretary of Rozanne's divorce attorney—relayed the news. Miller, who said she had become friends with his sister-in-law, was crying as she spoke.

"It doesn't look good," she said in a whispered voice.

Hanging up the phone, Steve made his way to the kitchen table. He sat, shaking, pondering the unwelcome task that had fallen to him. A patrol officer with the Framingham Police Department for two years before resigning to join his father-in-law's insurance firm, he had made such calls before, alerting relatives of accident victims, providing them the name of the hospital where their loved ones had been taken. And always the response had been the same: disbelief and stark terror.

Now he faced the dilemma of phoning his wife, a nurse working the night shift at Children's Hospital in nearby Boston, and telling her to come home immediately. Finally, he dialed the number of the hospital and waited for Paula to come on the line.

Calming his voice with great difficulty, he quickly assured her that the children were fine. He was okay. But it was important that she come home immediately.

"What's happened?"

"Just come home, we'll talk about it when you get here."

"Steve, what is it?"

"Just drive very carefully," he said, and hung up, feeling a stabbing awareness at the cruelty of his action. Paula would, he knew, imagine a multitude of horrible possibilities before she arrived home. None, however, would be as unsettling as the truth.

He then dialed the number of Henry Agostinelli, knowing he would awaken him from a peaceful sleep at his home on Cape Cod. Aware there was no way of cushioning the news he had to pass on, Steve immediately recounted the call he'd received as soon as his father-in-law answered.

For several seconds there was no response. Then, in the background, Steve heard Angela Agostinelli scream.

The remainder of the night passed with agonizing slowness as the family gathered at the Donahue house. Paula placed several calls to the Dallas hospital but, despite identifying herself as Rozanne's sister as well as a nurse, was given only the same basic information: condition critical. Calls to the Richardson Police Department resulted only in explanations that an investigation was under way and that an officer would return their call as soon as time permitted. Even before Henry and Angela Agostinelli arrived, Steve had phoned to book reservations on the first morning flight leaving Logan Airport. After a brief discussion, it had been decided that he would remain at home with the children while his wife accompanied her parents to Dallas.

It was past midnight when Paula answered the phone to hear a voice she'd never heard before. The caller identified himself as Larry Aylor. In recent telephone conversations with her sister, Rozanne had spoken of him often. They had been dating, she had said, and he was wonderful. She was anxious for Paula to meet him. On several occasions, following lengthy talks with her sister, Paula had remarked to Steve that Rozanne sounded happier than she had in years. Maybe, with her second troubled marriage almost behind her, she had finally met the right man.

Aylor asked when their plane would be arriving and said he

would be there to pick them up and drive them directly to the hospital. He had already made arrangements for them to stay at the home of his parents, he said, assuring Paula they would be far more comfortable there than in some impersonal hotel.

Under the circumstances, Paula thought, the kindness of strangers was something to be gratefully accepted.

Bypassing the turnoff to his office, McGowan had driven directly to Loganwood Drive. The secret to most crimes, he knew, remained at the scene. Perhaps, he thought, he might learn something in the light of day that had gone overlooked in the previous night's confusion.

For a half hour he wandered about the house, his own footsteps the only invasion of the quiet that had settled over what had, just hours earlier, been the site of frantic activity.

Again entering the bedroom, he stood silently, his attention finally drawn to the closet door, which was slightly ajar. Inside, he found the dress whose pattern matched that of the belt that Rozanne had been strangled with. Over the arm of the nearby rocking chair, several belts hung limply.

McGowan felt the anger returning. *You took your sweet time, didn't you?* he thought. *You went through her closet and found just the right thing to choke the life out of her. You enjoyed this, didn't you, you sorry sonuvabitch?*

The scene had, indeed, affirmed something he had left the house wondering about the night before. This, he was now sure, had not been a quick, in-and-out assault. Whoever had done this had spent a considerable amount of time in the house, savoring the dominating power he felt over the helpless woman whom he had bound and gagged.

Later, as McGowan drove toward Presbyterian Hospital to check on the status of the victim, he found himself wondering what sadistic horrors she had been forced to endure before her assailant's gunshots had finally ended her misery.

At Presbyterian, Dr. Morris Sanders stood in the hallway of the intensive care unit, shaking his head at McGowan's question. "It's over," the neurosurgeon said. "Quite honestly, the surgery we performed last night was a futile exercise."

He had, he said, already spoken with Rozanne's family. To keep her on the life support system, he had explained, would do nothing more than prolong the inevitable.

McGowan found Paula and her parents seated in a nearby waiting room with Larry Aylor and introduced himself. It was Angela Agostinelli who spoke first: "Do you have any idea who did this?"

"Ma'am, we're just beginning our investigation."

The woman, exhausted and clearly still in a state of shock, looked at the detective with piercing black eyes. "The doctor had something to do with this," she said in a cold, flat voice. Though he had no question about whom she was referring, McGowan was surprised that she had not spoken of her son-in-law by name or even as Rozanne's husband. For whatever reason, it was clear that "the doctor" had suffered a long fall from grace in the minds of his in-laws.

It was a state of affairs McGowan would want to know more about in the days to come.

Instead of responding, he suggested they continue their conversation in a small conference room down the hall. As Aylor rose to follow, the detective paused and turned toward him: "I'm sorry, but I'd like to speak privately with the family."

Aylor slumped back into one of the waiting room chairs. When Paula and the Agostinellis were out of earshot, Morris reminded him of his promise to come by the police station later in the day. "Don't forget to bring the gun," he said. If Aylor did voluntarily produce the .25 as he had promised, there was little likelihood that it would prove to be the weapon used in the assault. Still, McGowan was eager to see if he would, in fact, bring it and to learn what ballistic testing might reveal.

"I'll be there," Aylor said.

In the privacy of the conference room, McGowan recounted the events of the previous evening, assuring the grieving family that all available manpower had been assigned to the investigation.

Again, Rozanne's mother returned to the question of suspects. "Do you think it was the doctor?"

McGowan hesitated before answering. "In an investigation

23

of this nature, it is very important that we keep an open mind and not lock into any one suspect. At this time, all I can tell you is that we don't know who did it."

With that he handed her one of his cards. "Please feel free to call me at any time. At some time in the near future I'd like to sit down with you and talk more about your daughter."

The request drew a puzzled look from the mother.

"It would help me," McGowan explained, "to get to know her."

For the first time since they had entered the room, Henry Agostinelli spoke, his voice unusually soft for a man of his imposing physical stature. "You would have liked her."

Already, he was talking of his daughter in the past tense.

It was not until that evening, sitting in the den of the home of Aylor's parents, that the family discussed what had to be done. Paula, because of her nursing background, had been the one who had talked with the doctor, then relayed the hopelessness of the situation to her mother and father. "She is brain-dead," Paula said. "There's no miracle great enough to bring her back. The respirator is the only thing that's keeping her breathing."

That said, she looked across the room at her parents, waiting for their response. Her mother began to cry. Her father said nothing, only nodding his head.

Henry Agostinelli, concerned that his distraught wife was near collapse, suggested that he return her to Boston the following morning so that funeral preparations could be made. Paula, who had displayed remarkable strength through the grim ordeal, would remain in Dallas and accompany her sister's body home.

"I'll call the hospital," she said.

Before Larry could direct her to the hallway phone, it rang and was answered by his father. Following a brief conversation, Aylor's father entered the den and looked across the room at his son. "That was Joy. She'd just heard what happened and wanted to pass along her condolences."

If Larry was surprised that his estranged wife had phoned, he did not show it.

"She said to tell you she hopes they find the person who did this."

Contacting Dr. Sanders, Paula was told that it was the policy of the hospital to wait twenty-four hours after such a decision was reached before a patient was actually removed from life support.

It would be done, they agreed, at seven the following evening.


Morris McGowan did not arrive home until well past nine, too tired to accept Sandy's offer to prepare him something to eat. Instead, she sat with him in the living room, listening intently as he briefly described the day's hectic activities.

When the ten-o'clock news came on, they fell silent, interested to see if the Dallas television stations deemed the case worthy of a follow-up of the previous night's story.

Apparently it was not. Yesterday's violence, in the medium of thirty-second sound bites, was old news. The assault of crime on the metroplex had not ended at 804 Loganwood Drive.

Instead, an intense-looking young reporter, clutching a microphone, stood in front of a residence in the Casa Linda area of Dallas, detailing the city's most recent homicide.

A young woman, also a registered nurse, had been bound and strangled to death in her bed. Apparently, he reported, her ten-year-old daughter had been in the house when the murder occurred but had not been harmed.

McGowan, stunned by the similarities, was on his feet before the report ended, dialing the number of the Criminal Investigation Division of the Dallas Police Department.

After several long minutes of waiting Detective Pat Herring came on the line. McGowan quickly briefed the Dallas officer on the case he was working, making note of the similarities.

"How was the woman killed?" McGowan asked.

"Strangled with panty hose."

"No gunshot wounds?"

"No."

Neither did they have anyone in custody or a good suspect, Herring volunteered.

For several minutes the two officers discussed the possibility that their cases might be somehow related, then agreed to stay in touch.

Hanging up the phone, Morris looked across the room at his wife, slowly shaking his head.

That night he slept fitfully, waking to the disturbing thought that some nameless, faceless maniac might be stalking the streets, randomly seeking out victims.

To the growing list of things that would need to be done, McGowan added another. He wanted to know if there was anything, however remote, that connected Rozanne Gailiunas to the Casa Linda woman.

Thursday passed at a numbing pace for Paula Donahue. After seeing her parents off at the airport, she had met McGowan at Rozanne's house to select a dress in which her sister could be buried.

Though it had been her intent to make the dreaded visit to the scene of the crime as brief as possible, she was surprised to find herself lingering at the Loganwood address, wandering from room to room, drawn to so many familiar objects that brought a flood of memories of happier times.

Only when she entered Rozanne's bedroom did she make a concentrated effort to avert her eyes from the horrible remnants of the tragedy played out there: the bed, its bloodstained mattress removed; the residue of graphite left by those who had dusted every inch of the room for fingerprints.

Quickly gathering clothing from the closet and bureau, she felt a sense of relief as she walked back into the hallway, her eyes silently meeting those of McGowan, who had said nothing since they entered the house.

Stopping at the doorway of Peter's room, she stood for several seconds, then walked toward a bedside table where two small goldfish swam lazily in a bowl. Nearby, in another container, a salamander raised its head and blinked at the surprise visitor.

Paula found herself wondering if anyone had thought to feed her nephew's pets.

As if reading her mind, McGowan said, "The officer assigned to watch the house is looking after them."

"I need to get out of here," Paula replied.

Returning to his office, McGowan was anxious to learn what, if any, new information Cynthia Percival had learned during her morning interview with the child.

Her report was a disappointment.

Arriving at the Children's Shelter with several toys she had stopped to purchase, she had spent almost an hour with Peter, playing games and drinking soft drinks, before slowly turning his attention to the activities leading up to the assault.

He again told her of accompanying his mother to ChuckE-Cheese's, a fast-food restaurant, for lunch, then going to his ice-skating lesson. "I acted bad," he admitted, "and Mommy took me home and made me take a nap." When he woke, he had gone into the living room, wanting to watch a cartoon video but, not knowing how to activate it, had gone to his mother for help.

At that point, Officer Percival said, his stuttering grew worse. "Ss-she was ss-sick," he told her. "I cc-called mm-my daddy."

Gently, the officer coaxed answers from the distraught youngster. Had he heard any noises?

"Somebody bb-banged a-aa ham-mmer on the wall. Two times. The Coo-ookie Mmm-onster was doing it."

"Peter, I want you to think very carefully about this before you answer. It's very important. Did anybody come to your house that day?"

The little boy shook his head. "No."

Asking leading questions, Percival knew, violated the most basic of interview techniques. But how could she apply adult reason to a frightened, confused four-year-old? Tossing the rules aside, she continued.

"Did Larry Aylor come to your house?"

"No."

"Did your daddy come to the house?"

Peter again shook his head. "The ff-fire tt-trucks came, and then the pp-policemm-men." He paused for a moment, as if thinking. "Th-then, a hh-helicopter came and took my mm-mommy away."

Cynthia Percival looked down at the toy helicopter in the child's hand, one of the gifts she had just purchased for him. She smiled wearily and hugged him. There had, she knew, been no helicopter summoned to the scene that evening. "Okay, Peter, that's enough questions for today."

McGowan had listened in silence as Officer Percival re-created the interview, any hopes he had that the child might prove to be a valuable witness vanishing.

"He could be blocking things out," Cynthia offered, "or maybe he could be saying what someone told him to say. But I just don't think so."

For a time, the two fell silent. Finally, Percival said, "You know, it was really hard. He kept asking me when he could go see his mother and wanted to know if his daddy was coming to get him soon.

"When I got ready to leave, he started crying and grabbed my leg, begging me to stay. He was still crying when I walked out the door. God, it just broke my heart."

An understanding nod was McGowan's only response.

Shortly before seven, Paula Donahue, accompanied by Aylor, arrived at Presbyterian's intensive care unit and quietly entered Rozanne's room. While she had been exposed to the death of patients numerous times during her nursing career, Paula had never experienced what lay ahead and found herself wondering about the procedure. Would a team of doctors be on hand to monitor the final moments of her sister's life, making certain they were spent in dignity and without pain? Was some somber ceremony attached to this final act?

At ten minutes after seven her questions were answered. With nothing more than a slight, unspoken acknowledgment of their presence, a young nurse entered the room, walked to the side of the bed, and unplugged the ventilator that had assisted Rozanne's breathing since her surgery.

In tearful silence the two visitors stood near the bed, looking down on the woman each loved, occasionally reaching out to touch her still body.

Since her initial visit to the hospital, hearing the doctor's hopeless diagnosis, Paula had fought to convince herself that the person now lying before her was, in truth, no longer the sister she had known. Already gone was the vibrant teenager with whom she had shared so many schoolgirl secrets, attended football games, and joined at social events; the partner she had teamed with on long-ago April mornings to offer up cups of water and freshly cut orange slices to the courageous competitors of the annual Boston Marathon, whose course ran through the heart of their hometown. The motionless body lying in this sterile, suffocating room was not the woman she had always looked upon as more beautiful and adventuresome than she'd ever been. That person, she determinedly tried to convince herself, was already gone.

The only distraction to Paula's private thoughts was the faint beeping of the machine monitoring Rozanne's heartbeat.

Twenty-nine minutes passed before the machine fell silent. On the digital monitor, a flat line signaled that the wait had finally ended.

Paula moved to a nearby chair and sat, her eyes still fixed on Rozanne's now lifeless body. Slowly, she felt an unexpected sense of relief sweep over her, fueled by the knowledge that whatever suffering her sister might have been feeling was over.

Aylor gently placed a hand on her arm. "She went peacefully," he whispered.

As they prepared to leave, Paula, picking up her purse, felt her attention again drawn to the nearby bed. She turned and, for a moment, thought she might faint.

Rozanne was suddenly sitting upright, her lifeless eyes wide open, her arms extended in front of her. Her hands, which had been hidden beneath the sheet, were still wrapped in the brown paper bags used to preserve evidence that might be hidden beneath the fingernails.

Paula's piercing scream echoed along the corridors of the intensive care wing.

Larry was returning Rozanne's body to a horizontal position and replacing the sheet as a nurse rushed into the room. She explained that the movement had resulted from involuntary muscle spasms. It was, she said, not at all uncommon.

Badly shaken, Paula stepped into the hallway and breathed deeply, trying to regain her composure. She knew such post-mortem activity occurred often, sometimes almost immediately, or even hours after death. But she had not been prepared to see it firsthand. Not there. Not from her own flesh and blood.

For a fleeting moment, in fact, Paula had imagined that Rozanne had risen in a desperate protest of the decision to let her die.

At a few minutes past eight McGowan received a call informing him that Rozanne Gailiunas was dead.

He was now officially investigating a homicide. And since a lengthy afternoon interview with the victim's husband, he had found himself narrowing his focus on the frightened, angry doctor.

# 3

THE PARENTS OF Peter Gailiunas, Jr., had fled occupied Germany when he was just three years old, and his only recollection of the seemingly endless boat trip that had finally ended in New York in the summer of 1949 was one of constant seasickness and a diet of nothing but oranges.

In America, his Lithuanian father and Bavarian mother insisted, life would be better.

The young boy was innocently unaware of the price his

weary parents had paid for their new start. Nor did he have any
frame of reference for understanding the dispirited attitude of
his father—a man who had once aspired to be a doctor but had
settled for an unsatisfying career as a village veterinarian—or
his mother, born into a modestly wealthy family she would not
likely ever see again.

In the United States, Peter Gailiunas, Sr., first labored at a
Lawrence, Massachusetts, mill by day and spent his evenings
washing dishes at a local restaurant. In a few years, he earned
a license to work as a government meat inspector in the Chicago stockyards and later in Albany, New York.

By age thirteen Peter junior, his English vastly improved
from those kindergarten days when he spoke the language not
at all, was enrolled in boarding school. Unknown to him, the
purpose was twofold: not only would the environment of strict
academic and social training bolster his chances of entry into
the American mainstream, it would also remove him from a
household that had become an unbearable battleground. His
father's drinking was fast moving toward full-blown alcoholism, compounded by a growing addiction to amphetamines and
barbiturates.

For Peter junior, academics became a refuge, a welcome
escape from the tensions of family life. His father's behavior
was, at best, confusing: a mixture of angry, drunken abuse,
self-pity, and on rare occasions, loving concern.

Long before he enrolled at Boston College, the young Gailiunas had set his sights on medical school. That, he had decided, would assure him the love and respect of the tormented
father he'd spent most of his young life trying to please. But
while home from college to celebrate the holidays, an argument—its cause long since forgotten—erupted during Christmas dinner. The elder Gailiunas, drunk and enraged, had hit his
son hard enough to knock him from his chair. Peter, saying
nothing, simply left the house and returned to the Boston College campus, privately vowing never to return home again.

It did not surprise him when, sometime later, he received a
letter from his mother explaining that she had left his father and
was living with relatives in Boston.

Carlton Stowers

During his junior year in college, Peter decided to marry a pretty Boston College coed he had been dating for some time, and again his father's drunken behavior disrupted what should have been a joyous occasion. Peter senior's alcoholism was to bring on his early death only a few years later, before his son's graduation from Loyola's Stritch School of Medicine, fifth in a class of 104.

His father's death was not the only unsettling event in Peter Gailiunas's life. His four-year marriage was headed for divorce. To push the disappointments aside, he focused every waking hour on his residency training, spending a year at a clinic in Cleveland, then returning to Boston General for the final stage of his studies.

Only when the prospect of becoming a licensed physician was finally in sight did Gailiunas allow himself to resume a social life. A nurse at Boston General had caught his eye and soon they were dating, then living together and talking of marriage.

That relationship, however, abruptly ended when he met a pretty, raven-haired Italian nurse at a suburban Boston hospital where he worked nights in the intensive care unit. Her name, she told him, was Rozanne Agostinelli, and her outgoing, fun-loving manner fascinated him.

She was the most beautiful woman Gailiunas had ever seen, and he was in love with her even before, just as his shift was ending, with a flirtatious smile, saying nothing, she handed him a folded piece of paper. Written on it was her phone number and the message "Call me sometime."

In time, a passionate relationship developed. That several months passed without her once inviting him to her home, as she insisted that they meet secretly in shopping malls and out-of-the-way restaurants, was mildly puzzling to Gailiunas but did nothing to discourage him.

No woman he had ever met so fascinated him. At the hospital she was the picture of professionalism, calm and businesslike in the most demanding crisis. Peter had never seen a nurse more thoughtful and caring with the patients, her quick smile and sparkling dark eyes almost magically chipping the hard edges from the life-and-death tensions that constantly shrouded the ICU. Privately, she was sexual, adventuresome, and exciting, as comfortable on the nude beaches off Cape Cod as she was in one of Boston's finest restaurants.

Gailiunas was, in fact, thinking seriously of asking Rozanne to become his wife when she finally admitted to him that she was married.

Her husband, also named Peter, had been her high school sweetheart, and they had married shortly after their graduation. He worked, she said with a noticeable lack of enthusiasm, as a cashier in a liquor store. Quickly cushioning the shock she saw on Gailiunas's face, she explained that they were separated and she had recently filed for divorce.

Yes, she told him, when the decree was final, she would marry him.

Already having accepted a teaching position on the faculty of the prestigious Southwestern Medical School in Dallas, Gailiunas looked eagerly to the start of his long-awaited professional life. Even before their June 1972 arrival in Texas, Rozanne had been offered a nursing job in the burn unit of Parkland Hospital, the famed emergency facility where President Kennedy had been taken on that November day in 1963. Married in the Walnut Hill Episcopal Church shortly after moving to Dallas, the young couple looked ahead to a new life, far removed from family ties and bygone disappointments.

Gailiunas found the rugged, new vitality of the Southwest invigorating and exciting. Here, he assured his new bride, opportunity abounded. And, while Rozanne had initial reservations—she fought an ongoing bout with homesickness, missing her family and the familiar sights and sounds of New England—she, too, was soon at ease with her new home and the challenges of her job.

In short order, her husband had advanced from the position of assistant professor to director of the kidney transplant program, and there was talk that Rozanne was a prime candidate for the job of head nurse in Parkland's burn unit.

The marriage of Peter and Rozanne Gailiunas, then, appeared

no different from that of hundreds of other upwardly mobile young couples in Dallas in the seventies. The doctor's starting annual salary of $36,000 increased rapidly, and with the addition of his wife's income, they lived comfortably, able to make frequent trips back to Massachusetts for visits with Rozanne's family.

In the late seventies, the couple's financial fortunes took a dramatic jump. Gailiunas and fellow Southwest staff member Harry Jacobson entered into a business partnership that turned quickly into a gold mine. Buying a struggling medical-equipment distributorship, the new partners worked long hours to revive it into a viable concern.

Gailiunas, determined to make the venture successful, launched into a work routine that staggered the imagination of his associates. By day he tended his clinical responsibilities, taught, and continued with a variety of research projects. In the evenings he devoted his attention to the newly acquired business. One-hundred-hour weeks were commonplace. It was not unusual for him to arrive home at three A.M. and be gone again by six.

The Herculean effort soon paid high dividends. In a matter of two years the business had expanded to include offices in Texas, Oklahoma, Arkansas, and Tennessee, grossing $4 million annually. For the young doctor, haunted by early childhood days of poverty and struggle, the achievement was intoxicating.

No more so, however, than the feelings he experienced when Rozanne told him she was pregnant. Dr. Gailiunas celebrated the news by purchasing his wife a new Cadillac. And, he said, since their family was expanding, it was time to begin looking for a house befitting their new station in life.

Friends of the couple, however, privately took note of Rozanne's lack of enthusiasm for all the good things that were occurring in her life. Her vivacious manner seemed to have disappeared, replaced by what was best described as weary disinterest. She began making more frequent trips back home to Massachusetts, staying for weeks at a time. She would always come back with a rejuvenated spirit, fueled by her close-knit family, only to have it fade quickly after her return.

She no longer made any attempt to hide the fact she missed being near her parents and sister. Adding to her loneliness was the fact that her husband continued working around the clock, his days and nights fractured into hospital responsibilities, the business, and the latest research project he had taken on.

When, on the night of April 18, 1979, she was rushed to the hospital to give birth to Peter III, who arrived five weeks prematurely, Dr. Gailiunas was in Chicago, finalizing the purchase of yet another franchise to add to his still expanding medical-equipment business.

It had been after midnight when a neighbor telephoned the doctor to alert him that his wife had gone into labor. Despite a furious attempt to locate a charter service that would fly him home immediately, Gailiunas was forced to wait for an early-morning commercial flight and arrived, on the verge of exhaustion, at St. Paul Medical Center two and a half hours after his son had been born and placed in intensive care where he would remain for the next five weeks.

Feeling guilty at not being on hand for the life-threatening premature birth, the doctor made a vow to cut back on his frantic schedule. The promise, to no one's surprise, was soon forgotten. Dr. Gailiunas, associates agreed, knew but one work ethic: obsessive and full-out.

At the same time, he was strongly urging his wife to dismiss plans to return to her nursing duties after the child was born. They no longer needed her income, he argued; her time would be better spent at home, raising their son.

Reluctantly, Rozanne agreed to set her career aside.

Meanwhile, the search for the ideal house had gone on for over a year without success. Though countless weekends were spent following realtors through many of Dallas's exclusive neighborhoods, nothing suited the doctor's specific demands. In the fall of 1982, Gailiunas decided to call off the search and build a house whose design he would be able to supervise closely. Whatever ills troubled his marriage, the doctor was certain, would be quickly healed by the majestic home he had long envisioned.

A $100,000 lot at the end of a block on Bobbitt Drive would

be the site of Gailiunas's dream home. The builder he had chosen was a man named Larry Aylor.

Even before blueprints were drawn, it had become evident that a new house was not the answer to the growing marital problems of Peter and Rozanne Gailiunas. The doctor refused to slow his almost around-the-clock work schedule. So demanding had his schedule become that it was not unusual for days to pass without his so much as sitting down to a meal with his wife and new son.

And on those rare occasions when he and Rozanne did talk, an argument was almost certain to erupt. She complained little about his work schedule but repeatedly expressed concern that his drinking had increased to a point where it was now out of control. The time had come, she had suggested on several occasions, that he seek professional help. On nights when her husband remained at the school, working in the lab until the wee morning hours, it was not unusual for him to consume several six-packs of beer. At home, he was seldom without a gin and tonic in his hand.

The doctor, on the other hand, was increasingly critical of her care of their child. Despite his insistence that little Peter's food be blended daily from natural ingredients, Rozanne had soon dismissed the time-consuming idea and turned to commercial baby food. Gailiunas was also frustrated by his wife's decision to enroll their son in day school when he was just a year old. It was too soon for him to be separated from a mother's constant nurturing, he argued. Rozanne countered by pointing out that she felt it important for little Peter to be around other children.

With few friends and little inclination to spend her days wandering through shopping-mall dress shops, Rozanne had become lonely and bored. Rarely did her once-exuberant personality show. Instead, she found herself becoming increasingly withdrawn, a prisoner in her own home. In lengthy telephone conversations with her sister back in Framingham, she talked of how she missed the family and her work in the burn unit at Parkland. She also longed for the colorful seasonal changes of New England and simple delights like lounging on the beach or digging for clams at the Cape. Her husband, she said, had no idea how miserable she had become. That, or he simply didn't care.

As the calendar signaled the beginning of another year in Dallas, Rozanne had begun thinking seriously of divorce.

Such was the atmosphere at the Gailiunas home when Larry Aylor and his interior-decorator wife first visited to discuss plans for the house they had been contracted to build.

On that evening in January of 1983 the two couples sat in the Gailiunas den, discussing the building adventure that was about to begin. Aylor, professional and personable, talked enthusiastically of designs and building costs, even inviting the doctor to accompany him on a bird-hunting trip so they might get better acquainted.

Though Joy Aylor said little, Gailiunas turned his attention to her often, as if seeking her reaction to some point made by her husband. In truth, the doctor was privately fascinated by the paradox of her quiet, almost shy demeanor and the very apparent fact that she wore no bra beneath her thin silk blouse. It was obvious that Joy, just like Rozanne, was confidently aware of her striking good looks.

Still, as was customary in Texas, the men dominated the conversation, munching on fried chicken that Rozanne had prepared. The women sat passively, saying little.

Gailiunas, mixing a final drink before the meeting ended, asked how long construction would take. They would, Aylor promised, be in their new house by late spring.

Throughout the conversation, Larry could not help but notice that the doctor's wife had not shown the slightest sign of enthusiasm.

As they drove from the Gailiunas house, Joy said, "His wife is really pretty."

Larry Aylor only nodded.

"And very unhappy," Joy observed.

# 4

A NERVOUS, EMBITTERED Dr. Gailiunas sat in McGowan's office, all patience gone from his voice as he responded to many of the same questions he had been asked during his initial visit to the station. Mixed with his answers were angry threats of legal action against the police department and the City of Richardson if his son was not returned to him immediately, and frustrating disbelief that his own attorney had strongly advised that he stay away from the hospital where his dying wife had been taken.

Though he did not mention it to McGowan, Peter Gailiunas was also feeling a paranoia unlike any he'd ever experienced. And the doctor, by his own admission, had suffered some degree of paranoia much of his life.

Now, though, it had reached a new level. Every time there was a knock at his door, each time the phone rang, he was certain he was going to be placed under arrest and swept off to jail.

McGowan carefully studied the man as he battled a volatile mixture of emotions, clearly on the thin edge of exhaustion.

As the conversation continued, it became obvious yet another emotion was at play, one McGowan judged most significant to his investigation. Dr. Gailiunas was an extremely jealous husband, still not resigned to the fact the divorce that his wife had been seeking was to be final later in the month.

In the days since the investigation began, McGowan had mentally wrestled with various scenarios. He had, for instance, begun strongly considering the possibility that the attack on Rozanne Gailiunas might have been the act of some nameless, faceless stalker, a member of the ever-growing population of nut cases who fixate on a pretty woman after seeing her in the grocery store or walking through the parking lot after work.

And he hadn't completely dismissed the possibility that the crime had begun as a burglary, been interrupted, and escalated into mad violence. While visiting the house with Paula, she had mentioned that she had been unable to find Rozanne's engagement and wedding rings.

Still, despite the far-ranging possibilities that crossed his mind, his focus always returned to the doctor. His attitude, his alibi, even his body movements—all signaled suspicion.

And now, as he angrily spoke of the breakup of his marriage, Dr. Gailiunas was providing the element all investigators deem most essential: a motive.

In the spring of 1983, Gailiunas, preoccupied with work and the construction of the new house, awoke to the realization that his marriage was in serious trouble. Rozanne had grown increasingly distant, no longer waiting up for him in the evenings, rarely conversing. She showed little, if any, interest in the building project about which her husband was so enthusiastic.

Initially, Gailiunas passed it off as nothing serious. Rozanne, he knew, missed her work. She had developed few friendships since their move to Dallas, therefore had no social life. His wife was simply lonely and bored, he assumed, struggling with the new responsibilities of motherhood. It would pass. Soon, they would move into their dream house, magically making everything right. It would be like a new start.

In March, the doctor's concerns took a new direction. Despite their problems—his long hours, the drinking, her unrest—their sex life had remained good. Suddenly, without explanation, Rozanne had lost all interest in any kind of physical relationship.

Dr. Gailiunas began to suspect that his wife might be having an affair. His suspicion grew rapidly into an obsession, which he made no attempt to keep private. He confided his concerns to a few hospital associates, who responded by bluntly telling him he was persecuting his wife needlessly. Even his mother, who had recently moved to Dallas, admonished him for such thoughts, suggesting he get his imagination under control and start spending more time at home with his family.

If there were troubles with the Gailiunas marriage, those who knew the couple assumed they were the responsibility of the doctor, not his wife.

One late afternoon, while visiting the building site, Gailiunas even shared his worries with Larry Aylor as they stood at the curb, admiring the progress of the construction. In his attempt to develop a list of men his wife might possibly have become involved with, he had been told by a neighbor that "the guy who's building your house" was stopping in on Rozanne almost daily.

"I think Rozanne's fooling around on me," the doctor said, watching for Aylor's reaction. Revealing no interest in his client's domestic problems, Larry did not respond as he climbed into his pickup, turned the conversation briefly to small talk about the house, then drove away.

Aylor had not mentioned that he had marital difficulties of his own. Or that he and Rozanne had, months earlier, discussed their respective problems.

It had been shortly after construction of the house had begun when Aylor invited Rozanne to lunch at the Black-Eyed Pea on Greenville Avenue to talk about the selection of fixtures for the house. When she said little during the meal, Larry had finally asked if there was something wrong.

"No," Rozanne replied.

"Do you have some kind of problem with me?"

Rozanne shook her head. "No, I'm sorry. It's just that I really don't want to build this house. It's Peter's idea, not mine. As soon as it is built, I'm out of here."

Larry had smiled, then confided to her that he and his wife were also on the verge of divorce proceedings.

The idea of his wife having an affair began to consume Gailiunas, affecting his work and prompting an increase in his drinking. One evening when he returned home to find Rozanne and his son already asleep, he ventured into the laundry room and began sorting through a hamper of clothing waiting to be washed. Finding a pair of his wife's panties with small stains, he soaked them, then collected flushings from the stains into a syringe.

The following day, he summoned a fellow doctor to his microscope: "Tell me what you see here."

Puzzled by the request, the doctor peered down at the specimen slide mounted beneath the lens. In only a few seconds he recognized what he was looking at.

"Sperm," he said, wondering why Gailiunas would ask his opinion on something any first-year medical student would quickly recognize.

Pleased with his detective work, the doctor finally felt he had the evidence necessary to confront his wife. When he did so, however, she quickly labeled his accusations absurd and denied having had sexual intercourse with anyone. But, what she did admit was that she had been thinking of moving out for a while, having some time to herself so that she might think through some of the problems she'd been having with their relationship. She had become increasingly unhappy with the direction of their life together. She was not thinking of a divorce, she said; spending some time alone was the only step she'd decided on. That and possibly going back to work.

Early in May, Rozanne rented the house on Loganwood Drive. And though Dr. Gailiunas tried, there was no dissuading Rozanne from the course of action she'd clearly set her mind to. There was no one else, she continued to insist. She just needed time to herself, to get her life back in order. Further, she informed her husband, she had spoken with a doctor who had a small pediatrics practice and was in need of a part-time nurse. She was seriously thinking about applying for the job if she could arrange hours that would fit into little Peter's day-school schedule.

Her tone of voice made it clear that there was no room for discussion of the matter. All that was left to talk about was their son's schedule of visits with his father.

While far from pleased with the neighborhood Rozanne had chosen, the doctor agreed to pay her rent. He would also provide her with living expenses while they were separated and made sure she had whatever credit cards she might need. For the moment, his concern over any possible affair was overshadowed by thoughts of how to mend his marriage and bring his wife and child back into his home.

In time, however, he began to realize that any quick resolution to the problems he and Rozanne were having was not to be. On visits to her, she was increasingly distant. All warmth disappeared from her voice when he tried to talk with her about returning home.

On a Saturday morning, Dr. Gailiunas stood alone in Rozanne's tiny kitchen after having assembled his son's swing set in the backyard. In his wife's open purse, which lay on the counter, was a slip of paper with an unfamiliar phone number written on it. Hurriedly, before she returned from their son's bedroom, Gailiunas copied down the number.

Later that day, the doctor called the number and heard the recorded answer of a familiar voice. The number was for the recently installed phone in the apartment where Larry Aylor had been living since separating from his wife.

It was, of course, possible that Rozanne's having the number had something to do with the building of the new house, but the doctor doubted it. Since moving out, she had not once even mentioned the construction. Gailiunas was convinced that his wife was having an affair with Larry Aylor and stepped up his efforts to gather proof. He hired a private investigator named Jim Wright, who was immediately confused by his client's strange demands.

"I want to know if she's sleeping with that bastard," Gailiunas explained. The request was familiar enough to Wright. Gailiunas's additional instructions weren't: "I want you to follow her very closely. I want her to know you're there. I want her scared."

Long before the investigator would call to report seeing Rozanne and Larry together, Gailiunas had managed on his own to get the proof he needed. Despite their separation, Rozanne made frequent trips to their house while he was at work, picking up items she needed, bringing little Peter over for his visits.

Anticipating that she might use the phone while there, Gailiunas had a wiretap installed that would secretly record any conversations.

Just days later, he returned home to check the tape. On it he heard a ringing, followed by a man answering. Then there was Rozanne's voice, more cheerful than he'd heard it in months. "I love you, Larry Aylor," she said.

Numbed, the doctor sat alone in the darkening living room for some time, the conversation he'd just heard replaying over and over in his mind. Finding the answer to the question that had haunted him for months was far more devastating than he'd ever anticipated.

Only after he'd gotten very drunk did anger begin to replace his grief. With some difficulty he finally dialed Aylor's number and, in a slurred fit of rage, began hurling accusations.

Aylor, quickly taking the offensive, cut him short: "Look, you're nothing but a drunken bum, and if you ever call me again, I'm going to come over there and kick the shit out of you."

With that, Aylor slammed down the phone.

The threat was not enough to dissuade Gailiunas. A few evenings later while Aylor lay on his couch watching television, he heard someone at his front door. Moving down the hallway to a window, he looked out and saw Gailiunas and an elderly woman he would later learn was the doctor's mother.

"I want to see Rozanne," Gailiunas demanded as Aylor opened the door.

"She's not here."

"I want to talk to her."

Aylor shook his head in the direction of the woman standing behind the doctor and shrugged. "Come on in and see for yourself."

Upon realizing that his wife wasn't at the apartment, Gailiunas, clearly upset, slumped silently on the couch.

"Look," Aylor said, "I don't know what problems you're having with your wife, but you need to be working them out with her, not me. I'd appreciate it if you would leave now. And don't come back."

It was Kay Gailiunas who urged her despondent son to his

feet. "Let's go home," she said, speaking for the first time since entering the apartment.

Aylor stood in the doorway, watching as they walked away, bemused at the fact the doctor had deemed it necessary to have his mother accompany him.

She was not with Gailiunas the following morning when he drove out to Richardson and confronted Rozanne with the information he'd gathered. He detailed the report he'd received from the private investigator and told her of the phone conversation he'd taped.

Rozanne, defensive and angry at her husband's accusations, denied any romantic involvement with Aylor.

Yet, only two days later, during the first week of June, Dr. Gailiunas was served with divorce papers. What he didn't know at the time was that the same attorney representing Rozanne had also filed a divorce petition for Larry Aylor.

The dissolution of his marriage sent Gailiunas deeper into a dark downward spiral. He was going through a liter of vodka every two days and seldom ate. Having weighed 195 pounds when Rozanne had made the move to Loganwood Drive, he plummeted to 155 by August. Associates at the hospital whispered about the zombielike manner in which he went about his duties—on those increasingly rare days when he did not call in sick.

Then, there was the matter of the house being built by the man the doctor now knew to be Rozanne's lover. Though his enthusiasm was gone Gailiunas decided, to the dismay of those who knew the situation, to continue with the project. Construction, he explained, had gone well beyond the point of no return.

Adding to his miseries were growing concerns about his son. Peter III's stuttering had worsened dramatically since he and Rozanne had left, and his behavior at day school was, in the words of the administrator, becoming unmanageable. More than once, when Gailiunas arrived at the school to pick him up for the Monday and Wednesday overnight visits, he had found his son crying hysterically.

Gradually, however, Dr. Gailiunas began to accept the fact that his wife was gone and focused his attention on his son.

Initially, Rozanne agreed to his request for joint custody. But after the doctor's attorney had drawn up the papers, she had abruptly changed her mind. No, she said, her lawyer had insisted that she should be the child's managing conservator.

Slowly, the doctor began to take the offensive. Realizing that if he was to be a good father, it was imperative that he get his own life back in order. He quit drinking; he stopped taking antidepressant medication and launched into a fitness program, putting himself on a high-protein diet. He returned his attention to his career and contemplated a move into private practice. By doing so, he decided, he would have more time to devote to being a father.

And, despite the firm stance of his wife and her attorney, he continued to push for joint custody. One evening, as he and Rozanne stood on her front porch, beyond their son's earshot, he made it clear he was not going to give up the battle.

"In that case," Rozanne coolly replied, "we'll go to court."

Dr. Gailiunas reminded her of the incriminating tape. "You don't want it played in front of a judge and jury. I don't want to make you look bad in public. I don't want to drag you through the mud."

The threat had no visible effect. "Do whatever you feel you have to do," his wife said before turning to walk into the house.

Frustrated and angry, the doctor tried another tactic. Placing a call to Aylor's wife, he informed her of the tape and suggested she come to his home and listen to it. Perhaps, he said, they could both benefit by joining forces. Joy Aylor agreed to stop by.

In late August she sat in the den of the Gailiunas house, staring down at a tape recorder on the coffee table in front of her. As she listened intently to the conversation, with its verbal lovemaking and critical remarks about respective spouses, Dr. Gailiunas watched closely for her reaction. He was surprised at how controlled she seemed, demonstrating neither anger nor hurt at the things her husband was saying. Her only response was to ask that he replay those portions of the tape where her husband spoke of her shortcomings.

When the tape recorder was finally turned off, the doctor volunteered to make a copy, which she could provide for her lawyer. "I'll have to think about it," Joy replied.

The following day she telephoned to say she was not interested. She simply wanted it all to be over as quickly as possible.

Resigned, Gailiunas ended his battle. There would, he decided, be no more arguments, only brief, polite exchanges when he picked Peter up or she brought him to the house for visits. The divorce, he knew, was inevitable.

In less than two months—on October 10, 1983—his marriage to Rozanne would officially be over.

Despite his suspicions that the doctor was responsible for Rozanne Gailiunas's death, McGowan knew well the pitfalls of embracing a single theory too closely, of focusing his investigation too narrowly. For that reason, he continued to search even the most remote of avenues. Residents of the neighborhood were reinterviewed; a detective was assigned to collect information on every .25 automatic purchased from Dallas gun shops in the past two years; Rozanne's activities during the weeks leading up to her death were meticulously reconstructed, and people she had come in contact with were sought out and interviewed. Hours were spent on collecting the smallest details. An investigator was assigned to do nothing but learn the history of the brand of rope that had been used to tie Rozanne to her bed: who manufactured it, where it was sold locally, and what its general uses were.

The scattershot approach, McGowan hoped, would result in some collective answers that might ultimately lead him in a more specific direction.

Having seen little of her husband since the investigation began, Sandy McGowan coaxed him to take a break on Friday evening and go out for dinner. Getting him away from his office, even if briefly, she felt, was essential. She knew he was exhausted, physically and mentally.

Sandy was, however, not in the least surprised that their

conversation before, during, and after the meal rarely strayed from the case. Though she had long realized that Morris approached his work with an unusual degree of single-mindedness, the intensity with which he discussed the investigation concerned her. There was, in his voice, a frustrated tone she'd never before heard.

As they drove home late in the evening, he mentioned that an entire room at the station had been turned over to the investigation.

"Can I see it?"

McGowan looked at her silently for a moment, then turned the car in the direction of the police station.

A few minutes later, Sandy stepped into a small corner office that had once been used for polygraph examinations. Morris said nothing as her eyes slowly panned the room. On a blackboard was a time chart that detailed Rozanne's activities on the day of her assault. On a table, the contents of a purse were neatly laid out. An open filing cabinet revealed folders with written reports. Mounted on one wall were photographs taken at the crime scene; on another were the graphic autopsy pictures. Sandy turned her attention from them quickly, unaware that she had placed a hand over her mouth at the shock of what she had fleetingly viewed.

Other pictures, however, she examined closely, those that her husband had taken from the house on the night of the crime. Clearly, they were scenes from the little boy's birthday party, showing smiling youngsters—backdropped by a table filled with colorfully wrapped presents—eagerly awaiting cake and ice cream. One photograph, in particular, commanded Sandy's attention. In it, a pretty, smiling woman who she knew must be Rozanne sat, her son in her lap.

Only as she surveyed the silent, airless room did Sandy McGowan realize just how thoroughly the case was being investigated.

As Morris closed the door and locked it, his wife, overwhelmed by what she'd seen, asked if such measures were taken in every homicide investigation.

"No," he admitted.

That night, as they prepared for bed, Sandy gave the place she'd just visited a name.

From that evening forward, it would be referred to as Rozanne's Room.

The following Monday, while Rozanne's funeral was being conducted in Massachusetts and Peter III was finally being returned to his father's custody, McGowan drove to the Oak Lawn area of Dallas to meet with Joy Aylor in her divorce attorney's office.

He wanted to hear her perspective on her husband's involvement with Rozanne.

Polite and poised, she was an even more attractive woman than McGowan had expected. No, she insisted, she had not known of the affair until she'd received the call from Dr. Gailiunas about the tape recording.

"I went over and listened to it," she confirmed.

"Did the doctor appear angry to you?"

"Not really. He seemed pretty resigned to the whole matter and just wanted us to team up against them in some kind of counterdivorce action. I wasn't really sure what he had in mind, but I told him I wasn't interested."

McGowan then asked what her reaction had been to her husband's filing for divorce.

"At first, I was hurt and angry. After Rozanne's husband played that tape for me, I went home and called Larry and asked him to come to the house. I had decided to confront him, to let him know that I was aware of what was going on. And, I wanted her to know.

"We talked and he just kept trying to deny everything. Finally I suggested he call her. I got on the other extension and the three of us had a brief but very interesting conversation.

"That's how I found out why my husband was divorcing me."

She spoke freely, in a matter-of-fact tone that suggested whatever pain the breakup might first have caused was now past. She talked like a woman who had come to grips with the situation and had made up her mind to go on with her life.

"Can you tell me what you did last Tuesday?" McGowan asked.

It was immediately obvious that her attorney had warned her to expect the question.

"That morning," she began, "I got up and cooked a tuna casserole for my son, Chris. Then, around eleven-thirty, Sherry Bradshaw, one of my neighbors, came over and we watched a soap opera together. I think the postman came a little after noon.

"The reason I was staying around the house was that I was expecting a repairman. He arrived at around two-thirty and was there a half hour or so."

As she approached the critical time frame, McGowan shifted in his chair but said nothing.

"It was shortly after the repairman left that Chris got home from school. He'd brought a friend and they went to his room to study. Then my father stopped by to say hello, getting to the house about the same time the kids did. He stayed until five-thirty or so."

McGowan made a mental note to contact Henry Davis to confirm the time he'd spent with his daughter, then thanked Joy for her cooperation.

As he prepared to leave, she extended a hand and smiled. "Thanks for being so nice," she said. "I must admit I was expecting someone much older—and a lot more unpleasant."

Returning to his office, McGowan placed a call to Henry Davis and, careful not to mention his conversation with Joy, asked if he could recall what he'd done on the previous Tuesday afternoon. Without prompting, Davis confirmed that he'd been at his daughter's house from three until at least five-thirty on the previous Tuesday. He'd been spending quite a bit of time with Joy since her bastard of a husband had moved out on her, he added.

McGowan sat, contemplating the tangled web of bitterness he'd ventured into since beginning the investigation. Rozanne, he concluded, was not the only victim in this increasingly bizarre scenario.

In the wake of his interview with Joy Aylor—pretty, charming, and intelligent, a woman who comfortably fit the definition of *class*—Morris found himself pondering still another question:

*What the hell's Larry doing leaving her?*

# 5

IT WAS ONE of those teenage romances that normally bloom quickly, then fade with the discovery of someone or something more interesting. Joy Jeannine Davis, a pretty and vivacious junior, member of the Honor Roll and Future Teachers, daughter of a well-to-do developer–home builder, had been lobbying her friends to introduce her to a popular senior she found attractive.

On a fall Friday night in 1966, during a Hillcrest High School football game, Joy Davis first met Larry Aylor.

Soon the two were dating exclusively, and by the end of the spring semester it was obvious to everyone that the relationship between Joy and Larry was no passing thing. They were in love, in the romanticized view of their youthful friends, "the perfect couple." They had, in fact, already begun making plans to marry as soon as Joy completed her senior year.

When Larry graduated, Joy drove him to the family ranch just south of Dallas and proudly presented him with a gift that was the envy of all his friends. She gave him a registered gelding, launching the salesman's son on a lifelong interest in horses.

That they came from dramatically different financial backgrounds seemed not to matter. While aware that Joy's parents had money, perhaps a great deal of it, Larry's interest seemed focused on her striking good looks and engaging personality. That she doted on him like no other girl ever had—and seemed always eager to feed his already sizable ego—pleased him. She was, in his eighteen-year-old's judgment, everything a wife should be.

Following his brief stint in the navy as Joy completed her final year of high school, they were married in 1968. Larry was almost twenty; Joy had just turned nineteen.

And, while Larry Aylor was warmly welcomed into the fold of his wife's family, he learned quickly, that they held to the values of hard work and one's making one's own way. Their considerable wealth had not been earned to ease their children's path to adulthood. Such had been the case with Joy's older sister, Carol, and her husband during the early stages of their marriage. The same, apparently, would apply to Joy and Larry.

Leasing a small apartment, both went to work in clothing stores, Joy in a women's boutique in the fashionable NorthPark shopping center, Larry in a men's store nearby. For him, it seemed the ideal job despite the modest paycheck it earned him. Labeled a "clotheshorse" even in high school, Aylor commonly changed as often as three or four times a day. In their closet, his wardrobe occupied twice the space of Joy's. While she was comfortable in faded jeans and men's tailored shirts, her husband favored the starch and spit polish of a young banker or corporate executive. If, indeed, clothes made the man, Larry Aylor was clearly destined for bigger and better things.

Privately, his father-in-law was already making plans to steer him in a more financially rewarding direction than the clothing business. The transition, however, would be made on Henry Davis's timetable, only after he became fully convinced that his daughter's husband was deserving of his help.

He'd already been burned once, setting Carol's husband up in the home-building business only to see him fail miserably. Compounding the disappointment was thousands of wasted dollars invested in a college education that his eldest daughter had shown little interest in. Not a man to throw good money after bad, Henry had no intention of reliving the experience through Joy and her husband. This time he would patiently wait and watch before committing himself and his money.

Henry and Frances Davis were, to those long established in Dallas's financial and social circles, something of an oddity. Both products of rural upbringings, they had made the move from Ellis County at the end of World War II as the small tile-setting business co-owned by Henry and his brother, Hugh, continued to grow. In the mid-fifties, they began to expand, building a few custom homes in the booming Casa View and Lake Highlands sections of north Dallas. A shrewd businessman with a willingness to take a gamble, Henry soon recognized that the big money was in land development and began borrowing money to buy up prime plots of land for resale to home builders. Just steps ahead of the building boom of the sixties, the country boy was soon on his way to becoming a millionaire. In time, the Davis fortune increased with investments in a small, thriving insurance company, and Henry was made a director of one of Dallas's up-and-coming banks.

When his brother died of a heart attack during a bird-hunting trip in south Texas, Henry forged ahead alone, steadily climbing the ladder of Dallas's financial elite. Estimates of his wealth ultimately ranged from $10 to $25 million.

Though he lacked the formal education and social polish of many of his competitors, Henry had the primary skills necessary for success: vision, a knack for deal-making, and a strong competitive drive.

He rarely let anything, even friendships, get in the way of business, but he commanded the admiration of virtually everyone with whom he came in contact. While his manner might be appraised as ruthless by an occasional outsider, those who worked with and competed against him on a regular basis simply judged him a damn good businessman. He invested wisely and rarely spent a dime that he didn't have to.

Occasionally, for instance, he rewarded those working for him with a barbecue-and-beer gathering on his thousand-acre ranch south of Dallas. The workers would, in fact, be treated to food and drink aplenty, but also wound up spending a good portion of the day at such chores as clearing brush or mending fences. That they had been manipulated by their boss seemed to bother them little. Henry Davis was fun to be around. They loved hearing him tell his stories of small-town mischiefs as a boy and wartime exploits as a firearms instructor. An expert marksman, he was always willing to share his shotguns and give lessons to interested guests. Dressed in his khakis and worn boots, talking the salty language of the common man, he served as proof that they, too, might one day catch the brass ring.

Henry Davis, then, was one of the good ol' boys, a man of simple pleasures. When he wasn't making money, he was bird hunting at the ranch or seeking the peaceful solitude of the family cabin he'd purchased on Cedar Creek. On Fridays, he would invite carpenters and bricklayers to gather at some unfinished house he was building for an evening of beer-drinking and dollar-limit poker.

Frances Davis, however, was attracted to the brighter lights of the big city. Her husband's money was her membership card into local society. An attractive woman who enjoyed the arts, she became a regular at local theater productions, art exhibits, and charity functions. Occasionally, she would be accompanied by Henry, looking uncomfortable and out of place in a suit or tuxedo. More often, however, she arrived alone or in the company of other women whose husbands had also balked at attending such activities.

As a board member of the Dallas Summer Musicals, Frances enjoyed hosting cast parties in her home, always careful to invite writers from the society pages of the local newspapers. Playing host to such show business luminaries as Lauren Bacall, attending functions like the annual Cattle Barons' Ball, and planning occasional trips abroad provided the fuel for Frances Davis's life.

That and her grandchildren.

The Davis house had become the home away from home for elder daughter Carol's child, Michelle, shortly after she was born. And when in 1970 Joy gave birth to son Chris, it was Frances who insisted that Joy and Larry move out of their apartment and into the Davis house with her and Henry so she might lend a hand with the baby.

Shortly thereafter, Henry Davis decided it was time to take

charge of his son-in-law's career. If Larry was willing to learn the construction business from the ground floor, Henry would supply the start-up financing to put him and his wife into their own business. Larry could build homes and Joy could double as bookkeeper and interior designer. The young couple, having hoped that such an offer would eventually come, eagerly embraced Henry's proposal.

The only downside to the proposition, however, was Davis's firm insistence that Larry agree to an arrangement his father-in-law had worked out with friend G. W. Billingsley. Aylor was to work under Billingsley's supervision for a period of one year, learning all aspects of the business.

So while Joy continued to work part-time at the boutique, her husband toiled long hours alongside architects and carpenters, roofers and plumbers.

In 1978, Larry W. Aylor Custom Builders, Inc. was finally born. Henry Davis saw that Larry was assured a generous line of credit at the same bank where he did business, spread the word to subcontractors that a new builder was on the Dallas scene, and stood ready to offer any advice needed.

Henry immediately liked the enthusiasm his son-in-law displayed, seeing an energetic, ambitious young man with all the talents necessary to provide his daughter and grandson with a good and comfortable life. What he failed to see were the darkening clouds forming on the horizon of his daughter's marriage.

Friends who observed Joy and Larry in social situations saw an obvious tension. Around her husband, Joy always seemed nervous, careful not to upset him. When not in his company, she was outgoing, even gregarious.

In the view of many who knew them, Larry was a dominating husband, quick to fly off into harangues of jealous rage without the slightest provocation. To a few close friends, Joy confided that her husband seemed to delight in making her feel unattractive and intellectually inferior. He constantly criticized her abilities as a mother and business partner. Rarely did a day pass when he didn't phone several times to check on her whereabouts.

Such things were not seen by her tunnel-visioned, all-business father. In his presence, Joy carefully played the role of a contented daughter and happy wife. In fact, the picture Henry Davis viewed pleased him greatly. He saw a young, hardworking couple, building a family and establishing a solid reputation in the home-construction community.

Indeed, the trappings of their success were soon very much in evidence. Larry and Joy moved into a $250,000 home on Arbor Trail, just around the corner from the Davises. Joy decorated it tastefully, then turned the mundane upkeep chores over to a Hispanic maid. With a fellow home builder as his partner, Aylor purchased a small farm in Kaufman County where he kept his horses and the cattle he'd begun buying at the livestock auctions he enjoyed attending. While Joy drove a Porsche, it was her husband who seemed most intent on collecting the toys of wealth. He had a Jaguar as well as a motorcycle, a Jeep, a pickup, and a ski boat. He proudly wore a gold Rolex watch.

Early in 1982, Joy quietly made a purchase that pleased her more than any of the material items she and her husband had accumulated. Secretly entering Baylor Medical Center, she emerged with cleavage. "If your husband is always drooling over other women's breasts," she explained to a friend after the enhancement surgery, "you start thinking how nice it would be if he would do the same at home."

To her disappointment, the "new Joy," as she began referring to herself, seemed to have little effect on her husband's roving eye.

It would, in fact, be Larry Aylor's flaunted interest in other women that, in time, resulted in a dramatic fall from his father-in-law's favor.

Those who attempt to pinpoint the time when Henry Davis's attitude toward Larry abruptly changed refer to a hunting trip his son-in-law made to south Texas. Aylor, hosting several clients for a weekend getaway to a deer lease near the border, had led a Saturday-night visit to several Mexican whorehouses.

Upon learning of the trip, Davis was outraged. But, before

confronting Larry, he sought out confirmation of the story. What he got was far more than he had suspected. Business associates, when asked by Henry, were surprisingly frank about the "womanizing" of his son-in-law. The trip into Mexico, they assured him, was hardly his first association with prostitutes. One of the regular hangouts of Larry and a plumbing-contractor buddy of his, Henry learned, was a topless joint on Northwest Highway called The Doll's House. "See, Larry considers himself a real ladies' man," one longtime business associate of Davis's volunteered. It was common knowledge, Davis was told, that Aylor tried to sleep with every woman he built a house for.

When, several days later, Joy angrily made her husband aware that she had learned of his "partying" across the border, it was not difficult for Larry to determine how she had found out.

Henry Davis had sent his message.

The warmth that had previously existed between father-in-law and son-in-law immediately disappeared. A man with a long-standing reputation for intolerance and grudge-bearing, Davis no longer bragged of Aylor's progress as a businessman. When he did mention Larry in the company of associates, he generally referred to him as "the little sonuvabitch."

Only because his daughter seemed determined to make her marriage work did Henry keep his new feelings about Aylor in check. Making an effort to avoid his son-in-law as much as possible, he would stop by the house to see Joy only when he knew Larry was still at work. At holiday family gatherings, traditionally hosted in the Davis home, Larry was treated with cool tolerance.

The only member of the Davis clan who seemed to genuinely enjoy Larry's company, in fact, was Joy's fifteen-year-old sister, Elizabeth. When he wanted company during a late-afternoon trip to the farm or a Saturday visit to the lake, it would often be Liz, not Joy, who accompanied him.

Long before Rozanne Gailiunas came into his life, Larry's marriage had begun to dissolve into more of a business partnership than a loving husband-and-wife relationship. Increasingly, the couple seemed to go their separate ways, Joy keeping busy with the bookkeeping and a new window-shutter business she had started, Larry spending long hours overseeing the construction of the homes he was building.

To friends he began confiding that were it not for his son, he would have left Joy long ago. He spoke of her increasingly demanding manner, a trait he'd long seen in her mother. "I'm damned if I'm going to let her treat me the same way Frances treats Henry," he regularly vowed.

Most quickly dismissed his complaints, privately assuming that Larry, who made no attempt to hide his love for the good life, would never divorce himself from the financial comfort of the Davis family. But it was obvious to all that the marriage was seriously troubled.

One Saturday morning, as he sat in a Dallas coffee shop with friend Don Kennedy, Larry first spoke of Rozanne Gailiunas. She was, he said, the most beautiful woman he'd ever met. And the nicest. In the days to come, talk of her dominated his conversation.

Kennedy had never seen his friend so happy. Nor was he surprised when Larry told him that he had moved into an apartment and was planning to file for divorce.

What McGowan had seen in Larry Aylor in the days following the attack on Rozanne was a man grieving deeply over the loss of a beautiful woman whom he had planned to marry. Since the night of their first meeting in the front yard of Rozanne's house, Larry had repeatedly talked of how much he had loved her.

Still, the detective was puzzled. Never in his career of investigating homicides had he witnessed such unusual behavior by those directly affected. How could the doctor, obviously furious over Aylor's role in the breakup of his marriage, continue in a business agreement with him? And why, if so certain that Gailiunas was responsible for Rozanne's death, had Larry been so quick to summon his own attorney?

Too, McGowan had found it strange that the Agostinelli family, upon their arrival in Dallas, immediately embraced the young home builder whom they had never before met while hurling a barrage of angry accusations at Rozanne's husband.

There was, McGowan confided to his wife one evening as they sat discussing the case, much about these people that he did not understand. Maybe, Sandy had jokingly replied, they were lucky not to be rich.

By the time Larry had left for Boston, assuming with Paula Donahue the responsibility of accompanying Rozanne's body home for burial, McGowan had all but dismissed him as a possible suspect. Instead, he judged him a heartbroken victim of the tragic event that had occurred on Loganwood Drive.

A few days following his return from Rozanne's funeral, Aylor paid a visit to McGowan's office, eager to learn if any progress had been made in the investigation. They talked for a half hour, Morris reviewing the information that had been gathered, Larry quietly describing the funeral ceremony, then continuing to insist that all efforts should focus on proving that Dr. Gailiunas was the murderer.

Not until Aylor rose to leave did he make an almost offhanded statement that so stunned McGowan that for a moment he was unable even to rise from his chair.

"By the way," Larry said, "Joy and I sat down and had a long talk. I've moved back home."

# 6

WITH THE INVESTIGATION well into its second week, frustration continued to mount as results of polygraph examinations administered to Dr. Gailiunas and Larry Aylor reached McGowan's desk. Both had, at the recommendation of their respective lawyers, agreed to be tested, and neither had shown the slightest deception when responding to the three key questions:

1. *Did you kill Rozanne Gailiunas?*
2. *Were you present in her house when Rozanne Gailiunas was attacked?*
3. *Do you know who killed Rozanne Gailiunas?*

Even Joy Aylor, following the advice of her attorney, had volunteered for an exam and had demonstrated no deception in response to the same questions posed to her husband and the doctor.

Surprisingly, it was Dr. Gailiunas who had scored highest on the test, conducted by Eric Holden, one of Dallas's best-known and most respected polygraph examiners. In a cover letter accompanying the results of Gailiunas's test, Holden went so far as to make a highly personal observation: "If anyone seriously suspects him in this case, they are barking up the wrong tree."

Reluctantly, McGowan was beginning to agree.

With each new phase of the investigation, the case against Gailiunas weakened. Checking to see how the doctor might benefit financially from his wife's death, McGowan had learned that a $150,000 life insurance policy, part of the standard benefit package all doctors receive upon being hired to work at the Southwestern Medical School, was the extent of the coverage on Rozanne.

Initially, McGowan had been led to believe that Rozanne had been shot sometime after four P.M., most likely during the brief time when her husband's activities were unaccounted for: the forty-five-minute nap. Later, however, Dr. Mary Gilliland, the medical examiner who had performed the autopsy, had ruled that the shooting had most likely occurred sometime *before* 4 P.M. A number of people had seen the doctor in and about the hospital during that time.

Still, on the chance that Dr. Gilliland was wrong, McGowan had driven the seventeen and one-half miles from the hospital to 804 Loganwood on numerous occasions. Making the trip during the critical time and taking every conceivable route he could find, the best one-way time he could make was twenty-eight minutes.

If a case was to be made against Gailiunas, McGowan had determined, it was going to be necessary to put the gun in his hand. Searches of purchase records of Dallas gun and ammunition shops had revealed nothing that would indicate Gailiunas or anyone associated with him had purchased either a .25 automatic or the Federal-brand cartridges used in his wife's murder.

McGowan was, in fact, surprised that several of the investigators assigned to the case steadfastly held to their belief that Gailiunas was the guilty party despite the mounting evidence that he was not involved.

Secretly, and for reasons he could not really explain, the detective could not shake the same feeling.

Forcing himself to focus on other possibilities, McGowan began a review of Rozanne's activities in the days preceding the assault, searching for some indication that her assailant might have been someone who had recently developed a fixation on her and had been following her, planning to fulfill some twisted sexual fantasy. Yet, even as he pursued that avenue of investigation, he desperately hoped it would lead nowhere. If Rozanne had been the victim of some random, nameless stalker, McGowan knew well the odds against solving the case grew astronomically.

Since moving to the Loganwood house and taking the part-time job in Dr. Aaron Kreisler's office, Rozanne's activities had been remarkably routine.

She would drop Peter off at the Cornerstone Child Care Center in the mornings, arriving at work no later than eight-thirty. After getting off at five P.M. she would pick up her son and take him directly to his father's house. On those evenings when Peter was not scheduled to spend the night with his dad, Dr. Gailiunas would drive him home at eight o'clock.

When not working, Rozanne had spent most of her free time in the company of Larry Aylor, either visiting him at his apartment or traveling with him to inspect job sites. On the nights and weekends when Peter slept over at his father's, Rozanne stayed at Larry's apartment.

A recent addition to her routine was to drive to the nearby Prestonwood Center mall where her son was taking ice-skating lessons.

Not until the last Wednesday in September, McGowan learned, did anything unusual occur. Returning home from a visit to Aylor's apartment, Rozanne entered her house to find that a window near the back door had been broken. Fearing a burglary, Rozanne had looked through the house in a frantic attempt to see if anything was missing. The only thing she could not find was an extra set of house keys.

She immediately strongly suspected that the break-in was the responsibility of her estranged husband. The following day, September 29, as locksmith William Dawson changed the locks on her house, she asked him, "Who would break in and take nothing but the keys? Do you think it could have been my husband?"

Dawson's only response was to suggest a dead-bolt lock for the doors and the installation of a peephole on the front door so she could see who was outside.

Then, a few days later, as she prepared to leave for work, she discovered that one of the tires on her Cadillac was flat. She had phoned Dr. Kreisler's office to say she would be late, then called a nearby Texaco station to ask that they send someone to change the tire. Checking with the attendant who had responded to Rozanne's call, McGowan learned that the flat had resulted from nothing more than a nail. He had traveled down yet another dead-end trail.

Still, he was convinced that somewhere hidden within the maze of information collected was something that would point the investigation in the right direction. For the next couple of days he focused his attention on everyone's activities the day of Rozanne's assault.

After dropping her son off at the day care center that morning, Rozanne had met Larry Aylor and accompanied him on his inspection rounds of job sites. At eleven, she picked Peter up, stopped by an automatic teller machine at a bank near the day care center, and withdrew $30.

The doctor's morning had been equally routine. At seven-thirty he had called to talk briefly with his son, a ritual he'd fallen into shortly after the separation. Then, en route to the office he had stopped by his broker's office to check on some stocks. Arriving at the hospital shortly after nine, he immediately involved himself in the regular activities of his workday, paying visits to the dialysis unit and the transplant clinic before having lunch at the staff dining room.

At noon Rozanne telephoned Aylor, leaving a message on his answering machine: "Hi, handsome," she had said in a cheerful voice. "I'm home, but I forgot to tell you that little Peter has ice-skating today. We're going to get a bite to eat then go to his lesson. I'll be home around three. Call me."

After having lunch at a fast-food restaurant, Rozanne and her son arrived at the Prestonwood Center skating rink at one-thirty P.M.

Midway through the lesson, instructor Olivia Maxwell was forced to send Peter from the ice because his behavior was disrupting the class. For the last thirty minutes of his scheduled lesson, he had been forced to sit and watch the other youngsters.

The teacher had hoped to explain to Peter's mother why he had not been permitted to complete the lesson but did not see her seated among the other mothers. By the time Rozanne—who had apparently decided to shop in the mall while her son's lesson was going on—returned, Maxwell was busy with the other children on the ice.

She had noticed Rozanne removing Peter's skates, but by the time she could get over to where they were seated, Rozanne and her son were gone. Maxwell made a mental note to phone Rozanne later to explain what had occurred.

Thus, the last time anyone had seen Rozanne Gailiunas was at the skating rink at approximately two-thirty P.M.

According to the recollection of Peter, they had driven directly home, and upon arrival his mother had immediately sent him to his room to lie down for a nap.

Aylor had stated that he first called Rozanne's home from the phone in his truck at a few minutes past three. Getting no answer, he had tried at three-thirty from a phone at a repair shop where he'd taken his bicycle, which had been damaged during a traffic mishap earlier in the day. An erratic driver had forced him off the road.

From three-thirty to four P.M. Aylor had called every ten minutes, becoming increasingly concerned. Stopping by the home of his parents, he had tried again to reach Rozanne, then, with his sister Karen joining him, had begun to drive toward Loganwood Drive. The North Central Expressway traffic, however, had been so congested that he eventually turned back, deciding to return to his apartment to await Rozanne's call. By five-thirty he was calling her number every five minutes.

Peter's skating instructor had also called twice, still hoping to explain to his mother why he had not been allowed to complete his lesson, but had received no answer.

Neither caller was aware that Rozanne, having received a number of hang-up calls in recent weeks, had instructed Peter not to answer the phone.

At Southwestern, meanwhile, several associates had spoken with Dr. Gailiunas in his office or had seen him in the lab during the afternoon. The only nonbusiness phone call his secretary recalled him making was to a local cable-television company, informing them that he wished to cancel a movie channel to which he had previously subscribed.

Except for the troubling four-to-four-forty-five nap he claimed to have taken while seated at his desk, virtually every minute of his day could be accounted for. People saw him enter the elevator to leave work at around five, and a neighbor, out watering her lawn, recalled seeing him arrive home just before five-thirty.

After changing clothes he had telephoned his attorney to discuss the final wording of the custody agreement, then spoken briefly with a woman he had taken to dinner a few times in recent weeks.

Sometime after six Dr. Gailiunas's mother had called, and their conversation was interrupted by a series of clicks from his call-waiting. Putting his mother on hold, the doctor had answered to hear little Peter say something was wrong with his mother.

Gailiunas had urged his son to wake his mother and ask that she come to the phone. Minutes later, Peter said, "She won't wake up . . . and there's stuff coming out of her mouth."

Fearing that Rozanne had attempted suicide, Dr. Gailiunas got back on the line with his mother and instructed her to immediately call 911. Records at the Richardson Police Department indicated the call from Kay Gailiunas had been received at 6:33 P.M.

Aylor, meanwhile, recalled that it was sometime between six-thirty and six-forty when Peter answered his call.

"Little Peter," he said, "this is Larry Aylor. Let me speak to your mom."

"She can't. She's sick."

"Well, go get her. She'll want to talk with me."

"She can't. She's bad sick."

Before Aylor could reply he heard a voice in the background. "Hang up the goddamn phone," someone said. Then the line had gone dead.

The voice, Aylor would say later, sounded very much like that of little Peter's father.

Everyone, it seemed, wanted Dr. Gailiunas to bear the responsibility for the death of his wife. For Morris McGowan, however, the possibility had gradually dimmed throughout the course of the investigation.

Then, in the midst of a sleepless night, he had become certain the doctor had not been the assailant.

As he lay in the darkness beside his sleeping wife, McGowan's thoughts had again returned to the crime scene. Some things about it had troubled him the moment he entered Rozanne's house; things that made no sense. Despite the assurance of those who knew her that Rozanne was a strong, tough, spirited woman, there had been no sign of a struggle, no indication that she had attempted in any way to fight off her attacker. Why?

During their talks the doctor had, on several occasions, assured McGowan that he had resigned himself to the end of the marriage and that the only reason for the delay in the divorce proceedings was the custody arrangement.

Despite Gailiunas's sometimes strange behavior and suspicious actions, McGowan was certain that the doctor loved his son very much. As he lay there, images of the attack again playing in his mind, the detective was convinced that it was highly unlikely that the doctor's unhappiness over the situation could have prompted him to torture and murder his wife while little Peter slept only a few feet away. Dr. Gailiunas would never have chanced having his son see such a brutal act of violence.

Rozanne, at the same time, would likely have fought off any attack from the doctor, confident that the presence of their son would ultimately serve as her safety valve from even the most crazed behavior of her husband.

Suddenly, it was clear. Why, McGowan asked himself, had he not understood before?

*Rozanne had not fought off her attacker for fear of awaking little Peter, protecting him from the madness being played out in her bedroom. In an act of remarkable courage, she had remained silent, perhaps even passive, to keep her child from harm's way. In doing so, she had given her life to save her son.*

Dr. Gailiunas, McGowan was now certain, had not murdered his wife.

This realization sent the investigation back to square one, to the scattershot approach that promised little hope of immediate resolution. The already difficult case had suddenly become even harder.

Sending out Teletype messages in an effort to determine if any crimes similar to the one on Loganwood Drive had been committed, McGowan soon found himself looking far afield for some clue that would lend direction to the investigation. Several promisingly similar cases were uncovered in Texas and nearby states, but if there was, in fact, a tie-in to any of the other assault cases, it remained frustratingly elusive.

While the possibility of a faceless rapist—randomly choosing his victims—existed, linking him to the Gailiunas murder was a stretch. The medical examiner had found no indication of sexual assault while performing the autopsy on Rozanne.

"Dammit," McGowan confided to Deputy Chief Jim Bellamy, "I feel like I'm trying to put square pegs in round holes."

Bellamy suggested the formation of a task force of a half dozen officers who would collectively devote their efforts solely to the case for the next several weeks. "You'll head it up," he told McGowan. "Work the case until you solve it . . . or until you run out of leads."

To McGowan, the message was simple: solve the case or get on to other matters. The clock, he knew, was now ticking on the investigation. If the combined efforts of a handpicked group of officers didn't result in something solid pretty quickly, the murder of Rozanne Gailiunas, while not abandoned, would take a dramatic slide down the priority list. There were, after all, other crimes that the taxpayers of Richardson wanted investigated and solved.

None, however, would command McGowan's interest. Never in his career had he found himself so fixated on a single case. Right or wrong, it had become the only one that mattered. He eagerly welcomed the formation of the task force, hopeful that someone in the group would see something he'd missed, would serve up a fresh perspective to the investigation.

During the next several weeks, an elaborate computer record was made of every detail of the case, cross-indexing items that might somehow combine to form a new lead. Names of everyone who had purchased a .25 automatic in Dallas during the past four years were collected and checked. Supplemental reports were read and reread, compared, and discussed during the regular meetings of the task force. The Loganwood Drive neighborhood was again canvased in hopes that someone, somewhere, might remember something they'd not already told to the officer who originally interviewed him or her. Fruit vendors seen in the area on the afternoon of the murder were tracked down and questioned. A man who had been seen sleeping at the wheel of his car, two blocks over from Rozanne's house the morning before the attack, was found and interviewed.

But as the year neared an end, they were no closer to solving the case than they had been the night the assault was reported. In truth, the entire matter had become even more confused.

Dr. Gailiunas had telephoned McGowan to inform him that the mystery of Rozanne's missing engagement and wedding rings had been solved. "She had hidden them," he said flatly, "probably from me."

He explained that he'd had her furniture moved from the Loganwood house and stored in his garage, and while going through the items left in her dresser drawer, he had found one of Rozanne's rings taped to the back of her jewelry box, the other attached to the bottom of a bottle of fingernail-polish remover.

The possibility of robbery as a motive, always remote, was dismissed.

Then, there was Larry Aylor, who continued to stay in touch, regularly stopping by to see if any progress had been made. In truth, McGowan had come to like him despite the fact that at times he found his behavior every bit as strange as that of Dr. Gailiunas.

More than once, during the course of a visit, Aylor would talk openly of how deeply in love he had been with Rozanne, pointing out that he had arranged for a local florist to place fresh flowers on her grave monthly. Then, almost in the same breath, he would mention that his reconciliation with Joy was going better than he'd dared expect. They were, he confided, more in love than they'd been at any other time during their marriage. He often prefaced some new observation on the case with, "Last night, Joy and I were talking about it and . . ."

While a lifetime of training served as a reminder to McGowan that he should never lose sight of the fact that both Aylor and Gailiunas had to be considered suspects so long as the case remained unsolved, it was his gut feeling that both were nothing more than men who marched, ever so wobbly, to a different drummer.

For all their involvement and interest, McGowan had become increasingly certain that neither knew the secret of what had happened on Loganwood Drive.

With the Christmas holiday season approaching, the task force was disbanded, leaving in its wake a new level of frustration and a monumental stack of paperwork. Late one evening, after the office had cleared, McGowan dutifully carried the folders and computer printouts down the hall to Rozanne's Room.

Standing alone in the silent room, hands buried deep in his pockets, he let his eyes slowly wander over the montage of photographs he had attached to the wall almost two months earlier. As was always the case when he visited the small office, his attention finally came to rest on the picture of Rozanne with her smiling young son seated on her lap.

*God,* he heard himself saying, *I'm not going to solve this one.*

Shoving his hand against the light switch, he turned to leave the room, slamming its door behind him. In the deserted hallway he forced himself to breath deeply and focus his shattered thoughts on other things.

At home, he knew, Sandy was waiting to trim the Christmas tree.

# 7

THE EARLY MONTHS of 1984 saw public interest in the murder of Rozanne Gailiunas fade. Reporters, who had once routinely checked in to see if any progress was being made on the case, had long since stopped calling, their attention drawn to other, more immediate concerns. Even within the police department the investigation came to the mind of those not directly involved only when they happened to pass the solemn-faced

McGowan in the hall or noticed him at his desk, slumped over written reports they knew he had read hundreds of times before.

For one of the few times in his career, McGowan had reached a dead end. Even the most far-reaching attempts to breathe new life into the investigation yielded nothing.

At his request, Dr. Ralph Somodevilla, chief psychologist for the Dallas Police Department, had reviewed the case file and prepared a brief profile of the assailant. The description—a white male, mid to late twenties, probably a common laborer with no more than a high school education—McGowan determined, could have been assigned to three-fourths of the criminals he'd encountered during his career.

In April, while in Dallas attending an FBI-sponsored conference on the bureau's newly formed Violent Criminal Apprehension Program (VICAP), McGowan had taken along his case file and approached speaker Pierce Brooks during a break. A legendary Los Angeles Police Department detective who had been involved in some of the nation's most celebrated murder cases, Brooks had been hired as a consultant to aid the FBI in establishing its national computer network of information on criminal activity.

By the end of the day-long conference, Brooks had spent considerable time listening to McGowan's recap of the case and was clearly fascinated, even suggesting they make a trip out to the crime scene following his final lecture of the day.

"I think," Brooks said, "there's a strong possibility that you're looking for a serial killer."

Aware that the likes of Ted Bundy, the handsome, articulate young law student from Seattle, had recently been thrust on the public consciousness, lending a frightening awareness to a new breed of brutal, highly mobile criminal who randomly chose his victims, committed murder without motive, then moved on, McGowan admitted that he had no expertise in dealing with such crimes.

Brooks suggested he contact Ann Rule, a former policewoman whose best-selling book on the Bundy case had been praised as the definitive work on serial killers. "She's the expert," Brooks said.

"Hell, I'm not looking for someone to write a book," McGowan argued. "I'm just trying to solve a case."

"Just listen to what she has to say. She could point you in the right direction."

Where Rule pointed him was to a detective on a police task force in Seattle that had been formed to investigate what newspapers in the Northwest had begun to call the Green River killings, the murders of numerous prostitutes found dead in a seedy area near Seattle's Sea-Tac International Airport.

While a series of phone calls and correspondence with Seattle officials provided McGowan with a crash course on serial murderers, he learned nothing that enabled him to move his own case off high center.

He was, McGowan determined, simply making angry stabs in the dark.

With no new leads to follow, he reluctantly returned to the routine duties of his job, unsuccessfully trying to shove the Gailiunas case to the back of his mind.

Finally, McGowan wrote a lengthy summary of the investigation, carefully detailing even the most minute aspects of the case.

It was, in a sense, his admission that there was nothing more to do. What he had written, he hoped, might benefit some future investigator in the event a new piece of evidence breathed life back into the case.

In August of 1984, McGowan was, at his own request, transferred to a special deployment unit and began studying for the sergeant's examination.

Still, he could not completely escape the recurring thoughts of the case. It was a ghost that reached out to touch him at the most unsuspecting times. Occasionally, Larry Aylor still stopped by or Dr. Gailiunas would phone. And there were long-distance calls from Rozanne's father and sister, always to inquire if there had been any progress.

McGowan, spun into a period of depression by each call, nonetheless ended each conversation with the same sincere promise: "We're going to solve it. I can't tell you when, but we will."

Thousands of miles away, Rozanne's family had their doubts.

By June of 1985, twenty months after the death of his daughter, Henry Agostinelli's patience had reached an end. Despite the telephone conversations with McGowan, in which the soft-spoken Texas officer continued to assure him the investigation was ongoing, the still-grieving father had become increasingly skeptical with each passing call.

If, as McGowan freely admitted, there had been no new leads, what was there to investigate? And how many new crimes had occurred since 1983, each one pushing the murder of his daughter farther down the priority list?

For Henry and Angela, the issue was clear: both remained convinced that Rozanne's death had been caused by Dr. Gailiunas. If the Richardson Police Department couldn't find the proof, perhaps it was time they began looking for someone who would.

Agostinelli contacted his nephew Robert Muto, a Massachusetts state trooper, for advice. Muto suggested they hire a private investigator, and the man he considered the best around, he said, lived only a short distance from the Agostinelli's Falmouth home.

Snow-white hair provides the only hint that Frank Joyce—a small, athletic-looking man with a gravelly voice and a no-nonsense style—is in his mid-seventies. He began his storied law enforcement career with the Boston Police Department just before the outbreak of World War II. And, with the exception of a three-year stint in the navy, he worked as a criminal investigator until 1981, when he retired from the office of the Plymouth County district attorney. Among the numerous high-profile cases Joyce had successfully investigated was that of infamous serial killer Albert DeSalvo, the Boston Strangler.

While retirement to the Cape Cod community of Bourne, near Falmouth, was a longtime dream, Joyce had soon found himself at loose ends. The switch from the demands of law enforcement work to lazy days of gardening, fishing, and digging for clams had been too abrupt. To ease the transition, he decided to offer his services as a private investigator, taking occasional jobs that he found interesting.

The unsolved murder of Henry Agostinelli's daughter was such a case.

Before agreeing to make the trip to Dallas, he had sat in the living room of the Agostinelli home, listening as Rozanne's family outlined the events that had led to her death. The tragedy, they assured him, had actually begun with their daughter's decision to accompany Dr. Gailiunas to Texas, a part of the world Henry Agostinelli, in particular, judged as primitive and hostile. It was made clear to Joyce that the marriage of Peter Gailiunas and Rozanne had not been blessed with their approval.

"What we want you to do," Henry said, "is determine if, in fact, the doctor had anything to do with our daughter's murder."

Agostinelli had already made arrangements with a friend in Dallas to meet Joyce at the airport and provide him transportation during his visit. The friend's name, he was told, was Larry Aylor.

For five days, Joyce endured the blistering Texas heat, retracing the steps of the investigation. Visiting the Richardson Police Department, he was pleasantly surprised to find McGowan not only hospitable but co-operative, almost eager for any new input. For several hours the officer painstakingly detailed the events of the crime and the frustrating investigation that had followed.

Long before leaving McGowan's office, the most important question Joyce had pondered before his arrival had been answered: the police had, in fact, done their job thoroughly and professionally.

Still, he set about to learn answers for himself. He went to the hospital and spoke again with the associates of Dr. Gailiunas who had accounted for his activities on the day of the crime, carefully comparing their recollections to those given investigators in October of 1983. With Aylor doing the driving, he retraced the route from Gailiunas's office to Loganwood Drive in an attempt to determine for himself whether it would have been physically possible for the doctor to have made the fatal trip in the unaccounted time span of forty-five minutes. He spoke with the polygraph examiner who had tested Dr. Gailiunas and checked when the life insurance policy on Rozanne had been taken out.

Joyce interviewed Dr. Mary Gilliland, the medical examiner who had performed the autopsy on Rozanne, questioning her again about her estimate of when the attack had occurred, whether sexual assault was indicated, and if toxicology tests had indicated the presence of any drugs in the victim's system. She had never seen the test results, she admitted, but would check with the hospital and notify the Richardson police in the event they revealed anything positive.

Finally, Joyce interviewed Dr. Gailiunas.

Sitting in the living room of his home, his mother at his side, the doctor made no attempt to hide the bitterness he felt toward the Agostinellis. He remained angered that the decision to take his wife off life support had been left to Paula when he, in fact, was legally the nearest of kin. That the headstone placed on Rozanne's grave bore her maiden name instead of Gailiunas, he felt, was inexcusable.

Dr. Gailiunas stubbornly refused to allow Joyce to tape-record the interview and answered his questions in a hostile, clipped fashion. Why, the doctor finally asked, should he co-operate with someone who was clearly attempting to prove him guilty of a crime he had nothing to do with?

Joyce responded to the question sympathetically: "Frankly, I wouldn't blame you if you threw me out of the house."

Even before he left, Joyce had reached a conclusion: nothing indicated that Dr. Gailiunas had murdered his wife. Instead, what Joyce saw was a man waging war with myriad demons let loose by his wife's brutal murder and an obvious battle with alcoholism.

It was not, he knew, the report the Agostinelli family anxiously awaited.

On the evening before Joyce was to leave Dallas, Aylor suggested that he join him and his wife for dinner. Though weary and anxious to return home, Joyce readily accepted the invitation. Since agreeing to look into the case, he had found it curious that the Agostinellis had developed such a close relationship with a man who had freely admitted being their daughter's lover. He found even stranger the fact that Larry Aylor, who had apparently professed his love for Rozanne to them, had decided to reunite with his wife only days after returning from the funeral.

Frank Joyce was anxious to meet Joy Aylor, to see what kind of woman would not only be so quick to forgive her husband's affair but tolerate his continued involvement with the former girlfriend's family.

As they sat in one of Dallas's most exclusive restaurants, the conversation was light and pleasant, with idle comparisons of the weather in Dallas to that on the Cape. Larry talked of his concern for the faltering economy, and Joyce assured his hosts that Dallas had, in fact, been far more cosmopolitan and impressive than he had anticipated.

Throughout the dinner, the investigator found himself stealing glances at the woman seated across from him. Attractive, stylishly dressed, she had appeared gracefully attentive throughout the evening's conversation. But she had said little. Joyce, in fact, quickly surmised that she was going to great lengths to hide her boredom.

Although a lifelong student of the nuances of verbal responses and body language, Joyce left the restaurant having learned little about Joy Aylor.

During the course of the evening, suddenly abbreviated when the restaurant's air-conditioning went out, nothing had suggested that in less than a week Joy would file for divorce.

After he had returned home and reported his findings to the Agostinelli family, Joyce sat at the kitchen table one morning, drinking coffee with his wife and discussing his trip.

"I've got a question to ask you," he said.

"What's that?"

"If I'd had an affair with a beautiful woman who I'd told

everyone I was deeply in love with, then she'd suddenly died, would you be willing to take me back?''

An expression of mock deep thought briefly spread across his wife's face, then she playfully tossed a napkin in his direction. ''*Absolutely* not.''

Frank Joyce nodded and smiled. ''That's kinda what I figured.''

A week later Joyce received a copy of the toxicology report from the medical examiner's office. As he read it, he found it odd that traces of the antipsychotic drug Thorazine had been found in Rozanne's system.

Placing a call to the Richardson Police Department, Joyce learned that McGowan, who had read the report before it had been forwarded, had also found the presence of the drug somewhat perplexing. No one, he said, had ever mentioned the possibility that Rozanne was taking any kind of prescribed medication. Nothing found in the search of her home suggested it.

He had, he explained to Joyce, already talked with the medical examiner about the finding and had been told it was likely that the toxicology report had been in error. McGowan did not see it as a matter that merited any follow-up.

Joyce agreed. Still, he would inform his clients of the report.

# 8

IN TRUTH, THE reconciliation of Larry and Joy Aylor had quickly turned into the stuff from which soap operas are scripted. Even as he was insisting to McGowan that things were going well at home, Larry had confided to a friend over morning coffee at BeeJee's Restaurant just two weeks after moving back in with his wife that he ''had to get out of there.'' Joy, he said, had been acting strangely, staying up late with a neighborhood girlfriend, talking as loud rock music blared through the house. It also angered him that she seemed to have lost all interest in the business.

Too, he had become increasingly irritated at returning home late in the afternoon to find Joy and her father seated in the living room or kitchen, engaged in conversation that always abruptly ended when he entered. No longer making any pretense of tolerating his son-in-law, Henry Davis would routinely leave as soon as Larry arrived.

His wife, Larry confided, had become a different person.

In truth, Joy Aylor was indeed harboring secrets from her husband. While separated from Larry, a friend from her high school days had introduced her to a Dallas plumbing contractor named Jodi Packer at a wine-tasting party. Formerly the husband of a Dallas County District Court judge, he had the look of a long-distance runner: slender, almost gangly, with narrow hips and shoulders and an angular face framed with blond hair. Soon after their first meeting, he and Joy had become romantically involved.

Their affair had not ended with Larry's decision to return to the Arbor Trail house shortly after Rozanne's death.

While Joy hid her own affair, she was also wrestling with a dark, sordid episode from the past, a story concerning her husband's secret life that she had learned about from her older sister, Carol.

At one time, Joy learned, Larry had had an affair with her younger sister. Elizabeth, when confronted by Joy during lunch at the Dixie House restaurant, had tearfully admitted her involvement with Larry years earlier, when she was still a teenager. Guilt ridden, she explained that the relationship had gone on for several years before she finally ended it.

"You must hate me," Liz said.

"No," Joy replied, reaching across the table to touch her sister's shaking hand. "It wasn't your fault."

Biding her time before confronting her husband about the matter, Joy had quietly made up her mind that she would file for divorce, including her husband's sexual wanderings in the petition.

In time, it became clear to everyone who knew the couple that any hopes of mending the marriage were gone. One evening at a dinner held in conjunction with their high school class reunion, Joy had remained quiet through most of the meal. Then, to the surprise of the others at the table, she had suddenly turned to Larry, staring at him angrily for several seconds before saying, "I don't want to be here with you."

With that she had pushed away from the table and hurried from the banquet room, leaving her husband speechless and embarrassed.

A few weeks later Joy joined the family at a restaurant to celebrate Liz's birthday. Immediately following the meal, Joy had abruptly left without telling anyone where she was going. When she had not returned home by the following morning, Larry phoned the Davises and several of Joy's friends and had then driven out to her parents' lake house to see if she might be there.

Not reappearing until late that afternoon, she arrived home to explain that she had, in fact, driven to the lake house but, realizing that she didn't have the door key, had decided to just drive around all night.

There were things on her mind, she had said.

When, in 1985, Joy learned that she was pregnant, she said nothing about it to her husband. Instead, she explained that she had been invited to accompany a friend to New York on an antique-shopping trip that would last several days. While there she checked into an abortion clinic, using a fictitious name.

"I just couldn't bear the thought of having another child with him," she later confided to a girlfriend.

Don Kennedy, a bearish, good-natured man who loved hunting and the outdoors, was among those friends of Aylor's who had been surprised at his decision to return to his wife following Rozanne's death.

A county-road foreman and husband of a *Dallas Times Herald* reporter, Kennedy had initially developed a friendship with Larry's father-in-law while accompanying his wife, Maggie, to a Summer Musicals cast party hosted by Frances Davis. It was during the gathering at the Davis home that Kennedy overheard

Henry discussing quail hunting and quickly joined the conversation. He was delighted to find that Davis shared his discomfort in social settings, and the two men struck an immediate friendship. Soon they were meeting regularly for morning coffee and planning hunting trips together.

In time, Larry Aylor had also become one of the coffee shop regulars and soon developed a friendship with Kennedy as well. The two men soon learned they had common interests, including teenage sons the same age, both named Chris. As their friendship developed, Kennedy and Aylor spent an increasing amount of time together, bird hunting, attending cattle auctions, and watching weekend football on television. Soon, Don had even volunteered to sponsor Larry as a candidate for membership in the Masonic Lodge.

It had taken Larry little time to confide his marital difficulties to Kennedy. Were it not for his son, he admitted, he would have left Joy long ago, freeing himself not only from an unhappy marriage but the Davis family as well.

Ultimately, his friendships with both Larry and Henry Davis had placed Kennedy in an awkward position. Even before Joy and Larry separated, Henry had made it clear he had no use for his son-in-law. On several occasions, Davis had launched into an angry tirade against Larry, suggesting that Kennedy pass along some caustic message.

"Look, Henry," Don had finally said, "you're my friend, and Larry's my friend. I'm not going to get into the middle of whatever business you two have with each other. You got something to tell Larry, by God, you tell him."

Thereafter, Kennedy saw Davis rarely. In Henry's mind, Don had taken sides.

Aylor, meanwhile, was making a barrage of accusations about his vengeful, domineering father-in-law; he was certain that Henry was having him followed. Davis, Larry said, had threatened to have some of his "henchmen" take care of him if he didn't "leave that black-haired bitch [Rozanne] alone and get back home" where he belonged. The banks, according to Aylor, had suddenly begun refusing him loans for new building projects. He felt certain they were acting on orders from Henry Davis.

Though Larry had refused to admit it, Kennedy became convinced that his friend harbored a genuine fear of Henry.

That fear had not waned following Rozanne's murder or during the rocky attempt at reconciliation with Joy.

In time, Kennedy began to believe that Larry's concerns were justified.

On the Saturday morning of June 14, 1986, they sat drinking coffee at BeeJee's. "You got anything to do this afternoon?" Aylor asked.

Kennedy shook his head.

"Joy says that she and her mother want to go horseback riding this afternoon. She asked me if I'd go down to the farm and saddle the horses for them." For a moment both men silently considered the image of Frances Davis on horseback, then began to laugh. It was something neither could imagine.

"Hell, it might be worth the trip just to see it," Larry said. "You want to ride down there with me?"

"I've got nothing better to do," Don said, adding that it would give him the opportunity to drill Larry on questions he would soon be asked when he sought membership approval from the Masonic Lodge. "We'll just do a little studying while we're down there."

Shortly after noon Larry picked up Don and they began the forty-five-minute drive to the Aylors' Kaufman County farm, saddles loaded into the back of Larry's four-wheel-drive Suburban.

Since Joy had indicated it would be midafternoon before she and Frances arrived, the two men had time to take a leisurely horseback ride themselves, checking fence lines and looking over the small herd of cattle Larry had begun to assemble. Returning to the barn, they climbed the stairs that led to the loft and sat to await the women's arrival. Enjoying the warmth of the early summer sun, they sipped from a bottle of bourbon that Kennedy had brought along and discussed the lengthy series of questions Aylor would need to answer properly if he hoped to gain favor with Don's fellow Masons.

Only the rumbling of an old pickup, slowly making its way down the dirt road beyond the farm's entrance, interrupted the quiet of the bucolic setting.

As the sun began sinking behind the thin row of post oaks that bordered the farm, Larry rose, muttered a curse, and said he was going to unsaddle the horses. "Shit, they're not coming."

"Reckon they got lost?" Kennedy said as he climbed back into the Suburban after having locked the gate.

"Joy hasn't been down here that often, so she had me draw her a map. More than likely they just found something better to do." With that he turned onto the dirt road that would lead them back to the highway.

They had traveled less than a mile before reaching a bend in the road that gradually sloped toward a wood bridge stretching over a small, brush-tangled creek bed. As they neared the bridge, they noticed a brown Ford pickup parked in the middle of the road ahead.

"Looks like somebody had to stop and take himself a leak," Don observed as they crossed the bridge.

Any response from Larry was lost in the sudden cracking noise of a gunshot and the sound of the side window bursting behind him. Immediately, another bullet hummed past Aylor's head, shattering the Suburban's front window. "Sonuvabitch," he yelled in response to a jarring thud against the back of the car seat just inches from his shoulder.

Turning to look out the back window, Kennedy saw a figure standing in the middle of the road near the bridge, pointing a gun in their direction.

"Get the hell out of here," he yelled. As he spoke, a side window shattered and he felt a sudden, stinging sensation in his left elbow, which had been pressed against the armrest of his seat. "Goddammit, I've been shot."

For a moment Aylor, too, thought he might have been hit as he felt a warm trickle of blood slide down his forehead. Placing his hand to his hairline, he was relieved to find that the bleeding was only the result of several small pieces of glass that had been blown into his hair when the front window had exploded.

Stomping his boot to the accelerator and turning his head-lights on bright, he spun up the incline in the direction of the parked pickup.

Even in his panic, Aylor recognized it as the truck they had seen slowly pass by the farm several times earlier in the after-noon. Whoever was in it, he was certain, was part of the am-bush they had driven into. "If some sonuvabitch gets out of that truck," he said, "I'm running over his ass."

As they sped past the pickup, Kennedy, slumped in the pas-senger seat with the pain in his arm blurring his vision, glanced over. He thought he saw a figure duck down, but wasn't sure.

Though soon out of the gunman's range, Aylor continued down the darkening back road at high speed, adrenaline pump-ing, fearful that their assailants might decide to give chase.

His destination was the police station in nearby Terrell. "We'll get you to a doctor as soon as we can and report this," he said to his now silent passenger.

They had reached the highway before Larry spoke again. Anger had replaced the stark fear that had swept over him back at the bridge. "Henry Davis is behind this," he said through gritted teeth. "I'll guarantee you that. This is his doing."

Don Kennedy did not immediately reply. Instead, he turned to stare at the shattered windows, then reached over to feel the bullet hole that had been torn in the back of the seat. Briefly distracted from the throbbing pain in his arm, he felt a sudden rush of relief that their sons had not accompanied them. Had they, he thought, they would have been seated in the back, directly in the line of fire. He and Larry, he knew, had been lucky to escape with their lives.

What kind of insanity, he wondered, had he been thrust into?

At the Terrell Police Department, a paramedic dressed Kennedy's wound while an officer listened to Aylor's account of what had transpired, then took a number of photographs of the damaged Suburban.

"Based on what you're telling me," the investigating officer finally observed, "there's a good chance you boys ran up on some kind of drug deal that was going down. That, or you jumped some poachers who were afraid you might be able to identify them." Since the shooting had taken place outside the city limits, he explained, it would be the responsibility of the Kaufman County sheriff's office to investigate.

Kennedy, concerned with the numbness developing in his fingers, suggested the officer pass the information along to the sheriff so he and Aylor might get on their way back to Dallas. "I called Maggie," Don said, "and she's going to meet us at Presbyterian Hospital."

Aylor, too, had called home to tell his wife what had occurred but had gotten no answer.

It was past midnight when the two men arrived in Dallas, detouring by the darkened Aylor house to leave the Suburban. With the windows shattered, Aylor was concerned that the saddles might be stolen if he left them unattended in the hospital parking lot.

Entering the house through the garage, he telephoned the Davis house and asked for Joy. Coming on the line, she quickly began explaining that she had forgotten about the plans for horseback riding. They had, in fact, just returned from a day at the lake. Larry interrupted her to explain what had happened. "I need to get Don to the hospital."

"Are you okay?"

"I don't know. My head's bleeding some."

In minutes, Henry Davis pulled his station wagon into the driveway, Frances and Joy in the backseat. Aylor quickly climbed in beside his wife while Kennedy sat up front with Henry. Don thought it strange that in the first few minutes of the trip not a word was spoken. Finally, Davis broke the silence. Turning to Kennedy, he shook his head and said, "Don, what in the hell were you doing down there with Larry in the first place?"

Don considered a response but instead turned his face to the window. It was, he thought, an odd question to ask.

At the entrance to the emergency room, Maggie and Chris Kennedy had been waiting for over an hour. Though her husband had assured her that he was not seriously hurt when he had phoned from Terrell, she felt a rush of relief when he walked toward her and kissed her on the cheek.

"God," she said, "what happened?"

Her husband smiled and put his injured arm around his son's shoulder. "We just drove through World War III. Apparently we interrupted some poachers."

Maggie Kennedy found the atmosphere of the emergency room disconcerting. While doctors X-rayed Don's arm and picked the tiny shards of glass from Larry's forehead, she sat quietly with Joy and Frances Davis. Henry paced endlessly.

While they were there, a young man suffering a stab wound to the stomach was rushed in. Then a woman who had attempted suicide. As unsettling as the view of human miseries was, it was the silence that most disturbed Maggie. *There should be some conversation*, she kept thinking, *someone should say something, if only to release the tension.*

Thus she welcomed the doctor's invitation to join her husband in the examining room. There, she listened as he explained that the bullet had lodged near a nerve that controlled the movement of the hand. He advised against surgery.

In an attempt to lighten the mood and assure the patient and his wife that the matter was not serious, the doctor gently slapped Don on the shoulder. "You may have a little problem getting past the metal detectors at the airport. But, otherwise, I don't think you'll have any difficulties."

In an adjacent cubicle, there was no levity. As Larry prepared to leave, Joy folded her arms across her breasts and stared at her husband. "Come on, let's get out of here," Larry said.

Joy shook her head and focused her attention on the tile floor. "Larry, somebody's trying to kill you. I'm scared. I'm not going home with you. I'm going to stay with Mother and Daddy."

Aylor stared at his wife, offering no response. He had a phone call to make, he finally said.

The dispatcher's call had awakened Morris McGowan from a deep sleep, advising him that Aylor had phoned, insisting on speaking with him immediately. "Can't it wait until Monday morning?" the groggy McGowan asked.

"He says it's an emergency."

"Okay, patch him through."

The first words he heard as Aylor came on the line were, "The doctor's tried to have me killed."

The following Monday morning, McGowan sat in his office, listening as Aylor carefully detailed the ambush, insisting that there was some tie-in between the attempt on his life and the murder of Rozanne Gailiunas.

The detective listened patiently as his visitor again voiced his suspicion that Dr. Gailiunas was somehow involved in the Kaufman County incident. Aylor, however, said nothing of the observation he'd made to Kennedy Saturday night. If, in fact, he still suspected that Henry Davis had played some role in the event, he had chosen, for whatever reason, not to mention it to McGowan.

And while McGowan promised to contact Kaufman County authorities about the case, he admitted doubt that the two crimes were, in any way, related. In the first place, he explained, there was not the slightest similarity that would link the attack at Loganwood Drive and the shots fired near Larry's farm.

Though he made no mention of it, McGowan was certain that Dr. Gailiunas had nothing more to do with the attempt on Aylor's life than he had the death of his wife.

"You know, Larry," Morris offered, "there is a possibility that you did just accidentally drive into some kind of drug deal or poaching activity."

"I don't think so," Larry quickly replied, making no attempt to mask his frustration. Nothing McGowan could say would convince Larry the ambush on the Kaufman County bridge wasn't as thoroughly planned as the attack on Rozanne.

For Aylor, life became a study in paranoia. In addition to his suspicions about Dr. Gailiunas, he confided to friends that he was certain Joy and her father were also plotting against him, perhaps even involving the doctor in their plans. He hinted that sizable amounts of money were disappearing from his business account, and his wife, he was sure, was somehow secretly draining the profits. Though he had no evidence, he had begun to wonder if Joy and Henry Davis had entered into some kind of drug-dealing partnership.

And just days after being shot at, he learned that his wife was having an affair.

Returning home one afternoon he stopped in his son's room to make a phone call and accidentally hit the redial button. On the other end of the line, a voice answered, indicating the call had been made to the office of the Levy Plumbing Company.

Puzzled, Larry asked, "Can you tell me where you're located?"

Given a Mockingbird Lane address near Love Field, he immediately drove there and found his wife's red Porsche parked at the side of the small, nondescript building. Pulling into a parking space on the opposite side of the street, Larry had been there less than a half hour when he saw a pickup pull up in front of the building. The driver leaned across the seat and kissed Joy.

Aylor recognized the man as a plumbing contractor named Jodi Packer.

Shortly thereafter, Larry Aylor again moved out of the Arbor Trail house, making plans once more to file for divorce.

Yet, despite his insistence to friends that he was relieved to be away from Joy and anxiously looking ahead to the finalization of the divorce, there were those who viewed his observations as nothing more than a cover for the jealous rage he had felt upon learning that his wife had been unfaithful.

For all his own infidelities and mistreatment of Joy, many were convinced that Larry Aylor was still in love with her. Perhaps more so than ever.

Indeed, his actions in the days following his filing for divorce would indicate as much. One afternoon, he had stopped by the house, unannounced, to check on his hunting dogs. Letting himself in, he had found Joy and Jodi in bed together. Hurling curses and threats, he attempted to lure Packer into a fistfight before Joy calmed him with threats to call the police.

Returning to his apartment, the still-angry Aylor had placed a call to the office of Packer's ex-wife. "Get your goddamned husband out of my house," he yelled, "or I'm going to blow his fucking head off."

Stories he shared with friends grew increasingly bizarre. He had, he said, seen a man looking into the bedroom window of his apartment one evening and was convinced the intruder's purpose was to kill him. To avoid making himself a target, Larry began sleeping on the couch, a handgun at arm's reach.

The Davises, aware that a custody battle was soon to begin between Larry and Joy, had urged Chris to move in with them, seducing him with the promise of a new car and other expensive gifts. "They've always bought his affection," Larry pointed out to anyone who would listen. "And they've made him very aware that should he choose to leave and come live with me, the ride on the gravy train would be over."

To make his point, he delighted in telling a particular anecdote that, he felt, clearly demonstrated how his son's grandparents had lavishly spoiled him:

The summer after Chris just turned thirteen, he had found an expensive racing bicycle that he badly wanted. While it was a gift Larry could have easily afforded, he opted to teach a lesson in financial responsibility, offering to pay Chris an hourly wage for doing cleanup work at several job sites. Once he had earned enough money to pay half the cost of the bike, Larry agreed he would pitch in the remaining half.

"Like most kids," Larry would recall, "he wasn't crazy about the idea of spending all day in the hot sun, raking trash and tossing scraps of lumber into a pickup, but he did it.

"Then, one day I got home and there were *two* bikes sitting in the driveway. When I asked Chris where they'd come from, he said that his grandmother had bought them for him.

"I was livid. I called Frances Davis to find out what the hell was going on. She eats my ass out for making her darling little grandson do such menial work.

"Finally, I ask why, in God's name, she'd bought the kid two bikes. Just as calm as you please, she explained to me that when she'd taken him down to the bicycle shop, Chris had not been able to choose between two colors. So she bought them both."

Henry and Frances Davis, he had no doubt, were prepared to move heaven and earth to keep his son away from him.

And there was the matter of Joy's continued strange behavior. She was, he claimed, calling him at all hours of the night, sometimes angrily berating him, at others declaring her love and pleading for him to once again come back home.

McGowan, having long since wearied of the finger-pointing and charges and countercharges of the domestic warfares of both Dr. Gailiunas and Larry Aylor, began to distance himself from the two. If they wanted to discuss something relative to the case, his door was open, but their personal problems were not his concern.

He had made several phone calls to the Kaufman County Sheriff's Department in an attempt to see if they had learned anything new and was assured each time that the incident had all the earmarks of a panicked reaction from drug dealers or poachers who, without witnesses who could identify them, would likely never be apprehended. If they heard anything, they promised, they would be in touch.

The Richardson detective, careful not to intrude in another agency's investigation, had no way of knowing that, in truth, absolutely nothing had been done after statements had been taken from Larry and Kennedy.

In fact, a county game warden named Jerry Hinojosa, who lived near the site of the ambush, had offered help after hearing about it at a dance he and his wife had attended in Terrell that Saturday night. Hinojosa recalled that he had traveled the road adjacent to Aylor's farm earlier that day and had noticed a brown pickup parked in a pasture near the bridge. Slowing to see if it might be someone he knew, he hadn't recognized the driver and had continued on his way.

After learning that shots had been fired at Aylor's Suburban, Hinojosa had driven back to the area the following day and, after a brief search of the roadway near the bridge, had collected a half dozen spent .22 casings, which he carefully placed in evidence bags.

He had telephoned the sheriff's office to report his findings but sensed no interest. For months, the casings would sit in the glove compartment of his pickup.

In time, the Richardson Police, greeted by the same lack of concern, quit calling.

As the months passed, McGowan busied himself with new duties, sometime managing to go for several days without thinking of the Gailiunas case. There was, he had finally accepted, really nothing more to do except occasionally review the now-worn case file in the unlikely chance that he might happen on some shred of information he'd previously overlooked, or scan the NCIC computer from time to time, searching for some new homicide similar to the murder of Rozanne.

For all practical purposes, the investigation of the Rozanne Gailiunas murder was at a standstill, no longer a topic of conversation at roll call or in the halls of the Richardson Police Department.

Aylor, in fact, had finally stopped dropping by the station, and Dr. Gailiunas, having moved into his new house and a private practice, no longer called.

Such was the distance that had grown between the detective and the men he had once judged to be his prime suspects, McGowan had not even been aware that Joy and Larry had divorced. Nor did he know that Larry and the doctor had each remarried, both to women whom they had met just months after Rozanne's death.

Aylor's new wife, Jan, had been involved in a divorce herself during the time Larry was dating Rozanne, and a casual friendship had developed. After Aylor was divorced, Jan had run into him again and asked if he was seeing anyone. Larry responded by inviting her and her young son and daughter to dinner. Soon they were dating regularly and eventually decided to marry.

The doctor's new wife, Pat, had a friend whose son attended school with little Peter. The friend, troubled by the sadness she saw in Gailiunas's face, had given him Pat's number. "It's time you quit being lonely," the matchmaking friend had said. In short order, the doctor and Pat began dating and ultimately married. Little Peter was doing well in private school, had developed an interest in soccer, and enjoyed the loving attention showered on him by his new stepmother. Only rarely did he speak of his mother, though a framed photograph of her was on a nightstand near his bed.

Joy Aylor, meanwhile, continued to live at the Arbor Trail house, sharing it with her son, Chris, and her lover, Jodi Packer. Joy was keeping books for Packer's plumbing company and had become a silent partner with him in a newly established remodeling business. Several of her friends remarked they had not seen her so happy in a long time.

On the surface, then, it seemed that all had managed to put the tragic event of that long-ago October 1983 evening behind them.

Such, however, was not the case in Framingham, Massachusetts. In the late spring of 1987, Morris McGowan received a lengthy letter from Paula Donahue. Though her words were not angry, they straightforwardly addressed the lingering feeling of frustration felt by the entire family. Was it possible, she asked, that the murder of her sister would never be solved? Would her still-grieving parents be forced to go to their graves never knowing who had taken Rozanne from them?

McGowan was still contemplating a proper answer to Paula's letter when, for the first time in months, he was contacted by Larry Aylor.

"When I got home this evening," he said, "there was a strange message on my answering machine. Some woman with a thick Southern drawl said, 'If you want to know the riddle of Rozanne's death, I have the answer.' "

McGowan was surprised at the calmness in Aylor's voice. "You have any idea who the woman is?" the detective asked.

"None whatsoever."

"I'd like you to bring the tape in tomorrow."

While he knew it was unlikely that the strange message passed on by Aylor had been anything more than a crank call, McGowan felt a rush of new energy, the lighting of an ever-so-faint flame of hope that someone out there might, in fact, have valuable information and be willing to share it.

If nothing else, McGowan realized, the call from Aylor had provided him with an answer to Paula's letter.

The case, he wrote, had not been forgotten. Once again he assured her that it would someday be solved.

# 9

---

SITTING IN MCGOWAN'S office, Larry Aylor listened as the brief message was played over and over. The caller was obviously disguising her voice, speaking in a drawl that would have caused Southern belles everywhere to roll their eyes.

"No idea who it might be?"

Aylor shook his head. "Somebody's fucking with me. I don't know, maybe one of Joy's friends just trying to give me a hard time about the divorce." Once eager to jump at the slightest hint of a clue to Rozanne's death, Larry demonstrated only mild interest when McGowan suggested putting a trap on his phone that would trace any future calls.

"If she's legit," McGowan observed, "she'll call back."

Aylor shrugged and welcomed the detective to have the telephone company install the trap.

In truth, neither man thought it would accomplish anything more than perhaps to discover who was making the harassing calls and put an end to them.

When several weeks passed with no new word from the mystery caller, they were both convinced the message had been nothing more than the work of some idle prankster. The phone trap was removed and the matter forgotten.

Nine months later, on the Sunday night of April 24, 1988, Aylor answered his phone and immediately recognized the caller's voice.

"It was her," he told McGowan. "The same faked Southern drawl and all. But this time she sounded really scared. She says she's afraid this guy's going to kill her next."

"What guy?"

"Somebody named Bill Garland. She says he's the one who killed Rozanne . . . and now he's threatening to kill her."

"Do you know this Garland?"

Aylor shook his head. He'd never even heard the name before. "Morris, I don't know what the hell this is all about, but I think maybe there's something to it this time. This wasn't just some prank call. She sounded scared to death."

Aylor's new wife, who had accompanied him to McGowan's office, nodded in agreement. She had listened in on the conversation on another phone. "It was frightening," Jan said.

McGowan pondered the strange turn of events, trying hard to maintain a noncommittal expression that he hoped would mask the sudden swell of new hope he was feeling. It was crazy, he knew; most likely a long shot that would lead to another dead end. But his gut instinct was to agree with Aylor. Maybe—and he privately attached a great deal of caution to the word—this woman, whoever she was, did know something.

"If you hear from her again—"

"She said she would call back tonight."

"—your job is to convince her to talk to me. Tell her we'll see that she gets protection if she's in danger. Tell her whatever the hell it takes."

With that he gave Aylor the number of his pager.

Draining the final sip from his coffee cup, Larry stood to leave and began shaking his head. "You know, I thought everything had settled down. But now, all of a sudden, there seem to be an awful lot of funny things going on."

McGowan gave him a puzzled look. "Like what?"

"Chris has been telling me there've been some weird things happening at Joy's house. He says one afternoon he saw some man looking over the backyard fence. When Chris yelled out to him, he ducked and apparently took off running down the alley, got in a car, and drove away. Chris says he followed him, trying to get his license plate number.

"Then there was some guy who Chris says pulled up beside his car and tried to force him to the curb. Chris is a black belt in karate, you know. He jumped out, pulled the guy from his car, and decked him right there in the middle of the street.

"And now he's talking about how strange his mother's acting. Very nervous. She keeps the shutters closed all the time and has apparently been getting some phone calls that seem to really upset her.

"Then, he told me, she'd found a dead fish in their mailbox. Why would someone do something like that?"

The detective shook his head. "Beats the hell out of me."

Within an hour after Larry and Jan had left the station, McGowan and Mike Corley, who had recently been moved into Criminal Investigation, felt they had a pretty good idea who Aylor's caller might be. Checking with the Dallas Police Department to see if it had any criminal history on someone named Bill Garland, a computer search had yielded two men with that name, one a black with a history of small-time drug dealing, the other a white male whose name had only recently gone into the files.

A man named William Wesley Garland, a local pest-control exterminator, had been booked into the Dallas county jail after his wife had filed assault charges against him.

It was his first arrest.

"You know, what we've probably got here," Corley cautioned, "is some highly pissed off woman who just wants to see how much hot water she can get her old man in. Don't get your hopes up."

Since accompanying McGowan to the Loganwood Drive crime scene on that long-ago night, Corley had watched as the Gailiunas murder consumed his friend. More than once, over an after-work beer, he had gently suggested that Morris take some time off. "Get away from this thing for a few days—hell, maybe a week. Nobody's going to think you've walked away from the case just because you take a little vacation." McGowan had only smiled and insisted he was fine.

Finally, Corley had tried a more straightforward approach. "Dammit, Mo, you've got to lighten up. You're taking this thing way too personally, walking around telling yourself that if this case doesn't get solved, it will be your fault."

McGowan had offered no argument. How could he? Mike,

who knew him better than anyone else in the department, was absolutely right.

Now, with the prospect of Aylor being contacted again by this woman who, in all likelihood, was Bill Garland's estranged wife, Corley knew that Morris's hopes would again soar. In truth, Mike himself felt a new rush of excitement for the long-dormant case.

For a number of reasons, both personal and professional, he silently prayed this would not be another false alarm.

Sandy McGowan had for weeks been looking forward to the evening. A longtime fan of pop-rock entertainer Michael Jackson, she had dutifully stood in line to purchase tickets, then counted off the days until she and Morris would drive into Dallas to attend the concert.

Long before they reached Reunion Arena, McGowan had convinced himself that the possibility of the woman contacting Aylor again was a long shot. Certainly, the chances that she would call back so quickly were, at best, slim. It had, after all, been nine months between her first and second calls.

The detective fought to put the matter out of his mind and enjoy the music. Only a few times during the evening did he sneak a look at the tiny screen of his beeper.

Not until they were on their way back home did it sound and an unfamiliar number appeared. Pulling off North Central Expressway, he found a bank of pay phones near a service station, jumped from the car, and dialed the number.

A busy signal. Hanging up, he called Aylor's house. Another busy signal.

Sandy had left the car to join him when his beeper went off again. This time he recognized Aylor's number and quickly dialed.

"Larry, this is Morris."

"Jesus, man, she's hysterical. She says she's next. I gave her your beeper number and made her promise to call."

As if on cue, Morris's beeper went off again. Glancing at the number, he immediately hung up, took the quarter that Sandy was holding out to him, and dialed.

After a single ring, a woman's voice came on the line.

"Ma'am, my name is Sergeant McGowan." It was the last sentence he would utter for several minutes as the woman immediately launched into a tirade of accusations. This time there was no coy Southern drawl, only the sound of crazed fear.

She spoke so fast and in such a high-pitched voice that it was difficult to understand everything she was saying. "Bill Garland . . . *he's after me* . . . he's going to kill me, *just like he did that nurse*. . . . See, I met him in this bar and he started talking. . . . He told me about that, you know. *He told me* about how she was killed . . . they went in her house . . ."

Finally, McGowan managed to break in. "Just calm down. I'm going to do whatever I can to help you."

"Calm down? Don't you understand what I'm saying? He told me *I would die*. . . . He said it would make what happened to that nurse look like a tea party. . . . He's killed a lot of people. *Goddammit,* how am I supposed to calm down?"

For over a half hour the bizarre conversation continued, McGowan saying little as the woman, alternately crying and screaming into the phone, continued her rambling horror story.

"Ma'am," the detective interrupted, "listen to me for just a minute. I want to help you, get you some protection if you need it, but I can't do anything if I don't know who you are."

"Just call me Mrs. Mud," she replied sarcastically. "My name's M-U-D."

"Look, we're not getting anywhere this way. Why don't we meet somewhere we can sit down and talk?"

Suddenly, there was silence on the other end of the line. As he waited for the woman to reply, Morris quickly wrote a note to Sandy, instructing her to use one of the other phones to contact the police station and have them attempt to trace the call and to notify Mike Corley to meet him at the station.

Finally, the woman spoke. "Where?"

"There's an all-night restaurant out on North Central and Spring Valley. JoJo's."

"I know where it is. What time?"

Morris looked down at his watch. It was already after eleven. "Whatever's convenient with you."

A sudden calm came over the caller and McGowan thought he heard her laugh. "Aren't meetings like this supposed to take place at midnight?"

"I'll be there," McGowan said.

Driving to the police station, McGowan kissed Sandy good-bye and sent her on her way. "Don't wait up," he said as he saw Sergeant Corley's car pulling into the parking lot.

"Mo," Sandy said, "be careful. This woman sounds nuts."

That, her husband quickly explained, was why he wanted someone to accompany him as a backup. Corley would find a spot in the restaurant parking lot from which he could monitor the meeting.

"I'm not even sure she'll show up," Morris added.

He had been waiting inside the all-but-deserted coffee shop for only a few minutes when he saw a Mercedes pull into a parking space near the front entrance. An attractive blonde, dressed in black, hurried inside, searched the booths, and began walking toward him.

She was hardly what McGowan had expected.

"Are you Sergeant McGowan?"

Standing, he extended his hand. "Yes, ma'am. Are you Carol Garland?"

"I see you've done your homework." She was smiling, her voice calm and pleasant. There was no trace of the accent or the hysteria the officer had heard over the phone less than an hour earlier.

Smoothing her dress as she slid into the booth, she asked another question: "Do you know who *else* I am?"

Puzzled, McGowan lifted his palms and shrugged. "No."

"I'm Joy Aylor's sister. She's the person you're after. Joy is the one who planned the murder of the doctor's wife."

Stunned, the sergeant did not immediately respond. Instead, he studied the face of the woman seated across from him, wondering what kind of insanity he had allowed himself to be lured into. Was she, as he had already begun to expect, just another one of those crazies who seem always to come out of the woodwork during the course of every high-profile investigation? Or was it somehow possible that she might actually have information that would give his investigation new life?

"I think," he said, "that it would be best if we continued this conversation at the police station."

If nothing else, Morris wanted Corley to hear what the woman had to say. Lord knew, no one would believe him if he alone tried to pass on the woman's story to his superiors.

The two detectives sat into the early morning hours listening to Carol's rambling, mazelike story. Early in 1986, she said, Joy had approached her, asking a favor. If a man phoned and asked for "Mary," Carol was to get in touch with Joy immediately. Initially, she had assumed Joy was involved in an affair. Only later did she learn that the caller was a self-professed hired killer named Bill Garland. Over a period of months, Carol and Garland had talked at length on the phone, and he had finally confided to her that it had been her sister who was responsible for the death of Larry Aylor's girlfriend.

"Did Garland tell you that *he* killed Rozanne Gailiunas?" McGowan asked.

"All I know is he said, 'We did it.' "

The detectives listened as she recalled details of the crime, all of which they knew had been reported by the media.

"Did he tell you how they got into the house?"

"I think they told her they were utility repairmen."

Why, McGowan wanted to know, was she so concerned that her own life was now in danger?

"Because he's afraid I'll do exactly what I'm sitting here doing, for God's sake. He's afraid I'll talk about all the things he's told me and the things he made me do. Like blackmailing Joy. He forced me to help him with that."

McGowan rubbed his face. Keeping pace with Carol's train of thought was impossible. "What blackmail is that?" he finally asked.

"Last October, Bill needed money and decided to jack Joy around a little. He was going to contact her and say that a girlfriend of one of the guys who they had hired to kill Larry—''

McGowan bolted forward in his chair. *"Wait a minute.* Now you're telling us Joy was also involved in the attempt on her husband's life?''

Carol nodded and continued with her story.

"So, what Bill decides to do is send her this note. It said something like, 'I'm coming for a visit. Am strapped for money. Think you could loan me twenty-five thousand dollars? Would you and your son like to come visit me?' and was signed 'Roxanne Gailiunas.' '' Either Garland had been confused about Rozanne's first name or had, for whatever reason, chosen to alter it slightly.

"Joy really bought it. She called Bill and told him that she was certain that Carl Noska—the man who had originally put her in touch with Bill—was trying to blackmail her and that she wanted him killed right away. Bill plays along, telling her he'll check into it. He waits a few days and calls her back, saying he'd had a drink with Noska and is convinced he's not the blackmailer. Now Joy's even more frantic and asks Bill if he can find out who it is.

"He waits awhile, then calls her and gives her this cock-and-bull story about the girlfriend of one of the men he'd hired to do the hit on Larry. The guy was dead now, and the girlfriend wanted twenty-five thousand dollars to keep her mouth shut about what he'd been involved in.

"Now, Joy's asking Bill if he can arrange to have this woman killed.

"It was getting nuttier by the minute. Joy's telling Bill that his name was also mentioned in the note—which, of course, he and I both knew wasn't true. She starts negotiating with him to kill this woman who she says is now threatening to expose both of them.

"This goes on for weeks. Bill keeps sending more letters. One said, 'I'm coming to visit soon. Think you need to have the same kind of rest I'm having. R. Gailiunas.'

"Joy's going nuts.

"Finally, Bill agrees to find someone who can get rid of this blackmailer and says it's going to cost the same amount the woman was asking for. Joy throws another fit and tells him that since the woman's threatening to expose him, too, he should pay half.

"She even sends him copies of the notes she's been receiving. Hell, they didn't even resemble the ones Bill had written. His name was mentioned in each of them, as if the blackmailer was threatening both of them.

"Bill argues and raises all kind of hell with Joy, then finally agrees. He tells her he will send me over to pick up the twelve thousand five hundred dollars.

"See, she didn't know Bill and I had married. In fact, she still doesn't know.

"So, anyway, a couple of weeks later, Bill phones her and tells her the job's been taken care of. God, he loved it—getting twelve thousand five hundred dollars to kill someone who didn't even exist.

"Pretty crazy, huh?"

With that, Carol finally took a deep breath, stood up, and asked directions to the rest room. As soon as she had disappeared down the hall, McGowan turned to look at Corley.

Anticipating the question, Mike began shaking his head. "Ain't no way."

McGowan agreed. Aside from naming a suspect, all of what Carol knew about the Gailiunas murder could have been taken from newspaper reports. And unless this guy named Bill Garland was ready to throw up his hands and confess, there was little they could do to substantiate her story.

"There are a couple of things we might check out," Morris offered. While discussing the blackmailing of Joy, Carol had mentioned renting a post office box in the name of "Roxanne Gailiunas." Too, maybe it wouldn't hurt to find out something about Carl Noska, the alleged go-between she had mentioned.

"Mo, dammit," Corley said, "the lady's a blue-ribbon nut case."

"Yeah, I know."

In a matter of minutes both men had cause to reconsider. Carol was looking at her watch as she returned from the rest room. "I had no idea it was so late. I've got to be at work in a few hours. Is it okay if I go now?"

McGowan nodded and began walking her toward the door.

As she stepped into the darkened parking lot, she stopped. "I forgot to tell you about one of the things we did to scare Joy into going along with the blackmail deal." She was smiling as she spoke. "It was Bill's idea. We left a dead fish in her mailbox."

With that she turned to walk away, leaving McGowan to reflect back on what Larry Aylor had said just the previous day: "Chris says there have been some strange things happening at Joy's house . . . phone calls making her nervous . . . *a dead fish in the mailbox.*"

Standing in the doorway, McGowan was unaware of the disbelieving look that had spread across his face. "Sonuvabitch . . ."

Corley laughed. "Welcome to the twilight zone, partner."

"I think we'd better talk to the captain in the morning."

# 10

WHERE HAD THIS strange woman, cool and calculating one minute, panicked and paranoid the next, come from? Was she really whom she claimed to be? And what could her motive be? Was it possible that her life might actually be in danger? Or was she, as some in the department were already suggesting, just another angry, vindictive wife inventing new miseries to inflict on a hated husband?

The questions intrigued McGowan enough to schedule another meeting for the following evening.

Having reviewed all the newspaper reports on the Gailiunas murder, he determined that much of her story could have been pieced together after reading the articles. "Toss in a lucky guess here and there,'' he told Capt. D. E. Golden, ''and someone could come up with a pretty plausible story. She may well be a certifiable nut case. But I think there's at least a possibility that there's something here.''

Golden listened with mixed feelings. A patrol sergeant at the time of the murder, Golden, too, had been among those early arrivals at the Loganwood Drive address. The scene in Rozanne's bedroom had been unlike any he'd ever walked into. Nothing he'd experienced in the line of duty, before or since, had so affected him.

For that reason, he understood McGowan's determination to resolve the long-standing case.

At the same time, the toll that the investigation had taken concerned him greatly. Like Corley, Golden had lost track of the times he'd spoken privately with McGowan about the case. The captain knew how personally involved his friend had become, taking the case home with him, waking in the middle of the night to pace a darkened house in search of answers that would not come. He'd seen an easygoing, even-tempered man become snappish and overreactive. More than once he had felt that Morris had stepped very near the emotional edge.

Candidly, Golden had expressed concern for McGowan's health, both physically and mentally, as well as the potential problems the investigation might be causing his marriage.

Though the man standing in his office spoke casually, tempering his story with an air of cautious doubt, Golden knew that McGowan was hiding a newborn enthusiasm. And it concerned him.

''Get a couple of detectives to do some of the legwork for you,'' the captain said. His unspoken message was clear: he wanted to find out as quickly as possible if Carol Garland's story had any validity. If not, he didn't want McGowan or anyone else spending undue time agonizing over something that was ultimately going to do nothing more than refuel old frustrations.

If, in fact, Golden had realized at the time that he had several years earlier encountered the same woman who was now promising to shed new light on the Gailiunas case, he might well have dismissed the idea of spending time with her at all.

Her last name had been Walker then, and she had reported a burglary to which he had been assigned. When he arrived at her house, he found it deserted and seriously damaged by fire. Contacting fire department officials in an attempt to locate the complainant, he was told that she was viewed as an arson suspect and had disappeared.

The lady, who never got back in touch with him to follow up on the alleged burglary, had, he was told, a lengthy history of wild claims and strange behavior.

To some who knew her, the observation was a classic example of understatement.


The first child born to Henry and Frances, she was, by her own admission, the outcast of the Davis family. For as long as she could remember, her relationship with her parents had been a destructive series of fights and forgivings. Little that Carol did met with approval. And, in many cases, for good reason.

When she had pled with her father to be allowed to attend Southern Methodist University, he had agreed to pay for her college education. When, in time, he learned that she was not even bothering to attend the classes his hard-earned money had paid for, he became furious. A man who lived by a credo of not throwing good money after bad, Henry closed his checkbook and informed his daughter that she was on her own. Yet, when Carol would next find herself in financial trouble, a grumbling but willing Henry Davis always came to the rescue. In 1979, he paid the bills when she entered Baylor Hospital for psychiatric treatment, then funded the outpatient therapy she received for the next two years.

Such had been the pattern of their stormy relationship for years.

When she married a man named Michael Walker, Henry had provided them a house, ever ready to dispatch members of his crew to take care of any repair work necessary. Davis, in fact, had even financed his son-in-law's brief and unsuccessful attempt at the home-building business.

Yet when her seven-year marriage finally ended in divorce, Carol felt the weight of blame from her family.

Suddenly on her own and with a two-year-old daughter to raise, Carol had once again gone to her parents for help. After all, Joy and Larry, struggling through the early days of their own marriage, had been welcomed into the Davis home during financial hard times. While they both worked, their young son, Christopher, was cared for in the Davis home.

Such help, however, was denied Carol. She was forced to place her daughter in a day care center while she worked, first as an insurance company secretary, then as a passenger service representative for Southwest Airlines. Frances Davis's explanation had been that there was simply no way the maid could be expected to watch over two small children on a daily basis. Only later had the Davises, concerned for the well-being of their granddaughter, decided to take her into their home.

For Carol, it was just another in a long line of reasons to feel betrayed by her family.

The resentment, born during her childhood, continued to intensify. In time it was targeted not only at her parents but also her sister. Joy, two years younger, was, Carol felt, clearly the favored child.

In childhood, a pattern had developed in which Joy would get into mischief and Carol would be blamed. For instance, six-year-old Joy, playing with matches in an upstairs bedroom, had accidentally set a closet on fire. She had tearfully claimed her innocence, blaming her sister, and, as usual, Carol was ultimately disciplined.

Later angered that her parents clearly favored Joy's child over hers, and weary of the constant criticisms of her lifestyle, Carol finally made up her mind to distance herself from the family. For long stretches of time, she would only visit the Davis house on Christmas day, forcing a festive smile for a few hours as turkey and dressing was served and presents exchanged.

By the mid-eighties, she no longer even saw her family during the holidays. The self-proclaimed "black sheep" of the Davis family disappeared into her own world, leaving behind what she perceived as a collection of cruel, vindictive, and manipulative people.

She was surprised, then, in the early weeks of January 1986 when she received a phone call from her sister.

"I need to talk with you," Joy said.

Carol at first suspected it had something to do with her absence from the family Christmas gathering. No, Joy said. She wanted to talk about her husband. "What do you know about Larry?"

Carol paused for a moment. "You know I don't like him," she frankly answered. "I never have."

"Can you come over?"

Joy had appeared happy to see Carol when she arrived at the front door, still perplexed by the urgency she'd heard in her sister's voice. Joy confided that she didn't feel comfortable talking in the house and suggested they take a walk through the neighborhood. As they walked in the crisp afternoon air, Joy calmly talked of a bizarre sequence of events that had occurred since they had last spoken. Larry, she explained, had left her for another woman and filed for divorce. Then, suddenly, the girlfriend had been mysteriously murdered and Larry had come back home. She feared that Larry was responsible for the woman's death and, despite their reconciliation, was now concerned that her own life might be in danger.

For the first time, it struck Carol just how much distance she had managed to place between her and her family. "How come I never heard anything about this?"

Joy ignored her and continued. She apologized to Carol for not believing her long ago when she had been the first to suggest that Larry and Elizabeth had been romantically involved. For the first time, Joy talked of the physical and mental abuse she had suffered throughout her marriage. She desperately wanted to leave her husband but was deathly afraid of what he might do to her if she did.

Carol listened intently, surprised at the sudden outpouring from her sister. Throughout their adult lives, Carol had been the one so often accused of paranoia. Now, as they walked side by side through the quiet Arbor Trail neighborhood, the roles had suddenly reversed. Joy, she was convinced, was genuinely frightened.

"Do you know someone who can scare Larry?" Joy asked.

"Why?"

"Maybe if he's afraid someone might hurt him, he would leave me alone."

"Jesus, Joy, that's crazy."

"I know."

Carol stared at her sister for a long time. *Why come to me about this?* she wondered.

As she drove home, pondering the strange conversation she'd just had with her sister, Carol could not help but smile. At least they now had one thing in common:

Neither could stand Larry Aylor.

Weeks would pass before Carol again heard from Joy.

They met for lunch and lingered over coffee for an hour or so before any mention was made of their previous conversation.

Finally, just as they were leaving, Joy said, "Oh, by the way, I've found someone."

Carol noticed a twinkle in her sister's eyes that she'd not seen before. "Fine."

"You may get a call from a man," Joy continued, "asking to speak to Mary. If so, call and let me know."

For a moment, Carol contemplated asking for an explanation, then decided against it. She left the restaurant wondering if perhaps her sister had dismissed the idea of divorcing Larry and, instead, had entered into an affair.

In early April, a man phoned and asked to speak to "Mary."

"She's not here," Carol replied, "but I'll see that she gets the message you called."

It was the first of several such conversations that slowly lured Carol Garland into an insane nightmare that seemed to have no end.

Following a second meeting with Carol, McGowan had become convinced her story had a basis of truth. Though she could not remember the specific address of the mail drop used in the blackmail scheme, she did recall the shopping center in which it was located and was able to direct him and Officer Ken Roberts to it.

The next morning, Roberts, accompanied by Detective Ken MacKenzie, interviewed the mail-drop manager, who acknowledged that a box had been rented to a "Roxanne Gailiunas." His description of the woman who had rented it matched Carol Garland. He remembered her, he said, because she had come to the counter wearing several Band-Aids on her face. "I didn't see any indication of any cuts or bruises," he said, "and I wondered at the time if maybe it was an attempt at some kind of disguise."

In the second meeting with McGowan, Carol had told of taping a number of her husband's telephone conversations. Though she said that Garland had found most of the tapes she'd hidden, she thought she still had at least one of Garland talking with Joy.

McGowan and Roberts accompanied her home to search for the tape.

While they were at the Dalhart Street address, which was vaguely familiar to Roberts, new light was shed on Carol Garland's identity. As she searched, Roberts walked into the dining room where a large collection of mail was strewn on the counter. Thumbing through the assortment of bills and past-due notices, he saw that many of them were addressed to "Carol Walker."

Catching McGowan's attention, he motioned to him. When they were out of Carol's earshot, Roberts whispered, "We're in deep shit here. I know this woman."

Back at the station, he said, there was a thick file of oddball complaints that had been filed from this address. Carol Walker, he confided, had been a pain in the ass of the Richardson Police Department for a long time.

Neither was surprised, then, when she was unable to locate the tape.

Later, back in McGowan's office, Carol's story grew even stranger.

During the spring of '86, she said, the messages for "Mary"

had come sporadically, and each time her conversation with the caller had been brief.

"Then, one day he calls and, out of the blue, strikes up a conversation. He tells me I have a nice voice and wants to know my name. He says his name is Bill Garland. We talked for, maybe, fifteen or twenty minutes."

Thereafter, the conversations would stretch on for as long as an hour, sometimes more. Bill talked at length of his experiences in Vietnam, his love for hunting and fishing, always ending with a flirtatious suggestion that they should meet someday soon.

"For some reason," Carol said, "he apparently got the impression that I knew far more about what was going on than I really did. That became very clear one day when he called to say that 'Mary' had not been in touch with him for some time."

It was obvious that he was irritated.

Bill, she said, told her to tell Joy that he needed the "other instructions. Since we're having trouble getting this goddamn job done," he said, "I need the other list."

"What other list?"

"You know, the other five people."

Carol felt her chest tighten but tried to maintain a calmness in her voice. "Do you know their names?"

"No, dammit, that's why I need the list."

Then, suddenly, he was off on a tirade against her sister, weaving a story that left Carol speechless.

Joy, he said, still owed him money for the job they had done on the woman whom her husband had been messing around with. He was getting damn tired of her stalling. Adding to his frustration was the fact "his people" had been trying to get rid of Larry Aylor since sometime back in '84 and still hadn't gotten the job done.

He recalled that they had almost succeeded one afternoon as Larry rode his motorcycle through the neighborhood. "We were in a Jeep, waiting for him at the corner. But just as he rode up on us, these kids walked by. We didn't want any witnesses."

Sometime in '85, he said, they had tired of following Larry around, waiting for the ideal time, and had considered simply walking up to the house, kicking the door in, and getting the job over with. Joy had said no to the idea and, in fact, had told him she had changed her mind. She wanted them to forget about it.

"The two people I brought in to do the job stayed in a hotel for a fucking month and never could get the guy alone long enough to take care of their business."

Frankly, he said, he was relieved when she had canceled the deal.

But now, suddenly, Joy had again decided she wanted her husband killed yet still hadn't paid him the $11,800 in expense money owed him. "You remind her we agreed on two hundred dollars a day," the caller said. "And tell her I want my goddamn money right now."

Frightened, Carol said she would pass along the message, then hung up the phone. She sat on the edge of her bed for some time, the incredible story she'd just been told replaying in her mind.

Late the following afternoon Carol drove to Joy's house and was pleased to find that neither Larry nor Chris was there.

"Look," she said, "your friend Bill isn't very happy. He wants the money you owe him . . . and some kind of list."

Joy smiled and said things had been taken care of. She had spoken with Bill earlier in the day.

Though they were alone in the house, Carol lowered her voice to a whisper. "Jesus, Joy, he says this has been going on since 1984."

Joy replied with a nonchalant nod. "It has."

Carol began pacing, her arms folded across her breasts. "Look, whatever goes on between you and Larry is your business. I don't really give a shit, one way or another. But why am I involved in this? Why did you do this to me?"

"Hey, no one's ever going to suspect you of anything. I just needed someone for him to contact. I couldn't have him calling here."

"What's the list about? Who are the five other people, for Christ's sake?"

"There's no list," Joy said in an assuring tone. "I told him that so I could make a better deal."

"A *better deal?*"

"See, if he thinks we're going to be doing more business, his rates are cheaper."

Carol slumped into a chair and stared across the room, suddenly frightened of the woman curled on the couch, sipping iced tea. Dear God, she thought, her sister was talking about discount murder as calmly as if it were some ten-cents-off bargain she'd happened on at the supermarket.

"I need you to do me a favor," Joy said, placing an envelope on the coffee table. "Would you deliver this on your way home?"

"What is it?"

Joy ignored the question. "Someone will be waiting for you at the Gulf station on the corner of MacArthur and Highway 183. Just see that he gets it."

Though reasonably sure she knew what the envelope contained, Carol said nothing. Instead, she walked aimlessly around the tastefully decorated living room, stopping to study a painting above the fireplace. Finally, she turned to her sister.

"Tell me who you really think killed that doctor's wife."

"I've already told you, I think it was Larry," Joy replied, "or, maybe, the woman's husband." With that she picked up the envelope. "Are you going to deliver this?"

Carol shrugged. "Sure, why not?"

In truth, she was afraid not to.

The envelope contained $3,000—thirty $100 bills. Carol had opened it before arriving at the service station and parking near the car wash. She had not even had time to turn off her engine before a young man with long blond hair leaned into her window. "Do you have the package?" he asked.

Carol handed him the envelope without a word and quickly drove away, easing into the late-afternoon traffic. Joy's debt, she knew, had been whittled to $8,800.

Carol was unlocking her front door when she heard her phone ringing. Thinking it was probably her sister, calling to make sure the delivery had been made, Carol made no attempt to hurry into the house.

When she did finally pick up the receiver, she was surprised to hear Bill Garland's voice: "I must say, you're a very good-looking woman."

He described the white silk skirt and navy blue jacket she was wearing, even mentioning the flower-shaped pin attached to her lapel.

"Where are you?" Carol demanded.

Ignoring her question, he said, "I also like women who wear those dark stockings."

"Goddammit, where are you?"

"Not far."

In truth, he was speaking from a phone in his car, parked just across the street from the service station where he had watched her pass the envelope to an unsuspecting office clerk less than a half hour earlier.

With the aid of a pair of high-powered binoculars he had managed his first look at the woman whose voice he had found so intriguing. Now he wanted to get to know her better.

In the days to come, he began calling more regularly, continuing to compliment her on the way she had dressed that day, mentioning that he'd watched her as she shopped during her lunch break or when she walked her dog in the evening. He told her how pretty he thought her daughter was.

There was a new tone to his voice—part amused, part sinister—that she found unsettling. That he was obviously following her, playing this I-know-you-but-you-don't-know-me game, unnerved her. Several times he asked her to dinner, and on each occasion she turned him down. "I'm already seeing someone," she would explain.

"I'm a patient man," he replied.

It would not be until September, four months after their first telephone conversation, that Carol finally met Bill Garland.

After a drug-related shooting in her neighborhood one evening, she had mentioned it to him when he called later that night. He suggested that she should have a gun for protection and volunteered to purchase her one and teach her to shoot it. When she failed to accept his offer, he took another approach: "You know, your daughter sure looked cute walking home from school today. I thought about stopping her and saying hello.''

Carol was certain she detected a threat in his voice.

''I think it's time that you and I meet,'' he continued. ''You should go out with me.''

Already, Carol had begun to harbor a genuine fear of this man, who now seemed determined to force his way into her life. She saw no way out.

When, finally, she met him, her concern had immediately magnified. A dark-haired man in his early forties, he stood six feet six inches and weighed almost three hundred pounds.

As the bizarre relationship continued, Carol became increasingly convinced that his intent was not to court her, but instead to kill her. The motive, she was sure, was her still sketchy knowledge of the nurse's murder and the unsuccessful attempts on Larry's life.

Buying time to decide how she might free herself from what she now perceived as a dangerous situation, Carol accepted his invitation to dinner and a movie.

When he demanded she spend a weekend at a friend's small farm north of Dallas, learning to shoot a handgun, she reluctantly agreed. Later, two things would stand out in her mind about the trip. She would return home with her right hand throbbing and her arm badly swollen from the repeated impact of firing a .357 magnum more times than she could remember. And, Garland had made a comment, disguised as a joke, that chilled her.

There had been a county-owned bulldozer on the property. Pointing to it, he had said, ''You know, way out here a fella could climb up on that thing, dig him a deep hole, bury a body in it, and nobody would ever know.'' Then, he laughed.

Carol felt helplessly trapped, the target of this huge, chain-smoking man's cruel mind games.

Two weeks later, standing in the living room of a justice of the peace in the tiny town of Sunset, an hour's drive north of Dallas, she became Mrs. Bill Garland. Though he had not said as much, she had felt his message was clear: either she marry him or he would kill her.

Becoming Mrs. Bill Garland, she felt, provided her the only chance of staying alive long enough to devise some plan of escape from the insanity she'd been swallowed into.

She was careful not to tell anyone in her family, neither her parents nor her sisters, that she had married.

For the safety of her preteen daughter, who by then was spending most of her time with her father or at the Davis house, Carol did not even contact her when she moved into Bill Garland's house in nearby Greenville, Texas.

McGowan and Roberts had listened to the woman's meandering, improbable story, each fighting the urge to stop her and ask the dozens of questions that had come to mind as she spoke. Why had she not simply told Joy she didn't want to get involved as a go-between? Why even talk to Bill Garland if she found him so frightening? How could she agree to deliver money that she was certain was payment for a crime and think she would not be viewed as a party to what was going on? Had there been some incentive offered her that she was conveniently not bothering to mention? How could she marry someone who so terrified her?

Her story, the officers felt, was as unbelievable as it was fascinating. Yet, it would become even more tangled.

Carol explained that her marriage to Bill Garland had been an endless succession of physical and mental abuse, macabre mind games, and horrifying threats. "He always slept with that .357 magnum under his pillow," she recalled, "with the barrel pointed toward me."

As she spoke, it became obvious to the officers that it would be difficult to substantiate much of what she was alleging. According to Carol, her husband enjoyed scaring her with stories from his past.

Having left the exterminating business after developing allergies to the chemicals he used, Garland had entered the oil-and-gas business but without much success. Yet money, he assured his wife, would never be a problem. Since returning from Vietnam, he had been supplementing his income as a professional hit man.

There had, he bragged, been a job over in Tyler. And a man

and wife he'd killed in Waco in some kind of insurance scam. He'd fired shots through a living-room window one night, killing a man in Dallas. A woman in Houston had hired him to do away with her father and uncle. And a couple of times he'd traveled up to Oklahoma to do some work.

And there had been the woman in Richardson. After killing her, he claimed, he had tossed the gun away in Lake Lavon, just outside of Dallas.

One evening, during the course of an angry exchange in the backyard, Carol had briefly mustered the courage to say she was planning to leave. Garland had grabbed her by the arms, putting his face inches from hers, and said, "If you ever do, what happened to that lady over in Richardson will be nothing . . . fucking nothing . . . compared to what will happen to your pretty little daughter. And I'll make damn sure you're there to see it. Then, if you're real nice, I'll kill you quick."

As he spoke, she remembered, his eyes were colder than she'd ever seen them.

On one occasion he had even confided to her that Joy had already paid him to kill her. He had simply been waiting for the right time. Her death, he explained, would look like a suicide. Aware of her fear of heights, he mentioned that she might "fall" from the roof of a building. Or perhaps she would die in an automobile accident.

Regularly, he would wake her in the middle of the night to tell her of a recurring dream. They were somewhere far out in the country and he saw her at the end of a partially completed bridge, several hundred feet above the ground, making preparations for a picnic. As he walked toward her, she would stand up, lose her balance, and fall. In the dream, he said, he always tried to catch her but without success.

Too, she had overheard portions of a telephone conversation in which he told someone that he had made up his mind he was going to "get rid" of her.

At times, she said, she was certain that her only way out was to kill him before he killed her. However, she had not been able to bring herself to do it.

Instead, for over a year she had continued to endure his

abuse and threats, even participating with him in blackmailing Joy.

After they had moved from Greenville back to Dallas, Carol began secretly recording her husband's telephone conversations. She had hired an electrician to tap into the phone and run a line through the bedroom closet to a recorder she had hidden in a dresser drawer.

The tapes, she had decided, might one day serve as her insurance to survival.

On the morning of April 19, 1988, she had finally become convinced nothing could assure her safety any longer.

An argument, which had been ongoing for several days, had erupted when Carol confronted her husband about the overheard phone conversation in which he had mentioned getting rid of her.

Flying into a rage, Garland lunged at her as she ran toward the bedroom, hoping to reach the closet where the gun he'd given her was hidden in the pocket of one of her jackets.

She had just found the gun when she felt a huge hand wrap around her arm, pulling her back into the room. Garland grabbed the gun away and, with a menacing smile, pointed it at her and pulled the trigger.

Terrified, her heart was pounding as she faintly heard the click of the hammer hitting an empty chamber. Tossing the gun aside, he again reached out for her and hurled her against the open closet door, with such force that the doorknob embedded in the wall.

As Garland moved toward the bed, she was certain he intended to get his .357 magnum. Escaping into the living room, she hurriedly picked up the telephone and dialed 911. "He's got a gun and he's going to shoot me," she yelled. "Please, help."

She had managed to give the dispatcher an address before her husband yanked the phone from her grasp and placed a thumb on the disconnect button.

For several seconds he stared at her, saying nothing. Then, as if on cue, he became remarkably calm. While Carol sat in the middle of the living-room floor, shaking and in tears, he methodically began gathering personal items and moving them onto the front porch.

He was packed and preparing to leave when a Dallas police car pulled up in front of the house. Bill greeted the officers and explained that his wife was crazy and that he could take no more of it.

After surveying the house and determining that a struggle had, in fact, taken place, the officers listened to Carol's story. Learning that she wished to file a complaint, they handcuffed Garland and took him to jail.

That, she said, was when she began seriously thinking her only chance of staying alive was to make the authorities aware of his involvement in the murder of Rozanne Gailiunas and the attempt on Larry Aylor's life.

After a friend had bailed him out of jail, Bill had immediately called Carol. "I told you that I'm a patient man. It may be a year or two, maybe longer. But someday you're going to open your door and it will be someone wanting to collect for the newspaper or to read the meter—"

She had hung up on him.

In the days to come she lived in constant fear, taking different routes to work daily, sleeping fitfully behind locked doors, refusing to answer the phone. Whether real or imagined, she was convinced he was again following her. More than once she was sure she had caught a glimpse of him in downtown crowds as she returned from lunch. One morning she had walked outside to find a dead cat lying on her front porch. As she was returning home from work, a car driven by a man she didn't recognize pulled up beside her and honked. When she looked over at the driver, he had pointed a finger in her direction and mouthed the words, "Bang, bang . . . you're dead."

Her husband was, she knew, still playing his cruel games.

Looking across the desk at the silent McGowan, she explained that she was convinced the only reason she was not already dead was Garland's fear that she still had phone tapes of him and Joy discussing the murder of Rozanne Gailiunas.

Pushing a phone across the desk toward her, the sergeant said, "Call Joy. See if you can get her to talk about it."

"What the hell am I supposed to say?"

"Tell her something's come up. You're worried. Just see what she has to say."

As if reacting to a challenge, Carol dialed the number and waited for her sister to answer.

"We've got a problem," Carol said.

"What are you talking about?" Joy replied. "I'm very busy right now. I have people coming over for dinner."

"Joy, we've got to talk."

After a moment's silence Joy said, this time in a whispered voice, "Is this about Larry?"

"Yes."

"I'll call you back later."

McGowan felt a combined rush of excitement and sudden impatience. Though Joy had said little, the tone of her voice, particularly when she'd asked if Carol wanted to talk about Larry Aylor, had caught his attention. For a brief moment, he even considered driving immediately to the Aylor house to confront Joy.

Instead, he asked that Carol return to the station again the following evening after she got off work. He wanted Ken MacKenzie to interview her, to also hear her story.

Afterward, MacKenzie felt even more strongly than did either McGowan or Roberts that an element of truth ran through her story. During his lengthy career as an interrogator, he had never encountered anyone with an imagination vivid enough to create such a complex scenario.

When, after a couple of days, Carol had not heard from Joy, McGowan suggested it was time to press the issue.

"Call her again," he said, "and do whatever you have to to convince her that the problem is major and not going to go away. See if you can get her to meet with you somewhere."

To the surprise of everyone, Joy agreed to meet Carol the following Friday evening at nine at JoJo's restaurant in Richardson.

From their vantage point in a van parked in front of the restaurant, McGowan and MacKenzie could see Carol seated in a corner booth.

Throughout the day they had made elaborate preparations to get the meeting on both audio and videotape. One microphone had been placed in Carol's purse, which lay on the seat beside her, another in a stamped envelope that lay on the table with her checkbook.

Four officers, recruited to work undercover, stood by to enter the restaurant after Joy and take a seat as near them as possible. One carried a briefcase that contained a tiny hidden camera.

In the van, a second camera was trained on the booth where Carol was seated.

Several times they had checked to make sure the envelope microphone was working properly. To activate it, one had only to press the corner where the stamp was attached. To turn it off required pressure applied to the opposite end of the envelope.

For several hours that afternoon, McGowan had talked with Carol, carefully explaining the importance of not indicating that she was attempting to solicit specific information. "Don't ask questions," he instructed. "Just talk yourself around the subjects and let her respond."

Still, throughout the preparation it had been McGowan who remained most skeptical. When Carol had been sitting alone for almost a half hour, he was convinced that Joy was not coming.

"Who's that?" MacKenzie asked, nodding toward a parking space near the restaurant entrance.

McGowan turned to see Joy Aylor step from a red Porsche and move toward the front door. "I'll be a sonuvabitch," he said as he watched her walk to the booth where Carol was seated.

For the first few minutes, Joy made it clear that she was unhappy that she had been forced to come out so late at night. Quickly, though, she calmed, and the conversation was no different from any that two sisters might have upon seeing each other for the first time in quite a while. Joy made approving mention that Carol appeared to have lost weight and complimented her nail polish.

Soon, however, Carol managed to turn the subject to the concerns she had alluded to on the phone. "Joy, I know what's going on."

"What are you talking about?"

"I'm talking about that woman out in Richardson . . . and about Larry, the money, everything."

A hostile tone crept into Joy's voice. "Are you wearing a wire?"

Carol slid from the booth to stand up. "Do you want to frisk me? Hell, no, I'm not wearing a wire."

"Sit down," Joy said, nervously glancing around the room.

Carol returned to the booth and for several seconds sat studying her sister. Though Joy did not immediately speak, a question was written across her face: *How do you know this?*

Before she could say anything, Carol continued, "Bill told me."

"Why would he tell you something like that?"

The question provided Carol the opportunity she'd been waiting for. "Joy, Bill and I are married."

Even through the viewfinder of the video camera, MacKenzie could tell that Joy was visibly shocked.

Speaking more softly, she leaned forward. "What has he told you?"

"Everything. I just don't understand how you could have gotten involved in such a thing."

"Believe me, if I had it all to do over again, I wouldn't. You just don't understand . . . what he did to me."

With that, the conversation turned to Larry Aylor. Joy spoke of the hurt she had felt upon learning of his affair with her younger sister. In response, Carol confided that he had, years earlier, made advances toward her as well. Then she began to describe the nightmare of living with Bill Garland. "You just don't know what it's like to be intimidated and beaten."

Joy nodded. "Oh, yes, I do."

As they talked, several couples entered the restaurant and moved into the booth directly behind Carol. Suddenly their loud talk and boisterous behavior was also being picked up by the hidden microphones. Straining to hear above the noise, McGowan swore. The high-pitched laughter of some woman prompted him to throw a styrofoam cup still half-filled with coffee against the wall of the van.

MacKenzie assured him that while they might not be able to hear clearly, the microphone in the envelope was sensitive enough to pick up everything being said.

Moments later, however, the envelope mike went dead. Inside the surveillance van pandemonium erupted. Fists were slammed against walls and curses flew. McGowan became like a caged animal.

While they could still pick up bits of the conversation from the mike in Carol's purse, both knew the quality of the recording would be dramatically reduced.

MacKenzie urged McGowan to calm down and continue listening while he frantically tried to think of something that might salvage the situation. He considered going into the restaurant and posing as a waiter. Perhaps he could somehow place another mike on the table while pretending to refill salt and pepper shakers. He dismissed the idea as quickly as it had occurred. It was too risky. He feared that Carol might react to suddenly seeing him there, arousing Joy's suspicion.

They would, it was finally decided, have to hope that the secondary mike would do the job.

McGowan, meanwhile, pressed the headset hard against his ears, still catching pieces of the conversation. He heard Carol saying, "Bill says you told him you had a partner . . . that you had to get some of the money from the doctor."

"That was a lie," Joy replied. "I just told him that to buy some time. . . . I needed time to get the money together."

McGowan glanced across the van at his partner, who had also heard the exchange. "She's doing a pretty damn good job," MacKenzie observed.

"Was Bill the one who did it?" Joy asked.

That was her impression, Carol replied. "But he had somebody else with him."

For the next half hour, Carol dominated the conversation, explaining how concerned she was for her safety. Joy, meanwhile, had adopted a sympathetic, even concerned tone.

Then, finally, it was over. Joy rose to leave, suggesting that Carol call her the next day.

MacKenzie smiled for the first time. "She's leaving the door open." Already, he was thinking of some way to schedule another meeting.

After Joy had driven away, he met Carol behind the restaurant and took the tapes. "You did a good job," he said, "but we may have to do it again."

"Like hell," Carol replied.

Back at the station, the officers sat listening to the tapes late into the night. Though still frustrated by the malfunction of the equipment, they shared a sense of excitement. Carol Garland's story, they now knew, had been true.

And they had clearly heard Joy Aylor admit her guilt.

But, with the quality of the tape a concern, they immediately began planning a second meeting between Carol and her sister. The next time, they agreed, it should take place somewhere free of distracting noises. And since they now believed that Carol's life might, in fact, be in danger, they would hide her away in some out-of-the-way motel that could serve as a temporary safe haven as well as an ideal place for a second meeting with Joy.

They decided on Richardson's Continental Motel, an aging, nondescript lodge just off North Central Expressway.

Carol, making no secret that she felt the failure of the microphone at JoJo's was a result of police incompetence, was not easy to convince. Only after a lengthy conversation with MacKenzie did she finally agree to contact Joy again.

This time she would insist that she was now certain Bill was trying to have her killed and that she had gone into hiding. She had to talk, to come up with a plan that would somehow assure her safety.

She phoned Joy on the following Wednesday, asking that she meet her in room 224 of the Continental the following day. Fearful that Joy would be even more suspicious of a second meeting, McGowan was surprised when she agreed. If nothing else, he thought, Carol was damn persuasive.

McGowan vowed that nothing would be left to chance. Several bugs were planted in the room where Carol would stay. The adjacent room was rented and listening equipment set up. A third room, directly across the motel parking lot, would serve

119

as a location from which video cameras could film Joy's arrival and departure. Plainclothes officers would be stationed at various points around the motel.

With everything in place, the wait began. And Joy failed to show. Early in the evening, Carol, nervous and angry, phoned and heard her sister explain that she had made a sudden decision to go to the lake house for the day and had just arrived home minutes earlier.

Carol exploded. "Joy, we've *got* to talk. This is serious."

"It'll have to be sometime in the afternoon. I've got a dinner party tomorrow night."

"Just be here," Carol said before slamming the phone down and gathering her things to leave.

For MacKenzie, the night was far from over. After leaving the Continental and stopping for a late dinner, he had gone home and was in bed when the dispatcher called to say that Carol was demanding that he contact her immediately.

The detective quickly dialed her number. Once again, Carol was hysterical, her words running together as she spoke. She had returned home, she told him, to find the burners on her stove turned on and the house filled with gas. "He's trying to kill me," she screamed into the phone.

MacKenzie instructed her to leave the house immediately and return to the Continental. Hanging up, he contacted the station and had one patrol officer check Carol's house and another go to the motel to stand watch until he could get there.

Carol was nervously pacing the tiny motel room by the time MacKenzie arrived. Looking at the shotgun he was carrying, she asked, "What are you going to do?"

"I guess I'm your bodyguard." For the remainder of the night, he sat in a chair in the adjacent room, the shotgun across his lap.

During the course of his sleepless night, the detective made two decisions. First, he would tell McGowan that he was now convinced that Carol Garland did, in fact, need protection. Second, he would tell the sergeant that he was taking the next day off to catch up on his sleep. Someone else could help to monitor the meeting between Carol and Joy. If there was one.

\*     \*     \*

Surveillance cameras were trained on Joy's Porsche the following afternoon as it pulled into a parking space in front of Carol's room. Next door, the recording equipment clearly picked up Joy's knock and Carol's greeting.

As McGowan listened, it was immediately clear that Joy was not only irritated but also highly suspicious. This time she wasted no time asking her sister if she was wearing a wire.

"Why would I do that?" Carol responded with a believable display of indignation.

"It just seems strange to me that you always want to meet in Richardson. How do I know you haven't gone to the police?"

Carol waved a hand to dismiss the idea and went straight to the point. "Joy, what are we going to do?"

"About what?"

"About that lady in Richardson."

"I don't want to talk about any of that."

"Dammit, Joy, Bill says he's going to kill me."

"Why?"

"Because of what I know."

"Carol you don't really know anything."

"Come on, Joy, get real."

On his headphones, McGowan could hear shuffling about in the room as the conversation went silent for some time. He was visibly relieved when he again heard Carol's voice.

"You know, all you had to do was divorce Larry."

"I wish I had." With that, Joy paused briefly, then continued, "One of us is loony, you know. You were sitting right there when we talked to Morgan Holmes about this. I said I wanted someone to scare Larry. You were the one who said you would kill him."

In the next room, McGowan was shaking his head. Who, he wondered, was this new character suddenly being dropped into the story?

"Don't you talk like that," Carol shot back angrily. "I'll smack your face."

For the first time Joy raised her voice. "Carol, you were there. Remember?"

Clearly, Joy was now playing a game. For several minutes, they argued about what had been said to the man named Holmes. Obviously growing frustrated, Carol managed to direct the conversation back to her fear that her husband was going to kill her.

"He says you were going to kill some other people. Five other people."

"I've already told you, that was just talk." Joy's patience was clearly waning. "I've got to go."

"What am I going to do?" Carol pleaded.

Joy heaved a frustrated sigh. "Let me talk to Bill Garland and I'll straighten this out. I don't want anything to happen to you. Give me his number."

Instead, Carol dialed it and handed the receiver to her sister. "Talk to him now."

On his headset, McGowan could hear Joy's voice as clearly as if she were standing next to him: "Is Bill there?" Then, "When he gets back, please tell him that Mary called."

McGowan waited until he'd been radioed that Joy had left the motel parking lot, then ran to the adjacent room. Carol was seated on the bed, her face covered by shaking hands.

"Who the fuck is Morgan Holmes?" the sergeant demanded.

For several seconds Carol only glared at him.

It had, she finally began to explain, been shortly after Joy approached her about finding someone to "scare" Larry that she had introduced her sister to Holmes, a Houston-based import-export dealer she had been dating at the time. On several occasions, Holmes had mentioned a man he used to collect delinquent payments. Without going into specifics, he had strongly intimated that, if necessary, a cracked rib here or a busted kneecap there went with the job description.

Carol had told Joy he would be in Dallas on business soon and offered to introduce her.

They had been seated in a dimly lit hotel dining room a few nights later as Joy listened quietly while Carol explained the situation to her friend and asked if he knew anyone who might be willing to carry out the task. "Look," she had said, "all she wants is a divorce from the guy and for him to leave her alone."

Carol spoke bitterly about her brother-in-law, describing his reputation as a womanizer, telling of the affair he'd had with their younger sister, and expressing fears that one day he might become interested in her own fifteen-year-old daughter.

"If," Carol said, "he were ever to so much as lay a hand on my little girl, I swear I'd kill the sonuvabitch. I'd do it in a minute, in cold blood and in broad daylight."

Holmes, taken aback by Carol's anger, admitted that the stories he'd told of his strong-armed bill collector might have been somewhat exaggerated. He didn't know anyone who would be willing to take on the kind of job she was describing.

"My advice," he said, turning to Joy, "would be to just divorce him."

"I'm afraid he'd kill me," she had replied in a calm, steady voice, then excused herself.

The story told, Carol again glared up at McGowan. "That is who the fuck Morgan Holmes is."

Morris smiled and extended a hand to help her to her feet. "We're going to move you to another motel. Somewhere that you'll be safe."

Now convinced beyond doubt that Joy Aylor had set in motion the plots to have Rozanne Gailiunas and Larry murdered, McGowan pondered ways to make his case airtight before making an arrest. And since Bill Garland and perhaps one or more others were involved, he wanted to learn more. Even Carol, who had gained a great deal of credibility in recent days, was not certain that Bill had actually killed Rozanne. He had, at various times, said that he and someone else had entered the house on Loganwood Drive, then changed the story to make her think that it was "his people" who had committed the crime.

With no way of knowing where the chain might end, McGowan wanted to bide his time a bit longer. Suddenly, his list of things to do, once empty, was growing longer by the minute. He wanted to know more about this man named Carl

Noska, who had apparently put Joy and Garland together. Morgan Holmes would have to be interviewed. And law enforcement agencies in the various cities where Garland had supposedly carried out hits would have to be contacted to see if any such crimes had actually occurred.

Already, MacKenzie was looking into the possibility that the quality of the tape made at JoJo's might somehow be technically improved.

Topping Morris's list, however, was a plan to lure Bill Garland to a meeting with Carol and Joy.

In a matter of days he would be convinced that such an idea had no chance of working.

Despite the fact they were moving her from hotel to hotel, Carol's fear was fast growing out of control. The slightest noise in the hallway outside her door would prompt a middle-of-the-night call. Responding officers would routinely arrive to face a fit of angry accusations that they were not doing their job properly.

Even McGowan's suggestion that he would look into the possibility of having her placed in the federal witness protection program failed to calm her.

With the passage of each new day, he became more and more convinced that they would not be able to control Carol much longer. That fear became a reality when he learned that she had gone to the Davis house to see her daughter and, while there, had confided to Frances Davis that the police were hiding her.

"How long do you think it will be before Joy hears that?" McGowan asked MacKenzie. The luxury of moving ahead methodically, they agreed, no longer existed.

"I'd say it's time we get our ass in high gear," MacKenzie suggested.

On the afternoon of May 24, 1988, McGowan was seated in the tiny office of assistant district attorney Kevin Chapman, an athletic-looking man in his mid-thirties.

Though McGowan had never met him, he had liked what he had heard about the man. Chapman, he had been told, was considered by many in the courthouse to be the most aggressive and conscientious of the new young felony prosecutors on the DA's staff.

McGowan waited silently as the assistant DA began reading the typed statement that had been taken from Carol Garland.

Chapman finally pitched the folder on his desk: "Give me a thumbnail sketch of the case."

McGowan had been rehearsing for the request for days. For the next hour, he reviewed the past five years of the investigation, adding brief profiles of the many characters involved in what he freely admitted was the most fascinating and frustrating case he'd ever worked. Finally, he carefully recapped the first meeting with Carol, his early doubts, then the telling conversations between her and Joy Aylor.

At no point did Chapman interrupt. He had made an occasional notation on a yellow legal pad, but had demonstrated little reaction until McGowan was finished.

Leaning back in his chair, his hands locked behind his head, Chapman silently pondered the complicated, almost unbelievable story he'd just heard. "In my opinion," he finally said, "you have probable cause to arrest Mrs. Aylor."

Pleased, McGowan stood to leave. "That's exactly what we're going to do."

# 11

JOY AYLOR WAS relieved to see a familiar face.

Just a half hour earlier she had been pulled over after leaving her house and, while standing in a church parking lot, was told she was under arrest.

She had said nothing to Detective MacKenzie during the drive to the Richardson Police Department except to ask what was being done about her car. MacKenzie explained that Ken

Roberts would remain with the car until it could be towed to the police impound.

For the remainder of the trip she had stared out the car window, her lips pursed in silence.

Then, as she was escorted into the interrogation room, her mood changed abruptly when she saw McGowan seated at a table in the middle of the room. "It's good to see you again," she said, ignoring the sterile surroundings, the video camera mounted on a tripod in the corner, and the tape recorder that sat in the middle of the table.

"Hello, Joy," McGowan replied. "Have a seat."

Even as she walked toward the table, Sergeant Corley was explaining that she was under arrest for capital murder and reading her her rights. "You have the right to remain silent . . . you have the right to . . ."

Joy frowned at Corley, then turned back to McGowan.

"It's over, Joy," he said.

"I'm sorry, but I don't know what you're talking about."

McGowan ignored her and continued, "Right now, we're just going to talk for a little while. I'm not asking for you to give a confession. We just want you to help us."

"With what?"

"I want you to help us get Bill Garland."

"Who? Do you think I've done something wrong?"

"Yes, I do."

"What?"

Morris leaned slightly forward, his eyes fixed on hers. "You were involved in the murder of Rozanne Gailiunas and the attempted murder of Larry Aylor."

For the first time, she acknowledged the presence of the tape recorder on the edge of the table and shook her head.

McGowan reached across the table and turned it off.

"What proof do you have?"

"If you like, I can play you tapes of some conversations you've recently had with your sister."

Anger flickered briefly in Joy's eyes at the mention of Carol, but just as quickly she was back in control. The only sign of nervousness she displayed was the constant clicking of her well-manicured fingernails. "Are you telling me that you're believing what Carol is telling you? You know she's crazy."

"Joy, the only thing I believe is fact."

Again she fell silent for several seconds before asking, "How do I get out of here?"

All interrogators dread that question, which most often leads to a quick end to information gathering. They are also required, by law, to answer it.

"You call a bondsman or an attorney," McGowan told her.

"I need a phone book."

He was relieved when she began looking in the yellow pages for the number of a bonding company. Immediately after hanging up, however, she looked across at McGowan and asked if he thought she should also contact a lawyer.

"It's your choice. But right now I want to make something very clear to you, something I don't think you fully understand. I think that Bill Garland is a very dangerous man. For your own safety, it is very important that we do something about him right away."

It was as if Joy had not even heard him. "Am I going to prison?"

Corley, who had been standing off to one side, moved toward the table. From the moment Joy had entered the room he had not liked her. In a matter of minutes he had judged her to be one of the coldest people he'd ever encountered. Her businesslike manner, the ease with which she lied, and the complete lack of any sign of remorse had quickly angered him.

"Mrs. Aylor," he said impatiently, "make no mistake about it. At the very least, you are going to prison for a long, long time. And there's a very good possibility that you will receive the death penalty."

Joy looked coolly at Corley. "Then, maybe I should call a lawyer."

While Joy was being interviewed, Chris Aylor and his father sat in Ken MacKenzie's office. McGowan had telephoned Larry Aylor the night before and asked that he bring his son to the station the following morning. When Larry had demanded to know what was going on, Morris had only explained that Chris was in no trouble or danger: "I just want to ask him a few questions."

McGowan wanted to hear firsthand from Chris about Joy's strange behavior.

Puzzled, the youngster answered MacKenzie's questions. Yes, his mother had seemed nervous lately, keeping the shutters closed. There had been strange phone calls that seemed to unnerve her. He had found the fish in the mailbox, And, yes, he'd seen someone looking over the backyard fence.

When he got to the story of being forced off the road by another car, however, his story differed dramatically from what his father had recounted to McGowan earlier: "Yeah, some guy did try to curb me. But, no, I didn't jump out and knock him cold. Hey, I'm just a brown belt, not a black belt. I didn't even get out of the car."

MacKenzie had glanced over at Larry Aylor as the teenager told his version of the story. Aylor avoided the detective's look.

Down the hall, meanwhile, an attorney and representative from the Allied Bonding Company had arrived almost simultaneously and were escorted into the interrogation room.

McGowan and Corley rose to leave, giving them and Joy a few minutes of privacy. Morris, eager to telephone the DA's office to let Kevin Chapman know that the arrest had been made, said nothing as he left. Corley, however, stopped in the doorway and looked back at Joy. "When you're finished," he said, "I'll come back and take you down to a jail cell."

"I don't want to go in one of those cells," Joy shot back instantly.

Corley simply turned away, shutting the door behind him, pleased that he had touched a nerve. It would, he knew, likely take the bondsman and attorney several hours to arrange for her release. In the meantime, she would clearly prefer sitting in the interrogation room to being locked in a cell.

Sometime later McGowan returned and again took a seat across the table from Joy. "Everything, okay?" he asked, placing a glass of water in front of her.

Obviously, it wasn't. "You know what that lawyer just said to me? He says before he hears a word of what I've got to say he wants a check for six thousand dollars. That's all he was interested in—nothing but the money."

McGowan gave no response, listening.

"I wrote him a check, but you can bet your sweet life I'm going to stop payment on it the minute I'm out of here. I'm not going to let him or any other lawyer take what money I have left. I want Chris to have it.

"I know what I did was wrong and that I'm going to jail. I should be punished. But not my son."

Corley returned to the room and, catching the last part of the conversation, was confident that she was on the verge of confessing. Glancing at the tape recorder, he noticed that it still had not been turned on. Already, he knew, Morris had enough to at least seek an indictment, but he needed more details. To get these he had to proceed slowly, carefully. Saying nothing, Corley pulled a chair up to the edge of the table.

Upon Corley's return, Joy had fallen silent, looking first at him, then McGowan. After sipping from the glass of water, she pointed at Morris. "I don't know why, but I trust you." Then she turned toward Mike. "I *don't* trust you."

"Joy," McGowan said, "we're just talking right now. No tape, no notes."

She sighed and again began clicking her fingernails. "All my life, all I've known is my family. That's always been the only important thing in my life. My husband, my son . . . then, all of a sudden that woman comes along and destroys everything. She ruins my life.

"And they were rubbing my face in it. She called me to say that Larry had bought her a mink coat. She even told me that he'd had 'Rozanne Aylor' sewn on the name tag inside the collar. That's the kind of thing that was going on. Larry's giving me twenty dollars a week and he's buying her a mink coat.

"One day I was out working in the yard and they came over to see Larry's dad—he lives near me—and paraded around in the neighborhood, walking up and down the sidewalk in front

129

of my friends. I was so embarrassed, I had to just go in the house.

"That's what did it. That's when I got Bill."

"Are you going to help us get him?" McGowan asked.

It was as if she'd not even heard the question. Rather than answer, she launched into another rambling discussion of her family, criticizing her father's lack of generosity, her treatment by Larry, and Carol's behavior, which had made it hard on her.

As she talked, Corley fought to contain his frustration. Joy's carefully measured self-pity and placing of blame on everyone from Rozanne to her father lacked any ring of truth to him. Admittedly a man of far less patience than McGowan, he felt his partner was allowing Joy to manipulate him. Finally, Corley suggested a break, asking Joy if she wanted a sandwich.

She mechanically sipped at her water and shook her head.

"We'll be back," Corley said. It was a less than subtle signal that he wanted to talk to McGowan outside.

In the hall, he wasted no time making his feelings known. "Dammit, she's toying with you." He knew, he said, that it was Morris's style to go slowly with interviews, to make people feel comfortable, to gain their trust. "But you're being way too easy on her. She's guilty as hell and you're letting her play games. She's all over the map in there and not telling you a damn thing."

McGowan's voice was calm, giving no hint that Corley's criticism concerned him: "We sure as hell aren't going to get anything standing out here."

His point was clearly made: the interview would continue at the pace he felt most comfortable with. If he had to listen to bullshit about fur coats, a mean daddy, crazy sister, and a cheating husband to finally get to the story he wanted, that's what he would do. He'd waited too long to be in a hurry now.

There was little left for Corley to argue.

Back in the interrogation room, McGowan repeated, "Are you going to help us get Garland?"

Joy shifted in her chair and studied her interviewer carefully. The wear of sitting in the small room was finally beginning to show on her. She began to nod slowly, as if to indicate she had arrived at a decision.

"You get me out of here and let me go home and get comfortable. Then, come on over with your tape recorder and we'll talk. I'll fix you a sandwich. I'll tell you the whole thing."

Then, almost as an afterthought, she nodded toward Corley. "But not him. If he comes, he sits outside in the car."

When McGowan didn't immediately respond, she continued to bargain. "Look, right now, all I want to do is get out of here. I don't like this place."

She paused, her green eyes searching the room as if to make sure the walls were not closing in. "You know, your friend Carol is in this up to her neck. The deal was that she would get fifty thousand dollars from Larry's insurance policy. That was going to be her cut."

McGowan masked his surprise at the statement, quickly moving his questions to the blackmail scheme that Carol had described.

"I got this dead fish wrapped in paper. And some letters."

"You still have the letters?"

"I might have. I'm not sure. And I may have kept the wrapper. Don't ask me why." She also mentioned a copy of the map to the Kaufman County farm she had asked Larry to draw.

Corley, who had said nothing since the interview had resumed, waited a short time, then stood and walked from the room without explanation. He did not have to be told that the next order of business was to convince a judge to quickly issue a search warrant for Joy Aylor's residence.

Once again alone, Joy and McGowan fell silent. For a long time the detective stared at the beautiful woman seated just a few feet away, then he began slowly shaking his head.

"What's the matter?"

Morris shrugged and smiled faintly. "I just can't believe you did it."

"Believe me, I wish I hadn't. But I can't take it all back, can I?"

"But, why?"

"I guess I just broke." The mink coat, she said, had been the last straw.

Moments later her lawyer and bail bondsman returned and requested a few minutes of privacy with their new client. Jodi Packer had arrived with them, giving instructions and tossing out angry accusations about false arrests in a take-charge manner.

McGowan studied the lanky plumbing contractor and knew immediately that he'd made a mistake. Earlier in the day, after Roberts and MacKenzie had taken Chris's statement, he had sent them out to talk with Packer in the hope that Joy might have told him about her involvement in the crimes.

Instead of being co-operative, Packer had been defensive, even hostile. There was no way, he said, that Joy could be involved in such a thing, and he would personally see to it that there would be holy hell to pay for arresting her.

Now, in the lobby of the police station, he was ranting to anyone who would listen that his former wife was a district judge, that he knew the law quite well, and that Joy's arrest was an inexcusable abuse of the legal system.

McGowan turned away and returned to the interview room where Joy sat, writing a $40,000 check for the bondsman.

"This check is no good, you know," she confided, smiling for the first time. "But at least it's going to get me out of here."

Leaning in the doorway, his hands in his pockets, Morris asked what she wanted to do about her car. "You want me to take you over to get it or do you want to go with Jodi?"

"What do you think?"

"It's your decision."

"Okay, let me go with him. I'll get the car, go home, and get rid of him. Then, I'll call you. Give me an hour or so."

McGowan handed her a business card. "I'll be at this number." With that he walked her down the hall to where Packer waited.

As they left the building, moving down the steps and out onto the tree-shaded sidewalk, Corley joined McGowan in the lobby. "Jesus, Mo, this is a helluva gamble. I hope it pays off."

Morris looked at him, then turned his attention back to the couple walking away. Packer had a protective arm around Joy's shoulder. "I hope it does, too."

Minutes later, pandemonium erupted.

Throughout the day, Captain Golden had occasionally stopped by to listen in on the interview with Joy Aylor. Like Corley, he had been concerned that McGowan was being too easy, allowing her to deflect his questions with questions of her own, seldom pressing when Joy promised to talk about certain specifics later.

The captain, however, had weighed his doubts against his faith in McGowan's abilities and said nothing.

That quickly changed minutes after McGowan rushed into his office, shirttail hanging out, fist clinched and raised in a victory salute. A wide smile was on his face. "I've got it," Morris told his superior. "I've got the story. I know what happened."

With that he provided Golden a brief recap of Joy's admission.

Golden reached across his desk and shook McGowan's hand. "Where do we go from here?"

"She's going to call me."

The stunned captain, assuming Joy had been placed in a holdover cell, did not immediately understand. "Where is she?"

"I cut her loose. She's on her way home." Morris explained that she had promised not only to provide him a full confession but physical evidence she would turn over. "She thinks she's got some letters, a map . . ." As he spoke, he could tell that Golden was not pleased. "She'll call."

"Like hell she will. We need a search warrant as soon as possible. And let's get someone out there to protect whatever evidence might be in that house until the warrant arrives."

It was the closest thing to a direct order that Golden, struggling to keep his temper in check, had ever issued to his sergeant. Convinced that if there was, in fact, evidence in Joy Aylor's home, it would likely be destroyed immediately upon her arrival, Golden wanted officers to get to the address as quickly as possible and prevent her or anyone else from entering.

Legally, he knew, officers could not enter the house without a search warrant. The law did, however, provide police the right to protect the scene of a search while awaiting the arrival of the warrant.

Golden dispatched plainclothes officers to the Arbor Trail address with instructions to let no one enter. McGowan's elation had turned to angry frustration. *He knew what he was doing, dammit, and now everything was going to be fucked up.*

Only a few minutes had passed when one of the officers radioed in to report that Joy and Jodi Packer had already entered the house. They had, he said, driven into the garage, closed the door behind them, and entered through a back door.

Golden made no attempt to hide his anger. "We've got two choices now," he said as he paced his office, carrying a portable radio with him. "Either we talk our way in immediately or we bust the damn door down." He paused for a second, then yelled into the phone, "Ring the doorbell. If that doesn't work, do whatever you have to to get inside."

Already, McGowan was en route to the parking lot.

He was in his car when the officers radioed to say they had been allowed into the house by Packer. Everyone was seated in the living room.

While McGowan sped toward the house, a furor continued in Golden's office. A judge, alerted by Packer, phoned to ask what was going on and, after the captain briefly explained the situation, suggested that in all likelihood the actions of his officers were in violation of the property owner's civil rights. Golden immediately contacted the department's legal adviser and capsuled what was going on.

The legal adviser suggested that everyone inside leave immediately. Until a search warrant arrived, he said, the right of the officers to be in the house was questionable. On the other hand, he assured Golden that his officers were within their rights to seal off the property. "Tell them to get everyone outside until the warrant arrives," he advised.

The idea of being forced to stand in her front yard in the company of police while the entire neighborhood watched was less acceptable to Joy than having the officers in her house.

"It's okay if we stay in here," she said. She was, in fact, pleading with one of the officers to move his police car to the alley entrance to the house when McGowan walked in.

Seated at a small desk in the corner of the room, Joy quickly got to her feet. "I trusted you. I was going to call you, tell you everything. What's all this?"

"Joy, it's been taken out of my hands," McGowan replied. "We're waiting for a search warrant to be issued."

She turned and stormed away. "Now everyone in the neighborhood knows what's going on."

Across the room, meanwhile, Packer was on the phone to the Dallas Police Department, providing the dispatcher with an address and reporting a break-in. Hanging up, he glared at McGowan. "If you're smart," he warned, "you and your people will get the hell out of here right now instead of going to jail."

McGowan fought an urge to reply. In the confusion of the moment, he knew one thing for certain: he did not like Jodi Packer.

Contacting Golden, Morris was relieved to learn that the captain had already been in touch with the Dallas police, advising them of the situation. Instead of coming to make arrests, they were going to assist with the securing of the house until the warrant arrived.

Joy's reaction to their arrival provided one of the few amusing moments: "Do they *have* to park in front of the house?"

Packer, frustrated that the Dallas officers had refused to escort McGowan and his men from the house, turned his attention back to Joy. It was important, he told her, that she contact a good lawyer immediately. With that, he began naming off several of Dallas's most celebrated criminal-defense attorneys. All, he said, were personal friends.

He was obviously annoyed when Joy turned to McGowan and asked whom he thought she should call.

"If I was in trouble, there's only one man in town I'd call."

"Doug Mulder," Jodi said, attempting to regain control of the conversation.

Morris nodded. "Doug Mulder."

Packer already had the phone in his hand, dialing information, when McGowan motioned for Joy to step outside with him.

Standing on the backyard patio, he attempted to explain the sequence of events that had led to the arrival of the police. Now, with search warrants en route and lawyers being called in, things had become far more complicated.

For the first time since his arrival, Joy seemed calm, even pensive. "I still want to tell you."

McGowan shook his head. "I can't talk to you about it now." Inside, the phone was ringing.

Packer opened the door to tell Joy the call was for her, then joined McGowan on the patio, where he launched into another tirade. How, Jodi wanted to know, could anyone with a grain of common sense believe the screwy accusations of Joy's sister? McGowan and the chickenshit Richardson Police Department had damn well better get ready for a lawsuit that was going to end some careers. By God, he knew the law and people in high places and was going to see to it that people paid for this travesty. "You can bet your sweet ass on it," Packer yelled.

In time, things settled into an agonizing waiting game. With the Dallas officers on hand, McGowan sent the Richardson officers back to the station. The silence that had finally settled over the now crowded living room was interrupted only by Parker's occasional harangues.

Outside, darkness had fallen when the phone rang a second time and Jodi again answered. Looking across the room at Joy, he nodded to indicate that it was for her. "It's some man, but he won't give his name."

Glancing at McGowan, Joy said she would take the call on the kitchen extension.

Minutes later, when she returned, Morris smiled at her knowingly. "That was Bill, wasn't it?"

Ignoring his question, she walked to Packer and placed a hand on his arm. "There's something I've got to tell you," she said, her voice a soft whisper. Then, turning back to McGowan, she asked if she and Jodi might speak privately for a few minutes.

McGowan nodded and followed them to Chris's room. "I'll be right outside the door."

After twenty minutes, he opened the door and was greeted by a suddenly warm and friendly Jodi Packer. "Come on in, Morris," he said, all hostility gone from his voice. McGowan did not need to be told what the conversation had been about. Joy, he was certain, had admitted her guilt to her boyfriend.

"Look," Packer said, "I'd appreciate it if you would give me a straight answer to something."

"What's that?"

A forced smile spread across Jodi's face. "Do we really have something to be worried about here?"

"You're damn right you do," McGowan replied, watching Packer's smile disappear as he walked from the room.

Seated on her son's bed, Joy motioned for the detective to close the door.

"I'll give you Bill Garland," she said, acknowledging that he had phoned twice since they had returned to the house. "But I can't go to prison."

When McGowan did not immediately reply, she continued, "That's got to be the deal."

Morris was pleased to see that the roles had suddenly reversed. He had felt sure he could have eventually reached this point had he been left alone to deal with Joy in his own way. Now it was his turn to play games, to hint at things without making a commitment. "All I can do is see what the district attorney's office thinks."

With that, Packer reentered the room. "What's going on?"

"We're going to make a deal," Joy snapped, clearly displeased at the interruption.

Jodi began furiously shaking his head. "No. No deals until you've talked to an attorney."

By the time they returned to the living room, even the Dallas officers were aware that the mood had changed dramatically. Joy agreed to sign a consent form allowing the officers to remain in her house while awaiting the arrival of the search warrant, asking only that the patrolmen leave. "I just don't want a bunch of police cars sitting in front of my house."

Hiding his amusement at her concern over the neighbors' reaction, McGowan thanked the officers for their help and assured them there was no reason to remain.

For the next hour, McGowan sat impatiently awaiting Corley's arrival with the search warrant. The frantic, roller-coaster day had, with the arrival of darkness, fallen into an almost eerie calm. To the casual visitor, it would have appeared he was nothing more than a family friend who had stopped in for a visit. Joy brought him a Pepsi while Jodi called out for pizza. Packer repeatedly made attempts at small talk, which ended almost as quickly as they began.

Only minutes before Corley's arrival, Doug Mulder phoned, talking first with Joy, then Jodi. McGowan was not at all surprised when Packer informed him that Joy had been instructed to say nothing more.

He knew also that any hope of getting the confession he had once felt was forthcoming was gone.

Nor would any evidence result from the long-awaited search warrant. Joy had brought out a large file box, placing it on the dining-room table, insisting that she was certain she had placed one or more of the blackmail notes among the collection of papers. But she found nothing.

There was no map, no wrapper in which the fish had been delivered.

It was almost eleven by the time the officers, disappointed that the furious attempt to secure the search warrant had resulted in nothing, prepared to leave. As they moved toward the front door, Joy stopped McGowan and tiptoed to lean close to his ear.

"My deal still stands," she whispered.

Sandy McGowan woke from a light sleep to see her husband seated on the edge of the bed, a weary smile on his face. As was her habit on waking in the middle of the night, she glanced at the clock on the nightstand and saw that it was almost two in the morning.

"You look exhausted," she said, reaching out to touch the stubble of whiskers on his cheeks. "I want to know everything. Don't leave out a word."

"She did it," her husband began.

For the next hour, he talked nonstop of the conversation at the station, the scene with Golden, and the events at Joy Aylor's house. Fascinated, Sandy interrupted only when she feared he might have left out even the smallest of details.

There was, he explained, a great deal more work to be done. Joy's admission, in fact, served only as a new starting place for the investigation. Doubtless, there would be new obstacles in the days to come, but now the case had direction and purpose and the promise of resolve.

The five long years of frustration were, as if by magic, now replaced by a feeling of eager anticipation only a homicide detective could fully understand.

Sandy leaned across the bed to kiss her husband. "See," she said, a flip, playful tone to her voice disguising the flood of relief she was feeling, "I told you that you would solve it."

Morris smiled and buried his head in his pillow. In a matter of minutes he was asleep.

It was the last night of peaceful rest he would experience for months to come.

# PART 2

—

# Investigation

Human blood is heavy; the man that has shed it cannot run away.

—African proverb


All is a riddle, and the key to a riddle is another riddle.

—from "Illusions,"
*The Conduct of Life*,
Ralph Waldo Emerson

# 12

BILL GARLAND'S HUGE frame was squeezed into the chair opposite Morris McGowan's desk, the puzzled look on his face not at all what the anxious detective had expected.

It was late afternoon, and the sequence of events that finally resulted in Garland's arrival at the Richardson Police Department had been straight out of a bad television sitcom.

Aware that Garland was scheduled to appear in court for a hearing on the divorce suit filed by Carol, McGowan had sent a team of four officers, headed by Ken MacKenzie, to watch until Garland had parted company with his attorney and then follow him as he left the Dallas County courthouse. A computer check had revealed an unpaid traffic ticket, reason enough to stop him and bring him to the station.

Late in the afternoon Garland had finally emerged from the courtroom, walked briskly to the basement parking lot, and pulled into the downtown traffic. Following close behind were MacKenzie and Ken Roberts. Having earlier advised both the Dallas police and the sheriff's department of what was going on, Roberts radioed the Dallas Police Department with a request that they make what should appear to be a routine traffic stop.

However, the pilot of a Dallas police helicopter, monitoring afternoon traffic, heard the call and decided to join in the chase. And before a Dallas patrol car could reach the location radioed in by Roberts, Garland had made his way beyond the city limits into the suburb of Mesquite. A call to the Mesquite police did no good as the suspect's route soon took him into the jurisdiction of the neighboring Garland Police Department in another Dallas suburb.

Meanwhile, the helicopter pilot continued his pursuit and

radioed the Richardson dispatcher to ask what offense the driver had committed. The dispatcher, unaware of the plan to stop Garland on an outstanding traffic warrant, had explained that the subject was a suspect in a homicide investigation. The pilot immediately relayed the information to the Garland police.

Thus, by the time Bill Garland was pulled over, the episode had all the earmarks of a full-scale manhunt.

MacKenzie and Roberts were stunned to see the helicopter landing in a nearby vacant lot as a half dozen officers approached Garland's car with guns drawn. The passing five-o'clock traffic had already begun to slow to witness the excitement.

And, as Garland was standing outside his car being handcuffed, his divorce attorney happened by and pulled over.

MacKenzie rolled his eyes as he glanced over at Roberts. "Damn," he whispered, "this is not going to be easy to explain."

So it was that Garland was accompanied by lawyer Jim Conway as he was finally escorted into the Richardson Police Department. McGowan's hopes that the suspect might admit his involvement in Joy Aylor's elaborate murder plots immediately evaporated as Conway extended his hand and introduced himself.

Discarding the hard-nosed approach he had planned, McGowan adopted a mock display of friendly skepticism as he outlined the series of accusations that Carol had made against her husband.

Garland smiled and shook his head to demonstrate his disbelief on several occasions as the officer spoke. "She's fucking crazy," he finally said. "I've never been in trouble with the law in my life—until I met her. Then, suddenly, I'm arrested and thrown in jail for assault, and now I'm sitting here listening to you talk about some murder and blackmail and all kind of shit like that. It's unbelievable.

"All I can say to you is that you can't believe anything that woman says. She's doing everything she can to make my life a living hell. She calls me at all hours of the day and night, screaming at the top of her lungs. All I'm trying to do is get the hell away from her.''

It had, he said, been Carol who pursued him. She was the one who pushed the idea of their getting married. And, in fact, the marriage had been great for the first few months. ''But then she started acting weird. It went from bad to worse after that.''

Garland's attorney joined in, reciting a litany of vindictive behavior displayed by Carol Garland.

McGowan looked over at MacKenzie, who had been sitting in on the interview. ''Sounds to me like we've been royally duped,'' McGowan said. ''Why in the world would a woman do something like that?''

''If you find an answer to that question,'' Garland said, ''I'd like to know about it.''

Ten minutes later he had paid his traffic fine and was gone. The interview that McGowan had hoped would go on long into the night had lasted less than forty-five minutes. The dread of informing Captain Golden, who Morris privately knew would feel he should have pressured Garland harder, was overshadowed by his own disappointment.

Alone in his office, reflecting on the missed chances, first with Joy and now with Garland, he slammed his fist against the top of his desk and mouthed a curse. ''Where the hell do I go from here?'' he asked the empty room.

Later that night, as he sat in the darkened living room of his home, all the concerns expressed by his friends and fellow officers became suddenly justified.

For the first time in his life, Morris McGowan feared that he was losing it, that the pressures and frustrations, the roller-coaster course the case had traveled, had become more than he could handle.

Sandy's father was seriously ill and she had been at the hospital, visiting him, when her husband arrived home. Not even bothering to turn on the lights, McGowan had slumped into a chair and pondered his situation, slipping into the darkest mood he'd ever experienced.

Chances of solving Rozanne Gailiunas's murder, even now that he was certain he knew the motive and who had set the plot in motion, looked remote. Though incriminating, the tapes of Carol's conversations with Joy had not been enough to persuade Kevin Chapman to seek an indictment. Too much of his case, McGowan knew, rested on the word of a woman with a long history of strange actions and wild accusations. And though much of what she had said had proved to be legitimate, Carol had become more hostile and less co-operative with each passing day. Still paranoid, she had angrily accused everyone in the department who came in contact with her of not providing her proper protection. No one—not McGowan or Golden or MacKenzie or, finally, female officer Rhonda Bonner—had been able to maintain a congenial relationship with her for any length of time. Contacts with Carol had dissolved into a series of tantrums, telephone screaming matches, and door slammings. Now she was talking of taking her daughter and leaving town, disappearing.

An interview with cabinetmaker Carl Noska, the man Joy had supposedly first gone to in an attempt to find someone to kill Larry, had not moved the case forward. While Noska acknowledged that Joy had, in fact, approached him, confiding that she was having problems with her husband, he had no idea she was contemplating murder. He had put her in touch with Bill Garland, whose exterminating business was just a few doors from where he worked, but it had been his impression that Garland was being paid only to follow and harass Aylor. Noska had willingly taken and passed a polygraph test.

So it had boiled down to getting a confession from Joy or Bill Garland. Both attempts had ended in what McGowan knew was being perceived by many in the department as his failure to get something on paper—and signed—during those initial interviews.

Mixed with the crushing frustration, then, was his wounded ego. For the first time since he'd been sworn in, McGowan felt that his reputation had been severely damaged. Though never boastful about the cases he'd solved, he enjoyed a quiet satisfaction at knowing his peers judged him favorably. Now, after five years, the biggest investigation of his career was in a shambles. It would, he knew, be his legacy, and he found the prospect depressing. Then, there were the unfulfilled promises to Rozanne's family.

And, once again, the image of a four-year-old boy, frightened and confused, running from the scene of the unspeakable attack on his mother, played on his mind.

For hours he sat, the negative thoughts gradually overwhelming him. And frightening him.

Shortly before Sandy arrived home, he methodically removed the bullets from his service revolver.

For the remainder of the night Sandy McGowan sat, listening as her troubled husband confided his frustration and disappointment, vainly searching for some way to lift him from the dark mood that worried her far more than she dared admit.

Suddenly, the entire case and what it had done to her husband infuriated her. She was angry that he had taken charge of the investigation that long-ago night; angry at Joy Aylor for her long-standing intrusion into their lives; at Carol and Bill Garland; and those in the police department who doubted Morris's ability.

"Maybe," she finally suggested, "you should get mad, too."

Following a few hours' sleep, McGowan awoke to the same decision. As his anger mounted, he found it fueling a new sense of determination. If, he decided, it was necessary to start from scratch, beginning the investigation all over, that's what he would do.

For the next month, investigators were dispatched to check out every piece of information that had been gathered. In addition to working long hours in an attempt to decipher the mangled words on the troublesome JoJo's tape, MacKenzie traveled to Houston to talk with Morgan Holmes about the long-ago conversation he'd had with Joy and Carol.

To the best of his recollection, he said, it was Carol, not Joy, who had talked of killing Larry Aylor.

Kevin Chapman made several trips to the Richardson Police Department, carefully studying the case and offering continued encouragement.

And while the renewed effort yielded no real positive results, it did serve a purpose in providing a renewed, almost comforting, sense of accomplishment. Only when work was ongoing, the investigators collectively agreed, did the possibility of a break in the case exist.

Still, however, the overriding emotion that permeated the investigation was frustration. The only difference was that McGowan was no longer shouldering it alone.

MacKenzie, following a visit to the district attorney's office in early June, returned to McGowan's office to report a conversation he'd just had with prosecutors Kevin Chapman and Dan Hagood. Chapman, after researching all the case law available to him, still did not think they had the evidence necessary to gain a conviction. Hagood had expressed even more doubt than had his associate.

The observation, MacKenzie admitted, had depressed him to such a degree that the simple act of driving from Dallas back to the police station had been a chore. "You know what the last thing Kevin told me was?" MacKenzie snapped. " 'Don't get down,' he said. Don't get down. If he only knew."

McGowan, who had kept his own bout with depression secret, felt immediate empathy with the weary officer standing in his office. "Go home. Take a few days off and try to forget about it for a while. Get some rest and come back when you're ready."

Meanwhile, McGowan decided it was time to play a card he'd been holding since he'd first met Carol, one he hoped might serve as a way to reopen discussions with Bill Garland.

On one of her early visits to the Richardson Police Department, Carol had arrived in Bill's Chevrolet Blazer, asking permission to leave it there so that he wouldn't be able to find it. It was still parked in the lot behind the station, and no doubt, Garland would like to have it.

A trip to Richardson to pick it up just might provide a new opportunity for McGowan to talk with him.

Aware that Garland had been living with an old hunting companion named Billy Ray Newsome, owner of the Sunset, Texas, farm where he'd taken Carol to teach her to shoot a pistol, McGowan called in hopes of reaching Bill.

When Newsome informed him that Garland had moved to Sulphur Springs and was living with his mother, McGowan asked that he pass the word on that the Richardson police had the Blazer if Garland wished to come pick it up.

A day later, Newsome phoned to say that he'd relayed the message and that Bill had said he had no interest in it.

McGowan was not surprised days later to learn that Garland had come to the station over the weekend, when he was reasonably certain few homicide detectives would be working, and claimed the Blazer.

The following day, Morris invited Newsome to meet him for lunch: "I'd just like to talk with you about Bill."

Reluctantly, Newsome had agreed. "I'm not in any trouble, am I?"

"Not that I know anything about."

As they sat in the dining room of the Rockwall Country Club, Morris listened as the likable carpet layer assured him that there was no way his friend could be involved in murder. Bill talked a big game at times, he said, and you had to know how to dismiss the bullshit from the truth, but he was basically a good guy, a good friend. "Now, his wife's a different story," Billy Ray had insisted. "Based on what Bill's told me about her, I'd have to guess she's crazy as the day's long."

"Did he ever mention anything to you about some kind of blackmail scheme?"

Newsome sighed. "Yeah, as a matter of fact he did. You know what that was all about? He told me that Carol knew that her sister's husband had been messing around with their younger sister, Elizabeth. He said Carol told him she wanted to blackmail Joy, telling her she would go to her daddy and tell him all about it. Carol said she could get a lot of money for just keeping quiet about it, not letting the old man know that Joy had stayed with her husband even after she knew what he'd been up to with her baby sister."

"You've got to be kidding."

"That's all there was to it. At least, that's what Bill told me. Like I said, his old lady's nuts."

On the drive back to Richardson, McGowan let the conversation replay in his mind. *That's a great story, Bill,* he thought, *but what about the post office box? And using the name Roxanne Gailiunas?*

Even before arriving back at the station he was planning a trip to Sulphur Springs. It was time to play a long shot.


On July 8, in the interrogation room provided them by the Department of Public Safety of Sulphur Springs, the two men sat at a small table. McGowan slid an ashtray across to his visitor, a signal that it was okay to smoke.

"Okay, Bill, I want to go through the whole story again."

"What story's that?"

"How you met Carol, what you know about Joy, the blackmail . . . the whole business."

"Should I be calling a lawyer?"

"That's up to you. All I'm here to do is see if I can find out what the hell's going on."

Garland inhaled deeply on the cigarette he'd just lit, then leaned back to let the smoke escape toward the ceiling. "Okay, what is it you want to know?"

McGowan asked again how he and Carol had met.

It had been at a coffee shop, Garland said, again portraying Carol as the aggressor. The early stages of their marriage, he repeated, had been great. Then suddenly she had become suspicious of everything he did, constantly accusing him of seeing other women and keeping secrets from her.

"She was always telling me how rich her folks were, and what a wonderful cook she was. Hell, I never even met her family. It was like she was ashamed to introduce me.

"And I can damn well assure you she was no cook.

"After a while, she just went crazy. That day they arrested me after she told them I was trying to kill her, I never even touched her. She just flew into a rage and told me to get the hell out, and I was going about my business to accommodate her when the police showed up."

"Why did you stay with her as long as you did?"

"To tell you the truth, I don't really know."

McGowan then shifted the conversation to the blackmail

attempt, and Garland's version matched almost verbatim what McGowan had heard just days earlier from Billy Ray Newsome. "I know it sounds crazy," Garland added, "but that's the way it was. I couldn't believe she was doing something like that to her sister and her father."

McGowan rose from his chair and moved to sit on the corner of the desk. For several seconds he said nothing, as if digesting the story he'd just been told. Then, leaning forward to make direct eye contact with Garland, he spoke in a soft, measured tone.

"Bill, you're lying."

"I'm not."

"Listen to me," McGowan said, his voice louder, demanding full attention, "there are two women out there—Carol and Joy Aylor—who have you by the nuts. They want to give you to me in the worst way."

Garland's face grew suddenly pale as he studied the detective for a moment before responding. "What makes you think that?"

"Bill, the night we arrested Joy, you called her. Hell, you called her twice. I was standing right there by the phone."

Garland said nothing as McGowan, no longer the friendly, skeptical cop he'd encountered that evening at the Richardson police station, continued to drive home his point. "How do you explain that post office box? We checked it out, you know."

Mashing out his cigarette and leaning his head on the table, Garland slowly shook his head.

McGowan's voice was again suddenly soft, almost a whisper. "Bill, what happened to that woman . . . what that little boy went through . . . it wasn't right."

"I know," Garland acknowledged, lifting his head but avoiding the detective's eyes.

"I want all of it. I want the whole goddamn story."

Garland took a deep breath, a look of sudden exhaustion spreading across his face. "Okay, here's what happened."

He had been sitting in his office when Carl Noska came in and said that he had a friend who wanted someone followed.

"I told him to have them call me," Garland said. "He was real secretive about the whole deal. Wouldn't tell me who this 'friend' was. He just said that a woman would be in touch.

"A few days later, I heard from this woman calling herself Mary. She said she wanted someone taken care of."

McGowan interrupted for the first time. "What did that mean to you?"

"That she wanted somebody killed."

"Did you ever tell Noska this?"

Garland shook his head. "No, I didn't figure it was something he needed to know.

"I told her I'd see what I could do, what kind of information I would need, and how much the deal would cost. I told her it would be five thousand dollars, half up front, half when the deal was done."

Two days later, he said, Noska was back in his office, this time delivering an envelope that contained twenty-five hundred-dollar bills. There was also a photograph of a dark-haired woman, addresses of her home and where she worked, and the license plate number of the Cadillac she drove.

"I passed it along to a friend of mine—a guy named Brian Kreafle—who said he might know somebody who would be interested in doing the job."

"Did he say who it was?"

"I swear I don't know. I didn't want to know. I got the impression that he was going to contact somebody out of Houston, but I'm not sure.

"A week or so later, Brian calls and says the job was done. I phone Carl and tell him. Then this Mary calls and I tell her. I gave her my post office box number where she could send the rest of the money. But a day or so later Carl came by with another envelope. Another twenty-five hundred-dollar bills. I took five hundred out for myself, then gave the rest to Brian."

The almost casual manner with which Garland described the transactions took McGowan by surprise. That $5,000 could have bought the death of Rozanne Gailiunas repulsed him. A dozen questions raced through his mind, but he fought to suppress them, to allow the man seated before him to continue.

"Apparently," Bill said, "she was pretty pleased with the job because later that week I get another five hundred in the mail with a fucking thank-you note.

"That was the last I heard from her until sometime around the first of the year. That's when she called and said she wanted to do another one. I remember kinda laughing and asking her if she was planning to get rid of everybody in Dallas. She told me that she had five more after this one."

The new job, Garland had told her, would cost more. "I told her the price had gone up to ten thousand and she didn't hesitate for a second. She just said okay, and in a few days I got five grand."

"Did Noska deliver it?"

"No, she mailed it. Carl was out of it by then. She was dealing directly with me."

This time, Garland added, the money was accompanied by a photograph of Larry Aylor, a list of several places he frequented, and the various vehicles he was likely to be driving.

"I went back to Brian and told him we had another deal. He said okay and that he'd have to get back in touch with his man in Houston."

Garland said that he made no mention to Kreafle of the price increase, this time keeping half of the $5,000 for himself.

"I didn't hear anything for several weeks, so I started calling Brian to see what was going on. He finally told me that his guy had been killed by the Houston police. When I asked him what had happened to the money, he said that he had spent it looking for the guy.

"So, when 'Mary' called again, I had to explain that we hadn't been able to get the deal done and that the money was gone. She didn't really seem that unhappy. In fact, I got the impression that she was ready to forget the whole thing."

Garland had then assumed that was the end of it until he'd received another call from "Mary" months later. "She said that she had decided she still wanted the deal done—but she didn't want the price to go any higher than the ten thousand we'd previously talked about. I told her I'd have to think about it.

"A couple of days later I get this call from some woman who tells me her name is 'Miss Mud.' She says she's got something for me and we talk about a place to meet. There was this kid working in the office who was going out for cigarettes, so I asked him if he would pick up an envelope from this lady who said she would be driving a black Mercedes."

This time, Garland continued, Brian Kreafle managed to find someone to do the job. "But they fucked it up. They missed. When 'Mary' called to ask what happened, she was really pissed.

"I told her, 'Lady, I don't want nothing else to do with this. The game's over.'"

McGowan, now pacing the floor of the smoke-filled room, had heard enough. "Okay, Bill, we're going to go to the station and make this all neat and official. You're going to give us your statement, then I want you to take a polygraph test."

"Why?"

"To convince me that you weren't the shooter."

In Richardson, Captain Golden had given little thought to McGowan's mission. The odds of Garland's giving any information that might advance the case, he was certain, were astronomical. He was just preparing to leave his office when his phone rang.

"I just wanted to let you know that we're on our way," Morris said.

Golden was silent for a second. "Did you say *we?*"

"Yeah."

Suddenly, the captain had a mental picture of McGowan on the other end of the line, Bill Garland standing nearby. "Are you telling me he's going to give it up?"

"Yeah, that's right," McGowan said, maintaining the code language that his excited captain now fully understood.

"Jesus," Golden whispered. "We'll have everything set up by the time you get here."

"Great. See you soon."

Golden, unable to contain his excitement, rushed from his office, shouting orders. He wanted a video camera and a tape recorder set up in the interview room immediately. "Bill Garland's going to confess. I can't believe it, but it looks like it's going to happen."

On the drive to Richardson, Garland fell quiet, chain-smoking as he stared out into the late-evening darkness. They had reached the edge of Dallas before he turned to McGowan.

"That last time," he said, "when she called and said she wanted the hit done on her husband. It wasn't Brian who I called. It was a guy named Joe Thomas."

McGowan expressed his dismay at the ever-growing list of players. There was Brian Kreafle, who, if Garland was telling the truth, contracted with someone else to kill Rozanne. Now, still another name was being tossed into the confusing mix.

"Who the hell is Joe Thomas?"

"He's an old buddy of mine who's in the construction business. I took the deal to him and he said he thought he had a couple of guys who worked for him who might be interested.

"He got these two dumb-assed brothers to do it and they fucked up royally. They went out there drunk and with nothing but a fucking .22 pistol."

The links in the nightmarish chain continued to grow.

It was after ten P.M. by the time Garland's statement had been videotaped and recorded. Pressed for even more detail, he had again gone through the admission he had made just hours earlier.

Only toward the end of the interview did McGowan pose questions that had long piqued his curiosity.

"Why the fish in Joy's mailbox?"

"She didn't take the first couple of notes we sent to her seriously. Hell, she just tore them up and tossed them away. We figured the fish might rattle her, get her attention." With that Garland smiled slightly and sipped from a cup of coffee. "And, by God, it worked."

"Just how involved was Carol in the attempt on Larry Aylor's life?"

"She was supposed to get fifty thousand dollars after his insurance paid off."

The interview concluded, McGowan and Golden discussed the next step. Though the polygraph test would have to wait until Monday, they were both convinced that Garland's role had been that of a middleman. He had, in fact, offered his help in leading them to Brian Kreafle and Joe Thomas.

"Your job," Golden said, "is to find the person who killed Rozanne Gailiunas. He can't help you much if he's sitting in jail."

It was what McGowan wanted to hear. By not immediately placing Bill Garland under arrest, there was a far better chance that he would continue to cooperate. Also, it would keep the latest development from the media.

"I don't think he's going anywhere," McGowan said.

"One other thing," Golden said, extending his hand. "Congratulations."

Before leaving the station, Garland asked if he might call his mother to let her know that he was okay. Following a brief conversation, he returned to the hallway where McGowan and Golden waited.

"She told me that Joy's lawyer, Doug Mulder, has been calling." Garland smiled as if anticipating the officer's question. "That's where I was earlier today. Mulder wanted me to come talk to him. He knows the whole story."

McGowan, too, had a call to make before beginning the trip back to Sulphur Springs, and if the assistant DA was irritated at the lateness of the call, his voice gave no such indication.

"I drove over to Sulphur Springs today and talked with Bill Garland," McGowan said.

"And I suppose he confessed," Chapman said in jest.

"Kevin, *he did*. He gave it up. The whole nine yards." With that McGowan launched into a capsule recap of the statement Garland had given.

Chapman listened in silence, saying nothing until Morris told him that he had to drive Garland back to Sulphur Springs.

"Morris," the prosecutor finally said, "you just got Joy Aylor. Call me in the morning and we'll get to work." Working Saturdays had become routine for Chapman.

* * *

Captain Golden, buoyed by the turn of events, had volunteered to accompany McGowan on the drive back into east Texas.

The mood of Bill Garland, clearly relieved at not being placed under arrest, had lifted dramatically. He sat in the backseat reciting a litany of horror stories about his life with Carol, her insane jealousy and insatiable sexual appetite, the destructive rages she would fly into at the slightest provocation.

Glancing into the rearview mirror, McGowan made eye contact with his passenger. "I still can't understand why you stayed with her."

"It was the goddamn tape. She kept telling me that she had this tape of Joy Aylor and me talking on the phone. I couldn't leave as long as she had something like that hanging over my head."

McGowan nodded. Carol's involvement in blackmail, it seemed, had extended beyond threatening notes and dead fish in mailboxes.

Driving into the night, the detective found himself wondering if the tangled knot of lies and half-truths he'd been listening to since the earliest days of the investigation would ever be sorted out.

After he pulled into the driveway, he turned to face Garland, reminding him that he would return to Sulphur Springs on Monday. There were still things to discuss, he explained, and a polygraph test to be arranged.

Finally Garland asked the question that had been weighing on him since they left the station.

"What's going to happen to me?"

"Bill, that decision is not up to me."

Garland gave an understanding nod and stepped from the car.

A weary McGowan had, however, reached some decisions during the hour-long trip. As he headed back toward home, he discussed them with Golden. First, he said, he wanted to locate Joe Thomas. Then Brian Kreafle.

"It's your show, but you're going to need a lot of help," the captain acknowledged. "We'll get together first thing Monday morning and put a plan together."

For the remainder of the trip, McGowan looked forward anxiously to getting home and telling Sandy what had taken place. In his mind's eye, a happy image played.

Dominoes, stacked neatly in a row, were falling, one against another.

Standing at a blackboard, McGowan was outlining a plan that he'd been thinking about the entire weekend. With a good case against Joy Aylor now in place, the investigation would now focus on learning the identity of the person—or persons—who had actually murdered Rozanne Gailiunas.

The best way to accomplish that, McGowan had decided, would be to attack the weakest links first. In a sense, he wanted to back into the next phase of the investigation, going to the known middleman who had the least to lose.

If this man named Joe Thomas had, in fact, only arranged the attempt on Larry Aylor's life, he would likely find some degree of comfort, once confronted, in the fact that no murder actually took place. "What we want to explain to him and anyone else in the middle of this thing," Morris explained, "is that our primary interest is in just two people—the one who ordered Rozanne's murder and the one who committed it."

Ultimately, of course, all the parties involved would be arrested and serious charges were certain to result. What McGowan wanted most, however, was the person who fired the shots into the head of Rozanne Gailiunas.

Among those seated in the conference room was Investigator Rhonda Bonner, an eleven-year veteran of the force with a well-earned reputation as a thorough, hardworking police-woman. She was now in the midst of preparing for her sergeant's exam, and McGowan had followed her career with great respect. Bonner, he knew, would devote every waking minute to a case.

Intrigued by the investigation during the brief period she had been called in to deal with Carol Garland, Bonner was delighted when she was assigned to assist MacKenzie in the search for Thomas.

Before the day ended she knew that Joe Thomas, a construction worker in his late forties, had been a highly decorated infantryman during three tours of duty in Vietnam and suffered from the effects of exposure to Agent Orange.

She and MacKenzie also had an address.

When they located it, however, an elderly woman had answered and said that she knew no Joe Thomas.

After the officers had left, however, the woman, Thomas's mother, had telephoned her son in McAlester, Oklahoma, where he was working a construction job. "The Richardson police are looking for you," she said. "What's it all about?"

Joe had assured her that he had no idea, but that it was nothing for her to worry about.

The following day he placed a call to Bonner: "I understand you're looking for me." A tone of resignation was in his voice as he agreed to meet her and MacKenzie the following day at a Denny's restaurant in Sherman, Texas, a halfway point between Richardson and McAlester.

On the morning of July 13, McGowan was pacing the halls of the police station even before the officers had had time to make the drive to Sherman.

Early that afternoon Bonner telephoned to say that they were en route to Richardson and were bringing Thomas with them. "He's admitted it," Bonner reported.

The story that Joe Thomas—frail looking and nervously polishing his glasses—told would introduce a new and strange group of characters to the plot.

In the spring of 1986, Bill Garland, with whom he'd once been partners in the roofing business, approached him with a story about a wealthy family that was looking for someone to "take care" of a man who had been repeatedly sexually abusing his young daughter. Either the girl's mother or grandmother—Bill hadn't seemed sure which—had decided she didn't want the child put through the ordeal of a trial and had decided to take matters into her own hands.

159

Thomas had indicated to Garland that he might know some-one who would be interested in the job: "I'll ask around."

A few days later Thomas contacted fellow construction worker Kenneth Moorefield, outside his apartment. After a few minutes of work-related conversation, Thomas brought up the subject of the unknown man who was molesting his daughter.

"What do you think about a baby-raping sonuvabitch like that?" he asked, explaining that members of the family were ready to pay good money for someone to "put this guy in the hospital."

"I don't do things like that," Moorefield replied.

"Do you know anybody who does?"

Moorefield mentioned two brothers working for him who had more than once remarked that they would do almost any-thing for money. With that he had given Thomas the telephone numbers of Buster and Gary Matthews.

Contacting Buster, an ex-con and the older of the brothers, Thomas again outlined the sexual abuse story. "If the price is right," Buster said, "I just might be interested."

After talking with Garland and getting more details, Thomas arranged a meeting with Buster at a drive-in restaurant. He was surprised to see that both brothers were waiting for him when he arrived.

"What's their deal?" Buster asked.

"Five thousand dollars. Half up front, half when the job's done. How you do it is your business—gun, crossbow, or knife. Any jewelry and money you get, you consider a bonus."

Buster hesitated for only a few seconds before replying, "We'll take care of it."

"Just another search-and-destroy mission," added Gary Matthews, a demolition and weapons expert while in the ser-vice.

By the end of the week, Thomas had passed along a brown envelope containing $2,500 in cash, a photograph of a bearded, well-dressed man standing by a Suburban, and directions to a ranch in Kaufman County where the hit was to be carried out.

As his statement was being recorded, Thomas continued to

detail the sequence of events leading up to the country-road ambush.

"Bill Garland was to call and let me know when the guy would be going down to the ranch. The first time, Buster and Gary drove around for half a day and never could find the damn place. They came back and said the directions they'd been given were lousy.

"The next time, after we'd gotten a better map, it rained like hell and the guy apparently decided not to make the trip. They waited all day and he never showed up.

"Then, on the third try . . . well, you know what a fucking mess that turned into."

The day after the ambush, Thomas had met with the Matthewses at a Stop 'n' Go near his office, listening as they described their failure.

"When I called Bill to tell him what had happened, he was really upset. He said his people were really pissed. He apparently called them and was told that if the job couldn't be done at the ranch, maybe there was some other place. He had the names of a couple of coffee shops and a bar where the guy hung out.

"By this time, Bill was really pressuring me, getting to be a big pain in the ass.

"So, I met with the Matthews brothers and told them what the deal was. We drove around, going past coffee shops and the bar, and by the guy's house. Buster wanted to know why they couldn't just go up and ring the doorbell and when he answered, shoot him and haul ass. We talked about the possibility of catching him in the alley, near the entrance of his garage, and taking him out there. But Bill had said that one of the specific instructions he'd been given was that nothing was to be done at the house."

Shortly thereafter, Thomas said, Garland told him the deal was off. "I moved to east Texas in September of that year and never heard from Bill again."

Late into the night MacKenzie, Bonner, and McGowan sat discussing the events of the day. As in the case of Garland, they had made the decision not to immediately arrest Thomas. Instead, after a polygraph test to judge the validity of his statement, they would have him get in touch with the Matthews brothers.

That, however, could wait for a few days. They would go after Brian Kreafle next.

Bill Garland, having voluntarily returned to the Richardson Police Department, placed a call to Kreafle suggesting they meet later in the afternoon in a Kmart parking lot near Brian's auto repair shop.

Puzzled and suspicious when Garland refused to discuss anything over the phone, Kreafle, nonetheless, agreed to meet with him. "I wish you'd tell me what the hell this is about."

"Brian, goddamn it, just be there. It's important."

With a half dozen undercover officers in place throughout the parking lot, Garland, a wire hidden beneath his shirt, waited for a half hour before he finally saw Kreafle's car slowly approaching.

When it pulled up next to him, however, he saw that the driver was not Brian, but his wife, Cindy. Rolling down the window, she squinted into the last rays of the late-afternoon sun at the big man now standing next to her car.

"Brian had something come up," she said. "A friend of his called and needed his car fixed."

In the surveillance van several hundred feet away, MacKenzie looked over at Bonner. "The antenna's up," he said.

The following day, with the electronic equipment once again put away in the police department storeroom, the detectives knocked on the front door of Brian Kreafle's home.

It was easier than they had dared hope.

Hearing from Garland, he acknowledged, had alerted him that something was amiss. He'd been a nervous wreck since the call.

Seated on a couch in his living room, Kreafle listened as MacKenzie began outlining the information that Garland had provided them. As the detective talked, Kreafle buried his face in his hands and began to sob. Then, lifting his head, he looked up at MacKenzie. "I didn't kill nobody," he said. "All I did was pass the money on to this insurance guy I know."

Bonner phoned the station and told an excited McGowan to have the interview room prepared.

Garland had stopped by his auto repair shop with the envelope that contained the money and the woman's picture, Kreafle said.

"Bill first suggested that he and I do the deal. We even drove by the address that was in the envelope. But it just didn't feel right to me. The whole idea scared the shit out of me and I said so. But I told him I thought I knew somebody who might be interested. There was this guy I'd done some dope deals with, an insurance adjustor named Andy Hopper. He was a big talker. Said he was involved in all kind of heavy shit and knew a lot of badass people.

"One afternoon he stopped by and we started talking about it. He mentioned some buddy of his down in Houston, a guy named Cal, who would probably be interested. So, I gave him the envelope. He took it and tossed it on the front seat of his car and took off.

"The next thing I heard from him was when he stopped by the shop a week or so later to tell me that his guy had gotten the job done. I called Bill and told him."

MacKenzie, who was conducting the interview, pressed Kreafle about the Houston connection. Garland, he pointed out, had indicated that it was Brian who had mentioned knowing someone in Houston.

"What about the guy you were looking for down there? The one the police shot?"

For a moment Kreafle looked puzzled, then slowly nodded in acknowledgment. "You're talking about the second deal."

"The deal to kill the guy out at the ranch."

"I made that story up. Bill had brought me another envelope, another twenty-five hundred dollars. I told him I'd see what I could do, but, truthfully, I didn't want any part of it. When he called a couple of weeks later to see what was happening, I told him I'd spent the money trying to find the guy. I made up this bullshit story about him getting killed in a shootout with the police down in Houston.''

"What happened to the money?"

"Business was pretty bad back then." Kreafle had used it to pay off some debts.

MacKenzie glanced across the room at McGowan, who had been silently observing the interview, then turned back to Kreafle.

"Where do we find this guy Andy Hopper?"

# 13

THE SON OF a Houston auto repairman, he had been one of the most popular students in Sam Houston High School's class of '74, runner-up in the voting for Senior Class Favorite and a finalist in the annual Most Handsome Boy competition. George Anderson Hopper, Jr., called Andy by his wide collection of friends, played on the school golf team, was a member of the Thespian Club, and was considered by his teachers to be a bright and dedicated student.

While he was, at times, something of a braggart, it was generally judged to be a minor personality flaw far overshadowed by the "yes, ma'am, yes, sir" kind of manners that parents of his friends greatly admired.

Andy Hopper, those who knew him were certain, was a young man with a bright future. Few were surprised when he announced following his graduation that he was enrolling at Southwestern Assemblies of God College in Waxahachie, Texas, to study for the ministry. And no one was more pleased than George and JoAnn Hopper, deeply religious parents of two other sons and a daughter.

On the same college campus where rock-'n'-roll legend Jerry Lee Lewis had briefly flirted with a career in the ministry,

Andy's popularity continued. A good student, he immediately earned a spot in the school's traveling choral group, and the admiration of his fellow students. Many of the coeds made little secret of their eagerness to get to know him better. Among them was a diminutive, almost shy sophomore from the Texas Panhandle community of Pampa.

Becky Thompson, with her long and shiny auburn hair and warm, friendly doe eyes, had been pleasantly surprised when Andy first asked her out. She quickly became the solitary focus of his romantic attention and was soon deeply in love.

On April 19, 1975, they were married. Andy was nineteen, Becky eighteen. Dropping out of school, they moved thirty miles north to Dallas where Andy had found a modest apartment and a job managing a men's shoe store.

Hiding disappointment in her son's decision to give up the idea of becoming a minister, JoAnn Hopper turned her energies to making her new daughter-in-law feel welcome to the family. George Hopper, meanwhile, stood ready to help his son's career along.

During the summers when Andy was still in high school, he had worked long hours in his father's shop, learning the bodywork business. The young Hopper clearly had a talent for the trade. And as his dad would later point out, it paid far better than selling shoes.

When a job came open in the Houston Lincoln-Mercury dealership repair shop that George Hopper managed, he had no reservations about hiring his son, and by the end of 1975, Andy was settled into a line of work that he felt confident would offer a prosperous future. Indeed, he climbed the ladder even faster than he had dared hope. His reputation for quality work, a good business sense, and friendly dealings with customers spread quickly. Shortly after his twenty-first birthday he was hired to manage the body shop of a Ford dealership in Houston.

The married life of Andy and Becky Hopper also had all the earmarks of success. Their friends and family saw them as a happy, loving, churchgoing couple, fiercely independent and determined to make it on their own. Shortly before the birth of their first child, a daughter, Andy borrowed money to make a down payment on a house.

Few at that time knew that Andy Hopper had a dark side.

Becky confided to no one the frightening, uncontrollable temper she had first seen her husband display shortly after they had married. Nor did she mention the outrageous, often cruel treatment she received.

Her husband demanded that his clothes be laid out in specific order every morning. When he showered, he expected Becky to be standing ready with a towel of a specific color, still warm from the drier. If meals were not served on time or were not cooked to his satisfaction, he would throw food and dishes about the room in a fit of anger. A child's toy, hurled at Becky during one of his tantrums, had blackened her eye. Routinely, she hid bruises caused by his grabbing her by the arms or shoulders or the back of her neck.

Still, frightened and confused by her husband's mercurial mood swings, Becky refused to acknowledge that she was an abused wife, preferring instead to do everything she could to perpetuate the image of the perfect couple.

Hiding the truth about her husband, however, was not always easy, and shortly before their daughter was born, Andy had his first brush with the law.

In late March of 1976, Frances Ferguson, who managed an apartment complex near the dealership where Hopper worked, was busy cleaning one of the recently vacated units. Shortly after noon she was vacuuming the bedroom while her infant son lay sleeping on a quilt in the living room.

Looking up, she suddenly saw a young man standing at the bedroom doorway. Assuming that he was in the market for an apartment, she asked if she might be of help.

Saying nothing, the man smiled as he unzipped his pants and exposed his penis.

Panicked, the woman raced from the room, pushing the intruder aside. Pulling her son into her arms, she fled from the apartment toward her office. Once safely inside, she looked out a window to see the man still standing in the doorway of the vacant apartment. His casual appearance turned her fear to anger, and she opened the door and yelled out at him, "If you're through, you can leave now."

The man shrugged and began walking toward the parking lot.

Mrs. Ferguson, by now furious, raced next door to her apartment, found the pistol that her husband had bought her for protection, and hurried toward where the man was parked. He was already in his car, trying to start it, when she arrived with the gun in her shaking hand, pointed at him.

"You want to come back and try that again?" she screamed defiantly.

The man stepped from the car, the smile now replaced by a look of terror. "Lady," he pleaded, "please don't shoot me." Then he ran.

The apartment manager, after memorizing the license number of the man's car, phoned the police.

Later that afternoon Andy confided to one of the secretaries at the dealership that something strange had happened to him during his lunch break. He had, he said, gone to the nearby Winkler Drive-In for a hamburger and afterward decided to take a walk. As he passed a vacant apartment, a woman, hysterical and screaming, had accused him of exposing himself and began chasing him with a gun.

It was, of course, some kind of misunderstanding, Andy assured his coworker. He just wanted her to hear it from him in the event there was any kind of trouble later.

The secretary dismissed the story with a gesture of amusement. No one as nice and polite as Andy Hopper, she was certain, would ever do such a thing.

After her husband was charged with a Class C misdemeanor, Becky had borrowed money from her parents to pay the fine and court costs. She was careful not to tell them what the loan was for.

Andy, meanwhile, assured his wife that the woman at the apartment had lied to the police.

The all-American boy had dodged his first legal bullet, but not even Becky had any idea of the extent to which her husband had begun living a double life that went well beyond the private rages and abuses.

Sexual liaisons, often with women Becky thought of as friends, sometimes with casual acquaintances Andy made at work, became commonplace.

There was, for instance, Danny Colson and his teenage fiancée, Janie, whom the Hoppers had met at church. In time the couples began to see each other for backyard barbecues and evenings of watching rented videos. When, however, Becky left for a weekend visit to her parents in Pampa, Andy had invited Janie to the house and seduced her, beginning an affair that would last well into the early days of her own marriage.

She was neither the first nor the last to help satisfy Andy's ever-growing sexual appetite.

Publicly, however, Andy's image remained that of an upwardly mobile young man. At age twenty-one, while many of his friends were still working toward college degrees, his annual income climbed to near $40,000, thanks to his father.

George Hopper had opened his own insurance appraisal company and immediately set about teaching his son the business. In time, the company flourished and the elder Hopper opened a branch office in Dallas, managed by his son. Unknown to his father, Andy took something else to Dallas along with his family: a secret marijuana user even during his Bible college days, he now had a fast-growing and expensive addiction to methamphetamines.

Though still well hidden, the dark side was gaining control of his life.

In Dallas, the financial burden of a second daughter, rent on a fashionable three-bedroom home, and the cost of drugs soon began to weigh heavily. More desperate with each passing month, Andy began to search for a new means of supplementing his income.

That need led him to look up a man named James Carver, a former employee of his father's who had, years earlier, moved to Dallas and begun a business far more lucrative than repairing dented fenders.

Carver, seven years older than Andy and now weighing over

three hundred pounds, was surprised to hear from the young man he had long ago served as a mentor, teaching him the auto repair business during summer months.

Though Carver still professed to be in the paint and body-repair business, grease was no longer evident beneath his manicured fingernails. He now wore diamond rings and a Rolex watch, drove a fancy car, and lived in a home that cost over $2 million.

Andy immediately realized that the rumors he had heard were true: James Carver had established himself as one of the leading marijuana dealers in the United States, earning a reported $50,000 per week.

Although he dealt only with dealers in California and the Midwest who routinely made purchases well into six figures, Carver listened sympathetically as Andy detailed his financial woes. For old times' sake, Carver said, he would regularly provide Andy with a pound of marijuana—which normally sold for $650—on a pay-later basis. Build up a small but regular clientele, Carver advised, and you can do nicely.

What Carver was proposing, then, was a small-time involvement in the drug trade, a way to handsomely increase one's income without great risk. The Drug Enforcement Administration and the IRS, he explained, weren't likely to spend much time bothering people selling nickel and dime bags.

Andy welcomed the opportunity and in short order was spending more time selling dope than he was tending to the business of appraising damaged cars. James Carver's lifestyle impressed him far more than that of his hardworking father.

Having glimpsed life in the fast lane, Andy wanted to be a part of it. Newly prosperous, he and Becky made skiing trips to Colorado and moved into a larger home, complete with a swimming pool. And Andy was talking of joining several new friends in investing in a Dallas nightclub to be called Beethoven's.

Debts, however, soon began to grow faster than Andy's income as his own drug habit ate deeply into the profits from his marijuana sales. By the early eighties, a disappointed George Hopper had decided to close the Dallas branch of his appraisal company, surprised that his son had not been able to build the business into a profitable concern. He encouraged Andy either to find another, more solvent company to do insurance adjustments for or to return to the stability of the body shop business.

Once considered a young man on the rise, a shop manager at age twenty-one, Andy Hopper, now ten years older, was forced to deal with the ego-deflating fact that his career was headed in the wrong direction. To help make ends meet, his wife had taken a sales job in an arts and crafts store in Richardson.

On July 21, 1988, Officers MacKenzie and Bonner approached Andy Hopper in the body shop of Steakley Chevrolet in Dallas.

As had been the case when they first interviewed Thomas and Kreafle, they carried no arrest warrant. If there was, as Kreafle had indicated, someone involved beyond Hopper, they didn't want him alerted by news of an arrest.

Sitting in a small cubicle, MacKenzie carefully outlined Brian Kreafle's story, including the fact that Andy had supposedly told him that he had passed the assignment along to a friend in Houston.

"I'm going to tell you right now," MacKenzie said, "the middlemen in this deal don't have nearly as much to worry about as the lady who wanted it done and the person who actually did it."

"I don't know what the hell you're talking about," Andy argued. "I don't know why Brian would tell you something like that."

MacKenzie acted as if he'd not even heard Hopper. "Andy, who's Cal? Brian said you mentioned a buddy in Houston by that name."

A small table fan directly behind Andy was on high, but he suddenly began to sweat profusely, droplets falling from his chin onto the glass top of his desk. Calvin Hobson, he finally admitted, was a friend from high school days. A badass. Andy was, he said, always amusing people with stories about things Cal had done. In all likelihood, he had probably mentioned him to Brian at one time or another.

"The story I hear," MacKenzie continued, "was that you contacted him about doing the killing."

Andy, still sweating, did not respond. "I think I should call my lawyer," he finally said.

As Hopper walked to a phone in the rear of the body shop, MacKenzie looked over at Bonner. "He's pretty nervous," she said, as if acknowledging her partner's thoughts.

Ken MacKenzie kept to himself his own observation, one based on years of experience interviewing criminals. As he'd watched Hopper's nervous movements, a feeling had swelled in his gut that this nice-looking articulate young man was no middleman. Andy, he was convinced, had killed Rozanne Gailiunas.

Suggesting that Bonner phone McGowan to tell him they were going to bring Hopper in for further questioning, MacKenzie rose to walk back into the body shop.

Andy was nowhere to be found.

They were still searching the building and the car lot when a secretary approached MacKenzie to tell him that he had a phone call.

Rushing back into the body shop, MacKenzie picked up the phone to hear Andy's voice. Calling from a pay phone, he explained that he had spoken with his attorney's secretary. "She told me I should leave and not say anything until I've talked to my lawyer. I'm not coming back."

A flush of anger spread across the detective's face as the secretary told him that she had watched Hopper run out the back door, across the car lot, and climb over the fence.

Driving immediately to Andy's residence on Catalpa Drive, the officers found no one at home. However, a neighbor, working in her yard, volunteered that Becky might know where her husband was and could likely be found at work. She was a cashier in the hobby department of Michael's in Richardson.

As he drove toward the store, MacKenzie fell silent. The neighborhood where the Hoppers lived had been familiar. So had the house just across the street. He had made a long-forgotten arrest there.

"I'll be damned," he finally muttered to himself.

"What is it?" Bonner asked.

"I'll tell you about it later," her partner said, pushing hard on the accelerator.

As the officers entered the crafts store they were greeted by the sound of an intercom paging Becky Hopper. Quickly searching the counters, Bonner saw a small woman near the rear of the store pick up the phone and walked hurriedly toward her, hoping to eavesdrop on the conversation. Though the woman said little, it was obvious that she was upset.

Becky had clocked out and was in the parking lot en route to her car when the officers caught up to her and began explaining the situation. "It's important that Andy talk with us and get things straightened out," MacKenzie said.

"He didn't tell me where he was," Becky replied, her voice a soft tremble. "I don't understand—" She stopped abruptly and stared at the detective as if seeing him for the first time. "I know you."

MacKenzie nodded. "Yes, we've been through this before."

In mid-May of 1984, insurance salesman Glenn Johnston, just returning from an out-of-town business trip, had stopped by the Richardson Square Mall to purchase a birthday card for his cousin.

While standing in a shop called The Card Cage, browsing through the selection, a bearded young man had brushed against him. Johnston thought nothing of it. Nor did he give it much mind when, minutes later, the same man bumped into him a second time as he made his way back to the front of the store and out into the crowded mall.

Only when Johnston approached the counter to pay for the card did he realize the brushes had not been accidental but, instead, the act of a pickpocket. His wallet, which had contained $40 in cash and $200 worth of traveler's checks, was gone.

Not having had a good look at the man, Johnston decided that it would be futile to report the theft to the police, but he hoped that someone might ultimately find his discarded wallet and contact him. With luck, he might get back his driver's license and personal items, such as photographs of his wife and children.

Two days after the incident he received a call from a man who said he had, in fact, found the wallet in the mall. Relieved, Johnston asked where he might pick it up.

"I thought maybe there would be a reward," the caller said.

Johnston, initially surprised at the caller's mercenary attitude, suggested he keep whatever cash was in the billfold.

"There's not any cash," the man said. "I'll be back in touch."

The following day, Johnston heard from the man again. This time he demanded the insurance salesman's automatic bankteller code number. "I'll get the reward myself."

They argued for several minutes before Johnston, shocked and unsure what to do, gave the caller a bogus number.

That evening he answered the phone to hear an angry voice: "You lied to me. What you need to think about is the fact I've got all kinds of fucking information about you. I know where you live, where you work, where your wife works . . . and what your kids look like."

Now frightened, Johnston asked, "What do you want me to do?"

"I want you to meet me and endorse the traveler's checks over to me."

"I need to think about it."

"I'll be in touch."

Johnston heard the line go dead and stood speechless for several minutes. Then he dialed the number of the Richardson Police Department.

After driving to the station and detailing the extortion plot to Officer Ken Roberts, Johnston was told to go along with the plan to meet the caller. He was to find out where and when it was to take place and get back in touch as soon as he had the information. A team of undercover officers would set up in the area and move in to make the arrest.

Later that evening Johnston received a call instructing him to go to the Loehman's Plaza Shopping Center: "There's a lot of construction going on there. Near the corner just off Loman there's a stack of bricks near a utility pole. I'll leave the checks there with a note telling you how to endorse them.

"After you've done that, go to the JoJo's across the street and wait by the pay phone. I'll call you and tell you where to find your billfold."

As Johnston drove nervously toward the shopping center, he was closely followed by unmarked police cars driven by Officers Ken Roberts and Melody Acord. Two other plainclothes policemen waited in the restaurant. Ken MacKenzie, driving his pickup, had surveyed the parking lot of the shopping center and decided that his best observation point would be the southeast corner where he could watch both the alley exit and the side street.

While MacKenzie watched through binoculars, Johnston pulled up near the pile of bricks. In short order he found the traveler's checks and a card bearing a note telling him to make them payable to "A. Hopper." He pretended to sign each of the checks, then quickly drove away in the direction of the restaurant.

Only a few minutes passed before MacKenzie saw a brown Ford, driven by a man wearing a white shirt and blue shorts, pull up near the stack of bricks. The detective waited until he was certain the checks had been retrieved, then put his pickup in gear.

Seeing MacKenzie approach, the man quickly jumped into his car and sped off in the direction of the exit being blocked by Roberts and Acord, now positioned behind car doors with weapons drawn. The driver made a hard turn, jumped a curb, and was soon into the early-evening traffic, MacKenzie close behind.

As the chase reached speeds of eighty miles per hour, the detective got close enough to get the license plate number, then, at one point, was able to pull alongside the fleeing driver and signal him to pull over.

Instead, he had swerved in an attempt to hit MacKenzie's pickup, then turned onto a side street so abruptly that he lost a hubcap, taking the chase through a shopping-center parking lot, then into a residential area where the pursuing officer lost sight of him. Only when a man mowing his lawn pointed down an alley running behind Catalpa Drive did MacKenzie know how the Ford had disappeared.

Later that evening, after a check of the license plate had been run, MacKenzie, accompanied by Roberts and Acord, approached the front door of 3217 Catalpa and was greeted by Becky Hopper.

"We'd like to speak with Andy Hopper," MacKenzie said.

As he spoke, Andy stepped into the doorway. He had shaved his beard and mustache and changed clothes. "What's the problem?" he asked, forcing a smile.

MacKenzie did not reply, instead nodding to Roberts. "That's him."

Later, after Andy had been taken to jail, Becky had angrily retrieved the white shirt and blue shorts her husband had been wearing earlier as he had rushed past her and into the bathroom. She had turned them over to the police.

The following day she borrowed money from James Carver to post Andy's bail.

Ironically, Andy once again managed to dodge a legal bullet when, due to a paperwork snafu, no formal charges were ever filed in the case.


Clearly, the 1984 incident had come rushing back to Becky Hopper as she stood in the parking lot outside Michael's, again being questioned by MacKenzie. She quickly made it clear that she had no interest in talking to him.

Realizing that her partner's presence was an obvious liability, Bonner suggested that she and Becky walk to a nearby fast-food restaurant for a cup of coffee. "You need to know what's going on," the investigator said. "Your husband is in serious trouble."

For over an hour Bonner sat talking with the distraught young woman, who steadfastly refused to believe her husband could be involved in anything like what the investigator was suggesting. Slowly reacting to Bonner's questioning, Becky finally acknowledged that Andy knew a man in Houston named Calvin Hobson. For reasons she had never been able to understand, Andy had idolized him since high school days: "He's always talking about the awful things Cal does, how mean and bad he is."

"From the information we have," Bonner continued, "it's possible Cal is the person we're really looking for. The truth of the matter is, we think Andy was only the middleman. It would be in his best interest for him to talk to us."

Becky, looking fragile and exhausted, began to cry as she looked across the table at the officer. "I'll see that he comes to the police station."

Later that afternoon, Andy placed a call to the Richardson Police Department and promised Rhonda Bonner that he would be in her office the following day. Until then, he said, he would remain in hiding.

In the meantime, McGowan had met with Bonner and Mac-Kenzie to discuss their next move. Hopeful that Becky would, in fact, be able to persuade her obviously frightened husband to cooperate with the investigation, they agreed that it was too soon to seek a warrant for his arrest. Particularly if there was, in fact, someone he had passed the money on to.

"Let's see if we can find Cal Hobson," McGowan suggested.

Less than an hour later, Bonner took a long-distance call from Houston and heard a man on the other end identify himself as Calvin Hobson. He had, he explained, spoken with Becky, and she had indicated the police were looking for him. "I don't know what the hell's going on up there, but I want to get this mess cleared up, right now. I'm on my way."

"When can we expect you?" Bonner asked.

"I'm taking the next flight out."

"How will we recognize you?"

"I'll be the best-looking sonuvabitch walking off the plane."

Before nightfall Hobson was sitting in McGowan's office. Down the hall a polygraph operator was waiting.

"I ain't never hurt anybody in my life," Hobson insisted. "I'm a con man—three-card monte, pigeon drops, that sort of shit—but, hey, I don't hurt people. That's not my thing.

"Maybe me and Andy did a little dope together. He even

tried once to set me up with some dude he was selling for. But there's no way I'm getting involved in the kind of business you're talking about.''

Andy, he remembered, had phoned him sometime in late 1983 and mentioned something about a guy who was looking for someone to do a hit. The amount of money involved was peanuts. He had told Andy that not only was he not interested, but no one would be for that kind of payoff. "That's the last I ever heard about it, until Becky called.''

"Do you think you could get her to tell you where Andy is?''

"Hell, I don't know. I'll try.''

McGowan dialed the number and pushed the phone across the desk. In a matter of minutes he was convinced that Hobson was either genuinely angered at being involved or was the best actor he'd ever seen.

"Look, goddammit,'' he said into the phone, "I know what Andy's done and he's not going to drag my ass into it. You tell him I want to talk with him, right away. I know you know where he is, so get in touch with him and tell him he's got five fucking minutes to call me.''

Then, as if on cue, he changed his mind. "No, I don't want to talk to him on the phone. You tell him I'm coming to Dallas tomorrow night to get this straightened out. Tell him I'll be on the Southwest Airlines flight that gets in at seven. I'll meet him in the lobby by that big statue of the Texas Ranger.''

Hanging up, he looked across at McGowan. "She says she doesn't know where he is—he's at some motel—but he's supposed to call her.''

"Will he meet you?''

"He damn well better.''

Hobson readily agreed to wear a wire.

The Richardson police were not the only ones laying plans.
From a room at the Comfort Inn motel where he was in hiding, Andy was making a series of calls to friends in an attempt to borrow money. He needed it, he explained, to hire a lawyer.

After drinking heavily throughout the day, he telephoned Becky late in the evening to tell her he was not coming home. He was drunk, he said, and didn't want the girls to see him in such a condition.

"Are you going to be all right?" Becky asked.

"I'm thinking about killing myself." He had borrowed a .22 pistol from a friend, he said, then began reading from a long, rambling letter he'd written, apologizing for the hurt he had inflicted on his family. *Becky,* the letter ended, *I'm sorry that I've caused you so much grief. You've always been too good to me.*

Following their conversation, Becky returned to the girlfriend who had come over to keep her company.

Becky curled up on the end of the couch, then said, "He says he's thinking about committing suicide." After a long, thoughtful pause, she added, shocking her friend, "I hope he does."

This statement, born of fear and frustration, she immediately regretted.

Calvin Hobson arrived at Love Field two hours ahead of schedule and met with McGowan in a Dallas police substation located in the terminal lobby. The meeting with Andy, McGowan explained, would be monitored from the room located just across the lobby from the bigger-than-life-size Texas Ranger statue. "Your job is to get him to talk about the deal he made. If he handed the money off to someone else, we want to know to who."

Still angry that his name had been dragged into the investigation, Hobson showed no signs of apprehension. He was, he said, eager to see Hopper. "I'm ready to get this shit straightened out."

A half hour later he was standing at the base of the statue when he saw Andy enter the lobby and look suspiciously in all directions before walking toward the assigned meeting place.

Hobson wasted no time on a friendly handshake or small talk. He was pissed, he said. The police were trying to tie him into some woman's murder, and he wanted to know what the

178

hell was going on. For several minutes he railed at his old friend.

Finally, Andy spoke. "Are you wearing a wire?"

"Shit, no."

Hopper placed his hand on Hobson's breast pocket as if to check, and Cal brushed it away. "You asshole, I said I ain't wearing no fucking wire. I just want to know what this is all about."

Andy sighed and his eyes began to well up with tears. His shoulders slumped as Hobson continued to assail him. "Why the hell are you tossing my name around?"

Nervously scanning the almost deserted lobby, Hopper said, "Man, I'm really sorry about that."

"Sorry don't clear my fucking name. *What's the goddamn deal?*"

Hopper's voice fell to a whisper. "I know about it, but I didn't do it. Look, let's go into the bathroom. You prove to me you aren't wired and I'll tell you the whole thing."

Unprepared for that, Hobson replied, "Fuck that," glaring at Andy.

Saying nothing more, Hopper turned and walked away, his pace quickening as he neared the lobby exit. He felt certain that his old friend had been trying to lure him into some kind of trap, that the police had been close by, listening to their conversation.

What had made Andy immediately suspicious was that Hobson was wearing a suit for the first time since he had known him.

Inside the substation, McGowan removed his earphones and lifted his palms in a show of disappointment. All the meeting had accomplished was to emphasize further that Cal Hobson was a name that could be eliminated from the investigation.

The following Monday, July 25, Andy Hopper disappeared, again raising questions about McGowan's stubborn refusal to take people involved in the case into custody rather than wait until all arrests could be made simultaneously.

Kevin Chapman had contacted Hopper's attorney, urging that he persuade his client to come to the district attorney's office to discuss the allegations that had been made against him. Later that day the lawyer phoned to say he had been unable to locate Andy.

At almost the same time, Ken MacKenzie was talking with a Garland police officer who had phoned to advise him that a missing person's report had been filed by Hopper's father.

The last time anyone had seen Andy, the elder Hopper said, was when he had stopped by the house briefly to attend his oldest daughter's birthday party.

Walking down the hall to McGowan's office, MacKenzie was once again the bearer of bad news: "He's run."

For several days, Becky had tried to carry on normally, but with each passing day, her fear grew that Andy had, in fact, committed suicide.

Among those who tried to offer comfort was Lynda Whittaker, a pretty, dark-haired waitress at Beethoven's, the nightclub in which Andy had earlier invested. Several months before, Andy had introduced her to a longtime friend from Houston named Buddy Wright, and in short order Buddy was traveling to Dallas to see Lynda almost every weekend. They had spent a good deal of time in the company of the Hoppers, and Becky and Lynda quickly became good friends. Buddy, meanwhile, confided to Andy that he was seriously considering asking Lynda to marry him.

After Buddy called her to say that Andy was in trouble and had contacted him about a loan, Lynda went to Becky to ask if she could do anything to help. In the days following Andy's disappearance, she became Becky's almost constant companion, ever ready to listen to her troubled friend, offering solace and support.

She volunteered to help Becky prepare for a planned garage sale before leaving for Pampa to move in with her parents.

It was the only thing she knew to do, Becky explained, since Andy had emptied their small savings and checking accounts before disappearing. He had not even left her a gasoline credit card.

Only days before Becky's parents were to drive to Dallas and pick up her and the children, Lynda Whittaker had located

Andy's abandoned Nissan Maxima parked in a shopping center just a few miles from the Hopper house. The car had been unlocked, she first told Becky, then the authorities. She had been surprised to see that the car phone was still in place, and when she had checked the glove compartment to make certain it was Andy's car, she had found a .22 pistol.

Becky, growing more distraught and confused with each passing day, found Lynda's story troubling. For almost two weeks she had been driving through that same parking lot and was certain Andy's car had not been there.

On the third Sunday in August, McGowan was in his backyard grooming his Lab retriever, Macy, when he received a call from MacKenzie: "Lynda Whittaker wants to talk."

"What about?"

"Her boyfriend . . . Andy Hopper."

For a fleeting moment, what MacKenzie was saying did not sink in. "I'll be damned," Morris finally replied.

Accompanied to the police station by her mother, Lynda was in tears minutes after taking a seat in McGowan's office.

She and Andy had been lovers for some time, she admitted. They had met at the club and had begun seeing each other even before Andy had introduced her to his friend. She had pretended to be interested in Buddy only because it provided a way to spend more time in Andy's company without arousing suspicion.

"I love him," she sobbed, "and he loves me. But I'm scared. And I feel terrible about the way I've treated Becky."

Lynda had helped him leave town, driving him to a bus station in Oklahoma City. Upon her return, she had hidden his car in her mother's garage until the day she drove it to the shopping center.

She had spent so much time with Becky since Andy's departure so as to keep him posted on what was being done and said about his flight.

"And now, he wants me to come see him."

"Where is he?" McGowan asked.

"He wouldn't say. He told me he would call back tonight and tell me where to meet him."

"Do you want to see him?"

Lynda looked across the desk as tears slid slowly down her cheeks. "Yes. I want to help him. He couldn't have done the horrible thing you people are saying he did. Not the Andy I know."

McGowan rose and moved around the desk to stand closer to her. "If you really want to help him, here's the way it works. He doesn't know me, so if you go to see him, I go with you. And you try to get him to talk. If he won't talk to you, you're to try to convince him that it is in his best interest to talk with us.

"When's he supposed to phone?"

"At seven."

"Call me as soon as you've heard from him."

Lynda was still crying as McGowan and MacKenzie walked her and her mother to the station parking lot.

That evening she telephoned McGowan to tell him that Andy had called. He was somewhere in Montana, she said, and would call again on Tuesday to tell her where to meet him.

Two days later, Andy phoned with instructions to take a Saturday-morning flight to Boise, Idaho. He would meet her at the airport.

"Did he say anything else?" McGowan asked.

"He's really looking forward to seeing me." A heavy note of apprehension was in her voice.

For the remainder of the week, McGowan and MacKenzie worked furiously on preparations for the upcoming rendezvous. They contacted the Boise police, faxed them a photograph of Hopper, detailed the situation, and requested their help in setting up surveillance. Don Burcham, the Richardson Police Department's electronics technician, was already on his way.

At a Holiday Inn near the airport, they were told, Lynda Whittaker would have a room, which Burcham could wire for sound, reserved in her name. An adjacent room would be reserved to set up the monitoring equipment.

Undercover officers would be waiting at the airport to assist in any way they could.

Thus, by the time McGowan and Lynda boarded the United

Airlines flight, everything seemed in place. Though they had spoken on several occasions during the week, Morris carefully coaching her on the specific questions he wanted her to ask, the detective spent most of the flight going over them again in an effort to convince her that what she was doing was for Andy's own good.

Only when they began their descent did Lynda ask the question she had avoided for days. "Are you going to arrest him?"

"No," McGowan assured her.

His answer was only partially true. Still not convinced that Hopper was the final link in the Gailiunas murder chain, he was making the trip hoping to learn the name of the person Andy had passed the contract on to. With the Boise police poised to track Andy's movements, he could easily be picked up for questioning after Lynda was safely back in Dallas.

If, however, in the unlikely event Andy should confide to her that he was the murderer, McGowan would arrest him immediately.

Before entering the Boise terminal, McGowan allowed Lynda to move into a crowd of people well ahead of him. He remained close enough to see her but not be noticed himself. Though Andy Hopper had never met the detective, he was still careful to make it look as if Lynda had been traveling alone.

Soon McGowan saw a brown-haired man approach Lynda, smiling from beneath a heavy beard that looked recently trimmed. He kissed her, took the small bag she was carrying, and pointed in the direction of the terminal entrance.

McGowan felt a rush of excitement at seeing Hopper for the first time and increased his pace to keep the departing couple in sight. As he walked toward the door, a stranger wearing jeans and a cowboy hat stepped to his side. "You a police officer?"

Morris nodded.

"My car's parked in front," the Boise officer said. "Your boy's riding a motorcycle."

As they followed the couple, the officer assured his visitor that everything was in place. "The Holiday Inn's just a couple of miles up here on the right. The rooms are ready and we've got some people staked out in the parking lot."

A few minutes later, the motorcycle, which was less than a hundred yards in front of them, slowed as it neared the entrance to the Holiday Inn parking lot. Then, suddenly, Andy made a sharp left turn.

McGowan leaned forward in the passenger seat. "What the hell's he doing?"

The driver's answer was not what Morris wanted to hear. "He's going to the hotel on the other side of the fucking highway."

As they were riding from the airport, Lynda had explained to Andy that she had called ahead and made reservations at the Holiday Inn. He had, he replied, already checked into another hotel, paying in advance.

He had registered under the name of Bobby Drowns, a friend who had just a year earlier, committed suicide.

In a room down the hall from Andy and Lynda, McGowan paced the floor, exploring ways to salvage the situation. Somehow, he told the Boise officer, Lynda was going to have to convince Andy to move to the Holiday Inn. If that failed, they were going to have to find some way to get a wire to her.

"They're going to have to go out to eat sooner or later," McGowan finally said. "This place doesn't look like it's set up to do much in the way of room service."

Shortly, a female officer from the Boise police was summoned to the stakeout. Before arriving at the motel she had stopped at a convenience store and purchased a small box of Tampax in which to place a bug.

In the early evening Andy and Lynda emerged from the room and began leisurely walking toward a nearby Denny's restaurant. Just as they entered, Lynda saw a woman driver, accompanied by McGowan, pull into the parking lot.

The officers waited until Andy and Lynda were inside and seated, then entered and sat in a booth near the back of the restaurant.

Almost an hour passed before Lynda rose and walked past them en route to the women's rest room. The female officer waited a few seconds, then followed.

Inside, Lynda was hysterical, her arms folded around her

torso in an attempt to stop her shaking. Whispering, she explained that she had tried to convince him to go to the Holiday Inn but he had refused, saying he'd lose the money he'd already paid. "I didn't know what to do."

"You've got to talk him into moving over there," the woman explained. "Tell him you think the place is a dump, that you don't like the bed, anything."

"What if he won't do it?"

The officer reached into her purse and handed Lynda the box of Tampax. "There's a wire inside."

"He's already told me everything. I can't keep asking him questions."

The officer placed a hand gently on the distraught young woman's shoulder. "You'll do fine," she said, then turned and walked back into the restaurant.

For the remainder of the night, McGowan sat in the room adjacent to Andy and Lynda's, hearing nothing but the sound of the next-door television and the muffled noises of lovemaking.

While Lynda was able to convince Andy to move to the Holiday Inn the following morning, the detective's optimism that she would, in fact, try to steer him into a conversation about the murder had greatly diminished.

Throughout the day, McGowan and Burcham monitored the sounds of the wired room, cursing the fact that Andy constantly kept the television at an ear-bursting level while Lynda said little at all. By nightfall, the officers had begun to feel like electronic voyeurs as the sounds of youthful passion returned.

Telephoning MacKenzie back in Richardson, McGowan described the frustrating sequence of events. "All we've got so far is an X-rated tape that's not going to put anybody in jail for murder," he grumbled.

On the other end of the line, MacKenzie began to laugh.

"What's so damned funny?"

"Doesn't sound like you're having a very happy birthday. In light of everything you've said, maybe Rhonda and I should air-express you one of those inflatable dolls as a present."

McGowan, who had forgotten that it was his birthday, laughed. "Thanks for the thought."

The following morning, as soon as Andy left the room to tie Lynda's bag to his motorcycle in preparation for their return to the airport, McGowan phoned the room. "What the hell are you pulling?" he yelled. "Why aren't you doing what I asked?"

"I'm scared."

Morris ignored the pleading sound in her voice. "Goddammit, we're running out of time. You've got to get him to talk . . . right now."

A few minutes later, Andy returned to the room and once more turned up the volume on the television. Lynda completed her packing, then turned the sound down. "Andy, this whole thing scares me. I've got to know the truth."

A moment's silence preceded Andy's reply. "Okay, what do you want to know?"

"Did you kill that woman?"

"No, I didn't. But I did take some money. I'm involved, but I didn't kill her."

"How could you let yourself get involved in something like that?"

"I don't know. It just happened. But I didn't shoot her. I swear. The problem is, I can't prove my innocence right now."

Next door, McGowan slumped forward in his chair, letting out a long sigh of relief.

On the flight back to Dallas, Lynda said little. Clearly, she felt badly about what she had done. Only when McGowan pressed did she detail other things Andy had told her.

He had assured her that he didn't even know the woman who was murdered, nor had he ever been in her house. The man who had given him the money and asked if he would be interested in doing the job was someone named Brian.

The trip, then, hadn't yielded as much as McGowan had hoped, but Hopper's words were, if nothing else, enough to make a strong conspiracy-to-murder case.

It was a step in the right direction. Morris knew that with the license plate number of the motorcycle, the Idaho police could keep an eye on Andy. And while he was not yet ready to mention it to Lynda, McGowan was already mapping out a new plan. He was certain Andy would be calling again very soon, urging her to make another trip to see him. This time, however, she would remain in Dallas while McGowan, armed with a warrant, made the trip alone. He would arrest Hopper.

"Lynda," McGowan said, "I know this was hard for you—"

"I love him."

"—but you did the right thing. And you did a good job."

What McGowan did not know was that the distraught woman seated next to him had not told him everything.

While en route to the airport, she had been overcome with guilt and told Andy that police had been watching them throughout the weekend, probably even listening to their conversations.

She did not tell McGowan that she had advised Andy to leave Boise immediately and get rid of his motorcycle.

# 14

BACK IN DALLAS, Rhonda Bonner and Ken MacKenzie focused on locating the men who had allegedly fired the shots at Larry Aylor. Joe Thomas had agreed to cooperate, phoning Buster Matthews to set up a meeting.

On the morning of August 19, then, Thomas, wearing a body mike, traveled to Griff's, a Mesquite coffee shop that Buster regularly frequented. As the Richardson officers monitored the conversation from an adjacent parking lot, the two men drank coffee and talked about the roofing business for some time before Thomas finally suggested they step outside. There, the two men briefly discussed the unsuccessful attempt on Aylor almost two years earlier, then Thomas explained that he had received a call asking if "my people" would be interested in trying it again.

Buster, a stocky man in his mid-forties with jet black hair and a criminal record dating back to the sixties, said he would have to get in touch with his brother. "If we do it," Buster said, "the price goes up."

"Just let me know as soon as you can," Thomas replied.

Back at the station, Bonner placed a call to Don Robertson, a retired Mesquite police officer who she had learned had dealt with Buster Matthews off and on throughout his law enforcement career. Outlining the case, she asked his help in persuading Buster to talk with her.

Three days later, Robertson phoned to tell the investigator to meet him at Griff's the following afternoon.

Buster Matthews's attention was focused on the pinball machine when they entered and ordered coffee. Only when his game was over did he notice Robertson motioning him to the table where he sat with the female officer.

He introduced Matthews to the Richardson officer, then wasted no time getting to the point: "She wants to know about that guy out in Kaufman County that you and your brother tried to kill."

Matthews, obviously surprised, looked over at Robertson, then at Bonner. Now nervous, he ran his hand through his hair. "Hell, Don," he finally said, "I can't talk about that in front of her."

"Let's go outside," Robertson suggested.

Standing near the entrance to the restaurant, the retired officer spoke in a soft, friendly voice. "I'm out of law enforcement, so this isn't my deal. But these people aren't just fishing around. They've got a damn good case. If I were you, I'd go in there and tell her what you know and make the best deal you can."

"Can you help me?"

"Buster, that lady sitting in there is the only help you're going to get."

Back inside, Matthews continuously shifted in his chair as he spoke of the events at the ranch. Some well-to-do family, he said, had wanted a hit done on a baby-raper. They hadn't

**Joy Aylor** *Photo courtesy Richardson Police Department*

Joy and Larry Aylor attending the annual Cattleman's Ball benefit in Dallas *Photo by Andy Hansen*

**Larry Aylor and Joy Davis as high school sweethearts** *Photos courtesy Hillcrest High School Annual*

**Larry Aylor** *Pat Stowers photo*

**Chris Aylor at his high school graduation ceremonies** *Photo courtesy of the Bending Oaks School annual*

On a roll of undeveloped film taken from the crime scene was this photo of Rozanne and Peter III at his birthday party *Photo courtesy Richardson Police Department*

Rozanne Gailiunas
*Photo courtesy Paula Donahue*

The Loganwood Drive home where Rozanne was attacked  *Pat Stowers photo*

Crime scene photo taken at Rozanne's home. Note the pot of flowers on the floor between the front door and the couch.  *Photo courtesy Richardson Police Department*

**Dr. Peter Gailiunas** *Pat Stowers photo*

Elizabeth Davis, Joy's sister *Photo by Richard Pruitt, Dallas Morning News*

Carol Garland, Joy's sister *Photo courtesy Dallas County Sheriff's Department*

**Henry and Frances Davis** *Photo by Andy Hansen*

**Morris and Sandy McGowan** *Photo courtesy Sandy McGowan*

Ken MacKenzie, Richardson Police Department *Pat Stowers photo*

Joy and attorney Doug Mulder leave a pretrial hearing in the Dallas
County Courthouse *Photo by Richard Pruitt,* Dallas Morning News

**Andy Hopper** *Photos courtesy Richardson Police Department and Dallas County Sheriff's Department*

**Andy Hopper on trial** *Photo by John Rhodes*, Dallas Morning News

**Brian Kreafle** *Photo courtesy Dallas County Sheriff's Department*

**Bill Garland** *Photo courtesy Dallas County Sheriff's Department*

**Joe Thomas** *Photo courtesy Dallas County Sheriff's Department*

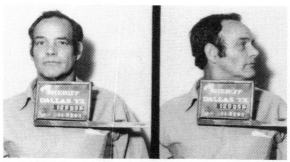

**Buster Matthews** *Photo courtesy Dallas County Sheriff's Department*

**Gary Matthews** *Photo courtesy Dallas County Sheriff's Department*

The Kaufman County road where Larry Aylor and friend Don Kennedy were ambushed
*Carlton Stowers photo*

**Mike Wilson after his arrest**
*Photo courtesy U.S. Attorney's Office, Dallas*

Headstone at the grave of Rozanne Gailiunas *Carlton Stowers photo*

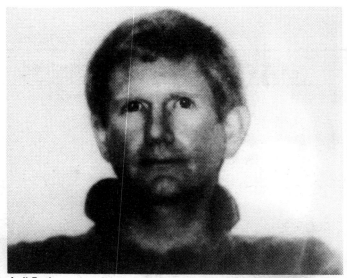

**Jodi Packer** *Photo courtesy U.S. Attorney's Office, Dallas*

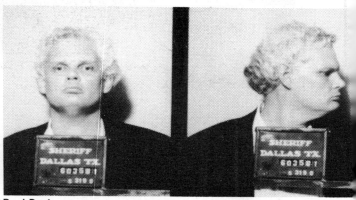

**Brad Davis** *Photo courtesy Dallas County Sheriff's Department*

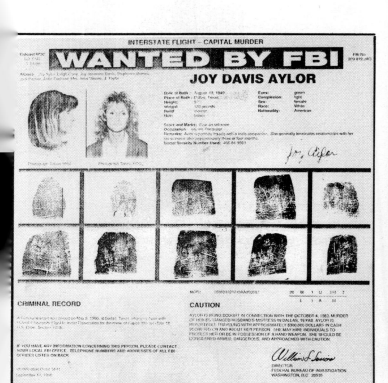

Joy Aylor's wanted poster *Courtesy FBI*

The Vence, France, villa where Joy was arrested *Photo courtesy Dan Hagood*

Assistant Dallas County D.A. Dan Hagood and Nice police officer Huy Decloedt in France
*Photo courtesy Dan Hagood*

Dallas County prosecutors Dan Hagood (left) and Kevin Chapman (right) with Morris McGowan  *Photo courtesy Morris McGowan*

Jim Oatman, Assistant D.A.
*Photo courtesy Morris McGowan*

Hopper's lawyers: Peter Lesser (standing) and Larry Mitchell *Pat Stowers photo*

State District Judge Pat McDowell *Pat Stowers photo*

On the evening of November 4, 1993, Captain Morris McGowan led Joy Aylor from Dallas–Fort Worth International airport following her long-delayed extradition back to the United States. *Pat Stowers photo*

wanted to put the child through a trial. He and his brother had gone to a horse ranch out in the country and shot at the man.

"Have you ever heard the name Joy Aylor?" Bonner asked.

Matthews shook his head. "No, I don't know her."

For several more minutes he talked of the ambush before Bonner stopped him and read him his rights.

"What happens now?" he asked.

"You'll eventually be arrested and indicted for attempted capital murder."

"Gary was the one who fired the shots."

That evening, seated in an interview room at the Richardson police station, Buster Matthews gave a formal statement, detailing his role in the attempt on Larry Aylor's life.

He also agreed to contact his brother and indicate to him that Joe Thomas had phoned to offer them a second chance to do away with Aylor.

Two days later, while sitting in the Richardson Police Department, Buster finally reached his brother. "Look, J.T. got ahold of me again, and those people are on his ass hot and heavy about us doing that whole thing again."

Gary waited a few seconds, then said, "It'll have to be COD, half up front and half after. And they're gonna have to furnish the equipment."

"You can't get ahold of the .22?"

"No."

"You sell it?"

"I don't know where it is. Listen, what kind of incentive are they talking about?"

"You think we ought to ask for more money?"

"Damn right. Ain't nothing free."

Buster ended the conversation with a promise to contact Thomas and arrange the financial details. He would insist on an additional $5,000.

They agreed to meet at a Waffle House the following Friday morning. Bonner explained to Buster that she would meet him in the parking lot of a nearby 7-Eleven prior to the meeting and fit him with a body mike.

But the evening before the proposed meeting, the Matthews

brothers left Texas on a spur-of-the-moment camping trip in one of the national forests in New Mexico. Quickly reverting to type, the brothers attacked a man camping near them, tying him up and leaving him zipped in a sleeping bag as they sped away in his pickup.

The victim, however, quickly managed to work loose from his bindings and phoned in a report of the incident along with the license plate number of his truck.

The Matthewses were stopped even before they found their way out of the park. Buster surrendered immediately, but Gary fled into the woods. On the following day, a shivering Gary Matthews flagged down a passing park ranger and turned himself in.

Bonner and McGowan were notified that the New Mexico authorities had already filed charges of kidnapping and auto theft against both men.

"They're not going anywhere," Bonner said with satisfaction to McGowan.

So, with what the DA's office now judged an indictable case against Joy Aylor, confessions in hand from Bill Garland, Brian Kreafle, and Joe Thomas, and the Matthewses in custody in New Mexico, the frantic roundup was fast coming to an end.

It was time, McGowan concluded, to arrest Andy Hopper.

Though still far from convinced that Andy had, in fact, actually murdered Rozanne Gailiunas, he was certain that he had played a role in the tragic conspiracy. And once in custody, there was a good chance he would provide the next link to the complicated chain.

Ken MacKenzie, meanwhile, no longer shared McGowan's reservations about Hopper. He was convinced that the former ministerial student was, indeed, the triggerman.

Among those he had interviewed since Andy's disappearance was James Carver. Recently convicted on drug charges and income tax evasion and confined to the federal penitentiary in Texarkana, Carver had, at first, been reluctant to concede that Hopper might be involved in such a crime. "Hell, the kid's a little unstable, but he's not crazy. He's just a big talker."

Andy, he said, was always trying to impress people. "He'd

bring his girlfriends by the shop, just to show them off. I remember him calling one afternoon just to tell me he was in bed with some gal he'd picked up. He even put her on the phone for a minute.

"Then one time I mentioned that I was having trouble getting my money out of some clients up in Baltimore. Andy got all excited about it and told me he'd go up there and collect it for me. Said he'd kill them if he had to."

He acknowledged that Andy had brought a friend named Cal Hobson to him, urging that he set him up in the drug-distribution business in Houston. Carver, angered that Hopper had so freely tossed his name around, had chastised him severely.

That was Andy, Carver said. A lot of big talk. Always trying to impress people.

Only after several nonproductive visits had MacKenzie managed to gain Carver's confidence. Finally, after the detective detailed the gruesome nature of the Gailiunas murder, Carver began to talk.

Dope dealing was one thing; killing a helpless woman while her little kid was in the house was something else.

Late in 1983, he recalled, he was leaving a motorcycle shop on North Central and Andy pulled into the parking lot to suggest they go across the street for a cup of coffee.

During their conversation Andy expressed concern over his growing financial problems and mentioned that he had been approached about a murder-for-hire.

"That's bullshit," Carver said, thinking it a ploy by Andy to get him to increase the amount of pot he had been providing. "You're no fucking hit man. I'll front you more marijuana. Get off your ass and get you some more customers. Forget about that other shit."

Carver did not hear from Andy again until three weeks later when he telephoned to suggest they meet again, this time at the Golden Eagle restaurant.

"You remember that hit I told you about? Well, I did it."

Stunned, Carver listened as his friend boasted of the manner in which he had carried out the crime. He had, Andy said, put a rope around the woman's neck and led her through the house for quite some time, even threatening to hurt her child, before taking her into her bedroom and shooting her. "Man, you have no idea the power you feel when you've got someone in a life-and-death situation like that. I wish you could have seen the bitch squirm."

Finally, Carver interrupted him. "Are you talking about that killing out in Richardson I read about in the paper?"

Andy smiled and nodded.

"Did you rape her?"

"No."

"Damn, Andy, does Becky know about this?"

"No."

Suddenly, Carver was angry. If on the off chance this was something more than another gesture by Andy to get attention and make himself sound like a tough guy, he didn't want to be drawn into it. "Goddammit," he whispered through clenched teeth, "I don't want to hear nothing more about this. Just shut up. Shut the fuck up, and whatever you do, don't say another word about it. You hear me?"

Hopper shrugged, a smile curling his lips. "Hey, it's okay. I've done this kind of thing before, you know."

For the first time in their fifteen-year friendship, Carver wasn't certain whether Andy was lying or not.


"Andy's our guy," MacKenzie insisted to McGowan. Rhonda Bonner agreed.

"Then let's bring him in and find out," the still skeptical detective suggested.

It was a task more easily said than done.

Before McGowan could contact Lynda Whittaker to suggest that she arrange another trip to visit Andy, a Teletype message arrived from Salmon, Idaho.

Immediately placing a call to the sheriff's department there, MacKenzie learned that Andy's abandoned motorcycle had been found, covered with brush in a wooded area outside of town.

"It's not wrecked or anything," a deputy said. "Looks like somebody just wanted to get rid of it."

Hopper, obviously, had followed Lynda's advice.

*     *     *

The interior of assistant district attorney Kevin Chapman's office was cluttered yet devoid of anything that might lend insight to the personal side of its occupant. Unlike the workplaces of fellow prosecutors, there were no framed photographs or mounted newspaper articles to remind of past courtroom victories, no plaques or touchstone souvenirs. The only touch of comfort was the two leather chairs arranged side by side in front of his desk.

Lined against the walls were stacks of boxes, each filled with folders that wouldn't fit into the two nearby filing cabinets. On most of the boxes, Chapman had printed *Gailiunas,* and for months he had poured over them, setting to memory every scrap of information collected by the Richardson police during the investigation.

Recently, he had begun spending weekends in his office, taking advantage of the quiet to categorize the evidence, research case law, and plan for the day when he would finally get the opportunity to weave his bizarre story for a jury.

Though he shared McGowan's frustration that pieces were still missing from the puzzle, pieces that only the on-the-run Andy Hopper could likely fill in, he had decided it was time to move forward with the case. Though early on he had agreed that immediate arrests might well slow the flow of information, he had recently become concerned with the possibility that others involved might soon decide to take off like Hopper and the Matthews brothers.

Chapman did not want anyone else to run. It was time, he informed a much-relieved McGowan, to seek indictments. The lone exception, he noted, would be Andy Hopper. Though there was ample evidence to secure a conspiracy indictment against him, the DA wanted to wait until he was apprehended. If, indeed, there was a participant beyond Andy, he would less likely be alerted if Hopper's name remained out of the court records and newspapers.

The first order of business, then, was to subpoena witnesses to a grand jury hearing.

After receiving her summons, Frances Davis made a trip to

Chapman's office to talk with him and McGowan. Impressed with the grace and strength of the woman, Chapman questioned her at length about any knowledge she might have of Joy's involvement in the crimes.

Mrs. Davis, her voice soft but firm, assured the DA that she knew nothing more than what her troubled daughter Carol had been telling her. She was, in fact, firmly convinced that the entire matter had evolved from some moneymaking scheme hatched between Carol and Larry Aylor.

As she stood to leave, Frances turned to Chapman, her eyes searching. "Can I ask you a question?"

"Yes, ma'am."

"Will this soon be over?"

Kevin stood thoughtfully for several seconds, a feeling of sympathy he'd not felt for some time for anyone involved in the case suddenly sweeping over him. The mother's question, he knew, had been asked without real hope. "I'm sorry, but I can't tell you that."

Frances nodded. "I appreciate your honesty."

On September 19, 1988—less than a month shy of five years since the attack on Rozanne Gailiunas—indictments were handed down and arrest warrants issued.

Joy Aylor was indicted on charges of capital murder, conspiracy to commit capital murder, and solicitation of capital murder, while Bill Garland and Brian Kreafle were charged with conspiracy and solicitation. Joe Thomas, Buster Matthews, and Gary Matthews were each indicted on conspiracy charges.

McGowan was to arrest Joy. Having located her Porsche parked in back of the Davis house, officers from both the Dallas and Richardson police sealed off the alley exits.

Down the street, McGowan, having made the decision to wait until she left the house before arresting her, sat waiting with two Dallas officers.

He had been there less than an hour when he heard the sound of a motorcycle and turned to see young Chris Aylor riding in the direction of the Davis house. Slowing as he neared, Chris immediately recognized McGowan seated on the passenger side of the unmarked police car.

"What's going on?" the solemn-faced youngster asked as McGowan got out of the car to greet him.

"Chris, I can't tell you."

"You're here to get my mom again, aren't you?"

Morris nodded. "I'm afraid so. Son, I know this is tough on you—"

"Hey," Chris interrupted, attempting to mask his feelings with a show of nonchalance, "you're just doing your job. I think I'll just go over to my dad's."

McGowan stood watching as the motorcycle disappeared into the early evening darkness. The excitement of the long-awaited moment faded as he contemplated the private agonies the young man had been forced to endure, the unanswered questions that no doubt haunted his dreams. *Someday,* McGowan thought as he returned to his car, *we'll sit down and talk about all this. There are things you have a right to know.*

Seconds later, his attention returned to the business at hand as a radio message informed him that Joy was in her car. She was only halfway down the alley when McGowan pulled up behind her.

She was already standing beside her car, silently staring in the officer's direction, as he walked toward her.

"Mrs. Aylor, you are under arrest. You've been indicted on five felony counts related to the murder of Rozanne Gailiunas and the attempted murder of Larry Aylor."

Briefly, Joy looked nonplussed. "I have?"

"Yes, ma'am." McGowan opened the passenger door of his car. "Let's go."

As McGowan made his way through the early evening traffic, Joy remained silent until the car turned off North Central in the direction of the police station.

"What happens now?" she finally asked.

"Since you now have a lawyer," McGowan explained, "I can't ask you anything unless you say you want to talk to me. I'm sure you've been made aware of that."

"My lawyer hasn't told me anything," she answered, the

first trace of anger edging into her voice. She again fell silent for several seconds, then said, "Okay, I want to talk to you."

It would have to wait, the detective explained, until they reached the station. There, he privately vowed, things would be far different from the first time they had discussed her role in Rozanne Gailiunas's murder.

Again seated in an interview room on the first floor of the Richardson police station, Joy's anger and apprehension disappeared, replaced by the same calm and control McGowan had witnessed during their first interview.

And her first question had a familiar ring. "Will I be able to get out of here?"

"Joy," McGowan replied, "I want to know what happened. I want you to tell me why you did this. That's all I'm interested in talking about. If you don't want to do that, I'll walk you over to the jail."

She began shaking her head. "No, I'll tell you. I don't even really know how it all got started. Larry and I had gone over to the house we were building for the doctor and his wife several times. Once, I remember, the little boy was very upset, crying. I offered to take him for an ice cream cone while his parents talked with Larry."

Once again, Joy was playing games, talking but saying little. The detective would not be lured into that trap again.

"Wait a minute, Joy. All I want to know is why you did it. Don't try to lead me down some primrose path. Why and how—that's all I want to know."

It was as if she had not even heard him. "Am I going to be able to get out of here?"

"Your attorney will have to help you with that."

With that she again talked of the house her husband had been building for Dr. Gailiunas. They had seemed like nice people, she said. For some time she had no idea that anything was going on between Larry and Rozanne.

McGowan got to his feet and smiled. "Joy, it's not going to work this time. I've got other things to do. Let's go over to the jail."

Moving toward the door, he turned toward her. "I've just got one question, and I'd like an honest answer," he said.

"What's that?"

"Was Dr. Gailiunas involved?"

Joy showed an amused smile as she stood, then shook her head. "No, he had absolutely nothing to do with it."

"You're sure?"

"I'm positive," she said as she moved past him into the hallway.

As they walked in the direction of the jail annex, McGowan saw Bill Garland standing near the booking desk and, saying nothing, gently steered Joy in his direction.

Seeing the detective approach, Garland nodded. "What's going on?"

"I just wanted to see if you two know each other," McGowan said, nodding in Joy's direction. "This is Joy Aylor."

Then, turning, McGowan said, "Joy, this is Bill Garland."

For a moment she stared wide-eyed at the hulking man standing only a few feet from her, then quickly stepped back as if suddenly repulsed.

Without a word, she had answered yet another question for the detective. Clearly, she had never before seen the man she had hired to carry out her murderous plots.

McGowan watched as Joy was locked into a cell, then moved close to the bars. "If you change your mind," he said, "someone will come find me."

Joy, her lips tightly pursed, offered no reply. Certain that he would not hear from her again, McGowan soon left the station. Walking into the warm night air, he was eager to get home where he knew Sandy waited to hear about his day.

The following morning, McGowan stopped by the jail before going to his office. Assuming that those arrested had, at some point during the night or early morning, been released on bond, he was surprised when he saw Joy walking down the hall in the company of a jailer.

"I can't believe your attorney hasn't bailed you out of here," he said.

"I just tried to call him again. He's supposed to be on his way."

With a blanket wrapped around her shoulders, she had undergone a transformation that briefly took McGowan by surprise. The aura of innocence was gone, as if at some point during the long night she had finally seen what her future held. Her voice seemed weaker, her almost mechanical movements suggested near exhaustion.

"You want a cup of coffee?" the detective asked.

"And something for a headache."

As she sipped at her coffee, McGowan silently studied her for some time. "You know," he finally said, "the thing that really amazes me is that you've gone through all this and I've never seen one bit of emotion from you."

Pulling the blanket tight against her, she shook her head as a gesture of disagreement. "It's been there. Plenty of it. You just don't know."

McGowan waited until she had finished her coffee, then returned her to the jailer.

Late that afternoon he answered his phone and heard her voice again. She was calling from home, free on $140,000 bond. "I wanted you to know that I truly appreciate the way you treated me. I just wanted to thank you."

The calm, pleasant tone had returned to her voice.

# 15

ANDY HOPPER FROWNED at the gas gauge of the old pickup, looked over at his traveling companion, and began buttoning an army fatigue jacket. Stranded on the shoulder of a highway somewhere in Montana, out of gas, and still several miles from their destination, they would have to hitchhike to the next town.

In the months that had passed since his rendezvous with

OPEN SECRETS

Lynda, Hopper had lived a vagabond existence. Correctly assuming that the FBI had joined in the search and that it was
likely law enforcement agencies throughout the United States
had been alerted to be on the lookout for him, he had stayed on
the move.

For a while Andy had traveled with a family of migrant
workers in a dilapidated old camouflage-painted bus. They had
taken an immediate liking to him, and their constant movement
suited his needs perfectly. But, soon, the dire conditions of
their day-to-day existence had begun to wear on him. Embarrassed by sharing food he knew they could not spare, Andy had
taken it upon himself to approach several churches and food
banks along the way, managing to amply stock the bus with
canned goods, warm clothing, and blankets before parting company with the grateful family.

Briefly, he found shelter in an isolated Idaho logging camp,
then was hired by the owner of a small traveling carnival. To
earn his $150-a-week salary, he helped erect tents, set up the
rides and game booths, and assumed the role of advance man.
On the day before the carnival was to leave one small town,
Andy would travel ahead to the next destination to put up
posters, check out where the carnival was to set up, and visit
the local schools to pass out free admission tickets.

It had been while en route to one of those dot-on-the-map
communities that he had run out of gas, and a friendly state
trooper had stopped to give him and his fellow carny a ride into
town.

While Andy slid quickly into the backseat of the trooper's
car, his companion opted to ride up front. Thus, when the
officer asked for identification, his routine curiosity was quickly
satisfied when the man seated next to him produced a driver's
license and explained the purpose of their travels.

The trooper did not even bother asking the smiling young
man in the backseat, who had introduced himself as Bobby
Drowns, for ID.

In Richardson, the emotional roller coaster had taken another
frustrating dip. The celebration that followed the arrests of Joy

Aylor and the middlemen lured into her plans had quieted, soon overshadowed by the frustration of losing Hopper.

For weeks, Officers Bonner and MacKenzie had interviewed Andy's friends and family members, hoping he might have been in contact with them. Bonner traveled to Pampa, where Becky and the children had moved in with her parents, but learned nothing about Andy's whereabouts. MacKenzie, in a discussion with George Hopper, came away with nothing more than the fact Andy's parents wanted desperately for him not to be harmed when he was captured.

"From what you've told me," the elder Hopper wearily confided to MacKenzie, "it looks pretty bad. My wife and I are praying that you do catch him, for his own good. But I have to tell you this: he's still my boy and I love him. Whatever happens, I'm going to stand by him."

Police and sheriff's departments in the Midwest provided Hopper's photograph, occasionally contacted the Richardson office to discuss an unsolved crime in their jurisdiction, hopeful that the Texas fugitive might be the man they were looking for. None of the calls, however, warmed the trail.

Not until November did the chase again move into high gear.

Don Price, an executive for a Dallas claims-adjusting firm, telephoned McGowan. "We need to talk."

"About what?"

"Andy Hopper has asked me to wire him two hundred dollars." It was time, Price decided, to learn what, if any, kind of trouble his friend might be in.

Despite a long-standing personal rule against socializing with business associates, Don Price had quickly made an exception when Andy began doing adjusting work for his firm in 1981. Price found Hopper's warm personality and child-like zest for life contagious.

Almost immediately the two men became friends, meeting frequently for lunch, playing golf almost weekly, and attending Texas Rangers baseball games together. Andy urged Don to join him on an amateur softball team sponsored by an old friend named James Carver.

Soon, Price's wife, Wanda, and Becky had also established a fast-growing friendship, sharing their respective interests in arts and crafts, their children, and talking almost daily on the phone.

Almost every morning, Andy would telephone Wanda with what he referred to as his "joke of the day." At first she found it a bit unusual that he called so regularly—husbands of her other friends rarely phoned, except maybe to ask for help selecting a birthday or anniversary gift—but she quickly dismissed her concern. The calls, she decided, were nothing more than harmless fun.

For the first year of their friendship, then, Wanda Price viewed Andy and Becky as a happy couple, coping remarkably well with the daily tensions of family life and the pressures of establishing a career in a new environment.

Shy at first, Becky had announced that she looked on Wanda as her best friend, a confidant with whom she felt comfortable discussing the most personal matters. In time, she was tearfully admitting that things were not as they seemed to be. She would call Wanda to talk of abuse, both physical and mental, that resulted from Andy's volatile temper. He constantly criticized the way she kept the house and cared for the children. And his increasing drug use—cocaine, crystal, and marijuana —caused mood swings that she had difficulty coping with. She told of a suddenly angered Andy chasing his visiting sister through the house with a butcher knife until she safely locked herself in the bathroom. At times, Becky admitted, she felt her only chance for a happy life was to leave her husband. A few days later, however, she would call and downplay the previous conversation, assuring Wanda that things were not nearly as bad as she had made them out to be.

With Wanda, meanwhile, Andy assumed a role more akin to a mischievous younger brother than the husband of a close friend. He began casually talking of relationships with other women, sometimes with teasing innuendo, at other times being more specific, giving names and places where sexual encounters had taken place. "But," he would always add, "don't tell Becky."

They had begun playing a game he called Secrets, wherein he would confess some indiscretion to Wanda in exchange for her admission of something dark and private in her life. While Wanda had little to contribute to the game, Andy used it to brag of "big-time" drug connections, friends of his who "would do anything for money," and talk of the women who were constantly coming on to him, of lunch-hour sexual encounters, and of evil deeds he fantasized performing.

The game's only rule, he explained, was that the secrets they shared be told to no one else.

Thus, Wanda played along, feigning amusement at his fantasies and claims of infidelity and connections to unsavory people, saying nothing about them to her husband or to Becky, until a few days after Christmas in 1983.

The Prices had been invited to the Hopper home for dinner to celebrate a recent reconciliation between Andy and Becky and to belatedly exchange Christmas gifts.

While Becky was in the kitchen, preparing dinner, and Don had excused himself to go to the bathroom, Andy moved to the living-room couch to sit beside Wanda. "I've got a secret to tell you," he said.

For the next several minutes he talked rapidly of recently having been in a house where someone was tortured. Though he had not participated, instead staying in a room to watch over a child who was also in the house, the scene had gotten far uglier than he had expected. "Something really bad happened."

Wanda stared speechless at the man seated next to her, then turned away, focusing her attention on the nearby Christmas tree. Generally, when Andy confided his secrets, they were with a smile and an almost flip tone in his voice. This time he had not smiled; he seemed genuinely upset.

Suddenly frightened, Wanda rose and went into the kitchen to offer to help with dinner.

Later that evening, as she and Don drove home, Wanda mentioned the strange conversation. Andy, her husband said, had also spoken with him about the same thing shortly before they left.

They agreed that it sounded as if he had been involved in some kind of drug deal. More than likely, someone had failed to make good on a debt and had been roughed up.

"Do you think Andy was really involved?" Wanda asked.

"Hell, you know Andy. He's always got some wild story."

As they made their way home that evening, Wanda found herself thinking back on the past several months.

Andy's drug problem, she knew, had grown worse. Becky had told her so. And the Hoppers' financial problems were apparently out of control. Despite the fact that at times they had a considerable amount of money, most often they were broke and struggling to make ends meet. Though Becky had not admitted it, Wanda suspected that Andy's drug dealing, not the adjusting business, provided the bulk of their income. Andy, in fact, had all but ruined his career as an adjustor with shoddy work, drawing complaints from virtually everyone he dealt with. Even Don had spoken of the possibility of no longer using him: "Friendship is one thing, and business is another. Andy's just not getting the job done."

When a frantic and distraught Becky had called one afternoon to say she could not find $3,700 that had been hidden in the house, Wanda was finally convinced of the drug dealing. Why, she had asked Becky, would she keep that kind of cash in the house?

It was, Becky had finally admitted, money Andy owed to James Carver.

"Could someone have stolen it?" Wanda asked. "Has there been anyone over there lately?"

Becky thought for a minute, then mentioned the name of a man Andy had recently introduced her to. "Brian. Brian Kreafle was here the other day." He was, she explained, the owner of a body shop called Brian's Car Care—a big, rumpled man whom she had immediately disliked.

Then there had been the strange sequence of events late in October when Don and Wanda had invited the Hoppers to attend a toga party with them.

Annually, the city of Dallas takes on a holiday atmosphere on the weekend of the Texas-Oklahoma football game played in the Cotton Bowl. Fans from Austin, Texas, and Norman, Oklahoma, converge on Dallas for a celebration that turns the downtown area into a scene straight out of Mardi Gras. Young and old march up and down Commerce Street, beer in hand, shouting cheers and promising victory for their team. The newspapers had, over the years, made a game of tabulating the number of arrests for drunkenness and disorderly conduct at the weekend bash.

In homes throughout the city, alumni parties go on until the wee hours. Indeed, one need not have any loyalty or ties to either college to join in the festivities.

Initially, Andy had seemed excited about the party. But as the date grew closer, his enthusiasm had waned, replaced by a level of anxiety even Becky had never before seen. Only after constant urging from both his wife and Wanda had he agreed to go.

On the evening of the party, the couples decided to go in two cars with Andy and Becky following the Prices.

Stopped at an intersection on Lemmon Avenue, Don had looked into his rearview mirror to see Becky running in the direction of the Friendly Chevrolet parking lot. Andy, having abandoned his car in the middle of the busy street, was close behind, yelling at his wife.

When he finally caught up to her, they stood, both dressed in bedsheets fashioned into togas, yelling at each other.

"This is crazy," Don said, making a U-turn and pulling up near where the arguing couple was standing. Writing the address of the party on a piece of paper, he handed it to Andy. "We're going on," Don said.

"Fuck it," Andy replied, "we're not coming."

"Yes, we are," Becky shot back.

Don, disgusted with the scene, rolled up his window and drove away.

Later that evening, with the party in full swing, Wanda was surprised to see Becky walk in. She had obviously been crying. "Andy doesn't want to come in," she explained, "so we're going on home. I just didn't want you to worry."

Angered by Andy's behavior, Wanda suggested that Becky

at least have a beer before leaving. "Let him sit out there for a while."

Becky, however, had not even finished her drink before one of the partygoers approached to announce that her husband was at the door, asking to speak to her. Again apologizing to Wanda, Becky moved through the crowd toward the front door and disappeared.

Distressed by Andy's irrational behavior and the embarrassment she had seen in Becky's eyes, Wanda was telling her husband that they should also soon say their good-byes when the hostess approached her. "The police are in the front yard," she whispered, "talking with your friends."

The argument between Andy and Becky had been re-ignited the minute she had stepped out onto the front porch. Andy had grabbed her by the arm and was pulling her toward the car when Becky threw the plastic cup of beer she still carried in his face.

Andy had responded by slapping his wife so hard that a small diamond earring she was wearing was knocked off. Kneeling in the grass, Becky had found it, only to have Andy slap it from her hand.

A neighbor, watching the scene from his front doorway, had telephoned the police.

By the time Wanda made her way into the front yard, Andy was standing near the car, his face awash with anger, while Becky used a police officer's flashlight to search for the lost earring.

Later that night, after she and Don had returned home and were preparing for bed, Wanda received a call from Becky: "I'm so sorry about what happened."

"It wasn't your fault. Are you okay?"

"I'm fine. By the time we got home, Andy had calmed down and was acting like nothing had happened. He's sleeping."

"Becky, what's going on?"

Becky's voice fell to a whisper. "I'm leaving. I can't stand this kind of behavior anymore. The girls and I are going to Pampa."

"Are you coming back?"

"I don't think so." Becky was crying as she spoke.

\*     \*     \*

By Tuesday, Becky was gone, taking her puzzled and crying young daughters with her. And while most, Andy included, assumed her retreat to the comfort of her parents' home in the Texas Panhandle was little more than a cooling-off period, it stretched into weeks, then months.

Her father had, in fact, finally accompanied her to Dallas where, with a U-Haul trailer in tow, he had helped her gather most of her belongings and taken them back to Pampa.

During long-distance phone calls, Wanda had become convinced that Becky had summoned the strength to end the marriage, putting Andy out of her life forever.

And while Wanda spoke with Becky only occasionally, she was besieged by calls from Andy. As many as a half dozen times a day he would phone, no longer to pass on some off-color joke, but to plead tearfully for her help in convincing his wife to return to him. He missed Becky, he said; he missed his daughters.

He was also, he admitted, frightened. "I've done something really bad," he would tell Wanda almost every time he phoned, "and there are some bad people who are going to come after me."

Wanda detected the trembling sound of legitimate fear in his voice, as if he were cold and shaking as he spoke. Possibly, she assumed, it was the drugs he was taking. Or maybe even a childish plea for pity. Whatever the case, she decided it was not a topic of conversation she wished to encourage. If Andy was, in fact, entangled in something dangerous, she did not want to know.

The "something bad," she assumed, was Andy's guarded way of finally admitting that he had physically abused his wife. Wanda had no intention of discussing that either.

She was, therefore, surprised two months later when Becky phoned to say she had spoken with Andy and agreed to bring the children to Dallas for a Christmas visit.

Even more surprising had been the call inviting her and Don for the post-Christmas dinner. "I've decided to stay," Becky said.

After that visit, after Andy's strange tale of someone's having been tortured, Don and Wanda decided to put some distance between themselves and the Hoppers.

Though Wanda and Becky still talked on the phone on occasion, Don made it a point to be busy whenever Andy suggested a ball game or a weekend round of golf. When Hopper called, eagerly inviting him to invest in the new club Beethoven's, in which he claimed a 14 percent interest, Don Price declined.

The people Andy had begun to associate with, he decided, were not people he was comfortable around.

Price, then, had been somewhat surprised when, on November 8, 1988, Andy had called him at his office, asking for money. "I need it to get back to Dallas. I want to come back and clear myself." Andy, who did not say where he was calling from, explained that the money could be wired to him by Price, using the name of Mike Hargrove, the Texas Rangers first baseman. "They'll have a question for me to answer, so tell them the money is for 'Rangers tickets.' "

"I'll have to think about it," Price replied.

Andy had told him he would call at the same time the next day.

That evening, Don discussed the matter with his wife. "Look," he said, "if this is some trumped-up deal, something that Andy's gotten himself into by shooting off his mouth, I'd like to help him get it straightened out. But if he's involved in something criminal, I don't want any part of it." He urged Wanda to phone Becky. "See if you can find out what's going on."

Becky's reaction to word that her husband had contacted Don was far from what Wanda had expected.

"Whatever you do, don't send him any money." Then Becky had begun to cry. "I had hoped he was dead. I was hoping someone would call me to tell me they had found his body."

Immediately after Price had phoned McGowan, the detective sent Rhonda Bonner to Price's office and Ken MacKenzie to Western Union. "We've got to have Price's cooperation,"

Morris explained with a suddenly renewed sense of urgency, "and we need to find out how to trace where the money is being sent."

Thus, while Bonner was encouraging Price to help with the effort to catch Hopper, MacKenzie was learning the tracking capabilities of the Western Union computer system.

When money is wired, he was told, it does not have to be sent to a particular destination. A person can walk into any Western Union office in the country and ask if money or a telegram has been sent from a specific person. It is not even necessary to show identification so long as the recipient can give the correct answer to a question on the form filled out at the point of origin.

"Your man can walk into any Western Union office and say he is expecting money from a certain party," a Western Union supervisor said. "The operator on his end will then ask if he knows the code word or phrase. If he answers correctly, the money is his."

"And if the code word is different from his answer?" MacKenzie wanted to know.

"Then the operator is not authorized to give him the money." By computer, Western Union could alert offices everywhere to be watching for the code MacKenzie would supply. When the code was given, the Dallas office would immediately be alerted.

MacKenzie took $200 from his wallet. He would send the money in the name of the Rangers first baseman, but change the code phrase to "Cowboys tickets." The confusion created by the switch, he hoped, would provide the time necessary to determine where Hopper had gone to pick up the money.

That done, he phoned the station to report to McGowan that everything was in place. He would, MacKenzie said, remain at the Western Union office to monitor their computers. As he spoke, McGowan detected an anxious note in MacKenzie's voice.

"Hey, don't worry, we're going to catch him," Morris said.

"Damn, I hope so. That was my own two hundred dollars that I used."

Two days later MacKenzie called McGowan from the Western Union office. "Andy's at the Shott's Crossroads Truck Stop in Minot, North Dakota." Ken then quickly read off the telephone number.

Cashier Julie Henson had just come on duty when the travel-weary man, carrying a battered backpack, entered and inquired about money that was supposed to have been wired to him from "Mike Hargrove." She had felt badly for him when he had been unable to answer correctly the question that she was required to ask. "I'm sorry," she said, "but 'Rangers tickets' is not the code I've been given."

Puzzled, he had walked to a pay phone located in a foyer connecting the truck stop and adjacent restaurant and attempted to make a call. The frustrated look on his face as he returned signaled to her that he'd had no luck.

"Maybe," he said, "it's 'Texas Rangers.' "

The young woman shook her head apologetically and he turned back in the direction of the pay phone.

Moments later her telephone, located behind the counter, rang.

"Ma'am, I'm Detective Morris McGowan with the Richardson, Texas, Police Department. Please be careful how you respond to my questions."

Momentarily taken aback, the cashier finally answered, "Okay."

"Is there a man there trying to pick up some money sent by Mike Hargrove?"

"Yes. He just stepped next door to get a cup of coffee. There's been some confusion with the code message."

"It's very important that you keep him there. Stall him, if you can."

While McGowan spoke with the cashier, a secretary had dialed the number of the Minot Police Department on another line. Stretching from the desk where he was standing,

McGowan took the receiver, hurriedly explaining the situation to a Minot officer.

Then, speaking into the other phone again, he said, "The police are on the way."

Less than twenty minutes passed before a half dozen police and FBI agents rushed into the truck stop.

"I'm sorry," the young cashier said, pointing in the direction of the parking lot. "He left just a few minutes ago."

The Minot police chief phoned McGowan with the bad news. "But there's no way in hell he's going to get far. The biggest snowstorm we've had in years just blew in. It's shutting everything down, including the highways."

The disc jockey on the car radio was announcing that the North Dakota chill factor had dipped to minus fifty degrees as Milton Melgrado drove his family eastward from Burlington toward Minot. The windswept snowstorm had just begun when the surprised driver slowed and squinted his eyes to be sure of what he saw in the distance. A lone figure, wearing only a fatigue jacket, was standing on the side of the highway, his arm extended in the customary hitchhiker's plea.

"He'll freeze," Melgrado's wife, Angie, said. "Pick him up."

Minutes later the grateful traveler, cold, dirty, and showing the early signs of a beard, was enjoying the warmth of the car's heater. He introduced himself as Bob Frost.

He was, he said, originally from Dallas but had left there several months earlier after his wife and daughter were killed in an automobile accident with a drunk driver. Shortly afterward, he said, he had made the decision to head north in hopes of putting time and distance between him and his overwhelming grief.

For a time, he said, he had stayed with relatives whom he'd not seen in years. But after learning that the husband was an alcoholic who abused his children, he had chosen to leave. For a while he had worked with a traveling carnival before the winter weather had abruptly ended the season. Since then, he'd just been wandering, seeing the country, trying to put his life back together.

He had owned a motorcycle, he continued, but it had been stolen along with his wallet, which contained all his money and identification. That recent theft, he said, had turned his thoughts toward home. He'd contacted his sister and she was wiring him money to get back to Dallas.

The Melgrados' teenage daughter, Melissa, had begun to cry as the sad-faced stranger told his story.

After leaving Minot, they drove south, staying just ahead of the growing storm, stopping in Bismarck only long enough to get gas while their traveling companion made a phone call. Then they turned east.

At a truck stop in Fargo a cashier had finally counted out money that had been wired to Hopper.

Andy's brother Joe, using another code, had come to Andy's rescue by sending him $200.

"Are you sure you have enough to get you back to Dallas?" Angie Melgrado asked. "We'd be happy to help you out."

"Thanks, I'm fine. I'm going to check into a motel and get some rest, then take a bus home tomorrow."

Before leaving him at the entrance of a Super 8 Motel, the woman pressed a piece of paper with their address written on it into his hand. "Please take care of yourself and drop us a note when you get back to Dallas."

"I will," he answered, then hugged her.

For much of their remaining trip, the family talked sympathetically about the nice but troubled young man they had met.

Back in Richardson, fellow officers were surprised at McGowan's quick dismissal of the disappointing near miss. "He's spooked now," the detective observed, "and will probably be more careful than ever. At least for a while. But we'll get him."

The holiday season, he knew, was fast approaching. Christmas was a time when one's thoughts—even those of a fugitive—turned toward family and loved ones. Andy, McGowan was certain, would soon be paying someone a visit.

With that in mind, he contacted a Texas Ranger stationed in Pampa, asking that he keep an eye on the house where Becky and her daughters were living. Houston authorities agreed to check in with Andy's parents as the yule season approached.

MacKenzie, meanwhile, spoke with Lynda Whittaker. No longer trying to help Andy maintain his freedom, she promised to call if she heard from him.

Clearly Lynda, planning to move into the apartment of her new boyfriend, had hoped the matter of Andy Hopper was behind her: "I don't ever want to hear from him again."

While the waiting game continued, another area of the investigation progressed.

Accepting a collect phone call from the Lincoln County, New Mexico, jail the day after Hopper had disappeared, McGowan listened as Gary Matthews identified himself and said that he wanted to confess his role in the ambush of Larry Aylor. He even volunteered the location of the pawn shop where he had hocked the nine-shot automatic .22 pistol used in the murder attempt.

Calling MacKenzie into his office, Morris related the surprising conversation and suggested Ken pick up the weapon.

"What kind of deal does he think he's going to be able to make with this?" MacKenzie asked.

McGowan smiled, then said sarcastically, "Ken, Gary's not trying to make any deal. He told me so. The only reason he wanted to talk was so he could get it off his chest."

MacKenzie smiled. "He's found God, right?"

"You've got it."

On a Sunday evening, December 18, Morris McGowan's prophecy about Hopper came true. Traveling under the name Robert Lee Kobb—a Dallas musician who had been among the Beethoven's shareholders—Andy arrived at the Richardson bus station shortly before nine.

Mike Wiley, a co-worker with Hopper at Steakley Chevrolet, had not heard from his friend since the night he had gone to the Comfort Inn to talk him out of a suicide attempt. Though he had been interviewed by MacKenzie and Bonner shortly after Hopper's disappearance, Mike knew little about the case and had remained convinced that the police's suspicion of Andy's involvement was nothing more than a mistake that could easily be corrected if only Hopper would turn himself in.

Therefore, when he received a call from Andy, who said he was in town and trying to get in touch with Lynda Whittaker, Mike immediately telephoned MacKenzie.

In less than an hour, the two detectives were seated in McGowan's office, explaining to Lynda and her mother how they hoped to apprehend Hopper. A trap that would enable the phone company to trace the origin of any incoming calls would be placed on their phone as soon as it could be authorized by a judge. In the meantime, MacKenzie would follow them home and station himself near their house in the event Andy paid an unannounced visit.

Even as the plan was being outlined, Andy was walking in the direction of the Whittaker house. From the bus station, located only two blocks from the Richardson Police Department, his course had taken him through the station's parking lot.

Finding no one at the Whittaker residence, he walked to a park located a block away and hid his belongings. That done, he crept down an alley until he spotted a clothesline, from which he stole a clean sweatshirt.

MacKenzie, meanwhile, had set up surveillance at the end of the block. From the cab of his pickup, he had a good view of the house, which Lynda and her mother had entered.

He was surprised, shortly after his arrival, to see a Garland Police Department cruiser driving slowly down the street. Fearful it might stop and thus alert the neighborhood to his presence, MacKenzie ducked across the seat as the car passed slowly. Minutes later, a second squad car appeared.

On his radio, MacKenzie contacted McGowan at the station. "What the hell is the Garland police doing out here?"

"I'll check it out."

Soon Morris was back on the radio. He explained that a Garland patrol officer had responded to a prowler call in the neighborhood and, a half hour earlier, questioned a man seen walking near the Whittaker house. While the officer was making a radio check of the name given him, the man had fled. "They're looking for him," McGowan told MacKenzie, adding that he had alerted them to Ken's presence.

The Garland patrolmen had been told to leave the area and would be on standby in case they were needed. "Backup is on the way to seal off the area," McGowan added.

Relieved, MacKenzie settled back to continue his watch. If Andy hadn't been scared away by his encounter with the Garland patrolman, he was somewhere nearby.

Only a few minutes passed before MacKenzie noticed a shadowy figure in his rearview mirror. A man, hands in his pockets, had crossed the street and was approaching along the sidewalk. Quickly turning off his radio, the detective again lay across the front seat in hopes he would not be noticed. The man stopped as he reached the pickup, moved near the driver's door, and looked in. Thinking the occupant was asleep, he had turned away, taking only a couple of steps before he heard the pickup door open. Without looking back, he began to run.

The fleeing figure was already into the street when MacKenzie shouted an order for him to halt. Moving to the front of his pickup, the officer yelled again, "Police, freeze . . . Andy . . ."

When he shouted the name, the detective became certain of the man's identity, for Hopper had emitted a scream, then begun running even faster, rapidly distancing himself from the pursuing officer. Racing down the sidewalk, Andy ducked into the darkness between two houses and vaulted a backyard fence. Despite the fact he was in good shape, a religious jogger, MacKenzie was no match for the man he was chasing.

He soon gave up the chase and hurried back to his pickup to radio for backup, not even reaching his truck before FBI agent Matt Chapman, alerted earlier by McGowan, arrived and was immediately joined by the Garland police officers.

A helicopter from the Dallas Police Department was already en route.

Climbing into the pickup, MacKenzie hurriedly flipped on

his radio and made contact with McGowan: "Goddammit, I lost him." With that, the detective slammed a fist so hard against the steering wheel that he momentarily feared he had broken his hand.

"We're on our way," McGowan replied.

The search of the neighborhood continued until dawn, but Hopper had magically vanished.

Curled beneath an overturned children's plastic wading pool in a backyard not far from where the chase had begun, Andy's charmed life continued.

He would remain in his hiding place until late the following day.

Merle Ward had arrived home from her job at TU Electric, fixed herself a sandwich, and had just turned on the television to watch her favorite show, "Designing Women," when she heard a knock at the door.

Since moving to the house she shared with a roommate, Rebecca Trammell, in the high-crime Dallas suburb of Pleasant Grove, Merle had quickly learned not to open her door before knowing who was standing outside.

She asked the visitor to identify himself.

"It's Andy Hopper. Does Merle Ward still live here?"

Though Merle had known Andy and his family for years, first introduced to them by Hopper's cousin, she had not heard from him or Becky in some time. Quickly opening the door, she was surprised.

Dressed in jeans and a gray sweatshirt, the man standing before her was much thinner than he had been when she last saw him. He badly needed a haircut and his beard was unkempt. Still, she immediately recognized the man who was once her primary source of marijuana.

"Can I come in and talk to you for a minute?"

"Of course. What's going on?"

"You don't know anything?"

Merle shrugged and shook her head.

"Good," he said, then walked quickly to the curb to pay the waiting cabdriver.

Seated in the living room, Merle listened silently as Andy explained that he and Becky had separated and that for the past several months he had been on the run. He wanted to know if she would allow him to stay with her for a few days.

"Andy, I've got to know what's going on."

"I'm in trouble with the law."

"Drugs?"

"No, nothing like that."

"Then what is it?"

Hopper rose from the couch and began pacing the room. "You've got to promise not to tell anyone. I got involved in a deal where I passed some money to have a person killed." He went on to explain that he had been strung out on crystal at the time. He told her of the police visiting him at Steakley Chevrolet and of his decision to leave. He talked of his travels, his experiences working with the carnival, and the fact that on several occasions, including the night before, he had almost been caught.

"If you're in such trouble, why did you come back?"

"I wanted to see my girlfriend. Then, as soon as the guy I've been working for wires me some money, I'm going to Mexico."

While Merle was in the kitchen, preparing him a sandwich, Andy turned his attention to "Monday Night Football." When she returned, he was seated on the floor in front of the television, criticizing the play-calling of Chicago Bears coach Mike Ditka.

Shortly before midnight, Rebecca Trammell returned home and was introduced to Hopper. While their unexpected guest took a shower, Merle briefly explained to her the troubles Andy had described.

"I don't like the idea of him being here," Rebecca said.

"It's just for a day, maybe two."

When Andy returned to the living room, Rebecca began questioning him. "Why are you running?"

"Because I don't want to go to jail."

"All you did was pass some money to someone?"

Andy nodded.

Rebecca, admitting she knew nothing of the law, offered the opinion that one couldn't get in *that* much trouble just passing money from one person to another, even if a murder had resulted. "I would think that the person who pulled the trigger would be the one who had to worry."

"Yeah," Andy replied, "he's looking at the death penalty."

At the Richardson Police Department, Monday had been one of the longest days of Ken MacKenzie's life. Weary from lack of sleep and still despondent over his failure to apprehend Hopper, he had lost track of the number of trips he'd made down the hall to McGowan's office.

Both men had felt reasonably sure that Andy would try to get in touch with Lynda. Should he call, they had explained to her, she had to keep him on the line long enough for a trace to be made on the call. If he asked her to meet him, she was to agree but do nothing until talking with them.

When there had been no contact by late Monday night, MacKenzie began to fear Hopper might have left town.

"He's come this far to see her," McGowan said, trying to lighten his friend's spirits. "Let's don't give up yet."

The following day their fears were replaced by renewed enthusiasm.

A few minutes after noon on Tuesday, as they were having a sandwich in a restaurant near the police station, McGowan's beeper signaled him to phone the office. "Mrs. Whittaker just phoned," a secretary said. "Andy told her to have Lynda go to a pay phone at a nearby convenience store and wait for his call."

By the time the officers arrived at the Whittaker house, Lynda had already returned. "There was something wrong with the receiver," she explained. "I could barely hear him and apparently he couldn't hear me at all. I finally just hung up."

Certain Andy would call back, MacKenzie immediately contacted Matt Chapman at the FBI office. As soon as they had a location where the next call was to come to, the phone company should be alerted to be ready to trace its origin.

Shortly before two P.M., Hopper phoned with directions to

another pay phone. With Garland police following at a discreet distance, Lynda drove to a shopping center and nervously waited.

She let the phone ring several times before answering.

"Hi, baby," Andy said.

"Where are you?"

Ignoring her question, he told her how much he had missed her. "I love you and I want to see you."

"You're here?" Lynda asked, hoping that her attempt at surprise sounded genuine.

"I'm here." He told her he had been by her house on Sunday night and of hiding his backpack in the park nearby. "I can't wait to see you, but I've got to be careful. I'll call you back at this number at six o'clock." With that the phone went dead.

The conversation had been too brief for the phone company to get an exact fix on the origin of the call. "All I can tell you," the operator said, "was that it came from somewhere in Pleasant Grove."

It would be four hours before they could try again.

Leaving officers to watch the Whittaker house, McGowan and MacKenzie returned to the police station for yet another planning session. This time, they would cover every possibility. A team of Garland patrolmen were dispatched to watch the park in the event Andy decided to go there to retrieve his belongings. Lynda would be fitted with a wire, just in case Andy decided to surprise her by showing up in person. Officers from Richardson, Dallas, and the local FBI office would be positioned in the shopping center parking lot, poised either to move in to make an arrest or to leave immediately after the phone company provided them with the location of the caller.

While the frantic preparation was under way on the north side of Dallas, Andy Hopper passed the time watching television and awaiting Rebecca's return from work. Before leaving for work that morning she had surprised him by agreeing to pick up his belongings.

Using a map he'd drawn for her, she had driven to Watson Park and found his hidden backpack.

She had, however, carried out the favor with much reservation, nervously circling the park several times to make certain she had not been followed. By the time she arrived at work, Andy's things hidden in the trunk of her car, she had reached a decision. When she got home, she would tell Merle that her friend had to leave.

Andy was on the phone when she arrived shortly after six that evening. Merle, having already sensed her roommate's discomfort over their visitor, was standing at the door. "He's leaving in just a little while," she whispered.

Several miles away, in the shopping center parking lot, McGowan heard Agent Chapman's booming voice on the car radio, reporting from the phone company where he had been monitoring the trace on Andy's call.

"We've got it. Three three three one James Street . . . Pleasant Grove."

"We're on our way," McGowan acknowledged.

"I'll be right behind you," Chapman said.

In the house on James Street, Hopper and the two women were seated at the dining-room table, having eaten a meat loaf that Merle had prepared. Dinner finished, they chatted as Andy waited for his laundry to dry. As he checked through the items in his backpack, he showed them a photograph of Lynda he'd taken during a trip they'd made to Mississippi and a faked Georgia birth certificate he planned to use as identification when he crossed into Mexico.

As they talked, the house was being surrounded.

It was Merle who answered the knock at the door, stepping onto the front porch. In a moment, Rebecca was at her side.

"Is there anyone else in the house?" McGowan asked.

Frightened, Merle shook her head. "No."

"Do you know a man named George Anderson Hopper?"

Again Merle shook her head.

"Would you mind if we come inside?"

Simultaneously, the two women moved to the side of the porch, clearing a path to the front door. While FBI agents hurried into the living room and kitchen, McGowan moved down the hallway.

Stopping near the end of the hall, he listened for a moment, then slowly pushed against the door. Inside, the room was illuminated only by the fluorescent lighting from a large aquarium. As McGowan attempted to enter the room, the door would not completely open.

McGowan turned his body sideways and moved quickly inside, placing his left hand firmly against the chest of the man standing in the corner, pinning him against the wall. The officer needed no light to know who stood before him.

"Andy, don't do anything stupid."

"I won't."

"I've got him," McGowan yelled, and in seconds an FBI agent was at his side, holding out a pair of handcuffs.

Only after he and fellow officer Mike Corley had escorted Andy to a waiting car did McGowan look back toward the front yard to see Ken MacKenzie returning from his assigned position at the back of the house.

Tired but smiling, McGowan walked back toward the front yard and waved. "Come on," he yelled to indicate that he wanted MacKenzie to join him on the ride back to Richardson. "Let's take this guy to jail."

# 16

DONE WELL, THE interrogation of a suspect becomes a fascinating study in extemporaneous theatrics. The officer asking the questions adjusts his behavior, even his language, to suit the situation. In a sense, he becomes an actor who must quickly establish his conviction that he knows the person he's speaking with is guilty. Then, based on the behavior of the suspect, the officer must make an immediate judgment about the role he is to play. If the suspect is hostile and belligerent, the response is greater hostility and belligerence. If he is frightened, comfort and understanding are offered; if he's weak, it is countered with strength; confidence is matched with confidence.

Andy Hopper, McGowan decided, needed a friend. Soon they were on a first-name basis.

For several minutes the detective outlined the case, explained that other indictments had already been handed down. The main character, he said, was a woman named Joy Aylor. A number of other people were involved, people whose names Andy had not likely even heard.

McGowan talked of the months of tracking; the weekend in Boise, the near miss in Minot, the countless interviews with friends and relatives. "I wish you hadn't run. Hell, you really don't even have a criminal history. But all that crap's over now."

"I'm tired of running."

McGowan leaned closer, his voice sympathetic. "I imagine you're tired of this whole fucking deal, just like a lot of people. Andy, I've been involved in this sonuvabitch for five years. And it hasn't been easy. That's where I got all this fucking gray hair. But now it's over. We know the whole story, except Andy's. So, now it's up to you."

"What do you mean?"

"You can get on our team and help us or not. That's your business."

"Shouldn't I be talking to an attorney before I do that?"

McGowan had anticipated the question from the moment he had read Hopper his rights. Under the strictest interpretation of the Miranda Rule, a suspect must ask for a lawyer in the most specific terms. Unless he makes a definite statement like, "I want to talk to a lawyer immediately and refuse to answer any more of your questions until I do," a seasoned interviewer has room to maneuver. It becomes a semantics game played within narrow but perfectly legal boundaries.

"Andy, I'm going to be up front with you." As soon as an attorney, hired or court appointed, entered the picture, McGowan explained, their relationship ended. The district attorney and his lawyer took over. "And, let me assure you, the DA's office is going to come down hard. You're holding the cards to your future and you better think hard about that. Andy's the one, his fucking lawyer ain't the one. Andy's the one who can make or break himself."

Hopper slumped in his chair and took a long drag on a cigarette. "I don't know what else to say or do."

McGowan smiled. "Well, let's just talk about some bullshit stuff that doesn't have anything to do with anything, all right?"

"Not on the record?"

"Nothing's on the record."

The detective, now convinced that Andy was far from ready to confess, simply wanted to keep him talking. If nothing else, McGowan wanted to satisfy some of his curiosities about the man seated across from him.

He listened as Hopper reflected on his travels through the Midwest. In addition to Idaho and North Dakota, he admitted he had spent time in Oregon, even briefly traveling south to Nevada and New Mexico.

Now more relaxed, the suspect began asking questions. How many police officers had been watching him and Lynda in Boise? Why hadn't they arrested him then? Did anyone follow him as he left town? Had Lynda's phone been tapped?

McGowan answered his questions, then observed, "I thought there would be a point where you would turn around, come back here, and do the right thing."

"Turn myself in?"

"That's what I thought would eventually happen. I get the feeling that you thought about it."

"Several times, but I couldn't bear to think of the embarrassment to my kids. I've got two really great daughters."

Hopper suddenly tensed, his relaxed posture giving way to visible anger as Ken MacKenzie entered the room. "I'm not saying another word with him in here."

McGowan rose from his chair and stretched. "I understand. It's okay. But you're going to have to trust *me*. When you do, a whole new world is going to open up to you. Think about it. In the meantime, I'm going to get me a cup of coffee. You want one?"

"I'll take a Coke."

MacKenzie, ignoring Andy's hostility, settled into the chair McGowan had occupied for the past hour. "I understand that I'm not your favorite person, but I know some things that you would probably like to hear. For instance, your kids are okay. They're in school, doing fine. And they have no idea what's going on."

Quickly, though, MacKenzie's tone became aggressive. Why, he wanted to know, had Andy risked so much to see Lynda while not even considering a visit to Pampa to check on his wife and daughters?

"You know," the detective said, "I've talked to a lot of people about you in the past few months. The one thing everyone said was that you were crazy about your kids. Hell, I got the impression you would walk across broken glass for them. But you didn't even try to make contact, to see them or find out how they were. I guess that's what surprised me most in all this."

When Andy offered no response, MacKenzie continued, "When you came back here, to the place where you had to know everyone was looking for you, it occurred to me that there must have been something in the back of your mind that was telling you it was time to give it up."

"I really don't know."

Unlike McGowan, MacKenzie made no pretense of liking the man he was speaking with. Pushing harder, making his point that he knew Hopper's background well, the detective talked of Andy's using and selling drugs, his lengthy list of infidelities, and criticized the fact that Andy had left Becky penniless when he ran. "You cleaned out the bank account . . . they even repossessed her car."

With that the interviewer briefly fell silent, studying the man seated across from him. "Why did you kill Rozanne Gailiunas?"

"I want to talk to my attorney," Hopper snapped, suddenly agitated. Only when McGowan stepped back into the room did he begin to relax.

The calm, however, did not last.

They had been talking casually for only a few minutes when

McGowan again got to his feet and moved closer to Hopper. "Okay, we're going to get first things out of the way first. I don't want you saying any shit about wanting to see a lawyer because I'm not going to use anything against you. This is all off the fucking record from this point forward.

"MacKenzie says you did it. Now I'm asking you straight out if you did and I want a yes or no answer. That's it. Nothing else."

"You want to know if I shot the girl?"

"Yes."

"No, I didn't."

McGowan paused for several seconds, as if pondering the answer. "In that case, you've got every fucking reason in the world to get on this fucking team, son. You're eventually going to have to prove to me that you didn't do it. We can get that done by doing a lot of talking. But if you don't resolve it with me, the ball game's over. If you're telling me the truth, you've got everything to gain because you're facing some tough shit right now.

"We've talked and we've beaten around the bush, but business is business."

Hopper, finally feeling McGowan's pressure, was near tears. "But don't you think I should have the right to at least talk with an attorney?"

"Sure, if that's what you want. But what I'm saying is that it all comes down to trust."

"Mo, if I'm going to trust anyone, you're the person. But I have it drilled into my head that I should talk to an attorney. Are you saying that after I talk to an attorney I don't have any chance to come over on your side?"

"See, Andy, you won't be dealing with me then. I can promise you that right now. Your attorney will go straight to the DA and our talks will be over with in a hurry."

As he spoke, Captain Golden, who had been monitoring the interview from an adjacent room, stuck his head in and motioned McGowan to the hall. "We're not going anywhere with this deal. Why don't we let him call an attorney?"

Despite his exhaustion, McGowan stiffened. "Because an

attorney is going to tell him to shut up and that'll be it. What I want right now is information.''

"Inadmissible information. He's asked for a lawyer so many times that he can drop to his knees and confess all day long and we can't use any of it.''

"All I'm doing is laying groundwork for the future.''

Golden finally nodded. "Let's go ahead and get it over with.''

For several more minutes the captain listened as McGowan emphasized to Andy the importance of his cooperation. If there was someone else involved, Andy was the only one who could name that person. It was his decision. His life.

"Let's face it,'' the detective added. "You've asked for an attorney enough times now that I'm not going to be able to use a fucking thing you say. Hell, even if you wrote out a confession, I couldn't use it. That's the law.

"But, Andy, I want you to know something. I'm going to lay the cards on the table. You can believe I'm going to shoot straight with you.''

Hopper would ponder that statement late into the night after he was placed in a jail cell.

The following morning, George and JoAnn Hopper were waiting to see him when McGowan arrived at the station. Once again, much as he had been on that afternoon when he'd first met Joy Aylor's mother in the district attorney's office, the detective was moved by the expressions of disbelief and sorrow. The Hoppers, he sensed, were good people, innocently drawn into a nightmare beyond their comprehension.

He immediately agreed to arrange for them to visit their son.

"How serious is this?'' George Hopper asked.

"Sir, at this point, I don't believe that it was your son that committed the murder we're investigating.'' The father's faint smile of relief quickly disappeared as the officer continued, "But, I think that you should know that I'm very much in the minority about that.''

McGowan then explained that he had learned little from their son during the previous night's interrogation. "While I'd like to talk with him again, he's asked for an attorney, so the matter is out of my hands.''

"Why's that?'' the elder Hopper asked.

"The only way I can talk with him would be for him to make the request.''

For the first time, JoAnn Hopper, clutching a Bible to her breast, spoke. "We want him to talk to you.''

McGowan had already returned home for the evening and was having dinner when he received a call from the jailer, informing him that Hopper had asked to see him.

Sandy was surprised when her husband remained at the house another thirty minutes before leaving for the station. Still excited over news of the arrest, her patience reached an end when Morris walked into the backyard to check on the dog.

Standing on the back porch, hands on her hips, she called out, "What in the world are you waiting on?''

"I don't want to appear too anxious." It was all part of the gamesmanship.

Flipping a package of cigarettes onto the table, Morris could tell Andy had not slept much, if any, since he had last seen him. His eyes were sunken and hollow, rimmed by dark circles.

"You know,'' McGowan began, "I've been thinking about you a lot today. You lasted a lot longer out there on your own than I thought you would.''

"It got pretty tough at times.''

"Hell, if you had stayed away from here—stayed away from Lynda —you might have made it.''

Andy lit a cigarette and exhaled smoke toward the ceiling. "I gotta ask you something. Did Lynda set me up?''

During an earlier conversation with Lynda, McGowan had warned her that, once captured, Andy was likely to ask just such a question. After considerable thought, she had told him to be truthful.

"Yeah, Andy, she did. But you've got to understand that we were putting a lot of pressure on her. I'm not sure I'd blame her if I were you.''

"Naw, I don't. I still love her. Can I call her?''

"Is that what you got me down here to ask?" McGowan slid his chair back as if preparing to leave.

Andy quickly shook his head. "I'm going to get me a lawyer, and if he says it's okay, I'm going to talk to you."

"Son, that might not be a good idea. If you're the killer, like most people around here think, you shouldn't talk to me."

"I've already told you, I'm not."

McGowan said nothing for a minute as he stared across the table at the sad-faced prisoner. "Come on," he finally said, "let's go make your call."

For the next twenty minutes Andy sat on the concrete floor of the book-in room, talking quietly to his girlfriend. Cupping his hand against the receiver, he looked across the room at McGowan. "Can I see her?"

At last, the game had switched to the detective's favor. "Not unless you're ready to tell me your part in all this."

Hopper stared at the floor for a minute. Finally, he looked up and slowly began nodding his head. "Deal."

"Tell her to come on."

Returning to the interview room, McGowan listened as Andy told of Brian Kreafle's giving him the envelope that contained the money, the note, and the photograph of Rozanne Gailiunas. "I just pitched it on the front seat of the car and didn't even look inside it until later. Then, a few days later, I was down in the Oak Lawn area, buying some crystal from this guy named Chip. I talked to him about it and he said he could get it done. So, I gave him the envelope. A few days later, I saw him again and he told me the deal was done."

"What's Chip's last name?"

"I don't know, but I think I can help you find him."

McGowan nodded. "I'm going to go check on Lynda and see if I can arrange a place for you to talk."

Locking Andy in, he went to a phone and called MacKenzie. "Andy's got a story I want you to hear."

When he arrived at the station, MacKenzie was surprised to see Andy and Lynda seated together in one of the upstairs rooms, holding hands and talking. McGowan sat on the edge of a nearby desk, silently watching them through the open door.

"I hope you know what you're doing," MacKenzie observed.

McGowan allowed twenty minutes to pass before telling Lynda it was time to leave.

Then, while MacKenzie passed the time at his desk, McGowan resumed his questioning. "Okay, Andy, I want to hear it from top to bottom."

Again, Hopper told of the encounter with Kreafle. "There was fifteen hundred dollars in the envelope. All hundred-dollar bills."

This time, however, his story changed. He had, he admitted, driven past the Loganwood Drive address on several occasions. One night, seeing that Rozanne's Cadillac was in the driveway, he crawled under the partially open garage door, thinking there was likely a doorway that led inside. Finding there wasn't, he had walked around to the side of the house and was looking in a bedroom window when the barking of neighborhood dogs scared him away.

The following night he returned to find the house dark and, using a glass cutter purchased at a nearby hardware store, attempted to cut through a back window. When the glass broke, he reached in to unlatch the lock, then climbed inside. For almost a half hour he wandered the empty house, using his cigarette lighter to illuminate each room he visited.

As he waited, he contemplated doing the murder. "I went into the kitchen and got a knife out of a drawer."

"You were planning to stab her when she came home?"

"I guess. I don't know. I was all fucked up. Anyhow, I chickened out. I got to thinking there might be somebody with her when she got there. A boyfriend or somebody. So, I got the hell out of there."

Saying he was shaken by the experience, Andy recalled driving to the Oak Lawn apartment of a drug dealer a friend, Blythe Dobbins, had introduced him to. "The guy's name is Chip. I was there to buy some crystal and just started talking with him about the deal. He said he'd do it, so I gave him the envelope. A few days later he told me everything had been taken care of."

Later, Andy had driven by Kreafle's shop to pass on the message. "Brian said something about the woman being in the hospital, still alive. I hadn't heard anything about that."

"What about the other half of the money?"

"I never got it."

Suddenly, Andy buried his face in his hands and began sobbing. When he raised his head, tears were streaming down his cheeks. "Mo, Chip told me if I ever told anybody about this, he would rape my daughters and cut them to pieces."

"If you'll just cooperate, let us help you, we'll make sure he doesn't get to them. But we've got to know where to find him."

"The last time I saw him was a few days after he told me he'd done the deal. Later, I heard that he'd moved to California."

"And you're sure you don't know his last name?"

"Chip's all I ever knew."

"What's he look like?"

"Five-nine or so . . . maybe a hundred and sixty pounds . . . black hair parted in the middle."

After returning Hopper to the jail, McGowan returned to his office where MacKenzie sat, eagerly waiting to learn what Hopper had said. Morris made no attempt to hide his excitement as he recapped the conversation.

"Ken, I want you to find this guy Chip."

MacKenzie's frustration over Morris's stubborn insistence that Hopper was not the triggerman finally erupted. "For Christ's sake, Mo, that whole story is bullshit. There is no Chip. I'm telling you, Andy Hopper is the guy who killed Rozanne Gailiunas. I've been sure of it from the first time I talked to him at Steakley Chevrolet."

McGowan's voice was controlled but firm. "Chip is real. Andy was too damn descriptive to be making it all up. I want you to find him."

The key to determining whether Andy Hopper was a middleman or a murderer, McGowan felt, lay in the truth about this mysterious drug dealer with no last name.

And while he understood MacKenzie did not share his feelings, McGowan knew that if the person existed, Ken would find him.

Even before Hopper was transferred from Richardson to the Dallas County jail, MacKenzie had attacked the search with a vengeance. Still, he felt he had been sent to look for a needle in a haystack. Nonetheless, he had begun to acknowledge begrudgingly that if the case was to move forward, the possibility of yet another person being involved had to be dealt with.

During the next several weeks his quest took him along the dead-end streets and back alleys of Dallas's Oak Lawn area, long the hub of the city's gay community.

Phoning Becky Hopper, he had learned that Andy's friend, the woman who had supposedly introduced Andy to Chip, had moved to Houston. Dozens of calls later, he found that Blythe Dobbins had moved again and was living in Florida.

When he finally reached her, he was surprised when she admitted that she had, in fact, introduced the two men sometime in 1983. "Chip lived in some apartments on Cole Street," she said. "I don't remember the address. He dealt meth and a little cocaine."

The description she gave was remarkably similar to that Andy had given.

"You might talk to Deena Lampley," she said. "She used to spend a lot of time at Chip's place."

"Where can I find her?"

"I have no idea. I heard she got married."

For days, MacKenzie drove along Oak Lawn, visiting the gay bars and coffee shops, talking with hollow-eyed hookers and brain-fried addicts who populated the area. Deena Lampley, he finally learned, had married and moved to another section of Dallas.

She was not pleased when the detective located her. Her previous life, she explained, was something she had carefully kept from her husband. Only when MacKenzie assured her that her secret would be safe did she admit that she had, in fact, known a drug dealer named Chip. "But all that was a long time ago."

"Do you remember where he lived?"

"I can show you."

For hours they drove through the Oak Lawn area, past run-down apartment complexes, dreary bars, and clapboard windowed barbecue joints. Slowly, memories of another time in her life came back to the woman seated next to him. "It was here," she said as they moved slowly along tree-lined Cole Street.

MacKenzie stared blankly at a vacant lot where once an apartment house had stood.

During the next week he searched in vain for records that might indicate the ownership of the apartment back in '83. And he continued to haunt the neighborhood in search of someone who might have known Chip.

Deena had mentioned two women—she only knew them as Joyce and Cathy—whom she recalled meeting at Chip's place.

"Christ, doesn't anybody around here have a last name?" the frustrated detective asked.

"Hey," Deena snapped, "back then I was out of it most of the time. All I was interested in was getting high, not formal introductions."

The thirtysomething lovers Joyce and Cathy finally gave direction to MacKenzie's search. Sitting in the living room of their tiny apartment, he listened as they reflected on time spent at Chip's, of drug parties and casual sex.

"I think," Cathy said, "that his first name was Steve. I remember just before Christmas, back in 1983, he was arrested over in Highland Park. I bailed him out."

If there was, in fact, a needle buried in the haystack he'd been sifting through, MacKenzie now knew how to find it.

Highland Park, an incorporated community of million-dollar homes located just a few miles from downtown Dallas, boasted one of the lowest crime rates in Texas. All-white, its pristine image was guarded not only by its own police department but neighborhood guardians quick to report even an unfamiliar car being driven down its streets.

MacKenzie doubted that there had been a great deal of police activity in the days preceding Christmas of 1983. Driving to the

Highland Park Police Department on a late-February morning, he began methodically going through old records, looking for anyone named Steve who had been arrested.

After two hours of pulling files he found what he was looking for. Steve Rennick, whose residence at the time was the since-demolished Cole Street apartment, had been jailed for unlawful possession of a weapon.

MacKenzie's next step was to contact the Dallas Police Department to see what, if any, dealings it might have had with Rennick. An officer in the narcotics division quickly confirmed that Rennick had been busted several times on drug-related charges and suggested that MacKenzie get in touch with retired officer Buddy Beckwith. "He worked that Oak Lawn beat forever. He's knows every sleazy bastard down there."

Visiting Beckwith at his home, MacKenzie found that the ex-officer not only knew Steve Rennick but—as do many retiring officers—had made copies of many of his files before retiring. Among his keepsakes was the criminal history of the man MacKenzie was searching for.

"He was a small-timer," Beckwith recalled as he flipped through the photocopied papers. "Sold a little here and there, but mostly used the shit himself or gave it away to his buddies. Last I heard of him, he'd moved to San Diego."

With that he handed his visitor a photograph. "That's your boy."

MacKenzie silently studied the mug shot for several seconds. Staring back at him was a slender-faced young man with dark hair, parted in the middle.

That afternoon Ken walked into McGowan's office, taking a seat before speaking. Sliding the mug shot of Rennick across the desk, MacKenzie shrugged. "You were right."

It had taken him almost two months of searching to confirm that.

Jan Hemphill, bookish and matronly, had, during two decades of practicing law in Dallas, gained a reputation as an aggressive defense attorney—a woman more apt to intimidate her male counterparts than be intimidated by them.

When she was appointed by the court as his attorney, Hopper learned quickly that he had been fortunate. Fellow inmates in the Dallas County jail, many of them self-proclaimed experts on the lengthy role call of local defense lawyers, assured him that Hemphill was "one tough broad" who loved to go up against the district attorney's office. "You got fucking-A lucky," he was told.

Hemphill had found Hopper pleasant during their first meeting—a bit cocky for one facing such serious charges, perhaps, but polite and well-educated. She was also impressed by the fact that, unlike so many of her clients, he had no criminal background to speak of.

After listening to his story of taking the money, then contemplating the murder himself before ultimately passing the job along to a drug dealer he knew only as Chip, she had met with prosecutors Chapman and Dan Hagood to discuss the case.

Briefly detailing the tangled story of murder for hire, they made it clear that their primary concerns lay in trying Joy Aylor and whoever had actually fired the shots that killed Rozanne Gailiunas. If Hemphill's client was, in fact, nothing more than another of the middlemen, it would be in his best interest to help them locate the man he claimed to have passed the job along to.

On February 22, 1990, Hopper telephoned the Richardson Police Department and asked to speak with McGowan. "My lawyer says for me to cooperate with you."

Andy made no mention of the fact Hemphill had advised him to limit that cooperation to helping the police find Chip.

A week later Andy was transported back to the Richardson Police Department and taken to the office of polygraph operator Robert Strauss.

A friendly, soft-spoken man, Strauss immediately set about making Hopper feel at ease. For several minutes he carefully explained the procedure, then read Andy the Miranda warning and had him sign a polygraph consent form.

"What we're going to do," Strauss said, "is just talk for a while, go over the whole thing before I even hook you up to the machine. I want you to be as comfortable as possible and to know exactly what questions we're going to be testing you on.'' There would, he promised, be no tricks.

Already briefed by McGowan and MacKenzie, Strauss was familiar with the basics of the Gailiunas murder case as well as Hopper's explanation that he had at one point considered killing the woman himself before passing the job along to his drug supplier.

For a half hour Andy answered a series of general questions about his family background, health, and education; the only fight he'd ever been in, he said, had taken place when he was in the seventh grade. He admitted lying to his parents when asked if he smoked marijuana. He was in good physical health and had only briefly seen a psychologist during a time when he and Becky were having marital problems.

Strauss then began questioning him about the events that had led to his arrest. Finally, the examiner went through the specific questions Hopper would be asked once the machine was monitoring his responses.

"Any problems with any of those questions?" Strauss asked.

"No, sir."

"Well, then we're ready to go."

Once Hopper was attached to the machine that would chart his breathing patterns, pulse rate, and the secretion of sweat glands, Strauss began the test.

"Do you understand that I will be asking only the questions that we've discussed?" the operator began.

"Yes."

"Regarding the murder of Rozanne Gailiunas, do you intend to answer all the questions truthfully?"

"Yes."

"Are you a citizen of the United States?"

"Yes."

"Other than what you've already told me, during the first twenty-five years of your life, do you remember ever trying to physically hurt anyone?"

"No."

"Do you know for sure who shot Rozanne Gailiunas?"

"No."

"Is your last name Hopper?"

"Yes."

"During the first twenty-five years of your life, do you remember ever threatening someone with physical harm?"

"No."

"Did you yourself shoot Rozanne Gailiunas?"

"No."

"Were you born in the month of October."

"Yes."

"Other than what you told me, during the first twenty-five years of your life, do you remember ever lying to anyone in authority?"

"No."

"Were you in Rozanne Gailiunas's house when she was shot?"

"No."

Strauss instructed Andy to relax and moved to the machine to mark a notation on the chart.

Over the next half hour, he would repeat the process, and the same questions—though asked in a slightly different order—three more times. When finally done, he had Andy sign his name to each chart, then turned him over to Brent Tourangeau, a Richardson investigator who had been assigned to sit in on the testing.

"I'm going to have you wait outside for a few minutes while I evaluate the charts," Strauss said.

Ten minutes later he called Hopper back in. "Andy, I'm afraid it didn't go well at all for you."

A look of mock disapproval spread across Hopper's face. "What does it say I'm lying about?"

"All three of the major questions about the murder. You reacted very strongly on each of them. Particularly the one where I asked if you yourself shot Rozanne Gailiunas."

"I don't know what to say."

"Detective McGowan is going to want to talk to you about this, of course."

Hopper looked pleadingly at the polygraph operator. "I'm telling you the truth. What else can I do?"

"Detective McGowan is waiting. The only thing I can suggest to you is that you level with him."

As Tourangeau walked him down the hall toward the interview room, Andy was still shaking his head. "I don't understand. I just don't understand . . ."

"Let's go back over it," McGowan suggested, "and see if we can figure out where things broke down. Tell me the whole story again, from the beginning."

Once more, Hopper started with his meeting Kreafle, then again detailed the late-night visits to Rozanne's house and finally his trip to Chip's apartment.

McGowan did not speak until Andy had told of seeing Chip again and learning that the job had been done. Slowly shaking his head, the detective looked across the table. "Son, I don't think you're telling me the truth."

"I am."

Standing, McGowan moved across the room as Andy's eyes followed him. "Let's say I find Chip. Let's say I bring him in and ask him about all this shit and he says he doesn't know fuck about any of this. Let's say I put him on the polygraph and he passes. If I do all that, where does it take me?"

Andy stared at his hands for a moment, then looked up at McGowan. "Back to me."

Moving to the table, McGowan reached into his shirt pocket and removed the photograph that MacKenzie had placed there minutes earlier. Placing it in front of Hopper, he asked, "Who's that, Andy?"

Hopper slumped in his chair as all color drained from his face. "That's Chip," he said, his voice barely audible.

"You're damn right it is, and I know where to find him."

"What do you want from me?"

"Andy, godammit, I want you to tell me the truth. What I want is for you to be able to get on the stand and testify against Joy Aylor. But first, I've got to have the truth."

"Can I go back and think about it?"

McGowan shook his head and leaned across the table, his face just inches from Hopper's. "*I want it now.* If you were there when Rozanne Gailiunas was shot, I need to hear it.''

The muscles in Andy's jaws tightened and he began nervously rocking back and forth in his chair.

''I've got to know, Andy.''

Hopper's reply came in a whisper. ''Mo, I did it.''

The admission had come so quietly, so suddenly, that the detective was momentarily taken aback. ''What did you say?''

''I did it. I shot her.''


On the afternoon of October 4, 1983, a Tuesday, twenty-one-year-old Kenneth Allen had been standing in the parking lot of Jerry Mason's Body Shop in Cedar Hill, Texas, for almost an hour, waiting for an insurance adjustor who was to appraise the damage to his Ford LTD.

When the man, who introduced himself as Andy Hopper, finally arrived, he seemed harried and disinterested, giving Allen's car only a cursory look before quoting a repair cost.

When Allen asked to discuss the appraisal in more detail, the adjustor quickly brushed him off. ''I'm sorry, but I have an appointment on the other side of Dallas.''

For days, Hopper had been functioning on nervous energy, fueled by an increased use of methamphetamines, sleeping little.

Such had been the case since he had told Brian Kreafle he could find someone to kill the woman in Richardson.

Before keeping his scheduled appointment in Cedar Hill, Andy had detoured by the north Dallas home of a friend and fellow adjustor named Terry Harmon.

Separated from his wife and living alone, Harmon had given Hopper a key to his apartment after repeated requests to borrow it. Though Hopper had explained that it provided him a convenient place to write up reports and make phone calls when in that part of town, Harmon strongly suspected that his place was being used by Andy and his endless parade of girlfriends for midday lovemaking.

On this particular day, however, it was not privacy that Andy was seeking. Instead, he wanted the .25 automatic that he knew Harmon kept in a desk drawer.

Taking the gun, he had then driven to a nearby mall and stolen a set of license plates from a car in the parking lot. On a secluded residential street, he had switched the plates to his car, stowing his in the trunk, before driving southward toward Cedar Hill.

Immediately after his business was finished there, he traveled to Richardson, stopping at a Safeway where he bought several lengths of cotton rope and a pair of surgical gloves. From there he went to a nearby florist where he purchased potted mums.

It pleased him that this time, he was executing a carefully thought-out plan.

When Rozanne Gailiunas had answered the doorbell, she found a handsome, smiling young man standing on the porch, a potted plant in his hand.

"Delivering flowers," Andy Hopper said.

As she pushed open the screen door, the smile suddenly vanished from the man's face. Shoving her backward into the hallway, he pointed the gun at her. Only then did Rozanne notice that he was wearing surgical gloves.

"Just keep your mouth shut," he said as he placed the flowers on the floor near the door. Then grabbing her by the arm, he led her down the hall toward her bedroom, stopping at the entrance of her sleeping son's room only long enough to gently shut the door.

"Take off your clothes and get on the bed," Hopper demanded as he reached behind him to push her door closed. He then watched silently as the terrified woman removed her robe. "Lie on your stomach."

Dazed by the sudden horror, Rozanne offered no resistance as he slowly, methodically tied her outstretched arms and legs to the cornerposts. Clearly, he was in no hurry. Only when the last knot was secured did Hopper realize she had begun to cry. Concerned that she might soon scream, he walked quickly to the bathroom and tore several tissues from a box.

As he prepared to force them violently into her mouth, she spoke the only word she would utter: "Why?"

Hopper gave her no answer, the urgency of his mission

fueled by the tantalizing rush of power that had seized him. He wanted to savor it, to inhale deeply the scent of fear and perfumes, to gaze down on the beautiful woman over whom he now had complete control.

He began to move slowly about the room, his mind cataloging the privacy he had invaded. At her dresser, he opened a drawer filled with silk scarves and lingerie, fighting the urge to remove his gloves and hold her things, rubbing their cool softness against his skin. Next, he moved to her closet. She liked bright colors and prints, he thought as he removed the belt from one of the dresses.

Turning back to the bed, he positioned himself over her and, removing the rubber gloves, began to masturbate. Semen soon covered his hand as he quickly ejaculated.

After he washed his hands in the bathroom, he returned and placed the belt around her neck. Only when he began choking her did Rozanne attempt to fight back, thrashing beneath him, finally managing to break her left hand free of its bindings.

Suddenly, as if some switch had been flipped, his euphoria drained away and was replaced by sheer panic. Hopper quickly reached for the gun he had placed on the nearby nightstand, pushed a pillow hard against her head, and fired two point-blank shots, which caused her body to go limp.

Not even bothering to see if the shots had been fatal, he ran from the house, past the still-closed door of the child's bedroom, and into the street where his car was parked.

In the bedroom, Rozanne's body began to convulse, knocking the pillow away. With her head now hanging over the side of the bed, she vomited around the Kleenex stuffed down her throat.

Driving to a nearby car wash, Hopper tossed the gloves and glass cutter he'd used during his earlier break-in into a trash bin. He then removed the stolen plates, threw them away, and replaced them with his own.

Finally, almost as an afterthought, he reached into his glove compartment and found the directions and photograph that Kreafle had given him and tore them into small pieces before letting them flutter into the bin.

Within the hour he had returned the pistol to Harmon's apartment, and the euphoric feeling, unlike anything he'd ever experienced, again swept over him as he drove back toward Garland.

After all the worry and planning it had happened too quickly, had been so easy.

Looking at the dashboard clock, he smiled and took a deep, relaxing breath. He still had plenty of time to pick up his young daughters from the baby-sitter's.

When Hopper mentioned the flowers, Ken MacKenzie, who was monitoring the interview from an adjacent room, rushed down the hall and retrieved a folder of crime-scene photographs he and McGowan had reviewed hundreds of times.

Thumbing through them hurriedly, he located a picture that had been taken in Rozanne's living room. Next to the front door, in clear view, sat the potted flowers. The answer to their single most troubling question—one McGowan had wrestled with since he first walked into Rozanne Gailiunas's home—had been there all along.

It was early evening by the time Hopper had given a formal statement of confession, first in writing, then on videotape.

Drained but happier than he could ever remember being, McGowan settled in his office to make a series of phone calls, first to Sandy, then to Paula Donahue, and finally to Kevin Chapman in the DA's office.

The following day the courthouse was abuzz with news that the final piece of the Gailiunas murder puzzle had fallen into place.

Only Jan Hemphill, Hopper's lawyer, refused to share in the enthusiasm. She had been in court most of the day when King Solomon, a public defender, saw her walking hurriedly toward an elevator and called out.

"You don't look happy," Solomon observed.

"I'm not," she said, adding that she'd just received a call from the district attorney's office. "I can't believe what those bastards did to me." When he heard of Hopper's confession,

Solomon wondered if it was the police Hemphill was angry with—or herself for not having accompanied her client to the polygraph test.

Upstairs, in the DA's office, Kevin Chapman was on the phone to McGowan, offering congratulations and reflecting on the unbelievable series of twists and turns they had followed to get where they were.

"You did a helluva job," Chapman said, "and you deserve some rest. It's time for you to sit on the bench for a while and let me play."

Already, the prosecutor was eagerly contemplating the trials that lay ahead.

# PART THREE

—

# Flight

Oh, that I had wings like a dove! for then would I fly away, and be at rest.

—Psalms 55:6

The efforts which we make to escape from our destiny only serve to lead us into it.

—from "Fate,"
*The Conduct of Life*, Ralph Waldo Emerson

# 17

THE THREE WOMEN had arrived early enough to find an empty table near one of the yawning picture windows at Chez Gerard, a trendy McKinney Avenue French restaurant where the lunch menu of soups and salads and croissant sandwiches caters to a predominately female clientele. It is one of those places to see and be seen, a favorite gathering place of Park Cities wives taking a break from the rigors of shopping and charity gala committee meetings. At the linen-draped tables, where rays of sunlight dance on fine crystal and polished silverware, the conversations range from the latest in fashion and academic accomplishments of the children to the most recent business successes of workaholic husbands. It is also a place to hear the whispered gossip about who's having an affair with whom or who might have paid a recent visit to her divorce lawyer or plastic surgeon.

However, little in the animated conversation at the window table indicated that its occupants—Joy Aylor, her cousin Vicki Kienest, and new friend Darla Green—were even mildly concerned over the fact each had, in recent weeks, been topics of just such gossip. Joy's arrest and indictment had been thoroughly reported in the local papers; the strongly worded divorce petition Vicki had filed against her husband, Jim, was public knowledge; and Darla's lawyer was trying hard to strike an agreement with federal authorities whereby she would receive reduced prison time for her role in fraudulent banking activities if she testified against fellow indictees.

If others in the restaurant stole occasional glances in their direction, they were ignored. All three women had quickly learned that a strong public display of confidence and well-being was their best weapon against the petty gossipmongers who took special delight in someone else's troubles.

245

Darla, a blue-eyed, blond divorcée, had first met Joy one evening after stopping in for coffee with her Autumn Oaks Apartments neighbor Vicki, and Vicki's mother, Victorine Davis. Though neither had discussed Joy's legal problems in any detail, Darla was generally aware of the charges against Joy and was surprised to find that she immediately liked this woman who was supposed to have set in motion an unthinkable murder-for-hire plot.

Soft-spoken and a bit shy, Joy seemed to be the strength in the family. Darla knew Joy had helped Victorine with personal and business matters after her husband, Hugh, had died of a heart attack while on a bird-hunting trip with his brother, Henry Davis. Joy had also helped Victorine's son, Brad, also a home-builder, through some financial hard times. But the relationship between Joy and Vicki was the strongest—more like that of sisters than cousins. When Vicki's teenage son committed suicide, it was Joy who had been there to help her through the ordeal. And when Henry Davis had suffered a sudden stroke shortly after her first arrest, it was Joy who purchased him an electric wheelchair and made daily trips to visit with him.

Darla was pleased that her friendship with Joy had blossomed. In short order they were meeting regularly for lunch, talking on the phone, and sharing problems. Darla, her assets frozen by government order, was badly in need of cash, and Joy had been quick to make her a $2,500 loan on some jewelry and later helped her sell a collection of rings, necklaces, and bracelets worth almost a half million dollars. In turn, Darla, a licensed realtor, had volunteered to help Joy sell her house.

Though they shared intimate thoughts on a variety of subjects, Joy avoided talk of the murder charge, limiting her personal confidences to occasional mention of her divorce. The reason she had thrown her husband out, she told Darla, was because she found out he had been involved in an affair with her younger sister.

Still, the better Darla came to know Joy, the more perplexing she became. At times Darla was certain that her new friend was nothing more than an innocent victim of a wayward husband who had likely committed the crime for which Joy was being charged. Then, just when she was sure that Joy was a kind, loving person, a cold, calculating side of her personality would emerge, causing Darla to reevaluate. And there was other behavior she could only describe as eccentric. When she visited Joy's home, Joy routinely pulled all the shades before they sat down for even the most casual conversation. A firm no-smoking rule applied to all visitors, and Joy appeared to be an obsessive housekeeper.

Early on, Darla came to realize that their relationship was not likely to last. Though Joy had not admitted it outright, she was obviously planning to leave the country to escape her legal problems. One evening she showed Darla an article she had clipped from the *Dallas Morning News* travel section about an isolated resort in Mexico, saying how much she would like to go there "and just disappear."

And she began inquiring about a first-rate cosmetic surgeon who might do reconstructive work on her nose and chin. Aware that Darla had recently had surgery done on her cheek following a horseback riding accident, Joy asked the name of her doctor. Joy had also wondered aloud if any surgical procedure could alter one's fingerprints.

Long before Darla accompanied Joy to the office of her doctor, introducing her—at Joy's request—as "Linda," it was obvious that a plan was formulating in Joy's mind: first, a new look, then a new locale. Darla was not surprised when Joy decided against using a local doctor and began talking of traveling to Los Angeles, New York, or perhaps Chicago, where there was less chance of her being recognized. From someone else she had learned of a famed underworld surgeon in Mexico who had made a career of providing new facial identities. Perhaps, Joy had said, she would pay him a visit.

If nothing else, Joy Aylor, was a careful planner, weighing all alternatives before making a decision.

Increasingly anxious about her own upcoming court date, Darla found herself occasionally wondering if perhaps Joy had the right idea. Darla's problem, she knew, was that she lacked Joy's courage and self-confidence. She would just have to sit tight and hope her attorney could make as painless a deal as possible.

Joy, meanwhile, had begun expressing growing frustration over the lack of attention from her own lawyer. Doug Mulder was seldom in his office when she phoned. If he was there, he was usually in a meeting and might not return her call for days. When they did talk, he rarely had anything in the way of encouraging news.

One evening as she and Darla talked on the phone, Joy voiced concern that she had not heard from Mulder recently. "Maybe what I need is a new lawyer."

What she didn't mention was that she had already placed a call to legendary Houston attorney Racehorse Haynes to discuss his taking over her case. Joy had liked neither the tone of Haynes's voice nor the fact that his retainer would be $100,000, so had not been back in touch with him.

Darla mentioned her attorneys, Denver McCarty and Mike Wilson. Wilson, she said, was a former prosecutor who had worked in the district attorney's office with Mulder for a time before leaving to enter private practice. He primarily handled criminal cases and, she had been told, had a reputation for being good at his job. "I'd be happy to introduce you," Darla said.

"I think I'd like that," Joy replied.

On a warm May evening in 1989, McCarty and Wilson sat in the den of Joy's house, sipping iced tea, each privately sizing up the woman seated on the couch, legs folded beneath her. During the course of their careers, both attorneys had long since learned that criminals and those charged with crimes rarely looked the part. Joy Aylor reinforced the rule in spades.

Relaxed and smiling, she introduced them to her teenage son, Chris, as he walked through en route to the kitchen, offered to prepare sandwiches, and showed not the slightest discomfort as she carefully outlined her legal situation. It was, Wilson found himself thinking, as if she were talking about the troubles of someone else, a girlfriend, perhaps, or a neighbor.

Only when a blond-haired man emerged from somewhere in back of the house to tell her he was leaving for a while did she seem to grow tense and quiet, even avoiding the formalities of introductions. Joy was silent for some time after the man had left, then, with the smile returning, offered an explanation: "I didn't want to talk about this with him around."

For almost an hour the men sat listening as the woman outlined the bizarre circumstances that had led to the death of Rozanne Gailiunas, occasionally interrupting her narrative to ask their legal opinions and their estimated cost of representing her.

As she spoke, McCarty found himself troubled by the almost constant smile, the casual manner in which Joy discussed the charges against her. Wilson, to whom she directed most of her conversation, found himself thinking of an observation from an old friend, forensic psychologist James Grigson. The doctor had once explained that some people, when talking about the most painful of things, smile, even laugh. "Inappropriate response," Grigson called it, a method some people use to hide their pains and true feelings.

Inappropriate or not, Wilson found the smile, and the woman behind it, fascinating.

When Joy began explaining that her mother was strongly advising her to continue using the attorney she had originally hired, McCarty, having quickly grown less than enthusiastic about handling the case, seized the opportunity to heap praise on Doug Mulder. Even at the risk of causing himself to lose a client, McCarty noted, he had to point out that Mulder's reputation as one of the country's premier criminal defense lawyers was well earned. He strongly advised her to give the matter a great deal of thought before dismissing her present attorney. Wilson nodded his endorsement to the advice.

Later, as they drove from Joy's house, the two men said little. McCarty finally said, "That's the coldest damn woman I've ever seen."

Wilson considered arguing the point, but instead remained quiet. He had seen a totally different person—a beautiful, frightened woman whom he had liked the minute she had greeted them at the door.

In the darkened ride back to the office, Mike Wilson leaned

back in the seat, closed his eyes, and let his mind drift back to Joy's smile.

Mike Wilson had grown up in Winnsboro, a former east Texas boom town, the son of one of the region's last remaining wildcatters. He quarterbacked the high school football team, dated the prettiest girls in town, and was one of the most popular students in his forty-seven-member graduating class. A favorite of teachers and townspeople alike, his determination to excel was evident even as a youngster. Such a young man, the locals agreed, was destined for things that Winnsboro could not offer. When he left to enroll in the University of Texas in the fall of 1963, his family and friends knew he wouldn't be coming back. Mike Wilson had a bigger world to explore.

As a collegian, he enhanced his reputation as one who worked and played with equal enthusiasm. He routinely scored high marks in the classroom and relished the active social life of the Phi Delt fraternity that he pledged, arriving early and staying late at the regular weekend beer busts. Pretty coeds were never more than arm's length away.

The prettiest was a petite blonde named Lucy Brants, a Fort Worth debutante whose family tree included the legendary philanthropist and newspaper publisher Amon Carter. Before their junior year, they married and moved into the Braesridge Apartments on the edge of the UT campus.

A few of their friends found it unusual that Wilson, despite his marriage, remained so active in fraternity life. He and Lucy were regulars at any social event the Phi Delts staged. And if Mike seemed always to drink a bit more than the others, few paid it much mind. After all, Mike Wilson seemed to be living the charmed life: he earned good grades and was happily married into a wealthy family.

Following graduation, Mike and Lucy loaded up their belongings, newborn son, Michael, and their basset hound and moved to Dallas. Keenly aware of the possibility of being drafted and sent to Vietnam where the war efforts were escalating, Mike had decided it would be prudent to remain in school a while longer. When a fraternity brother announced his plan to seek admission to Southern Methodist University's law school, Wilson decided to follow suit.

Though he had decided to study law on little more than a whim, Wilson soon found himself fascinated by the intricacies of the legal process, particularly those related to the practice of criminal law. He seized every opportunity to ride with Dallas police officers on late-night shifts, seeing firsthand the dangers lurking in the city's back alleys. He hung on every word of the well-known prosecutors who regularly visited the campus to address law students. Mike Wilson knew he had found his calling. As soon as he could graduate and pass the bar, he wanted to join the Dallas County District Attorney's Office.

In 1971, he achieved his goal and in the next three years quickly established a reputation as an aggressive but fair prosecutor. Wilson had what fellow attorneys called an uncanny gift for evaluating the merits of a case, determining whether a plea bargain or a trial was in order. A tireless researcher, he visited crime scenes, talked to witnesses and investigators, and seemed always to make time to assure victims that he was working diligently in their behalf. In the courtroom he was the picture of a sincere, fair, well-prepared attorney with strong convictions about his purpose. His closing arguments often drew admiring fellow lawyers to the courtroom to listen. And most important, he won far more often than he lost.

The only downside was the fact that promotions in District Attorney Henry Wade's office were notoriously slow in coming. Unlike many similar offices throughout the country where young, underpaid prosecutors use their time as assistant DAs only to gain enough experience to prepare them for more lucrative private practices, the top guns—Wade's chief felony prosecutors—were paid well, got the high-profile cases, and stayed on for years.

Impatient and eager to join the ranks of defense attorneys who commanded fees for a single case that exceeded his annual salary, Wilson resigned from the DA's office in 1974 and teamed with ex-prosecutors Bob Fain and Tommy Callan in private practice.

The move was disastrous. Potential clients with the financial resources to hire the best, he quickly learned, had little interest in an attorney just three years out of law school, regardless of his abilities or growing reputation. Wilson was forced to settle for an endless succession of court appointments, preparing defenses for clients for whom he felt little or no empathy. He quickly came face-to-face with the cardinal rule of criminal defense work: a good lawyer keeps his client—who is generally guilty—from being tried, plea-bargaining with prosecutors for the best deal possible.

What Mike missed most was the drama of the courtroom, the spotlight that seemed to shine only on the attorneys seeking to earn justice by putting the bad guys away. Soon, he was drinking more heavily than ever in an attempt to salve his disappointment in a career that he felt was going nowhere.

After three frustrating years, Wilson made two decisions. He would enter an alcohol treatment center to get his drinking under control, then he would go to Henry Wade and ask to rejoin the DA's office.

Though he was warmly welcomed back into the Specialized Crime Division, it was never the same. For the next five years he continued to enhance his reputation as a lawyer, successfully prosecuting murderers, rapists, child molesters, and drug dealers. When the Dallas Cowboys filed charges against producers of a pornographic movie titled *Debbie Does Dallas*, in which a young actress, dressed in the uniform of the team's world-famous Dallas Cowboys Cheerleaders, performs all manner of sexual acrobatics, prosecution of the case fell to Wilson. While he privately deemed the prosecution of X-rated movies a waste of his time and taxpayers' money, he pled the case to an enraptured jury with a Southern Baptist vengeance and won, earning nationwide publicity for his efforts.

Wilson's star was beginning to rise again. Its only tarnish was the drinking. Though it did not appear to impair his work, it had progressed well beyond his control. During the seventies he entered alcohol abuse treatment centers a half dozen times.

In 1981, the opportunity he'd long hoped for finally arrived. The Missouri-Texas-Kansas Railroad, looking for an aggressive, personable young attorney to head its civil litigation department, offered Wilson a job that would triple his income overnight. At last he was in a position to grasp the financial brass ring he'd aspired to since law school days.

In just six months, however, things turned sour again. At a Denver seminar for other railway lawyers, he made the mistake of accepting a drink in the hospitality room. One led to another, and by seminar's end he had made several public scenes before passing out in his motel room.

Upon his return to Dallas he was fired. Once again, Wilson found his career tumbling into a black hole of his own making. Finally convinced that the quick cures of treatment centers he'd previously visited were not the answer, he checked himself into a hospital for a month-long stay. By the time he was discharged, he had come to grips with the realization that he was a full-fledged alcoholic and even one social drink would be disastrous.

The binge that had cost him his job as attorney for the Katy Railroad was the last time he took a drink. Once again, Mike Wilson was on the rebound.

Again trying private practice, the going was easier the second time around. No longer a young, inexperienced attorney, he found himself in demand, his income increasing with each passing month. And when he wasn't working for his clients, he was serving as a counselor for other lawyers struggling with drinking problems. With fellow attorney John McShane, he formed an Alcoholics Anonymous chapter whose membership was made up almost entirely of men in the legal community. He made time in his increasingly busy schedule to speak to professional groups on the hazards of alcoholism. Clients with drinking or substance abuse problems were steered into recovery programs as part of his legal services.

Soon, Wilson's career was thriving. He and Lucy were living in a $300,000 lakeside home, and he was commuting to his fashionable Dallas office in a 924 Porsche. His wife drove a BMW. From all outward appearances, the young attorney who had just a few years earlier been a $50,000-a-year prosecutor had a firm grip on the brass ring.

However, a dark irony was attached to Wilson's skyrocketing success. His growing list of clients was made up almost entirely of big-money drug dealers. The same kind of people he had once prosecuted with a dedicated vengeance were now the chief source of his income.

In the early eighties, Wilson was hired to represent a Dallas drug dealer named Hollis Burns, a high-stakes gambler and pool hustler who annually made several trips to Colombia, returning to Florida via shrimp boat with large loads of cocaine. From there, a Californian named Michael Dawson, who had strong connections with the Colombian drug cartel, would fly the coke to his ranch for nationwide distribution.

When the Drug Enforcement Administration's investigation of Dawson's activities heated up, Burns convinced him to move from the coast to Dallas. Not only did the city offer a safer climate, Burns advised, but he also had a top-notch lawyer, Mike Wilson, who Burns insisted had "juice" in the courthouse and friends in legal high places who would alert him when any major drug investigations were begun.

In short order, a word began to spread through the legal community that Wilson was on retainer to two of the biggest cocaine dealers in the city. Many of his former associates in the DA's office expressed surprise that a lawyer of Mike's talents had "sold out" to the get-rich-quick fortune promised by defending drug dealers. Soon rumors ran rampant through the Dallas courthouse that Wilson was "dirty," that he had crossed the line and was involved in illegal dealings with the clients he was representing.

For Dawson, Dallas hardly proved to be the safe haven he had hoped for. In 1986 he was arrested by DEA agents following a high-speed chase. In the car with him at the time of his capture was his young daughter, his prostitute girlfriend, a gun, and $354,000 in cash. He was quickly extradited to California and ordered to stand trial.

Burns, too, was arrested and charged with possession of cocaine with intent to deliver and solicitation of murder for attempting to hire someone to kill the boyfriend of Dawson's estranged wife.

While Wilson was flying back and forth to California, trying desperately to arrange some kind of plea bargain arrangement for Dawson, Burns, out on bail, fled to Brazil.

Meanwhile, the "juice" that his clients thought Wilson possessed failed to materialize. Dallas narcotics agents refused to discuss any reduction of charges. He had no better luck with the DEA and FBI in California. Making a trip to Washington, D.C., he was told by Thomas Kelly, deputy director of the DEA, that there would be no deals for Mike Dawson. In fact, the unofficial word in the offices of the DEA was there would be no deals for any client Wilson represented.

Ultimately, Wilson convinced the angered Dawson to plead guilty to five counts, promising that he would somehow get the authorities to consider some kind of deal in exchange for information. Taking a new approach, he suggested to the authorities that his other client, Burns, not Dawson, was the key figure in the cases. With proper incentive, Wilson said Dawson would roll over on Burns.

In Rio de Janeiro, Burns heard rumors of what his attorney had proposed. Soon, Wilson, tangled in a situation that seemed to offer no exit, began receiving death threats.

And by the summer of 1987, his troubles were compounded by marital problems that had dissolved into a divorce action instituted by Lucy. He was ordered by the courts to make temporary support payments of $12,500 monthly to his wife and three children.

For the once up-and-coming young attorney, life's fast lane had become a rocky, treacherous road.

On July 2, 1987, Wilson was scheduled to appear in federal court with client Dawson for sentencing but failed to show. An irritated judge rescheduled the hearing for July 16. Again Wilson did not appear. Threatening contempt-of-court action against the attorney, U.S. district judge Edward Garcia set yet another hearing date, and on August 13, Wilson finally arrived in California, bringing with him affidavits from doctors that he was suffering from a bleeding peptic ulcer and prostatitis. Those in the courtroom needed only to look at him, gaunt and pale, to believe him.

Dawson was not among those moved by his lawyer's physical condition. Taking the stand, he angrily informed the judge that Wilson had assured him a deal had been made with high-ranking officials in the DEA that would allow him to go free in exchange for running guns to the contras in Nicaragua for the CIA and leading federal authorities to hidden drug labs in Colombia.

Dawson claimed a conflict of interest on Wilson's part since he was also representing co-defendant Burns and insisted that Mike had control of $980,000 worth of his assets. Stating that Wilson had provided him less than thorough representation, Dawson informed the court that he was firing his attorney, wished to withdraw his guilty plea, and demanded a jury trial.

Clearly shaken by his client's outburst, Wilson took the stand and explained that he had tried with no success to negotiate a deal for Dawson. There had never been any discussion of plans for Dawson to work as an agent for the CIA or to help the DEA in locating drug operations in Colombia. Wilson swore that he controlled no assets of his client, pointing out that they would have been subject to seizure by authorities. And since the charges against Burns were based in Texas, he felt no conflict of interest in representing the two men. Dawson's accusations, he added, were nothing more than the railings of a desperate defendant. Federal prosecutors, having already investigated Dawson's claims, agreed.

The judge ruled against Dawson's motion to withdraw his guilty pleas and ultimately sentenced him to seventy-seven years in prison.

In the hall of the federal courthouse, Wilson sat on a bench, sweating profusely, answering questions from newsmen who surrounded him following the hearing. "No matter what happens to Dawson or Burns," he told a reporter from the *Sacramento Bee*, "I'm a dead man. I've been called and threatened on four occasions. I'll spend the rest of my life as a marked man. I've lost my life and my practice. I'm snuffed."

Even when Burns was extradited back to the U.S., tried, convicted, and sentenced to five years in the federal penitentiary, Wilson's paranoia continued. Professionally, he dropped from sight, seldom seen at the courthouse.

Privately, friends began to wonder if he had actually been in as much danger as he indicated. Or was the paranoia the result of something else?

In the minds of some, the question was answered in the winter of 1988 when Mike and a client named Dean Young, who was on probation for cocaine possession, were arrested following a routine traffic stop in the Dallas suburb of Garland. In Mike's red Porsche was a bag containing cocaine residue, and he and his client were briefly jailed.

Though no charges were filed since police could not prove which of the men the cocaine belonged to, word of the incident spread quickly. Even friends and fellow lawyers who had long been giving Wilson the benefit of the doubt became convinced that he had stepped far over the line.

It was, many agreed, only a matter of time before Mike found himself in the kind of trouble that went well beyond expensive divorce proceedings and threats from angry clients.

What few knew was that Dallas DEA authorities, convinced that Wilson was as involved in drug activities as those he represented, had already made him the target of an investigation.

In the spring of 1987, Hollis Burns had introduced Wilson to a Vietnam War veteran named John White, a small-time Dallas drug dealer in need of an attorney. Their relationship had quickly developed beyond that of lawyer-client into a warm friendship. Mike delighted in White's war stories and talent at dominoes; White was also always willing to listen patiently to Mike's growing list of personal woes.

In time, John White became more than a friend and client; he also began supplying the cocaine Wilson had begun experimenting with. At first, he had used it to briefly dull his physical pains. Soon, he found that it also provided at least momentary escapes from the weighty personal and professional problems that were plaguing him.

Before long, however, Wilson was hooked, using the drug daily. Already labeled an addictive personality by those who had treated his history of physical ailments and alcohol abuse, Wilson had been easy prey.

Soon, even casual acquaintances began to take note of the dramatic change in the once friendly and admired attorney. Opposing lawyers who had previously faced a likable but aggressive and well-prepared Wilson in the courtroom found him sullen, disinterested, and generally ineffectual. More than once clients had fired him after he failed to appear for court dates. The tailored suits he wore hung loosely on a once-athletic body that seemed fifty pounds lighter than it had been just a year earlier.

Wilson, most agreed, was hanging on to his once-promising career by a very thin thread. And, if possible, his personal life was in even worse shape. Though he had recently remarried, there were already rumors that things were not going well.

Such was the troubled state of Mike Wilson's affairs when he and Denver McCarty had paid their visit to the home of Joy Aylor.

Keenly aware that his life needed no further complications, Mike had tried to put Joy out of his mind, despite the fact she had begun accompanying Darla on her visits to McCarty, always stopping into Wilson's office to say hello. Learning of his interest in bird hunting, she had quickly offered use of the family's ranch, urging him to stop by and get the key anytime he wished. She was being flirtatious, he knew, but in a way so innocently warm and friendly that it caught him off-balance.

Why would she be interested in him? She had long since decided to keep Doug Mulder as her attorney, so he could offer her no help with her legal problems. Too, he'd recently asked Darla and found that the man he'd seen leaving Joy's house that evening, Jodi Packer, was apparently now separated from his wife and living with Joy.

When Joy phoned to suggest they have lunch sometime, Wilson had told her he didn't think it was a good idea. When she had asked why, he had decided to be truthful.

"Because I might find that I like you too much."

"There's only one way to be sure," she replied.

# 18

LARRY AYLOR SLOWLY replaced the receiver in its cradle and stood silently at the living-room window, looking out onto the cold, darkening Virginia landscape. The lengthy telephone conversation with his son had marked the end of a wonderful Christmas day.

Though Larry had traveled to Dallas just a week earlier to see Chris, he had felt twinges of melancholy throughout the day, wishing his son could be there to share in the pleasures of the holiday.

Their talk, however, had washed away his private sadness. Chris had again spoken of visiting in the summer, perhaps even staying to work alongside his father and learn the homebuilding business. The maturity in the teenager's voice had pleased Larry Aylor.

As he stood at the window, lost in thought, he was unaware that Jan was standing next to him until she gently placed her arm around his waist. "How's Chris?"

"He's fine, except for a bad cold. He'd been planning to go out with some of his buddies later, but he's decided to stay in and go to bed early instead."

Not until the following day did Larry Aylor learn that his son had changed his plans.

For Joy Aylor, the holiday season had been a draining exercise in make-believe good cheer. Her legal problems were seldom out of mind and were compounded by the continued failure of her father's health and what was becoming a suffocating relationship with Jodi. By the time the traditional family meal, complete with labored conversation and strained attempts at making things seem normal, had ended at the Davis house, she was looking for an excuse to get away from the gathering.

She spent a few quiet minutes alone with Henry Davis, kissing him on the cheek as she prepared to leave. "Merry Christmas, Daddy," she whispered as she adjusted his blanket around his shoulders. "I've got to be running."

Henry nodded and smiled, his eyes signaling an understanding that he and his favorite daughter had long shared. If physically able, he, too, would be looking for an excuse to slip away from the gathering, maybe to drive alone down to his beloved ranch and do some bird hunting.

At the doorway, Joy turned and looked back at her ailing father. She stood for several seconds, then smiled. "I love you," she said.

There had actually been no pressing reason for her leaving so early in the day. Jodi, involved in Christmas activities of his own, would not be at her house until later in the evening. For now, Joy simply wanted to get away, to escape the oppressive atmosphere of her parents' home and the hollow ring of the false holiday cheer.

She felt better once she was in her Porsche, driving aimlessly through residential areas and finally onto the all-but-deserted North Central Expressway. As she drove, her thoughts turned to Mike Wilson.

Joy liked him. Talking with him was not like talking with the all-business Mulder. She enjoyed the friendly, understanding tone of his voice. During one of their conversations she had learned that he and his second wife had separated and that he was living alone.

On a whim, she dug into her purse and found the card he had given her. Handwritten on the back of it was his home number. Joy dialed the number on the car phone that Jodi had had installed in her Porsche.

His wife, Wilson explained, had gone to Alabama to spend the holidays with relatives, and his teenage son Clay was staying with him. "We're getting sick of sitting here, staring at each other," he joked as he looked across the room at his son. They would be delighted for her to stop by.

Joy stayed for a couple of hours, joining Wilson and his son in a game of dominoes and light, casual conversation. By the time she rose to leave, her mood had greatly improved. For Wilson, the feelings that he had experienced on that evening when he and Denver McCarty had visited her in her home were reinforced. She fascinated him. Though he knew that she had orchestrated a horrid, brutal murder—one for which she seemed to show not the least outward sign of remorse—Wilson saw, too, a warm, friendly, and beautiful woman.

Only when they walked into the front yard did the conversation turn into an uncomfortable silence. "What's wrong?" Joy asked.

"Since I'm not going to be your attorney," Mike said, "this is none of my business . . ."

"What do you want to know?"

Of all the rumors that had circulated through the courthouse and law offices around Dallas, one had troubled Wilson a great deal, one that suggested the murderer of Rozanne Gailiunas had followed a set of written instructions when he carried out the crime.

"Did you ask that Rozanne Gailiunas's death be carried out in some special way?"

Seemingly unfazed by the point-blank question, Joy smiled. "No. Of course not."

As he stood watching her drive away, waving to him as she left the parking lot, Mike Wilson realized that her all-too-brief visit had been the highlight of his Christmas. Joy Aylor had puzzled him from the first time he had met her. Now, he realized, he wanted to get to know her better.

He also knew that the only smart thing for him to do was make certain he not allow himself to become involved with her.

In just a matter of hours, that resolve—if it truly existed—would be forever dismissed.

The living-room telephone had rung only once before Joy, a light sleeper, had snapped awake to answer it. Restless and weary from the day's activities, she had finally been lulled to sleep by the crackling of the fireplace as she lay beneath a blanket on the couch. It was just after one A.M., and as she listened, the room's darkness—shadowed by the dying glow from the fire—turned cold. As she experienced every parent's worst nightmare, her breathing became difficult.

A friend of Chris's was speaking in short, hurried sentences. Joy was certain the young man was crying. There had been an accident, he said. Chris's car. He gave her a location on the LBJ Freeway. "Hurry. Oh, God, please hurry."

In the background Joy Aylor could hear the whine of ambulances.

She rushed into the bedroom where Jodi was sleeping and shook him awake. "Chris has been in an accident."

Packer raised himself on one elbow and glanced over at the bedside clock. "Those fucking kids," he muttered.

For a second Joy glared at him but said nothing. He was already sleeping again by the time she had hurriedly dressed in a pink jogging suit and tennis shoes and was rushing toward the garage.

Once in the car she dialed Wilson's number. "Mike, my son's been in an accident. I'm on the way there now. Would you go with me?"

"I'll be waiting outside."

As they approached the intersection of the LBJ Freeway and Marsh Lane, the all-but-deserted area took on the appearance of some cruel attempt at imitating the festive Christmas season. Multicolored lights flashed from the tops of police cars and fire trucks, and red flares placed around the perimeter of the accident still spewed their red-orange warnings. Near the guardrail, officers and firemen mingled, blocking the view of a mangled, burned burgundy Corvette. On the opposite side of the freeway, a growing crowd, many of them teenagers, watched the activity in grim silence.

Mike Wilson felt a tightening in his chest as Joy stopped her Porsche next to a Dallas police squad car. The news, he instinctively knew, was not going to be good. "Wait here," he told her. "I'll see what I can find out."

Joy had been alternately calm and hysterical during the short drive from his house. "He wasn't feeling well," she had repeated several times. "He wasn't even going out tonight. Why was he out here?"

"Just stay in the car," Wilson said as he stepped into the chilly night air and zipped his windbreaker. "I'll be back in a minute." She acknowledged him with a shake of her head, then muffled a pained cry with her hand.

As he walked toward a police officer, Wilson glanced in the direction of the teenagers standing nearby. For a brief second his eyes met with those of a young man dressed in jeans and a heavy sweatshirt. At the time Mike had no way of knowing that it was the same boy who had phoned Joy minutes earlier to tell her about the accident. The boy said nothing but slowly shook his head, then stared down at the pavement.

Mike Wilson already had the answer he feared.

The officer studied his notepad as he gave Wilson a brief, monotone description of what had happened. A young man named Raymond Slupecki had been driving the Corvette. The passenger, Chris Aylor, owned the vehicle. According to some of the youngsters whom investigators had spoken with, there had been a drag race in progress. The driver apparently lost control of the car and hit a guardrail and then a car parked on the shoulder of the freeway. The passenger had been thrown from the car on impact, and the car had then burst into flames.

An ambulance, the officer said, had already taken Chris to Parkland Hospital.

As the officer spoke, Joy approached. Hearing that her son was en route to the hospital, she glanced at Mike and turned to hurry back to the car. After a few steps, however, she stopped and turned to the officer. If Chris had gone out, she knew, he would have been with his best friend.

"Where's Raymond?" she asked.

"Ma'am," the officer said, "you should get to the hospital."

Wilson glanced in the direction of the still-smoldering car and saw a paramedic placing an orange blanket over the motionless, charred body that was still in the car.

"We'd better go," Wilson said, gently putting his arm around Joy's shoulder. He wanted to get her back into the car to shield her from the grim task that was being carried out in the front seat of her son's mangled Corvette.

"Would you drive?" Joy asked.

As he wound around the LBJ Freeway and on to Stemmons, Mike Wilson said nothing, trying desperately to sort out the situation he'd been drawn into. He knew what awaited them at the hospital. How would this woman—still a virtual stranger to him—react? And what role would he be expected to play? What he wanted more than anything was to postpone the scene for as long as possible. He wished he could think as clearly as he'd once been able to.

Beside him, Joy called the emergency number of Parkland. It was obvious she was getting few answers. Finally hanging up, she turned to Mike. "They wanted to know if I'm the next of kin."

Wilson's only reply was to press his foot against the accelerator. There was no way, he knew, to delay what awaited them.

They were barely inside the emergency room when a grim-faced doctor, still dressed in his green operating gown, approached.

"Are you Mrs. Aylor?"

"Yes."

"I'm sorry. We did everything we could."

Joy felt her body going limp and grabbed Wilson's arm for support. He gently guided her to a chair. "You'd better sit down."

"I want to see him," Joy said.

"Wait here for a minute." Wilson was surprised at the authority in his voice, that seemingly by rote he was suddenly taking charge of the nightmare.

He approached a nurse who was standing nearby. "Would she like to see him?" she asked as Mike approached.

"How does he look? Is he . . ."

He didn't have to complete the sentence. "He looks okay," the nurse said.

As they walked down the sterile hallway, only the faint squeaking sound of the nurse's rubber-soled shoes broke the silence until Joy spoke. "Where's Raymond?" she again asked Mike, this time in a whispered voice.

"He's dead. He was burned up in the car."

Joy made no reply. Instead, she simply took a deep breath before following the nurse into the room where her dead son lay covered with a bloodstained sheet.

For several minutes Wilson watched as Joy silently patted Chris, as if trying to render some final comfort. She smoothed his matted hair and bent to kiss his bruised forehead. "Well, Son, you've finally gotten yourself into something your momma can't get you out of." As tears blurred her eyes, she continued patting his body in a gentle, rhythmic motion. "I love you, Son. I love you more than anything in the world."

As she spoke, she was oblivious to the bloodstains on her own clothing.

For Mike Wilson it was the most moving, most intimate moment he had ever witnessed, a combined display of tenderness and strength he would never have thought possible. And it occurred to him that he had no right to be a party to it.

Moving over to Joy's side, he told her he would wait outside and assure her privacy.

For the next fifteen minutes he stood outside the door, barring anyone's entry to the room. From inside he could hear Joy's soft voice.

When she emerged, she looked at Wilson for several seconds, saying nothing. Then, as a faint, courageous smile crept across her face, she said, "I told him good-bye."

Before leaving the hospital, Wilson approached the officer who had accompanied Chris's body from the accident scene and asked if there was any property to be picked up.

The officer gave him a manila envelope that included $37, a ring that had been given Chris by his grandmother, a gold chain, and a Rolex watch that had been a graduation gift from Joy. Wilson signed for it and gave it to Joy. "You'll want these things someday," he said.

The trip back to Wilson's house was made in silence. Only when he pulled the Porsche into the driveway did Joy speak. "What happens next?"

"You shouldn't worry about that tonight."

"Will they do an autopsy?"

"Yes."

"Have you ever seen one done?"

The question took Wilson by surprise. It was as if she were making a purposeful effort to add to her grief. "You don't need to be thinking about things like that right now."

"It's something bad, isn't it?"

He only nodded in acknowledgment.

"I've got to make some calls."

A north wind had turned the early-morning hours bitterly cold. Wilson urged her to come inside and use his phone.

In the next few minutes he saw a transformation in Joy Aylor that amazed him. On the phone to her mother and her sister, she was calm and controlled as she spoke of the tragedy that had taken place just hours earlier, suggesting a family meeting to discuss funeral arrangements.

In a sense, the scene was as intimate as that he had witnessed in the hospital, one that provided him his first real insight into the complexities of Joy Aylor. She was, he determined as he listened to her giving instructions over the phone, a woman who could handle anything.

Though he offered to drive her home, she told him that she preferred to make the trip alone.

For some time after she left, Mike Wilson sat in his living room, letting his mind roll back over the emotion-charged sequence of events he'd just been through.

Finally he rose and went into the bedroom where his own son was sleeping soundly. He sat on the edge of the bed and woke Clay, helped him into a sitting position, then hugged him tightly.

Sixteen-year-old Clay Wilson did not understand why his father was crying.

During his career as a lawyer, Mike Wilson had, he thought, encountered every kind of criminal personality imaginable; the stone-cold psychopaths, the evil and perverted, the polished con artists, and the habitual liars. If anything, he felt he had

266

learned to quickly see past the facades worn by so many of those he had prosecuted and defended over the years.

Joy Aylor, however, was different. Nothing in his experience had prepared him for a woman like her. How could someone who he was convinced had planned and ordered two cold-blooded murders be as gentle and tender, strong and at the same time as vulnerable, as he had seen her in that hospital room?

How could someone supposedly so evil and uncaring be thoughtful enough to stop by the home of Raymond's parents, taking food she had prepared, offering consolation and assurance that she blamed neither them nor their son for the tragedy?

It seemed impossible to him that someone so beautiful and charming could be the target of a district attorney determined to see that she received the death penalty for her crimes.

These were the thoughts running through Wilson's frayed mind as he drove toward the home of John White, the client-turned-friend whom he'd agreed to represent back in 1987 after White had been arrested while trying to purchase a kilo of cocaine from an undercover officer. In time, the quiet, hermit-like man who had lived in the same tiny apartment for the past thirteen years had become Wilson's primary cocaine supplier. Now Mike wanted badly to clear his mind of the images from the previous night, to put this woman and her mounting tragedies aside. The white powder, he knew, would provide the escape he so badly needed.

For much of the afternoon the two men sat, playing dominoes, talking, and sharing cocaine. In time, Wilson began to reflect on the tragic death of Chris Aylor, finally describing the poignant scene in the hospital to his friend.

John White listened intently, his bearded face signaling no sign of emotion, his eyes void of compassion. He had gained a reputation as a cold, dispassionate man during his military career and had carried it with him back into civilian life.

Only after Wilson had finished did White look up from the row of dominoes he had been studying.

"Sometimes," he finally said in a slow, measured voice, "things have a way of evening out."

"What do you mean?"

White shrugged. "A life for a life."

The cocaine-induced warmth that Mike Wilson had been feeling was replaced by a sudden cold shiver that swept through his body as he rose to leave.

Upon his return home, the light on Wilson's answering machine was blinking. Rewinding the tape, he listened to the single message: Joy Aylor said she had a problem that she needed to discuss with him as soon as possible. "Please call me," the voice pleaded in a tone that hinted neither of sorrow nor desperation. What Wilson heard instead was anger.

Chris Aylor had loved his grandfather's ranch. Nestled in a beautiful corner of Ellis County where oaks and pecan trees shade the rolling countryside, it was a wonderful place to escape to. From early childhood he had accompanied Henry Davis on visits to the ranch, learning to shoot and hunt the dove and quail that abounded in the area. He had followed along as Davis tended his small herd of cattle, checked fence lines, and talked of his days growing up in a small town nearby. As he grew older and had a car of his own, Chris had often made the trip to Ellis County alone or in the company of friends, enjoying the comforting solitude the countryside afforded.

He had been pleased when his mother told him she was making plans to build a house on the property. They would, she said, go there to live "when all this other mess is over."

It was, he had often told her, his favorite place. When he died, he would like to be buried there.

As she went about the grim task of making funeral arrangements, Joy made preparations to grant her son's request.

In Virginia, Larry Aylor, who had learned of his son's death only after a friend in Dallas had heard the news on television and phoned him, had other plans. After calling Joy, he had telephoned his Dallas attorney, John Barr, demanding that he file a restraining order immediately to block the move to have his son buried on the Davis ranch.

"My life would be in danger anytime I wanted to visit his grave," Aylor yelled into the phone. "I want to be able to visit my son in peace. Tell them I'll agree to his being buried in any cemetery they choose. They can even buy up the plots next to him. But, dammit, I want him buried someplace where I can go see him whenever I want."

For Barr, the request was unlike any other he'd received in his legal career. But, acting on his client's request, he had set the judicial wheels in motion to block Chris's burial, filing a motion for a court order that would prevent removal of the body from the Dallas County morgue.

"They won't release Chris's body," Joy told Wilson. Her ex-husband, she explained, had flown into a rage when she told him of plans to have their son buried on the Davis ranch and was demanding that Chris be buried in a cemetery in Dallas. When she had gone to the medical examiner's office to begin making arrangements for the funeral, she had been told of the restraining order. They could not legally release the body until the site of burial was resolved.

Mike Wilson listened in disbelief. How, he wondered, could two people fight over the body of their only son just hours after he had died such a horrible death? "There's no way you would consider allowing the burial in a cemetery?"

"It has to be on the ranch. If he wants, I'll build Larry a four-lane highway leading to the gravesite and give him his own key to the place. But I have to do what Chris wanted."

Wilson sighed, trying to make some sense of the macabre battle he felt himself being drawn into. "Okay," he finally said, "I'll call John Barr."

In the office of Larry Aylor's attorney, the story of Chris Aylor's death had taken a far more sinister twist. Chris Aylor had supposedly been returning from a late-night trip to the airport when the accident occurred. He had apparently gone there to pick up a package for his mother. Barr, a close friend of many Dallas police officers, said that one of the patrolmen who had been at the accident site had observed something he thought strange. When Joy and Mike arrived, they had walked among the debris of the wreck, as if in search of something.

Though made aware that her son was en route to the hospital, in critical condition, Joy had remained at the crash site for an extraordinary length of time.

The implication was clear: Chris had gone to the airport to pick up a package of dope, and Joy and Mike were hoping to find it before the police did.

Also, Joy had supposedly told an administrator at the funeral home that she would make every effort to see that her ex-husband was not allowed to attend the services.

Barr also thought it suspicious that she seemed in such a hurry to have her son's body removed from the coroner's office. Was she concerned that an autopsy might reveal drugs in Chris's system when the accident occurred?

Morris and Sandy McGowan had spent the Christmas holidays in Florida, and while there, McGowan had come down with a cold that had developed into a full-blown case of flu before his return home two days after Chris Aylor's death. When he telephoned assistant DA Chapman to let him know he was back in town, he learned of the tragedy. "There are some people," Chapman said, "who think the whole thing's very suspicious."

Stunned by the newest twist in the case, McGowan immediately called Ken MacKenzie and Rhonda Bonner and was pleased to learn they had already begun investigating the accident. The officers had conducted interviews with a number of witnesses and gone to the police impound to thoroughly check out the car. It was nothing more, they had agreed, than a terrible accident. Everything was under control, they assured him. "Stay in bed and get well," Bonner urged.

Resting, however, did not come easy. The next call to the McGowan house was from John Barr. Almost frantic, the attorney spoke of Joy's suspicious actions at the crime scene, even intimating that Chris's death might not have been the accident it seemed.

McGowan, puzzled by the discrepancies in the story Bonner and MacKenzie had told and that outlined by Barr, placed a call to the Dallas Police Department and got the name and home number of the patrol officer who had worked the accident.

It was almost eleven P.M. when he reached the patrolman.

Apologizing for calling so late, McGowan repeated the story John Barr had told him about Joy's actions.

"That," the officer responded, "is pure bullshit. She acted like any mother would have under the circumstances. I was the one who talked with her when she arrived. And she didn't stay long. When I told her that her son had been taken to the hospital, she took off. Nothing like you're describing went on. Her lawyer friend was acting like a big shot, asking a lot of questions, but I've seen that before, too."

It was the first McGowan had heard of anyone accompanying Joy. "What was Doug Mulder doing out there?"

"Hell, it wasn't Doug. I know him."

"Then, who was it?"

The patrolman was silent for a few seconds, thinking back on the night of the accident. "A fella named Wilson," he finally replied. ". . . Mike Wilson."

McGowan then dialed Barr's number. "I've done some checking, and I think your fears are unfounded." Before the lawyer could argue his case further, Morris explained that he was sick and going to bed. He told Barr good-night, ending the brief conversation.

As he lay in bed, Morris's mind was again racing, the all-too-brief Christmas respite from the case over. And, he wondered, who in hell was this new person—Mike Wilson—who had suddenly been added to the cast of characters?

Wilson, meanwhile, was unaware of the rumors and suspicions when he placed a call to Barr. Though not close friends, they had been professional acquaintances for years.

"Have you ever met a pair like this?" Barr said as he took Mike's call. "This is a sad, sad situation. These people are just using the death of their son to inflict more injury on each other."

"John, all she wants is to grant her kid's wish to be buried on the family farm. She's not trying to be difficult. Hell, she'll even see to it that Aylor has a private entrance to the place. She'll agree to anything he wants so long as he agrees to the burial site.''

"I'll call Larry and get back to you.''

"John, if nothing else, make him aware that the body needs to be released to the funeral home for embalming as soon as possible. You know as well as I do that decomposition will start pretty quickly, even in that damn cold room.''

Barr was silent for a few seconds. "Yeah, I know,'' he finally said. He, too, had paid his share of visits to the Dallas County morgue. "Let me call Larry and I'll get back to you.''

For the next two days calls were exchanged by Wilson and Barr on an almost hourly basis. Every time Wilson thought the problem was nearing resolution Barr would phone to say that Larry Aylor had changed his mind and wasn't going to budge on the matter.

Finally, late on the second day of discussions, Wilson exploded. "I don't know this guy,'' he told Barr, "and I don't think I want to. But what he's doing is the most disgusting goddamn thing I've ever heard of. This business about the gravesite can be settled later on. But if you don't get him to agree to let that kid's body be embalmed—right away—I'm going to come over to your office and kick the shit out of somebody.''

The following day, the body of Chris Aylor was released to the Sparkman Hillcrest Funeral Home. Unknown to Larry Aylor or his attorney, an autopsy had revealed no evidence of any drugs or alcohol in the young man's system. Neither did they know that Joy Aylor had signed an agreement to donate some of her son's organs to an organ bank.

On a Friday afternoon, a funeral service attended by over four hundred people, many of them friends of Chris's from the Bending Oaks School where he had graduated as class valedictorian, was held.

As Chris's favorite song, "The Wind Beneath My Wings,'' played, several of those present were keenly aware of the family tension that marked the somber occasion. Joy and Larry took seats far apart, neither even acknowledging the other's presence. Many, aware of the ill-feelings between her and Joy, were surprised when Carol Garland arrived late and sat silently in the back of the chapel.

Throughout the service Joy, pale and visibly shaken, focused on the casket where her son lay. Only when she was escorted to the front to lead the procession of mourners viewing the body did she break down. Standing in front of the casket, she looked down at Chris's body for several silent seconds, then burst into tears. She leaned over, lifted her dead son into her arms, and wept until the minister gently escorted her from the chapel.

In the foyer, an announcement was made that there would be no immediate graveside service.

Absent from the crowd was Mike Wilson. Despite a call from Joy, asking that he attend, he had stayed away, still shaken by the events that had followed the accident.

Neither did McGowan attend. Unable to contact anyone at the Davis home, he had telephoned Elizabeth at her shop and asked that she pass on his sympathy to the family and explain why he could not be there. He'd also reached Larry Aylor at the Dallas home of his parents. And while Larry had briefly mentioned the suspicions raised by his lawyer, he had not dwelled on them. Larry's primary concern, it seemed, was the site of his son's burial.

The voice McGowan heard was neither angry nor accusatory, but simply that of a grieving father.

Larry had even tried to contact Joy, he said, to offer help with funeral arrangements, but Jodi Packer had answered the phone and, after a brief, hostile exchange, had hung up on him.

McGowan found himself feeling a new measure of sympathy for Larry as he tried to imagine the aching grief that accompanies the loss of one's only child.

But when he read the front-page story that appeared in the *Dallas Morning News* the following week, McGowan was glad he had stayed away.

A probate hearing had been held before Judge Robert Price, and he ordered that Larry Aylor be named administrator of his son's estate. The judge's ruling also allowed Larry to proceed with burial arrangements after his attorney had argued that the Ellis County ranch was "hostile territory."

Chris Aylor, it was agreed, would finally be buried at Restland Memorial Park in Dallas. On the bronze marker placed at the gravesite, Chris's middle name—Davis—was omitted.

Joy could not make herself enter her son's upstairs room at the Davis house for several days after the funeral. Once a comforting place where she and Chris had talked of his future and listened to music, she feared it would be another aching reminder that he was gone.

Yet she found herself drawn there. In time it became the place where she went to soothe her pain with the fond memories that the room offered. She would sit on the floor in front of Chris's television set, watching videos she had made of her son. In them he mugged for the camera, smiled, and did the silly things of youth. Again, for a brief moment, her son was alive, making her laugh.

She would sit at his study table near the window, surveying the room: the bookshelves, the VCR, the elaborate stereo system. And always her attention would finally focus on a photograph on the wall nearby. In it, her smiling son and several of his friends were at a party shortly before the accident.

It was the picture that made her cry—it and the contents of a small box she had found on the top shelf in his closet.

In it was his gold high school ring, a note from a girlfriend thanking him for a friendship ring—a gift he had purchased on his mother's credit card without her knowledge—and a letter addressed to his mother but never delivered.

He had always been proud that she was his mom, he had written. Not only was she the prettiest mother he knew, but it had made him feel good that she had always made his friends welcome in their home. They all thought she was great and that pleased him a great deal. She had always had time to help him deal with his problems and he appreciated it. Now, he knew, she was going through difficult times of her own, and he wanted to help in any way he could. He ended the letter with: "I love you very much, Mom."

As she sat reading, the telephone near Chris's bed rang.

Suddenly, Joy heard her son's voice on the answering machine: "Hi, this is Chris. I'm in the shower right now . . . but if you'll leave a message, I'll get right back to you."

For several days she considered erasing the message, then decided against it.

# 19

THAT JOY AYLOR had begun to speak of suicide troubled Mike Wilson greatly.

In late January of 1990 she first talked about driving her car into the garage, closing the door, and letting the motor run until carbon monoxide ended her life. She repeatedly asked questions about it: Was it really painless? Did you simply fall into a peaceful sleep and never wake? How long would it take?

The questions, so calmly posed, were as puzzling to Wilson as they were disturbing. Everything about Joy's personality had demonstrated remarkable strength and resolve. Her handling of the indictments and the publicity that followed had amazed him. He had watched as she dealt with her father's stroke without hysterics or self-pity. And the legal battles with her ex-husband had resulted in nothing more than what Mike had judged to be healthy, constructive indignation. Joy, in fact, had told him more than once that her self-image had greatly improved when her divorce from Larry became final. She simply did not strike Wilson as the kind of person who would take her own life.

"For God's sake, why?" he asked one afternoon as Joy sat in his office.

She slowly walked across the room and stared out the window for several seconds before answering. "Losing Chris was the one thing I hadn't prepared myself for. I just don't know how to deal with it."

Wilson rose from behind his desk and put his arms around

her. Suddenly fragile, even tearful, Joy buried her face against his neck and held to him tightly.

"Let me help you," he whispered.

Soon they were meeting regularly for lunches in quiet, out-of-the-way restaurants, taking afternoon drives down to the Davis ranch, slipping away to movies and talking on the phone several times a day.

Joy invented excuses to Jodi so she might accompany Mike on bird-hunting trips to west Texas and to San Antonio when he visited his father, who was seriously ill with cancer. During one weekend escape to Austin, Wilson gave Joy a nostalgic tour of the University of Texas campus and his old fraternity house. She had listened to his happy reflections of college life with great envy, again voicing her regret that she had not continued her education.

In fact, their search for new and exciting things to do together was almost frenzied. One evening, at Joy's request, they had visited the newly opened Cabaret Royale, an upscale "gentlemen's club" that featured a $12 cover charge, gourmet buffet, and topless dancers who entertained the predominately yuppie male clientele. Joy had been fascinated with the beautiful young dancers as they performed seductively to the gentle rhythms of New Age music. Surprised when Mike told her that some of the women earned as much as $1,000 per night, she said, "I could do that, you know. I think it might be fun."

For Wilson, any thought of salvaging his year-old marriage with Mona was lost in his fascination with Joy. His wife, in fact, had learned whom he was seeing and had telephoned Joy late one evening. The heated conversation had ended with Mona asking, "What are you going to do, have him killed, too?"

His life badly frayed, Mike felt he had finally found an escape from his mounting list of problems that was as effective as the cocaine he was using in increasing amounts. A few hours with Joy Aylor, engaging in the kind of courtship generally reserved for giddy teenagers, lifted his spirits greatly. Joy, who had seemed to sense instinctively the burdens he was shouldering, simply refused to allow him to dwell on the negative aspects of his life. She referred to his dark moods as "retreating into the cave'' and seemed always to have a quick remedy to bring him back into the light.

And if Joy's impending court date bothered her, she hid any apprehension well. The only real concern she expressed was about her choice of attorneys. The documentary movie *The Thin Blue Line,* which chronicled the wrongful prosecution and imprisonment of a man named Randall Dale Adams, was receiving a great deal of publicity that troubled her. Adams, convicted of the murder of a Dallas police officer, had spent twelve years in prison before investigations revealed evidence that the prosecution had used perjured testimony and withheld evidence to gain a conviction. Adams had finally been released and exonerated amidst a flood of publicity critical of the Dallas County district attorney's office in general and the prosecutor of the case in particular.

That prosecutor had been Doug Mulder, a former district attorney. On several occasions Joy had asked Wilson if he thought the unfavorable publicity Mulder was receiving might have a negative effect on her case.

Yet when Mike would call her attention to some article on Mulder or her case, she would simply ask, ''Is it bad?'' and if his reply was yes, she would neither read it nor allow him to read it to her. It was as if by ignoring the storm clouds looming in the distance, their threat could be made to vanish.

In fact, Joy had a kind of innocence that Mike found endearing. One evening as they sat watching television in the living room of his aunt, Doris Wilson, she had returned from the movies.

''What did you see?'' Mike asked.

''Oh, it was awful. It was a movie called *Body Heat,* about this terrible woman who has her husband killed and does all these awful . . .'' Doris stopped in midsentence, glanced at Joy, then rolled her eyes in embarrassment before she fled into the kitchen.

Joy's expression, meanwhile, had not changed at all as Mike's aunt described the fictional scenario that so closely paralleled Joy's life.

Only when Doris left Joy a note of apology the following day did the subject of the movie come up again. Joy had taken no offense and could not understand why Mike's aunt had felt such a strong need to apologize.

"Damn," Mike said with obvious admiration, "nothing effects you, does it?"

For Joy, her relationship with Mike was unlike any other she had ever experienced. No man had ever treated her so gently and with such simple kindness, accepting her for who she was. Mike Wilson didn't demand, abuse, or angrily criticize.

In turn, Joy asked nothing more than his company, his warmth, and his engaging sense of humor. She said nothing of his drug habit, never warning of physical or legal dangers, not even suggesting he cut back. Rather, she willingly accompanied him into some of Dallas's most hazardous neighborhoods where he replenished his cocaine supply.

With Mike's help, she had regained strength and laughter, and any thought of suicide was soon reduced to nothing more than a distant memory.

With her attention focused on Wilson, Joy decided to inform Jodi Packer that she had grown disenchanted with his domineering attitude and verbal abuse. She wanted time to herself, she said, and asked him to move from her house as quickly as possible.

That decision earned applause from friends like Darla and Vicki. Neither had ever liked Jodi, repeatedly telling Joy that he was nothing more than a leech attracted to her money. What she needed, they insisted, was someone like Mike, who treated her the way a woman was supposed to be treated.

Wilson, pleased to learn that Jodi was being evicted, was nonetheless surprised when Joy explained the arrangements she had made. Though he could well afford his own place, she had rented Jodi an apartment and purchased new furniture for him. Jodi would also be allowed to keep a key to the family lake house and could use it whenever he wanted. Aware that Mike found her generosity puzzling, Joy only shrugged. "What else could I do? My lawyer has told me to keep him happy."

For Mike, the implication was clear: Jodi Packer obviously knew a great deal about Joy's involvement in the murder of

Rozanne Gailiunas and the attempt on Larry Aylor's life. Mike privately wondered if Packer might have somehow been involved in the plots. Or had Joy, in some moment of weakness, simply confided her crime to him? Whatever the case, Wilson surmised, if Jodi was called as a witness at her trial, his testimony could do a great deal of damage. Like it or not, Wilson determined that Mulder had advised her well.

Unknown to either Mike or Joy, Packer already had strong suspicions about their relationship. In one of Joy's desk drawers he had found credit-card receipts from a hotel and several riverfront restaurants in San Antonio. With a couple of long-distance phone calls he had been able to learn the name of the man who had been accompanying Joy on her trips.

He had, however, waited several weeks after moving out before confronting them.

One evening near midnight, Joy and Wilson were wakened by a pounding on the sliding glass doors that opened into her bedroom. Joy, who had been aware of the noise before Mike, had turned on a bedside lamp and was already sitting up when the intruder, having pried the lock, appeared at the foot of the bed.

Wilson had bolted to a sitting position when he heard Joy cry out. The man was staring down at him, a pointed finger just inches from his face. "I want your ass out of here . . . right now," he yelled.

Trying to shake the tangled cobwebs of sleep and cocaine, Wilson finally managed to focus on the tall, blond figure. "Who the fuck are you?"

Joy placed a calming hand on Wilson's bare shoulder and answered for the jealous intruder. "This is Jodi Packer."

"And I'm telling you to get the hell out of here," Jodi repeated, glaring at Mike.

"Fuck you," Wilson replied, his anger at the intrusion mounting quickly.

Joy, having put on her robe, moved to Packer's side and immediately assumed the role of peacemaker. "Jodi, what are you doing here? What do you want?"

"I need to talk to you." The angry tone had disappeared from his voice, suddenly replaced by quiet pleading.

"About what?"

"I miss you. I want—"

"Jodi," she interrupted, "go home."

Packer's mood made yet another drastic swing as he returned his attention to Wilson. "What the hell's going on? Why is this guy here?"

"Because I want him here," Joy said calmly. "I've told him about us, about how things were, and why I asked you to leave. Jodi, you and I have been through all that, over and over. Do you want to discuss it all again . . . in front of him?"

Packer gave a quick, sarcastic laugh. "You love this guy?"

Joy nodded, then glanced over at Mike. "Yes, I do."

Suddenly, rage flamed in Packer's eyes and he began shouting frantic threats. Maybe, by God, he would have to pay a visit to the district attorney's office. Kevin Chapman would damn sure be interested in some things he could tell him.

Unfazed by the show of temper, Joy laughed. "Do you really think that would be a smart thing to do? Are you going to also tell him that you lied to the grand jury, that you committed perjury?"

As if he had not heard the question, Packer continued his tirade. Perhaps he would give John Barr a call to see if he might be interested in a chat.

Wilson had heard enough. Now on his feet, he walked calmly toward Packer. "You're one sick sonuvabitch."

Jodi stood his ground, staring at Wilson until Joy once again demanded that he leave. Without another word, he turned and quickly disappeared out the bedroom door into the darkness.

Joy slumped on the corner of the bed and looked across the room at Mike. "He scares me," she said.

Though the wild scene had been unsettling to Wilson, Joy's remark disturbed him even more. For a moment he considered demanding some explanation. Where did this discarded lover whom Mulder had insisted she "keep happy" fit into the scheme of things? What dark secret was Jodi holding over her?

Instead, Mike only suggested they return to bed.

As he lay in the darkness, listening to the rhythmic breathing that soon resumed next to him, Wilson came to a decision. If his presence in Joy's bed had enraged Packer enough to break in, even more violent encounters were not only possible but likely. For Joy's sake, he would do whatever necessary to avoid any such future confrontations.

It would, he decided, be the last night he would spend at Joy's home.

In mid-February 1990, Mike traveled to Lubbock with fellow attorney Brett Stalcup to defend a couple who had been indicted for the sale and distribution of anabolic steroids. Thirty-year-old John Hoffman, a graduate of SMU's Perkins Seminary, and his wife, Betsy, had long been active in bodybuilding circles, first as competitors, then as trainers. Ultimately, they had expanded their activities into the statewide sale of steroids to bodybuilders and power lifters.

When arrested, Hoffman, whose wife was being represented by Stalcup, had sought out Mike Wilson.

Awaiting the flight to Lubbock, where his client faced charges, Stalcup had not seen Wilson for some time and was surprised at Mike's physical appearance when he arrived at the Southwest Airlines terminal. He had aged dramatically and his face was drawn. Dark circles rimmed Mike's eyes.

Stalcup was also surprised that an attractive blonde, neatly dressed in a tailored suit, was accompanying Wilson on the trip.

"Brett," Mike said, "I'd like for you to meet a friend of mine. This is Joy Aylor."

It took a second for the name to register, but when Joy left to buy a magazine at the airport newsstand, Stalcup whispered to Mike, "Is that the woman who . . ."

Wilson nodded. "That's her."

Stalcup shook his head and smiled. "Jesus, you really know how to pick 'em."

In Lubbock, Stalcup first sensed Wilson might be having physical troubles when he had difficulty getting Mike up the following morning to make it to court on time. Only after repeated phone calls to Wilson's room had he finally appeared in the hotel lobby, looking even worse than he had the day before. Arriving late, the lawyers had been severely reprimanded by the judge, and Stalcup was relieved when, after an hour of in-chambers discussion, a plea bargain was struck, eliminating the need for a trial. Wilson, he had decided, was in no shape to argue the case.

As they flew back to Dallas that afternoon, Brett found himself watching Wilson closely. Restless and bursting with nervous energy, Mike was constantly up and down during the hour-long flight, repeatedly asking the stewardess for water.

Long before the plane set down at Love Field, Stalcup had concluded that the rumors circulating through the Dallas County Courthouse about Wilson were probably true. He would bet his next big retainer that the guy was on drugs.

Just before they landed, Hoffman, still free until the formal sentencing, approached Mike. He had a friend in Houston, he said, who was in trouble and unhappy with his lawyers. Would Mike be interested in talking with him?

"Tell him to come see me."

Mark Northcutt, the twenty-nine-year-old son of a Houston junior-high science teacher, was well known in Texas body-building circles. For years he had worked diligently to sculpt his body to a championship level, going so far as to undergo surgery for calf implants to improve the shape of his legs. Still, he had enjoyed only minimal success during his six years in the competitive arena and was ultimately banned from competition when he had tested positive for steroids.

Northcutt's reputation, then, was built not on athletic accomplishment but, rather, the fact he could supply large amounts of steroids and cocaine for an ever-growing list of clients who liked the cut-rate prices he charged. While most cocaine dealers were demanding as much as $1,000 per ounce, Northcutt rarely charged more than $700. His price for a kilo was considered a bargain at $18,000. His business had grown to a point where he was distributing as much as 25 kilos of cocaine weekly and was the overseer of a profitable lab where the synthetic drug Ecstasy was manufactured.

While attending Southwest Texas State University in San Marcos, majoring in criminal justice studies, Northcutt was first arrested and charged with the sale and distribution of steroids. Then, in September of 1989, his legal problems had been compounded considerably when Houston DEA agents arrested him and charged him with possession of twenty-five kilos of cocaine.

The handsome, enterprising college student, who drove a white Porsche, owned a condo in Houston, and rented a fashionable home in San Marcos, was suddenly looking at a long stay in the federal penitentiary—until the DEA offered an alternative.

If Northcutt would operate as a confidential informant, helping to successfully make cases on fellow drug dealers, a deal whereby he would receive a five-year probated sentence for the cocaine charge might be arranged. And if he performed his role exceptionally well, the state charges pending against him in San Marcos for possession and sale of steroids would be dropped. The underlying message was clear: if he harbored any hope of getting himself out of trouble, he needed to produce big results.

The desperate Northcutt eagerly seized the opportunity.

He had, in fact, already helped make cases against a half dozen dealers by the time he traveled to Dallas and, in the company of John Hoffman, paid a visit to Mike Wilson's office.

The story Northcutt told was convincing. He candidly admitted his guilt, pointing out that he had initially hired a young attorney, an old college buddy, to represent him. His friend, who had been practicing law only three years, had soon found it necessary to call another, more experienced lawyer in on the case. Ultimately, Northcutt said, he had paid out $100,000 in legal fees but had seen few, if any, results. Trial dates in both San Marcos and Houston were fast approaching, and he had no indication that any plan to beat the charges had been set in motion. In his frantic search for a new lawyer with experience in such matters, he had contacted several of his drug-dealing friends in Dallas, including Hoffman.

"Everyone tells me you're the best around," Northcutt said.

Mike arranged a second meeting for the following week. Scheduled to visit a potential client in the state prison in Huntsville, he could easily stop off in Houston.

As Wilson entered the fourth-floor room in the Houston Hol-

iday Inn shortly before midnight on February 27, he had no idea
that Northcutt had spent much of the afternoon at the Houston
DEA office, being fitted with a body mike and rehearsed by Special Agent Billy Joe Mundy on how to discuss payment of his
legal fees with his prospective new attorney. Nor did Wilson
have any way of knowing that two agents were stationed in the
parking lot, waiting to monitor their conversation.

Wilson listened as Northcutt once more outlined his legal
problems, his frustration with the work of his attorneys, and the
fact that none of his once-regular customers would respond to
his calls. He was, he admitted, painfully short of cash.

"Counting what I've already paid out to my lawyers and what
the government has seized—the condo, my car, bank account—
I'm out something like five hundred thousand dollars," Northcutt explained. "So, I don't have anything liquid, really. What
I do have is 'product' that's stored in a mini-warehouse.

"I've got twenty-one kilos that I haven't touched. I paid
fourteen grand apiece for them, so I've got two hundred and
ninety-four thousand dollars tied up in the deal."

Wilson, aware that Northcutt was talking about cocaine, became restless and paced about the motel room as he tried to
move the conversation in another direction. "Have you got any
cash at all? Mark, I'm willing to work with you as much as I'm
financially able to do, but I have to know what you can come
up with. See, most of us operate on a cash basis.

"If you're waiting for me to tell you how much I would
charge you, I honestly don't know at this point. You told me in
Dallas that you wanted someone who would get on this thing
and spend one hundred percent of his time on it. That's a big
statement. But if that's what you really want, let's strike a deal,
you get some cash up, and let me go to work.

"You don't want to go to jail, and what I do is keep people
out of jail."

Northcutt, eager to return the discussion to the warehoused
cocaine, tried another tactic. Could Wilson, obviously on a
first-name basis with a number of well-financed dealers, put
him in contact with potential clients? If he could move the
dope, he would have the cash to pay him.

"I'm really hinky about that sort of thing," Wilson replied. "It gets into the area of conspiracy, you know."

"Yeah, I know."

Wilson, like the young man with whom he was talking, was fast becoming concerned that the lifesaver deal was slipping away. "Now, I'm not saying I can't do it and not saying I won't do it, I'm just saying that it could be a problem. Let me get on back to Dallas and think a little about this."

He suggested that Northcutt give him a call the following week.

In the office of the Houston Drug Enforcement Administration, Mundy listened to the tape that Northcutt had turned over to them. It was not what he had hoped for. Mike Wilson had nibbled, but he had stopped far short of taking the bait.

During the next two weeks, Mundy and his fellow agents heard over a dozen taped conversations in which Northcutt continued to press the issue of the cocaine and Wilson still talked of the need for cash. Frustrated, the agents were beginning to have their doubts about the possible success of the operation. Concern mounted over whether Northcutt was, in fact, actually sharp enough to play his role convincingly. Or maybe Wilson was just too smart to be lured into such dangerous waters.

Still, the negotiations continued. And while the federal authorities were generally disappointed by the information the tapes were providing, Northcutt's recounting of an unrecorded conversation that he said had taken place in Wilson's office renewed their optimism.

According to Northcutt, both men had first opened their shirts to prove they were not wearing wires before Wilson had boastfully portrayed himself as a man on friendly terms with Colombian drug kingpins, who earned at least part of his $300,000–$400,000 annual income by selling drugs to clients, provided drug-dealing clients with mug shots of local DEA agents for their protection, and was well versed in extradition laws and ways to flee the country to avoid prosecution.

"He told me that he'd recently been the guest of Fabio Ochoa, the big-shot Colombian drug dealer, spending time on his yacht off the Florida coast," Northcutt relayed. "He talked about the money he was making, selling drugs. And he showed me this book that listed all the extradition treaties between the U.S. and other countries. He bragged about helping some guy who was under indictment escape to Brazil. He told me he knew where he could sell a kilo of coke in Dallas for twenty thousand dollars and said that he had moved a lot of Ecstasy for some guy and showed him how to launder the money."

Most important was Northcutt's insistence that Wilson had, during the conversation, finally agreed to accept the cocaine in lieu of money.

"How much?" the DEA officer asked.

"All of it. Eleven kilos to represent me on the San Marcos case and ten for the Houston case."

The portrait being painted by the eager informant was that of a lawyer every bit as dirty as those he represented. Northcutt, they were convinced, was finally on the verge of coming through with big results.

It was time, then, to shift to a higher gear.

On the afternoon of Thursday, March 15, 1990, Mike and Joy checked into the Park Suites Hotel on North Central Expressway, planning to spend a long, private weekend together, isolated from their respective legal problems. Joy had become increasingly anxious about an upcoming hearing in which she would appear before the probate judge to request that Larry be removed as administrator of her late son's estate. Mike, meanwhile, wanted to escape the fact that Mona had, just that morning, filed divorce papers against him.

Bingeing on cocaine, Wilson had slept little, pacing the suite constantly while Joy read and watched TV. He didn't leave the room until Sunday, when, after receiving a call from Northcutt, he dressed and drove Joy's Porsche to his Woodside Street office.

From his drug-induced haze had finally come a desperate plan. He would tell Northcutt that he would represent him in exchange for $100,000, which the client could pay out with money he could no doubt eventually earn from the sale of the warehoused drugs. Additionally, Mike would accept one kilo of

Northcutt's "product." The latter, he had decided, would afford him the opportunity to clear the $15,000 debt he owed John White for the cocaine he'd recently been supplying him on credit.

During the meeting, Northcutt agreed to go back to Houston and gather whatever cash he could, pick up the kilo of coke, and return to Dallas to sign a contract with his new lawyer.

On a Tuesday evening, Wilson and Northcutt met again in Wilson's office. Mike had drawn up a contract that stated that his client was to pay regular installments of $25,000 on the amount he was being charged for representation.

"I didn't have time to raise any cash," Northcutt said.

Disappointed, Wilson nonetheless altered the contract to indicate that the first payment would not be due until April first and assured Northcutt that even though no money had yet changed hands the contract would serve as proof that he was now officially representing him. "I guess we'll just have to be a little flexible," Mike said.

Northcutt then gave Wilson a key. "I made it real convenient for you. It's not far from here, at the Holiday Inn on North Central Expressway. Room nine oh nine. You come off the elevator, look to your right, and there it is.

"I think you're going to be very happy with what you find. It's called Royal, solid white. Right up there with the Reyna and Centavo. Ninety percent, at least."

"Sounds fine. When are you going back?"

"As soon as possible. But, I'd like to get the suitcase back before I leave. It's worth a thousand dollars."

For some time after Northcutt left, Mike sat in his office, feet on his desk, staring at the motel key that he slowly turned in his hand. He was sweating profusely but did not bother to turn on the air conditioner. Looking toward the ceiling, he breathed deeply, then exhaled a long sigh. "What the fuck am I doing?" he said, then dialed John White's number.

"I've got to pick up some money," Mike explained, "and I'd like someone to watch my back. Can you meet me in the parking lot of the Holiday Inn on North Central and Meadow?"

White replied that he had nothing better to do.

*  *  *

Earlier in the day, Dallas federal agent Rick Smith, alerted by the Houston DEA, had spent several hours making careful preparations for Wilson's arrival. He had rented two adjoining rooms at the Holiday Inn, checked the twenty-one kilos of cocaine from the DEA property room, put them in a Halliburton suitcase, and placed it in room 909. Additionally, he had installed a small camera with a wide-angle lens and a recorder in a lamp located on the dresser near the television set.

Next door, in room 911, which would serve as the command post, a final planning meeting was held and surveillance equipment was set up and thoroughly tested.

Peter Gronnebik, a short, balding agent with years of surveillance experience, was stationed in the motel parking lot, instructed to radio the ninth floor as soon as the attorney was sighted.

At 8 P.M. the red Porsche pulled into a space near the rear entrance to the motel. Almost immediately, a white Volkswagen, driven by a woman, pulled up alongside and John White got out.

Inside, Smith and fellow agents Tom Estep, Mike Holloway, and Mark Juvrrud were puzzled by the radioed news that Wilson was apparently not alone.

"I don't have a clue who the other guy is," Smith heard Gronnebik report, "but he's definitely with our boy. They were talking like asshole buddies when they went into the building. You should have company any second now."

The agents' attention was fixed to the small TV monitor as Wilson and White cautiously entered the adjoining room. Mike immediately dimmed the lights as White moved to close the drapes on the window, then turned on the television and turned up the volume to drown out conversation.

The agents watched in silent fascination as Wilson, a cigarette dangling from his mouth, looked behind a framed picture, then saw White stand on the bed to cover the overhead smoke alarm with a towel. When he stepped off the bed, White unbuttoned his pants and stood spread-legged for a moment as he calmly readjusted his shirt.

These guys, Smith thought nervously to himself, are no amateurs. He was relieved when neither man went near the table lamp in their search for bugging devices.

Finally, White briefly sipped from the soft drink can he was carrying, then approached the suitcase, lifting it as if to test its heft. He then placed it on the bed and opened it. Wilson watched in silent surprise as his companion counted the twenty-one brown packages it contained.

Neither spoke as White hurriedly replaced the cocaine in the suitcase and returned it to its spot on the floor near one of the single beds.

"Mike," White said in an urgent tone, "let's get the fuck out of here. Right now."

Seconds later the men left the room. Wilson made certain the room was locked, placed a plastic DO NOT DISTURB sign on the door, and walked hurriedly to the elevator where White had already pushed the down button.

In the parking lot, agents watched through binoculars as the two men argued briefly, White cursing Wilson for involving him before getting into the Volkswagen and instructing his female companion to drive away.

Wilson soon followed, his mind racing. Things had not felt right from the moment he had stepped into the room. Why in hell had Northcutt left all the cocaine there? Did he think that once Mike had seen it he would eagerly take the entire contents of the suitcase and forget their repeated discussions of cash payments? Or was it some kind of setup?

Cursing as he steered Joy's car from the parking lot and into the traffic of North Central Expressway, Mike made a concerted effort to put all thoughts of the past few minutes from his mind. What he planned to do was get back to the Park Suites as quickly as possible, back to Joy and his own supply of cocaine, back to what had come to fit his distorted definition of safety.

There was an ironic twist to the events of the evening which had gone undetected by either Wilson or the federal agents.

Having arrived in Dallas from Virginia just hours earlier, Larry Aylor was stretched on the bed in a third-floor room of the Holiday Inn, watching TV, unaware of the scenario being played out six floors above as he anticipated the probate hearing he was scheduled to attend the following day.

Conveniently located between the home of his parents and the downtown office of John Barr, Aylor had begun staying there regularly on trips back to Dallas. Increasingly paranoid and convinced that his ex-wife monitored his movements when he was in town, Aylor had felt reasonably comfortable that the modest hotel, located on the access road of one of the city's busiest thoroughfares, was not a place where she, nor anyone hired by her, might think to look for him.

Meanwhile, on the ninth floor of the Holiday Inn, Smith and his fellow agents made little attempt to hide their disappointment. "The guy with him got spooked," Smith observed.

The question thus became whether the deal had soured completely or if, perhaps, the DO NOT DISTURB sign Wilson had hung on the door was a message that he would eventually return. Discussing their next move, the agents decided that Northcutt should place a call to Wilson's hotel room. "Tell him you're wanting to pick up the suitcase so you can get back to Houston," he was told. "See what the hell he has to say."

Shortly before midnight, Joy, already in bed, answered the phone and called out to Mike. He had been sitting silently in the living-room area of the suite since his return, sipping from a glass of ice water laced with a powerful dose of cocaine.

"Mike, look, I'm sorry to call so late," Northcutt said, masking his nervousness with a cheerful voice, "but I was thinking about heading on back to Houston and wanted to know when I can get the suitcase from you."

Wilson, still mentally wrestling with the scene he'd walked into earlier in the evening, made no mention of the twenty-one kilos, nor did he tell his caller that the cocaine remained in the room. His voice was terse, unfriendly: "In the morning, probably around ten-thirty. Sound okay?"

"Okay."

Wilson returned the phone to the coffee table, mixed more cocaine into his glass, and slumped back in the oversize chair to prepare himself for another sleepless night.

Already, he had reached a fatal decision about what he was going to do.

The following morning Mike had already showered and was dressed casually in jeans and pullover shirt when Joy woke in an uncharacteristic foul mood. Scheduled to appear in probate court later in the morning, she was clearly dreading it. Mike tried with little success to cheer her, then said that he had to attend a breakfast meeting with a potential client.

Joy told him to drive the Porsche. She would tidy up the room, check out, and take a cab to her attorney's office.

Though Wilson did, in fact, have an appointment with a client who had been charged with a misdemeanor, he decided against keeping it and drove directly to John White's house.

They sat at his kitchen table, drinking coffee, discussing the previous evening's events for some time. Wilson was pleased to see that his friend's anger had subsided.

"You're not going back over there, are you?" White finally asked.

Wilson's refusal to reply provided a loud answer.

An hour later he entered room 909, carrying with him an empty canvas gym bag. Moving directly to the aluminum suitcase still positioned by the bed, he opened it and hurriedly began removing the hard brown packages, placing them in the bag.

In the next room, Rick Smith, his eyes again fixed on the surveillance monitor, silently counted the packages being taken from the suitcase: . . . *eight . . . nine . . . ten . . . eleven.*

Seconds later, as Wilson stepped into the hallway, he was looking squarely into the eyes of Smith, gun drawn, pointed toward him. "Put the goddamn bag down," the agent commanded, "and get on the floor. You're under arrest for violation of federal drug laws."

The next few seconds flashed in dreamlike fashion for Wilson. He felt his arms being jerked behind him and the cold steel of handcuffs locking around his wrists. Someone went through his pockets, removing his billfold and his pocket watch. Lifted to his feet, he was then hurriedly escorted back into room 909.

Sitting on the edge of the bed, sweating profusely, his body trembling, he looked up at DEA agent Bill Bryant, a man he'd known since his days as a prosecutor. No look of satisfaction was on Bryant's rugged face, no smile of victory. "I was beginning to wonder," he said, "if we were going to be able to arrest you before you killed yourself. God, Mike, you really fucked it up. Why?"

Wilson fought back tears as he stared at the floor. Finally, he lifted his head and looked squarely at the agent. "Bill," he said softly, "cocaine will turn a good person into trash faster than anything in the world."

As he spoke, a new flurry of activity erupted in the hallway. John White had been arrested as he stepped from the elevator, carrying with him a small, empty briefcase.

Though the door was shut, Wilson instinctively knew that it was his friend and shook his head.

Two miles to the north, at the entrance to the Park Suites, DEA agents who had followed Wilson there the night before stopped Joy as she was preparing to get into a cab. Showing their badges, they asked that she accompany them back to the suite where she and Wilson had been staying.

The search was fruitless. Despite the fact the hotel maid had not yet made it to that end of the floor, the agents were surprised to find that suite had been cleaned spotless.

They also found it unusual that Joy registered little, if any, concern when they explained that her Porsche had been confiscated and would be held as evidence.

Her only response was to ask if Mike was okay.

"Quite honestly, ma'am," one of the agents replied, "Mr. Wilson is in a world of trouble."


The following day, as soon as he read the *Dallas Morning News* report of Mike Wilson's arrest, Jodi Packer telephoned Frances Davis. He made no attempt to mask his delight in the stunning turn of events. Now, he told Frances, maybe Joy would see the guy for what he really was. She'd made a big mistake getting involved with Wilson. Probably Mike had been using Joy's money to finance his drug deals. Packer just hoped that she had not become a cocaine addict herself.

Frances, confused and distraught, had found Wilson likable

from the first time he'd accompanied Joy to her home. She thought back to his concern when Joy had repeatedly demanded to see the autopsy report that had been written following Chris's death; how Mike had quietly managed to secure a copy and read it first to make sure it contained no information that would deal her daughter added grief. Joy had worried over what the toxicology tests might reveal, fearing that drinking—something she had so often warned Chris against—might have played a role in his death. Frances had sensed that it pleased Mike a great deal to be able to report to Joy that neither alcohol nor drugs had been found in her son's system.

The Mike Wilson Frances had known, then, was a warm, kind man, not a drug user or dealer who would lure her daughter into even deeper trouble.

Still, she could not help but wonder about the accusations Packer was making. She liked him, too, and had continued to make him welcome in her home, letting him use the family lake house even after he and Joy had split up. Obviously, she felt, Jodi was still very much in love with her daughter and genuinely concerned for her well-being.

The lengthy interrogation Joy had undergone from the DEA officers who confronted her at the hotel the previous day had resulted in her missing the scheduled probate hearing. In her absence, the judge had ruled that Larry Aylor would remain as conservator of Chris's estate.

Weary and despondent, she had gone to bed early. Shortly after ten P.M. she felt a hand on her shoulder, shaking her awake. Seated beside her on the edge of the bed was the dark frame of Jodi.

At first he spoke in a quiet, gentle voice filled with concern. He was sorry she had been involved in Wilson's troubles and for the unfairness of the probate judge's ruling. He wanted to help in any way he could, he told her. He wanted to come back, to be with her. She needed him. They needed each other.

When he launched into his criticisms of Wilson, reiterating the observations he'd made to Frances earlier in the day, the conversation went out of control.

Soon, Joy was screaming, angry at his bold intrusion, demanding that he leave her house. "I've told you, I don't want you around here anymore. Just get out of here . . . and don't come back."

For a moment, Jodi stared dispassionately at her, then bent to one knee and reached beneath the bed where he knew she kept a loaded .20-gauge shotgun. Pulling it from its hiding place, he placed the barrel against her head.

"You're not through with me, goddammit, not by a helluva long shot."

With that he pitched the gun on the end of the bed, laughed, and walked from the bedroom.

Joy was still shaking as she heard the front door close.

Sleep eluded her for the remainder of the night as she mentally replayed the bizarre encounter. She could still feel the cold barrel against the side of her head and hear the ringing sound of Packer's departing laughter. She badly wanted it to be a dream from which she would awake, a nightmare she could dismiss.

Pacing aimlessly through the darkened house, she thought back on Doug Mulder's demand—"Keep Jodi happy"—and her fears turned again to anger. By the first gray hint of daylight she had come to two conclusions: money was the only thing that would make Jodi Packer happy. And, too, she was certain she would be seeing him again soon.

Mike, arraigned and freed on a personal recognizance bond, was in Joy's living room the following evening when Packer returned. Ignoring Wilson, Jodi launched into another plea to be allowed to move back in. Joy, who had not mentioned the previous evening's argument to Wilson, was clearly uncomfortable but stood her ground. She would, she told Packer, continue to pay rent on his apartment and he was welcome to use the family lake house anytime he chose. But, no, she did not want him back in her home. That part of their relationship was over.

Jodi could not accept that arrangement. Once more he turned angry and vengeful, at both Joy and Wilson. Again, he began to threaten. He knew Wilson's lawyer, he said, and would go to him with information that would no doubt convince him to withdraw from the case. "I've got friends in the DEA who would love to hear what I know," he said, looking across the room at Mike. He would visit the district attorney's office and talk with Kevin Chapman and tell him, among other things, that Joy had financed Wilson's drug dealings.

Joy, suddenly calm as she stood in front of the fireplace, looked on silently as Packer continued ranting. Finally, when he had finished, she posed the question she'd been planning to ask since his arrival: "Okay, Jodi, what's the bottom line? What's it going to take?"

Wilson sat staring at Joy, surprised at the control in her voice, puzzled by her question.

Packer leaned back on the couch, crossed his legs, and smiled as if already relishing the victory he'd come to win.

"For two hundred thousand dollars I'll just go away."

Wilson, suddenly enraged, did not wait for Joy's reply. Instead, he lunged across the room, grabbed Packer by the shoulders, and lifted the larger man into a standing position. "You miserable, sorry cocksucker," he yelled as he began shoving Jodi toward the front door. "Get the fuck out of here."

Stunned by the attack, Jodi finally managed to pull himself from Wilson's grasp as they neared the door. Mike quickly pressed an open hand against Packer's chest and shoved him onto the front porch. Then, moving his face close to Jodi's, he said, "If you ever . . . I mean ever . . . do anything to hurt her, I swear to God I'll find your sorry ass and I'll kill you."

For some time after Packer had gone, Mike and Joy sat in the living room, both silently rehashing what had happened. Though he said nothing, Wilson came to the realization that Joy had known exactly what button to push with her former lover. Her friends had been right: greed, not love or concern, was what motivated Jodi Packer.

In time, Joy began to laugh quietly, as if enjoying some private joke.

"What?" Mike asked.

"I was just wondering. What's the worst thing one man can call another?"

The question surprised Wilson. "Why?"

"I just wondered."

Now, for the first time in days, Wilson was also smiling. "A miserable cocksucker, I guess."

"That's what I thought," Joy said, a look of genuine satisfaction spreading across her face.

# 20

---

SINCE EARLY IN March, Kevin Chapman had been monitoring Joy's financial activities closely, following a paper trail that caused him great concern. Though unaware that she was selling off jewelry, pieces of furniture, and dishes, and giving many of her clothes to sister Liz, the alert assistant DA knew she was gathering cash.

For weeks, Joy had been transferring funds from various bank accounts to others, then, after a few days, making cash withdrawals. On several occasions, Chapman had noted, her cousin, Brad Davis, had helped with the moving of the money. The pattern had become predictable. Each transfer was just less than $10,000, the smallest amount that federal law required bank administrators to report.

By tracking the banks' cash-transfer reports, Chapman estimated that she had already accumulated well over $200,000 by mid-April.

"She's getting ready to run," he told Lieutenant McGowan.

Throughout the weeks of frantic transferring of funds and cash withdrawals, Joy had made a point of not discussing the purpose of the activity. Wilson instinctively knew, just as he had that first time he met Joy, that she had no intention of staying in Dallas to stand trial. With only days remaining before jury selection was to get under way, he was sure that she would soon be leaving. Yet they had never seriously talked about it, had never made even the most general plans for her escape. It was as if they had independently decided to avoid the subject that was obviously on both their minds.

The only question Wilson wrestled with was whether he would accompany her.

Brad, meanwhile, was still innocently certain that Joy was gathering the cash to pay her mounting legal fees. He had long since made up his mind that the idea of his cousin's doing the things he'd read about in the newspapers was absurd. The whole thing, he had decided, was a product of Larry Aylor's twisted imagination. Brad, in fact, had privately determined that Larry probably had far more to do with Rozanne Gailiunas's death than Joy.

Though he had never actually confronted her on the subject, someone as kind and gentle as Joy Aylor could not have been party to any kind of murder plot. Brad was anxious for the trial to be over and done with so that his cousin could be cleared of the charges.

Early on the morning of Friday, May 4, 1990, Joy received a call from Carol Cloud, a paralegal in Doug Mulder's office, with the message that yet another pretrial hearing had been scheduled for the following Monday.

Joy briefly expressed her irritation at the prospect of an additional trip to the courthouse, but told Carol to assure Mulder that she would be there. Hanging up, she immediately dialed Wilson's number.

"I don't like the way it sounds," Mike said. "Did she mention what the hearing was about? Anything about revocation of bond?"

"What's that?"

"That, darlin', is when they yank your pretty ass up and toss it in jail and don't let you go home. No more freedom." Though he didn't mention it, he felt sure that Joy's recent flurry of financial activity had been monitored, and the authorities were now concerned that she was accumulating money to leave town. "Get in touch with Doug and ask him what he knows about it."

"He's not in his office."

"Then find him," Mike said, a firm edge to his voice. "Do it right now. It's important."

Shortly, Joy's urgent message reached Doug Mulder on the front nine of the golf course, and he drove immediately to the clubhouse to return her call. No, he said, he had not yet learned the purpose of the hearing but would do some checking.

"Is it possible," Joy asked, "that it could have something to do with revoking my bond?"

Mulder was silent for several seconds. The thought hadn't occurred to him, but it made sense. As far as he knew, all pretrial motions had been filed by both the prosecution and defense, clearing the way for the selection of a jury to get under way on the fourteenth. Why else would another hearing be set so suddenly, so close to the beginning of the trial?

"Joy," he finally replied, "it could be."

"Well, I guess we'll know soon enough," she said in a resigned tone, then apologized for interrupting his golf game before hanging up.

Even as she spoke with Mulder, Mike Wilson was on his way over to talk with her. The subject could no longer be avoided, he had decided. If she was to make a run for it—if they were going to try to get out of the country—it had to be right away. If her bond was revoked, the judge would order that she be immediately taken into custody and escorted to county jail where she would remain through the duration of her trial.

Wilson would not have to explain any of this to Joy. When he arrived, she was already making preparations to leave. "We've got to go," she said. "Now. Today."

"How long will it take you to get ready?"

"Not long. Where are we going?"

"You know this is crazy, don't you?"

"Why?"

"Unless I'm wrong," Wilson said, "they've been watching both of us for quite some time. It will be a miracle if we get as far as the city limits."

"Are you willing to give it a try?"

Wilson laughed and shrugged his shoulders. "At this point, I don't have a damn thing to lose." Then he pulled her into his arms and hugged her. "If this is what you really want to do, I'll do whatever I can to help you."

"It's the only thing I can do."

"Well, then, let's get busy."

He was not surprised to find that she was several steps ahead of him. Joy had begun making a mental list of things that would have to be done before they could leave; she had already begun packing and had gone through a collection of personal papers and was methodically burning them in the fireplace when he arrived.

"I don't want to use mother's car," she said, "and yours is too small, so we'll rent one." She didn't mention that she planned to do so using a credit card that she'd taken from Jodi Packer's wallet during a recent visit to his apartment.

Wilson was relieved that Frances Davis's Cadillac, which Joy had been driving since her Porsche was impounded when he was arrested, would not serve as their getaway vehicle.

He sat on the arm of the sofa, listening and watching as Joy paced back and forth through the room, her energy almost electric as she talked about things she would need to do before they would be ready to leave. He found himself mesmerized by a calmness in her voice that suggested she was planning a weekend vacation instead of a desperate run from the law.

She was speaking more to herself than him: "It won't take me long to finish packing . . . get the money . . . some groceries to take with us . . . rent the car . . . go by Neiman's."

"Neiman's?" he asked, making no attempt to hide the incredulous look on his face.

"Well, I've got a six-hundred-dollar credit there," Joy casually explained, "and since we won't be coming back, I thought I'd buy this purse that I saw the other day."

Wilson rolled his eyes. "Jesus, Joy." It occurred to him to point out that desperate criminals on the run did not do things like stop by Neiman-Marcus to buy a fucking new purse for the trip, but he decided against it.

"We need to go over and talk to Brad," she said.

En route to the Davis town house a fuzzy plan finally began to take shape. They had agreed that any kind of commercial travel—plane, bus, or train—was out since they would probably be picked up even before they could purchase a ticket. And so the how of their escape was set. They would drive. But to where?

Despite her research of various countries abroad, Joy admitted that she had never seriously considered any place but Mexico. Mike insisted that odds were good the police would expect them to go there, taking the shortest geographic route to a U.S. border. If they headed south out of Dallas, they weren't likely to get as far as Waxahachie. They would, he said, drive north. Once they put some distance between them and Dallas, they could concern themselves with more long-range plans. They could go on into Canada or double back through Arizona and enter Mexico by way of Nogales.

"Okay, fine," Joy agreed, "we head north."

What Mike Wilson avoided mentioning was that his own planning entertained no real possibility of disappearing south of the border. During his legal career he'd heard too many stories of the horrors of Mexican jails. When they were caught—and his gut feeling was that they eventually would be—he didn't want to be at the mercy of the Mexican authorities. Such arguments, however, could wait until they were somewhere safe, somewhere he would have time to reason with Joy.

Brad Davis was at home alone, in the kitchen preparing himself a sandwich, when they arrived. Joy wasted no time in outlining the proposition she had for him. She needed a favor, and if he would do it for her, he could forget the $5,000 she had loaned him for the purchase of his new pickup.

"We need you to drive us to Denver," Joy said.

"When will you be back?"

"I'm not coming back."

A look of surprise and concern crept across Brad Davis's face. Finally, he turned to Mike. "You going, too?"

Wilson nodded.

"You coming back?"

"No, Brad, I'm not."

As they sat at the kitchen table, Wilson explained to Brad the need to leave as soon as possible in light of the hearing that was scheduled for the following Monday. "If we don't go now, there's a chance—a damn good chance—they'll put her in jail.

"But before you agree to help us, you need to think about what you're getting into. When she doesn't show up in court Monday, the shit's going to hit the fan in a big way. When they can't find her, they'll come looking for me. And when they can't find either of us, they're going to start asking everybody a lot of questions. If you decide to do this, it's important that you're back in Dallas before Monday morning."

Brad sighed and dug his huge hands into his pants pockets. "I've got to go to a wedding this evening. It won't be over until around nine o'clock."

"Go on to the wedding," Joy interjected. "As soon as you get home, we'll leave. We'll be waiting in the Tom Thumb parking lot down the street."

"You'll need a cover story when the police come to see you," Wilson suggested.

Brad was again silent for several seconds. "I'll tell 'em I decided to fly out to Las Vegas for the weekend."

That, Wilson knew, would float only for as long as it took the authorities to check plane reservations and make a few calls to Vegas. And, in time, there would be questions about his signature on the certificates of transfer. The DA's office and probably the Internal Revenue Service would want to know where the money had gone.

A rush of guilt swept over Mike as he looked at the big man so willing to commit himself to future legal problems to help out a relative he obviously adored.

Brad was still in the kitchen when Victorine Davis returned home and immediately noticed the sadness in his face.

"Something wrong?" she asked.

"Joy was just here. They really must have the goods on her." With no further explanation he walked out to his pickup, leaving the sandwich he had prepared untouched.

The remainder of the day was a blur of activity as Joy completed her packing, then drove over to her parents' house. For a half hour she sat with Henry Davis and chatted with Frances, revealing no hint that she was, in fact, paying a farewell visit.

Before leaving, she went upstairs and into the darkened gun

closet where she retrieved the purple leather bag from its hiding place on a back shelf. Not even bothering to turn on the light she hurriedly measured its heft as she pulled the drawstring tight.

Across town, Mike Wilson was packing and also contemplating how to handle his good-byes. He dialed the number of a friend in Highland Park with whom Clay had been staying since his father's arrest and was relieved when he heard a recorded message and not the actual voice of his son. Wilson spent several seconds in silence, trying to decide what kind of explanation his teenage son might understand. The answer, he knew, was that there really was none. "Son," he finally said, "I just want you to know I love you . . . and I'll be seeing you."

At a few minutes past nine P.M., Wilson sat slouched behind the wheel of the Budget rental car, privately surprised at the calm that had set in once the plan had been decided on and preparations made. In the darkness of the supermarket parking lot, he pondered their chances and felt sure they were slim at best. Surely the police were monitoring their activities. Somewhere—perhaps in the same parking lot where they awaited Brad's arrival—someone was watching, waiting for their next move. The whole idea was a long shot that they had waited too long to take. They should have left weeks ago, he thought. And there should have been more careful planning. He had tried earlier in the day to warn Joy of their chances—"We're going to be flying by the seat of our pants on this thing, you know"—and she had simply smiled. If she was in the least worried, it was well hidden.

Only when Brad failed to show a half hour past the time they had agreed upon did Wilson begin to show his agitation. Had he gotten cold feet, realizing that his involvement would likely result in legal troubles? Was it possible that, after thinking over the situation, he had tipped the police to the plan? "We can't sit here all goddamn night," Mike said.

"He'll be here," Joy calmly replied.

As she spoke, her attention was directed toward a man in a late-model pickup parked next to them. The driver had looked over at Joy, nodded, and smiled. She had smiled in return.

Wilson laughed. "I hope to hell that guy you're flirting with isn't an undercover cop."

"I wasn't flirting," Joy said with mock aggravation. "I made some sandwiches. You want one?"

As she was leaning into the backseat, searching the wicker picnic basket, all hell broke loose. Suddenly, three men were running from the entrance of the store as shoppers screamed and cleared them a path. Startled by the activity, Wilson sat upright and watched as the men ran in their direction.

Joy tensed as she turned to watch. "What's happening?"

"I don't believe this," Wilson finally answered as he heard the engine of the pickup next to them start up.

"What is it?"

"Those assholes have just robbed the place. And your buddy over there is the getaway driver."

They watched in stunned silence as the robbers, each carrying handguns, raced toward them, jumped into the pickup, then, with tires screaming against the pavement, disappeared into the night. In a matter of minutes several Dallas police patrol cars arrived in the parking lot. Wilson counted at least a dozen uniformed officers gathered at the entrance to the store, talking with employees and shoppers who had witnessed the robbery.

"Jesus," Mike finally said, breaking the silence, "this is crazy." Joy offered no comment on his monumental understatement.

At that moment Wilson spotted Brad Davis walking into the eye of the storm, strolling leisurely across the parking lot toward them, carrying a briefcase. It was a few minutes before ten o'clock.

"Sorry," he said as he climbed into the backseat. "The reception ran late. Look, you guys mind if we stop and get something to eat on the way out of town? I'm starving."

Wilson glared at his passenger through the rearview mirror. "Eat a fucking sandwich," he growled as he put the car in gear and slowly drove from the parking lot.

Long after the skyline of Dallas had disappeared behind them and the darkened north-Texas landscape turned to rolling grasslands, Mike Wilson could not shake the feeling of amazement that they had actually made their escape. Had he overestimated the attention the police were paying to Joy and him? Or had it just been some fluke, a freak accident that some momentarily distracted surveillance officer would pay dearly for once their absence was noticed?

Such were Wilson's thoughts as he drove into the late-spring night, through Wichita Falls, then on to Amarillo and finally into New Mexico as the first gray light of dawn broke across the flat, treeless plains. Beside him, Joy had been sleeping peacefully for several hours. In the backseat, Brad dozed restlessly, waking occasionally to complain of hemorrhoids that had been troubling him for the past few weeks.

The quiet night drive had finally given Wilson time to formulate a plan. Joy, he knew, still had her mind set on going to Mexico since among the carefully selected items she had packed were a small recorder and self-teaching Spanish tapes; the few clothes she had packed were for a warm-weather climate. He would, however, have to impress upon her the slim chance of reaching freedom by heading south. Their destination, he had resolved, would be Canada. If necessary, he would assure Joy that they would attempt getting to Mexico at some later date, but only after the initial search for them had died down. For now, though, their best chance of eluding the authorities lay north of the border.

For Wilson, the trip had already taken on the dreamlike quality of a final adventure doomed to failure. While every mile took them farther from Dallas, they were, he was privately convinced, heading closer and closer to their capture. In all likelihood, it would end at the Canadian border when they attempted to leave the United States. Only an unimaginable streak of good luck would see their hastily formed plan succeed. And Mike Wilson had not been that lucky of late.

To sweep the negative thoughts from his mind, he focused on what lay immediately ahead. In looking to the future, he found himself retreating nostalgically to the past. Their path was returning him to a part of the country where he had spent some of the most relaxing and memorable times of his life, fly-fishing in the streams of Montana and Wyoming in the company of lawyer friends. It would be good to see the region again, to breathe its intoxicating fresh air and look upon its calming, beautiful wilderness. Somewhere ahead were the majestic Canadian Rockies, which he wanted to see one more time. They would, he told himself, provide lasting memories to carry with him to the sterile confines of some federal prison.

As he drove, lost in thought, he turned to look at the woman beside him. Curled in childlike sleep, hair slightly disheveled, her shoes off, she was beautiful.

Reaching over, he gently touched her, then refocused his thoughts on cold mountain streams teeming with rainbow trout.

Stopping in Raton, New Mexico, for gas and breakfast, Wilson spread a road map on the restaurant table and outlined the remainder of the route to his passengers. By driving all day they should reach Cheyenne, Wyoming, sometime late in the afternoon. That would be the end of the line for Brad. In Cheyenne, Mike and Joy would purchase a car and continue their northward journey. The distance back to Dallas would allow Brad plenty of time to get home sometime Sunday, well before the Monday-morning court hearing.

As he discussed the day's route, Wilson was relieved that Joy made no mention of turning back toward the Mexico border.

When Brad excused himself to go to the rest room, she asked, "Where in Canada are we going?"

Mike smiled and shrugged. "Darlin', we'll know when we get there."

Joy nodded and returned his smile. "Brad and I can drive for a while. You get in the back and get some sleep."

Weary from the frantic preparations and the all-night drive, Wilson dozed as Joy and Brad shared the driving chores until they reached the outskirts of Colorado Springs. Only when aware they had turned off the interstate did Mike sit upright. "What's happening?"

"It's lunchtime," Joy replied. "You can't come to Colorado Springs and not have lunch at the world-famous Broadmoor."

Wilson's stomach tightened as he felt a wave of rage sweep over him. What was it going to take to convince these people that what they were doing was not fun and games but, rather, life-and-death serious? How in hell could they even think of lunch at the Broadmoor when the very real possibility existed that the authorities were already looking for them? He pursed his lips, deciding to say nothing as he leaned back against the seat and shook his head in disbelief.

"You hungry?" Joy asked in a cheery voice.

Wilson sighed. "Starved," he lied.

For the next hour he sat in the crowded dining room, picking at his food, wondering how many of their fellow diners might later identify them to the police, and listening as Joy and Brad argued over the quality of the wine list.

Late Saturday afternoon, Wilson pulled into a Jeep dealership in Cheyenne, identified himself as the owner of a Louisiana-based business called W&W Enterprises, and set about negotiating the price on a 1982 Grand Wagoneer.

The purchase quickly made, he returned to the rental car where Joy and Brad waited and began transferring the bags.

Finally, Brad spoke. "You think they'll believe that I was in Vegas?"

Wilson had long dreaded the question. From the moment he and Joy had first visited Brad, involving him in the transfer of money from one bank to another, then asking his help with their escape, Mike had felt a growing sense of guilt. "Brad," he said, "the honest truth is that nothing in the world is going to work if they figure out what you've done for us."

Brad Davis, a sad-eyed look of resignation on his face, stared at the pavement. "I can get in trouble for this, can't I?" It was more a statement of realization than a question. Joy bent into the car, pulled five one-hundred-dollar bills from her bag, and handed them to her cousin.

"I guess I'd better be heading back to Dallas," he finally said.

Joy put her arms around his slumped shoulders and thanked him.

"You guys be careful," he said, forcing a smile as he climbed behind the wheel of the rental car.

Standing in the car lot, watching Brad drive away, Joy turned to Mike. "Do you think five hundred dollars was enough?"

For several seconds Mike did not answer, focusing on the disappearing car. Then he shoved his hands deep into his hip pockets and shook his head. "Let me put it this way. If I'd gone looking for someone to take the chance Brad Davis just took for you, it wouldn't have cost a penny less then twenty-five thousand dollars."

If the observation surprised or troubled Joy, Wilson saw no sign of it.

Late that night they pulled into the parking lot of a Cody, Wyoming, motel, followed closely by a state trooper. He approached Wilson and requested that he get out of the car. "Could I see your driver's license, please?" the trooper asked.

The officer studied Wilson's Texas license in the beam of his flashlight as Joy sat silently in the car, not daring even to breathe.

"Mr. Wilson," she heard the trooper say, "are you aware that you were speeding?"

The ticket in hand, Mike glanced over at Joy as he got back into the Jeep. A relieved grin was already forming on her face. Then, as they watched the trooper pull back into the traffic, they each began to laugh uncontrollably.

Maybe, just maybe, Mike thought, they were going to be lucky after all. Already he'd left a damaging paper trail, first signing his real name to the purchase agreement for the Jeep, now the traffic violation.

Apparently, their absence had not yet been noted back in Dallas.

With hundreds of miles already behind them, Mike and Joy checked into the motel for the night. The last thing Wilson heard before falling into a deep, exhausted sleep was a question from Joy: "Mike," she whispered, "what's going to happen when they find out we're gone?"

"Well, my guess is that every sonuvabitch in the country with a badge is going to be looking for us."

In the darkened room he could not see Joy's face, but for some reason Mike Wilson was certain she was smiling.

\* \* \*

Sunday morning arrived with a welcome sense of relief for the two fugitives. With Brad well on his way back to Dallas, they felt a new freedom. Rested and his spirits renewed by the initial success of their escape, Wilson had wakened with a feeling that they just might make it into Canada after all. Now far past the point of no return, he was suddenly aware of a dramatic shift in his attitude. With a trial and a certain prison sentence awaiting him in Dallas, he had nothing to lose. Every day of freedom, then, should be viewed as a self-given gift; whatever time remained for him and this fascinating woman whom he wanted so badly to be near, to help and protect, was to be cherished.

The afternoon passed quickly as they wound northward into Montana, through Bozeman and Helena, each mile drawing them nearer their moment of truth.

Neither broached the subject of failure as they neared their destination, not wishing to dampen the positive attitude they had sustained throughout the day. Instead, they focused their attention on the grandiose landscapes they were passing through. While Joy appeared content to avoid any talk of what might lie ahead, Wilson occasionally felt the need to address issues they had not previously discussed.

There was, he said, no way to avoid using his real name at the border since he would no doubt be asked for some form of identification. He would say she was his wife, and if the authorities asked to see identification from her, they would explain that they were honeymooning newlyweds and she had not yet had her name changed on her driver's license.

Once in Canada, however, they would need to use a name other than their own. They would, he said, be Mr. and Mrs. John Storms.

"Who's John Storms?" Joy asked.

"An old Phi Delt fraternity brother of mine. For some reason, I was thinking about him the other day. His name just popped into my mind."

"You don't think he'll mind us using his name?"

Mike smiled. "Naw. Last I heard he was in the pen."

He pointed out it was also absolutely essential that they not contact anyone back in Dallas. Neither relatives nor friends.

Joy would have to erase concerns for Henry Davis's health and her mother's well-being, just as he would for his ailing father and other family he'd left behind.

"It's going to be very hard," Mike said, "but believe me, it's for their good as well as our own. We've got to just disappear from their lives if we're going to have any chance in hell of making this work."

He looked over at his silent and suddenly sad companion. "Can you do that?"

For a moment Joy didn't respond, then silently nodded.

After studying his map, Wilson had first thought of attempting a border crossing in the northern part of Glacier Park, then decided on a more sparsely populated region to the east. The dot-on-the-map community of Sweetgrass, located on the Alberta border, looked like the safest place to attempt their exit from the United States.

It was easier than he had dared expect. They were routinely passed into Canada with best wishes and hopes they would enjoy their visit.

"Joy, honey," Wilson said as he gleefully pounded his palm against the steering wheel, "I think we're on a roll."

She smiled, then leaned across the front seat to kiss him on the cheek.

The relief of actually making it into Canada was short-lived for Wilson, soon replaced by thoughts of things he would need to accomplish as quickly as possible. As they settled into an out-of-the-way motel in Lethbridge, he explained to Joy that he needed to return to the United States the following day to register the Jeep and get new license plates. Driving through Canada with only dealer's tags that were good for a maximum of twenty days, he explained, would serve as a glowing invitation to curious authorities.

The idea of his risking another trip across the border troubled Joy. "What if you don't make it back?"

"If I make the trip first thing in the morning, I think I'll be okay. With luck, they won't discover we've left until you fail to show for the hearing." Then, he explained, they would probably run all over Dallas looking for her before realization set in that she had, in fact, fled. Only then would law enforcement computers nationwide begin receiving all-points bulletins.

"Wouldn't it be better if we just stole a set of license plates off some car around here?"

Wilson shook his head and smiled. "Darlin', if I get arrested again, it damn sure ain't going to be for heisting license plates."

Mike woke early on Monday morning and dressed quietly. As he prepared to leave, he stood briefly at the doorway of the tiny motel room, looking over at the sleeping woman. They had not even discussed the possibility of his being apprehended when he tried again to cross the border, and he found himself wondering what she would do if he did not return. He briefly considered waking her to discuss some kind of plan, then discarded the thought. He decided to let her sleep, to hope their luck continued.

Closing the door quietly, he stepped out into a foggy Canadian morning. As he drove south toward the border, he began to prepare himself mentally for the mission at hand.

The young U.S. Customs agent manning the small border station was polite and businesslike, bidding Wilson good morning, then asking for identification. Mike smiled and handed the agent his driver's license and a card identifying him as a member of the Texas Bar Association.

"John Michael Wilson," the agent said as he looked at the license, then leaned forward to compare its photo to the man seated behind the wheel of the Grand Wagoneer. "Dallas, Texas. You're a long way from home."

Mike nodded, smiled, and explained that he was vacationing.

"Let me just run this through the computer, and we'll get you on your way."

"Great," Wilson said, suddenly realizing the dryness in his throat as he spoke. He watched silently as the agent returned to the small building and stood in front of a computer screen located near a single, open window. The agent slowly pounded at the keyboard for several seconds, then focused on the screen for what seemed like ages.

What information, Wilson wondered, would the computer

offer up? He was reasonably sure that it was still too early for their departure to be discovered, but what about his arrest on the cocaine charges? If they came up, how would he explain the fact that he was hundreds of miles from the jurisdiction he'd been limited to at his bond hearing? As time crept past, he felt all confidence slipping away.

While the agent continued to alternately press computer keys and frown into its bright green screen, Wilson slipped his hand into his shirt pocket and withdrew a business card bearing the name of the motel in Lethbridge where he'd left Joy. He'd brought the card along in the event he forgot the motel's name and location. Now, though, he was thinking it was a bad idea; it was the lone link between him and where Joy was hiding. If he did get caught, the last thing he wanted to do was lead the authorities to her.

Quickly folding the card, he put it in his mouth and began chewing on it until it was moist enough to swallow.

A few minutes later the agent approached, shaking his head. "Sorry to keep you waiting so long. I had no idea there were so damn many Wilsons in the computer. I still haven't found you. But, listen, since you're a lawyer, I'm going to let you go on."

"I appreciate it."

"You have a good day," the Customs agent said as he handed the driver's license and bar card through the window.

At the courthouse in Cut Bank, Montana, things were even easier. An elderly woman at the auto registration desk was reading the newspaper and still working on her first cup of morning coffee, obviously none too eager for her initial customer of the day. She gave the papers showing Wilson's ownership of the Wagoneer a disinterested glance, not even asking to see his driver's license. Sliding a form across the desk for him to fill out, she returned to her newspaper.

"I just got into town," Wilson said, "so I don't have a local address yet."

The woman didn't bother to look up. "Just write in General Delivery, Cut Bank, Montana," she said, then went into a well-rehearsed pitch for a commemorative license plate that was being offered at a price slightly higher than the standard issue.

Wilson handed the woman the completed form and said he'd take the cheaper plates. The woman frowned briefly at his decision. "That'll be seventeen-fifty, then," she said as she began typing his receipt.

Five minutes later, Wilson was around the corner at a service station, putting the new Montana license plates on the Wagoneer.

In another half hour he had been waved back into Alberta by a smiling Canadian Border Patrol officer and was on his way to Lethbridge. He stopped at a grocery store near the motel to pick up some doughnuts and coffee, eager to tell Joy of his recent good fortune.

The scene that greeted him as he entered the motel room caused him to stop in the doorway.

Joy, dressed in jeans and a sweatshirt, sat cross-legged in the middle of the bed, staring down at stacks of money arranged in front of her. He knew she had been crying, and there was a panicked look on her face Wilson had not seen since that long-ago night in the Parkland Hospital emergency room.

"You're not going to believe what I've done," she said.

Wilson let the grocery sack slip from his arms onto the small table near the door and sat on the edge of the bed. Seeing Joy suddenly frail and frightened, her composure shattered, unnerved him. His mind raced with possibilities. Had she called Dallas and turned herself in? Done something that would reveal their whereabouts to the authorities? "Joy," he finally said as he put his arms around her, "what's wrong?"

She began to cry again, her body heaving against him as she buried her face in his chest. "Hey," Wilson said as he gently rocked her, "you've got to tell me what's happened."

Joy pulled away and picked up the leather bag, angrily tossing it across the room. "I left half the money at mother's house."

As she counted the money she had taken from the gun closet, Joy had expected there to be over $400,000 in the bag. Instead, the total was far less. An additional $250,000, which she had hidden in her father's tool chest, remained in Dallas.

"We've got to get it," she said. "Who can we call to get it for us?"

Wilson sat speechless for several seconds, trying to absorb the frantic sense of desperation he had returned to. The woman he was holding, trying unsuccessfully to comfort, was nothing like the Joy Aylor he had known for months and had been traveling with for the past few days. With thousands of dollars in cash and Darla Green's jewelry spread before her, she still needed more. For the first time since their relationship had begun, Mike Wilson was forced to admit what he had suspected but refused to acknowledge before. Money, not him, offered Joy a calming sense of security and well-being. With money, she felt safe, invincible. Without it, she was vulnerable.

"Honey, you're just going to have to forget about it," Wilson finally said. "What's done is done. We can't risk contacting anybody back in Dallas, no matter what." He looked down at the money on the bed. "We're not exactly broke, you know."

His attempt to make light of the situation did no good. Joy pulled away from him, shaking her head violently. "We're going to need that money, Mike. We've got to figure a way to get it."

It did not surprise him that she had already been formulating a plan: "I'll call Lonnie and ask him to go over to mother's house and get it. He'll do it, I know."

A puzzled look crept over Wilson's face. "Who the hell is Lonnie?"

"A man I know back in Dallas. He loves me."

Wilson felt a wave of jealousy sweep over him as she spoke of the man not in the past but, rather, present tense.

Sensing his surprise at the mention of another man in her life, she quickly began to explain. Lonnie Fielding, an art and antique dealer in Dallas, was married and had children. They had known each other for several years, she said, and had met for lunches and dinners on a number of occasions. She had accompanied him a few times on buying trips to New York.

Eventually, Fielding had told her that he was in love with her. But, she insisted, they had never slept together.

"Does your mother know him?"

"No."

"And you want him to just knock on the door and say he's supposed to pick up a quarter of a million dollars in cash?"

Joy was suddenly angry. "Of course not. I could call mother and tell her he was coming."

"Goddammit, you can't call anybody," Wilson said as his frustration began to show. "We've already gone over that. We've gone over and over it. You've just got to forget it . . . right now."

Even as he spoke, it was painfully clear to Mike that she was not hearing a word he was saying.

Back in Dallas, Wilson's concerns that their every move prior to leaving had been carefully monitored had been unfounded. Officials in the district attorney's office, in fact, had stayed busy throughout the weekend preparing grand jury subpoenas to be served on those who Chapman felt might have knowledge of Joy's ongoing money-gathering activities.

After several lengthy meetings to discuss how best to keep their plan secret for as long as possible, they had decided to wait until early Monday morning before actually serving papers to key witnesses.

If Chapman's plan went as he hoped, the evidence presented to the grand jury on Monday morning would be sufficient to convince them Joy had, indeed, become a flight risk and that revocation of her bond was necessary. Then, during the scheduled afternoon hearing before Judge McDowell, the order would be made official and Joy would be placed under arrest.

The lone witness, in fact, whom authorities were genuinely concerned about was Jodi Packer. Locating him in recent days had become difficult. On several occasions when Ken MacKenzie had wanted to talk with him, Packer had managed to avoid him.

With it increasingly certain that Joy had discussed details of the murder-for-hire with him, he had to be among those who testified before the grand jury. Therefore, MacKenzie had gone to great lengths to make certain Jodi was served with his subpoena.

In the predawn hours of Monday morning, a Dallas city truck pulled up in front of the apartment where Packer lived, blocking his driveway. In the street, a manhole cover was removed and barricades set up as if work were getting under way on the city's plumbing. Dressed in a jumpsuit and wearing a hard hat, Ken MacKenzie posed as one of the workers.

Shortly before eight A.M., Packer emerged from the apartment to find that his exit was blocked. Clearly upset, he approached the group of workmen to ask how long it would be before he would be able to back his car from the driveway.

MacKenzie, who had kept his head down until Packer was standing almost directly in front of him, removed his hat and smiled. "Morning, Jodi." Ken handed him the subpoena. "I'll see you in court at ten o'clock."

Packer, at first stunned, then angry, wheeled and returned to the apartment while MacKenzie and his workers gathered their equipment and left.

Once again, Packer would be forced to face a grand jury's questions about his relationship with Joy Aylor.

For Brad Davis, however, it was a first-time experience. And one that would prove disastrous. Under oath, he admitted driving Mike and Joy out of state, thinking they only wanted to get away for a few days. He had, he swore, left them at a motel on the outskirts of Denver, Colorado.

Later that afternoon, after Joy failed to appear for the scheduled hearing, Judge McDowell issued a warrant for her arrest. Across town in the federal courthouse, Judge Tolle, briefed on Wilson's involvement, began preparing a federal warrant.

It was no longer just the Richardson police's case. Now joining in the hunt were the Dallas County Sheriff's Department and the FBI.

# 21

RECOVERING THE MONEY became an ever-growing obsession with Joy, constantly in her thoughts, even taking precedence over concern that the authorities might soon be close on their heels.

Despite Mike's insistence that the police were no doubt closely monitoring the Davis house, anticipating some kind of contact from Joy, she continued to devise plans for getting the money from its hiding place in Dallas.

"What if Clay were to decide to come up here on a skiing trip?" she asked one morning as they drove deeper into Canada. "He could go by, pick up the money—"

Wilson stopped her in midsentence. "No," he said, holding up one hand as if to ward off the idea. The suggestion that they involve his teenage son, already an innocent victim of the mess Mike had made of his life, infuriated him. "Absolutely not."

For several seconds he was silent, attempting to control his anger. It had troubled him when she had shown no remorse about involving Brad or any reservation at drawing her mother into the plot. And he was bothered by her suggestion that a man with a wife and children, Fielding, suddenly become an accomplice. No way would he allow his son to be drawn into this insane scheme.

They had driven several miles in silence before he spoke to her, calm finally restored to his voice. "Joy, how many more people are you going to drag down with you before this is all over?"

She did not reply, instead focusing her attention on the highway that stretched in front of them.

The mood of the trip had changed dramatically. For the first time since their departure, Wilson was having second thoughts about what he was doing. He loved the woman seated next to him and would, he knew, do everything within his power to keep her safe. But for the first time since he had met her, doubts were mixed with those feelings. Had this woman, who paid attention to the most minute of details, *really* left $250,000 behind? It made absolutely no sense, seemed almost impossible. And where did this man named Lonnie—someone he had not even known existed until days earlier—figure into her life? Why did he have this nagging gut feeling that this mystery man, whom Joy had apparently known for some time, might have been keeping the money for Joy all along? Was it possible that in the haste to get out of Dallas she had simply not been able to get the money from him before they left and was now looking for some way for him to get it to her?

While these questions and doubts troubled him, the new sense of panic he saw in Joy was the most unsettling. For the first time since he'd met her, the cool, calm facade had vanished, replaced by a kind of fear that he was unable to define.

From Lethbridge they drove north to Calgary, into the Banff National Park where they rented a small A-frame condo nestled in the Canadian Rockies. To Wilson, it was one of the most beautiful, invigorating areas he'd ever seen. To Joy, it was a prison. Ignoring the nearby boutiques and the majestic mountain scenery, she went on manic binges, pacing from room to room in the condo day and night. The money was all she spoke of.

Having her friend Lonnie go to her mother's house and get the money, she insisted, was the best plan. "I could call him and ask him to go over and tell mother that I need my fur coat. While she's upstairs getting it, he could get the money and she would never know. I trust him, Mike. I know he would help us."

The fury that Wilson had initially displayed toward Joy's incessant planning had long since been numbed. He spoke to her in a gentle voice, a lawyer advising a distraught client. "Honey, you're going to have to forget about it. It just won't work. Nothing will. You start making calls back to Dallas and we might as well just drive to the nearest police station and turn ourselves in."

Sitting in a chair, her legs curled beneath her, Joy hugged

herself and stared into the crackling fire as tears began to slide down her cheeks. "I'm so sorry about all this," she said, her voice barely a whisper. "I should never have gotten you into this. I should have stopped you the day you went to get those drugs. I shouldn't have asked you to come with me." Only then did she turn her attention from the fire and look across the room at Mike. "If you want me to, I'll take you to the airport right now and you can go back."

Wilson approached her, lifted her to her feet, and put his arms around her. "There's no turning back now for either of us. Dammit, that's what I've been trying to tell you."

In truth, the idea of returning to Dallas, giving himself up and facing the consequences of his actions, appealed to the wearied Wilson. He was, after all, only buying time until the inevitable. Why prolong it?

The answer stood before him: the most beautiful, fascinating woman he'd ever known.

Keenly aware of the dangers of staying in one place too long, they left the idyllic surroundings of Banff after four days, driving west toward Vancouver. It would, Wilson explained, be easier to hide in a large city.

Joy had finally stopped talking of the money or suggesting plans for getting it. But it was clearly still on her mind. As if resigned to a pauper's budget, they stole newspapers instead of buying them. She insisted they seek out two-for-one sandwich shops that offered free salad bars. The motels they stopped at were light-years removed from a four-star rating. The idea of going to a movie or visiting a bookstore, pastimes both had previously enjoyed, was suddenly out of the question.

One freezing afternoon as they walked across a busy street, returning to the Wagoneer after lunch, Joy stopped abruptly and hurried back toward the restaurant. Wilson stood watching as she reached a spot near the entrance where she bent over to pick up something from the sidewalk. She returned to him, smiling broadly.

"What the hell was that all about?"

"Somebody dropped a dime," she said, proudly showing him the coin she had picked up.

Wilson broke into uncontrolled laughter as they raced to get out of the cold. "Jesus Christ, Joy," he said, shaking his head in dismay.

The absurdity of her obsession with money both amused and grated on Wilson, but he had decided to say nothing more. After all, they were traveling on her cash. And he was resigned to the fact she was going to spend it frugally.

Arriving in Vancouver, Mike parked in front of a downtown Holiday Inn, leaving Joy in the Jeep while he went in to check on the rates before registering. When he returned to the parking lot, the Wagoneer would not start. Irritated at the price quoted by the hotel and now the possibility of repair expense, Joy suggested they take a walk in the downtown area and see if they might find a cheaper hotel. Two hours and several hotel lobby visits later, a weary "John Storms" returned to the Holiday Inn registration desk, rented a room for two nights, and asked the number of a garage that might do repair work on his Jeep.

The following morning he stood watching as a mechanic peered beneath the hood, sizing up the problem. Joy sitting in the garage's customer waiting area, was passing time by listening to a Spanish-language audiotape lesson when she heard a loud noise. Rushing into the service area, she found that the Jeep's battery had exploded and watched as Mike frantically helped the mechanic wash acid from his face and arms. Joy quickly rushed over to see if she could help.

While Joy fussed over the mechanic, insisting that he use an eyewash immediately, he assured her that he was fine. Their problem, he told the couple, could be solved with nothing more than a new battery.

As they prepared to leave the garage, Joy talked again with the obviously flattered mechanic, still expressing motherly concern and suggesting that he pay a precautionary visit to the doctor as soon as possible.

As they drove from the garage, the warmth disappeared from her voice. She glared across the seat at Wilson. "If you had just tried, I think you could have made a lot better deal on that battery."

For the first time since they had left Dallas, Mike Wilson

seriously considered the possibility that the pressures of running from the law might have caused Joy to snap.

In the days to come, in fact, he would begin to wonder if she might have dual personalities. At times the sexy, warm, and fun-loving Joy would reappear. Then with little warning, the smallest thing would trigger her paranoid side, bringing out the anger and fear he'd first seen that morning in the motel room back in Lethbridge.

In Dallas, Lieutenant McGowan received an excited call from a *Morning News* reporter late one afternoon: "They've caught her."

"Where?"

"Somewhere up in Canada. My editor said the wire service sent out an advisory that we would be getting a story on it shortly."

McGowan was certain that he would have been contacted immediately if Joy had, in fact, been apprehended. He refused to allow himself to get excited over the news.

And it was just as well. That evening he watched as the ten-o'clock news reported that Bambi Bembenek, a model turned Milwaukee police officer who had become something of a folk hero after her indictment for murder, had been arrested in Canada. The case of Bembenek, who was imprisoned for the murder of her husband's ex-wife, had gained the attention of the national media as well as a cultlike following, with some wearing "Run Bambi Run" T-shirts after she had escaped jail and fled the country. Bambi, not Joy, had been captured.

As he watched the TV report, McGowan looked across the room at Sandy and sighed. "Well," he said, "at least someone's having some luck up there."

The on-the-run life of Mike and Joy, meanwhile, was turning into a case study of erratic behavior that ran a gamut from the comic to tragic.

During moments of intimacy, they talked late into the night about the most private of matters. "How many women have you slept with?" Joy once asked.

"You don't want to know."

She then volunteered that her sexual experience had been limited. "You're my fourth."

She began to talk of her years of marriage to Larry Aylor, the knowledge of his infidelities, and her own endless battle to convince herself that she was, in fact, attractive, a good mother, and reasonably smart.

Joy had rarely spoken of her ex-husband after the bitter battle over Chris's burial and his property had been resolved. It was as though she had wiped him from her memory. Only when Mike broached the subject one afternoon as they were having coffee in a Vancouver pastry shop did she reflect on Larry.

"My dad once told me a story," she said, "that will show you exactly what kind of person he is. See, back before he got sick, Daddy and a bunch of his cronies—house builders, mostly—would meet for coffee every morning. Most of the time Larry would join them. One morning, the way I heard it, Larry and this other guy started arguing over something. This other guy finally got so mad at Larry that he invited him outside to settle the matter. His exact words, I think, were, 'I ought to take you outside and kick your ass.'

"Now, my dad, who is loving the whole thing, is sitting on the outside of the booth, and when the guy suggests Larry go with him into the parking lot and fight, he jumps up and says, 'Here, Larry, I'll let you out.' He's taunting him, of course. Anyway, this other guy gets up and storms out to wait for Larry. And what does Larry do? He just sits there with his head down, not moving a muscle, while all those other men look at him. He was still sitting there when everyone had finished their coffee and left.

"That's the kind of man Larry Aylor is."

But, her ex-husband was not the only culprit in her life.

If only her wish to attend college had been granted by her father, she said, her self-esteem might not have diminished so dramatically over the years. For that she blamed Carol. Had Carol not wasted time and Henry Davis's money during her unproductive years at Southern Methodist, her father would not have adopted the "I'm not throwing good money after bad" attitude toward higher education for her and Elizabeth. Carol, Joy said, had been ruining things for others all her life, long before she had gone to the Richardson police and helped them make their case against Joy.

The tone in her voice vibrated with the total distaste Joy had for her older sister.

As she spoke, Wilson thought back to a talk they had had shortly before leaving Dallas. Almost casually, Joy had asked what might happen if Carol was unable to testify against her. "What if she just disappeared?"

Uncomfortable with the direction of the conversation, Mike had attempted to laugh it off. "What are you going to do, have her whacked, too?"

Joy had rolled her eyes in mock dismay at his question. "Oh, no, of course not." But then, as if talking only to herself, she had said that she knew where Carol lived, what school her daughter attended, and could provide a recent photograph of her sister.

"Listen, sugar," Mike had said, cutting the conversation short. "You had better hope she doesn't get hit by a bus or even slip in the goddamn bathtub. If anything bad happens to her—I mean anything—you're the one they're going to come running after."

Joy nodded. "I know."

On occasion, without warning or provocation, she had also begun reflecting on Rozanne Gailiunas's death. Her motive had never been jealousy as her friends and the newspapers were saying. Everything would have been fine, she said, if Rozanne and Larry hadn't insisted she was a bad mother, if they hadn't begun threatening to take Chris away and have him come and live with them once they were married.

"She deserved what she got," Joy said without the slightest hint of remorse.

The calm, cold tone of her voice both disturbed and puzzled Wilson. It was as if some other woman were speaking the words—not the Joy Aylor he had fallen in love with, not the Joy Aylor he had seen shower love and kindness on family and friends.

He could not help but wonder what dark secrets he had not yet discovered about her.

Not all moments, however, were so serious.

Despite efforts not to draw undue attention to themselves, their distinctive Texas accents constantly prompted questions from strangers about where they were from. As they shopped in a Vancouver grocery store one afternoon, they were stopped by a polite produce clerk who had overheard them talking. "I was just wondering where you're from," he said.

"Louisiana," Mike replied. "Oklahoma," Joy said at the same time.

Reflecting on the faux pas, Wilson observed that they were "about the sorriest excuse for fugitives I'd ever heard of."

A few days later, after taking the ferry to Victoria to check out hotels there, they found themselves in an empty banquet room where a convention of Japanese businessmen had just completed a luncheon meeting. Joy walked to a table still filled with fruit and hors d'oeuvres and motioned for Mike to join her. She was already stuffing grapes, dinner rolls, and finger sandwiches into her purse.

Such lunacy had become a game. Despite carrying a great deal of cash, Joy had determinedly adopted an attitude rivaling that of a down-and-out street person. In the mornings she awoke early enough to scavenge motel halls until she found a newspaper to steal from the doorway of some other guest. From room-service trays left in the hallways she routinely took unused pads of butter, crackers, and packets of sugar.

Weary of arguing with her about her compulsive penny-pinching, Wilson had come to look on it as harmless folly and had reluctantly begun to join in.

In the banquet room he removed the western hat he was wearing and hurriedly began filling it with items from the table.

He was startled seconds later when he felt a hand on his shoulder. Assuming it was an employee of the hotel, he turned slowly, prepared to offer an apology. Instead, standing behind him was a small, elderly Japanese man smiling up at him, camera in hand.

Mike, placing one hand over his hat in hopes the conventioneer had not seen what he was doing, smiled back at the man, who was motioning with one hand and holding up his camera with the other.

"Honey, he wants a picture of you with your cowboy hat on," Joy said, trying to mask her amusement.

A puzzled look on his face, Wilson stared briefly at Joy, then at the smiling Japanese man. Finally, he shrugged. "Why the hell not?" he said, dumping the food back into a pile on the table, placing his hat on his head, and striking his best cowboy pose for the camera.

"God, I've never been so embarrassed in my friggin' life," Mike said as they hurried out of the hotel. Joy was laughing so hard she had begun to cry.

But the frivolous moments, once a mainstay of their relationship, were soon to end, replaced by a constant state of tension. Settled into a small, out-of-the-way resort motel called the Town & Country Inn near Victoria, Joy's mood blackened as the days passed. She began to take long early-morning walks alone, lost in thoughts that she refused to share. Though he did not confront her, Wilson had become certain she was in contact with someone back in Dallas. When they did talk, it was rarely about anything more than vague plans that would distance them from the authorities, of ultimately getting to someplace where a new life could begin without the constant need to look over one's shoulder. They spoke of the possibility of chartering a plane that would fly them to Costa Rica or perhaps Barbados. Someplace warm, Joy would always interject. Occasionally, she talked of one day establishing her own small interior-decorating business somewhere. And she still spoke of disappearing into Mexico despite Mike's repeated insistence that it was a bad idea.

In a halfhearted attempt to change his looks, Mike began to grow a beard. Joy talked of getting contact lenses that would alter the color of her eyes but never pursued the idea.

After only a couple of weeks, both tired of the island resort's solitude and decided to move back into Vancouver.

When they moved into a seventh-floor apartment in a downtown hotel, they began sleeping in separate beds.

\*　　\*　　\*

In the early morning of May 25, 1990, Joy stood at an outdoor pay phone, listening silently as a story from the *Dallas Morning News* was being read to her:

"A cousin of capital murder defendant Joy Davis Aylor was indicted Thursday on a charge of lying to a Dallas County grand jury about Mrs. Aylor's whereabouts. Hugh Bradford Davis faces one charge of aggravated perjury, a third-degree felony punishable by up to 10 years in prison and a $10,000 fine," the article began.

The story went on to explain how Brad had initially told of taking her and Mike to Denver, leaving them at a motel on the outskirts of town.

An unnamed source was quoted in the article as saying, "He [Davis] initially said he just thought they wanted to take a trip into the mountains."

Only recently, the story said, had Brad admitted the lie, which resulted in the indictment.

Mike, who had adopted a routine of staying up late into the night, long after Joy had gone to bed, was jolted awake by her frantic shaking of his shoulder. It was as if he had wakened to a nightmare instead of from one. Joy's face was ashen. She was clearly hysterical as her words ran together in a high-pitched voice.

Wilson sat up, pulled her to his chest, and tried to calm her. "Just slow down and tell me what's happened."

"They're coming."

"Who?"

"The police. They know where we are. I just talked to—"

"Lonnie." Suddenly, without further explanation, Mike's sleep-fogged mind was racing along with Joy's.

"Yes. They've arrested Brad. It's in the papers. He told them everything. We've got to get out of here."

Wilson sat on the edge of the bed, trying to sort out the sketchy information. It did not surprise him that Brad had told the police what he knew. Certainly, it would have provided them a trail to follow. By now they probably already knew that he had purchased the Wagoneer in Cheyenne and had located the registration records in Cut Bank. Even if Brad hadn't told the police that they were going into Canada, it would have been the most logical assumption. No doubt the Canadian authorities had already been alerted.

But there was no way, Mike was convinced, that they could have tracked them to their exact location so quickly.

"My guess is," he said, "that we've probably got at least a seventy-two-hour jump on anyone trying to locate us."

It was as if Joy had not even heard him. Already she had begun packing clothes and gathering the food she had stored in the room's small icebox. "We've got to get out of here," she pleaded. "Right now."

Swept up in the sudden frenzy, Mike dressed quickly. Any attempt at devising a long-range plan would have to wait. The first order of business was to get away from the hotel as quickly as possible. If the police had made the connection between Joy and Lonnie, his telephone might be tapped. And if, as Mike suspected, Joy had been calling back to Dallas on a regular basis, the calls could easily be traced.

While she continued to pack, Wilson went to fill the Wagoneer with gas.

Upon his return he found a scene highly reminiscent of the one he'd walked into weeks earlier back in Lethbridge. Joy was pacing the room, a wild, frightened look in her eyes. Her hands shook as she gathered things for Mike to load into the Jeep.

When she retreated into the bathroom and returned holding a package of razor blades, Wilson fully grasped the desperation she had attached to the situation.

"How long does it take you to die after you've cut your wrists?" she asked.

A knot formed in Wilson's stomach. "Goddammit, Joy, that's crazy. If you slit your wrists, all that's going to happen is you're going to bleed all over the fucking place until they bust in here and haul your ass to the hospital."

"How long?" Her voice was suddenly controlled, demanding.

"Too damn long," Mike replied angrily. "Just forget it. Forget it right now. What we've got to do is just get the hell out of here."

She refused to move. "Then you'll have to show me how to cut my throat. I'm not going to jail, Mike."

Wilson suddenly felt the sensation of being dragged down into a maelstrom of madness, grappling with a situation totally beyond his reach. He grabbed Joy's arm, took the package of razor blades from her, and tossed it across the room. "Help me get this stuff into the car," he demanded.

Joy was crying as she lifted a paper bag filled with canned goods, flour, and sugar. "Where are we going?"

The answer Mike gave surprised even him. "Mexico."

Caught up in Joy's paranoia, Wilson constantly checked his rearview mirror as he drove from the downtown area in the direction of the Vancouver airport. They would check into a hotel near there, he explained, and plan their next move. This time he would use the name of yet another of his old college buddies. In the event authorities had somehow been alerted to be on the lookout for "John Storms," Mike registered under the name of Leigh Curry, a resident of Sweetwater, Texas, whose greatest thrill in life was joining in his community's annual rattlesnake roundup.

Since Joy had awakened him with her panicked insistence that the authorities were no doubt nearby, Mike had been trying to formulate some workable plan. With the cocaine now out of his system, he was pleasantly surprised to find that he could think far more clearly than he had in months, applying some degree of logic to what was obviously an illogical state of affairs.

"I'm not sure we'll make it, but we've got to try to get on a flight out of here as soon as possible." He told Joy not to bother unpacking. "We're going to put the bags in a locker at the airport and check flight schedules." As an added precaution, they would take a cab to Vancouver International, leaving the Wagoneer in the hotel parking garage.

Joy, who had begun to calm as soon as they were away from the apartment, seemed pleased that Mike had taken control of the situation.

The cab ride to the airport provided the only break in the tension both were feeling. For reasons Wilson did not bother to ask, Joy had insisted on bringing the bag of food staples she'd collected before leaving the apartment, placing it in the trunk of the taxi along with the luggage. As the cabdriver was unloading his trunk, a sack of flour fell to the pavement, exploding into a mound of white powder at his feet.

The driver said nothing as he looked suspiciously at the substance, then nervously eyed both of his customers.

Wilson read the driver's mind and began to laugh. "Relax, pal, the only thing we're smuggling is Gold Medal flour."

Inside the airport, Mike rented a locker and stored their luggage while Joy went in search of information on flight schedules. "Look for the most obscure airline you can find," Wilson advised.

Japan Airlines, she learned, had a direct flight to Mexico City the next afternoon.

"That will have to do," Mike said.

Back at the hotel they began planning in earnest. Privately, Wilson was not at all optimistic about their chances. In all likelihood they would be arrested at the airport. If not, there was the very real possibility that Mexican Customs would detain them. He began to think that the great escape, once exciting and even romantic, had become a foolish, pointless exercise.

And though she had never mentioned it, Wilson had come to feel that Joy had expected him to provide a smoother getaway. Why hadn't he been able to simply telephone one of the high-rolling drug dealers he'd once represented, calling in a long-owed favor that would have them magically winging off to Guatemala or Europe on a private jet? Or hidden away on some yacht in the Caribbean? Why had he had no easy solution to retrieving the money she said she'd left in Dallas? And why had he lured her to the godforsaken cold of Canada when all along she had wanted only to flee to Mexico?

These instinctive feelings caused Wilson mixed emotions. On one hand he felt he had badly failed the woman he wanted more than anything to protect, to take to some safe place far beyond the reach of those who wanted to jail her, even put her to death. Still, he could not help wonder if he had been manipulated, lured into the kind of seductive trap one reads about in bad novels. Try though he did to push such thoughts from his mind, he pondered the possibility that Joy had never really been in love with him, but instead had only used him as part of her grand scheme for escape, even from the day they had met.

He had tried with little success to read her reaction to the plan he had mapped out for their flight. It was best, he had told her, that they travel separately. "They're going to be looking for us together, so we have a better chance traveling alone. We can't even get our tickets at the same time. If one of us makes it, he calls the other to come on. If things go wrong, at least both of us won't get caught."

He was only mildly surprised when Joy volunteered to go ahead of him. He could, she suggested, take a weekend flight.

"Joy, you've got to understand that there's a chance you won't make it."

"I'll make it."

Wilson secretly envied her confidence.

He thought about all this as he sat alone in the hotel room, waiting for Joy's return from a nearby travel agency.

He was not in the least surprised to see that she had purchased an excursion-rate ticket. What did give him pause, however, was the name it had been issued to: "J. Taylor."

"This could be a problem," he said. "Customs is probably going to check your passport, and they're going to wonder why the name on it and the one on your ticket are different."

Joy grabbed the ticket from his hand and stared at it. "Damn." It was the first time Wilson had ever heard her swear. "When the travel agent asked for my first initial and last name, I told her 'J. Aylor.' She must have just misunderstood. Damn."

She paced the small room, ticket in hand, for several minutes. "I can fix it," she finally said.

Taking a mascara pencil from her purse, she began trying to alter the name on her passport to match that on the plane ticket. Mike watched in amusement as she leaned over her task, her lips pursed as she concentrated like a schoolgirl trying her best to color within the lines. What resulted was a smudged mess that accomplished nothing more than proving to even the most casual observer that an amateur attempt had been made to change the name. Finally, Joy looked defeatedly at Mike. "Now what?" she asked.

Without speaking he walked over to the table where she sat, carrying with him a cup of coffee. Taking her passport, he opened it to the page she had been working on and held it over a nearby wastebasket and poured the coffee onto it. "People are always having accidents like this," he said. With luck, the coffee stains, once dried, would hide her aborted handiwork. "Hell, they probably won't check anything but your picture anyway."

He was suddenly aware of Joy looking at him in a strange way, as if seeking an answer to some question without having to risk asking it. She rose from the table and stood close to him, her arms around his neck.

Several seconds passed before she spoke. "You aren't coming, are you?"

Mike did not immediately respond. In truth, he was not certain of the answer.

"Are you going back to Dallas?"

Though he had in recent days considered returning and giving himself up, he wasn't ready to admit it to her. Actually, he wasn't even sure he wanted to do it. All he knew was that he was bone weary of being on the run, with no idea of what each new day might bring.

"Mike, I need to know what you're going to do."

The plan he outlined to her was simple. If she made it into Mexico without problems, she was to phone the Town & Country Inn and leave word. He would not risk returning there but would call to check for messages. If he learned that she was safely in Mexico City, he said, he would purchase his ticket and join her.

"And if I don't make it?"

"First, I'm going to write a long letter to Clay and try to explain some things. Then, I'll drive up into the Rockies, find me a nice quiet mountaintop, and kill myself." No hint of jest was in his voice. Nor did Joy, who had in the past expressed no discomfort at discussing her own possible suicide, make any attempt to dissuade him from such a plan.

"Then say a little prayer for me."

"Joy, I don't know if I even believe in God anymore."

"It doesn't matter. I think He hears you even if you don't believe in Him."

Wilson's greatest concern for the success of Joy's passage into Mexico was the large sum of cash she would be carrying with her. No vacationer or even a businesswoman could pass through customs with the amount of money Joy had without raising suspicion. At many ports of entry, travelers were required by law to declare amounts of $10,000 or more. Customs agents used this method to help keep track of "mules" carrying large sums of cash, earned from drug transactions, from one country to another. Many freelancing college students, girlfriends, and out-of-work thugs made dozens of in-and-out trips to foreign countries each year, never carrying more than the legal limit of less than $10,000 each time. For the life of him, Wilson couldn't recall if Mexico was among the countries enforcing such a law. He could only guess, but was almost certain that as soon as customs officials saw the amount of money she was carrying, they would likely detain her at least long enough to run some sort of computer check. If nothing else, they would question her. And in light of the way she had been behaving lately, Mike feared she might panic.

Late that night, after discussing the problem at length, they found a solution. Rather than carry the money, Joy would wear it beneath a loose-fitting dress.

Into the early morning hours she stood patiently, clad only in panties and bra, as Wilson arranged, then rearranged, the banded bills on her body, attaching them with adhesive tape. The trick, he pointed out, was to position the money in such a manner that it would not be obvious once she put on the dress.

At first humorous, the task ultimately took on erotic tones as Wilson attached the bills on her firm, youthful body—around her waist, along her legs, under her arms, in the small of her back, and between her breasts.

Finally satisfied, he stood back to watch as she slipped the dress over her head, struck a model's pose, then walked around the room.

"You look like a million dollars."

Joy laughed for the first time all day as she slipped out of the dress. "I wish."

For several more minutes she stood in front of him as he removed the bills, writing notations on each band to indicate where they were to be reattached the following day.

Not until the wee hours of the morning did Wilson finally convince her to try to get some sleep. As she lay in bed, Mike leaned over her and gently kissed her. She returned his kiss with more passion than she had displayed in some time. As he rose from her bedside, she looked up at him seductively. "Is that all?" she asked, a disappointed expression on her face.

"Get some sleep," Wilson whispered, turning out the lamp and making his way through the darkness to his own bed.

Long after, he would wonder why he had refused her obvious invitation to make love.

For the remainder of the night they lay silently in their respective beds, neither sleeping.

On Friday afternoon, as they stood near the Japan Airlines check-in counter, Joy displayed none of the exhaustion Wilson was feeling from the hectic past forty-eight hours. Before they checked out of the hotel she had again questioned him about his plans. If she made it safely into Mexico, he had repeated, he would follow. If he didn't hear from her, he would have to make up his mind whether to drive into the mountains and commit suicide or return to Dallas and turn himself in. When she had asked how much money he needed, he had told her $1,500 would suffice.

Waiting for her flight to be called, Joy looked at Mike from behind a pair of his sunglasses. He silently returned her gaze, saying nothing as he tried to push aside the feelings he had been struggling with. He could not help but feel that, despite what she might have said, Joy was secretly relieved they would no longer be together—that she had come to look on him as a disappointing and unnecessary accomplice.

When the boarding call came over the airport intercom, Joy put her arms around his neck and kissed him gently. "I hate to leave you here."

Mike returned her kiss but said nothing as she turned and

quickly walked down the concourse, disappearing in the mass of happy travelers en route to holiday sun and fun.

For almost an hour Wilson nervously waited in the airport, staring out its huge glass windows as the plane sat on the runway, awaiting clearance for takeoff. Only when it was finally airborne did he breathe a sigh of relief.

He stood at the window for several more minutes, focusing on the plane as it gained altitude and finally became only a small dot in the afternoon sky.

"Good-bye, Joy," he whispered, then turned to go back to the hotel and wait for the phone call that his gut feeling told him would never come.

Saturday passed with agonizing slowness. Registered in an out-of-the-way hotel on the outskirts of Vancouver, Wilson waited until midafternoon before phoning the registration desk of the Town & Country Inn to ask if he had received any messages. The operator's negative response gave rise to yet another strange mixture of emotions. While he felt a quiet confidence that she had not been apprehended—he had come to believe that her life on the run was almost magically charmed—it was no real surprise that Joy had not called. Still, he could not ward off the feeling of disappointment.

He took a long, solitary walk, ate dinner, returned to his room to watch an old black-and-white movie on television, then phoned the Town & Country again, only to learn there had still been no message.

Sunday was much the same, a lonely waiting game. As Wilson lay in bed that night, thoughts of past, present, and future racing through his weary mind, he again found himself thinking seriously about committing suicide. Never, during the dark moments of alcohol or cocaine addiction, marital problems, professional and financial disasters, or even when he was arrested, had he ever considered escaping his problems by taking his life. That he found himself dwelling on the thought—even feeling a strange sense of comfort from the idea—lent a new kind of fear to this situation.

The time, he knew, had come to seek help. He was ready to turn himself in. The only question that remained was how.

Bob Fain, having left the hectic pace of Dallas behind years earlier and moved his law practice and family to the relative peace and quiet of Billings, Montana, had been kept abreast of his ex-partner's troubles by former associates in Dallas. Still, he was surprised when he received the call from Mike.

Even more surprising was the exhaustion and resignation he heard in his friend's voice.

"Mike," Fain said, "I'm glad you called. Where the hell are you?"

Wilson refused to give him his specific location. "I'm still in Canada," he said, "but I'm thinking about turning myself in. The thing is, Bob, I don't want to get stranded in some jail up here for months. I want to get back to Dallas. Can you help me?"

"I'll sure try," Fain replied, already contemplating the best manner to deal with the federal authorities. He would, he said, contact a couple of FBI agents in Dallas he had stayed in touch with and see if it could be arranged for him to surrender in Billings.

"Mike," Fain said, "I've really been worried about you. I was afraid that woman you were with was going to kill you." He paused for a moment, then continued. ". . . or that you might have gotten crazy and decided to kill yourself."

"I've considered it," Wilson replied.

"You can knock that shit off, right now. We'll work something out, okay?"

"Yeah, I'm all right now. I've been thinking about driving to Calgary and trying to get a flight out of there to Dallas. I'll give you a call sometime tomorrow and let you know."

"Let me see what I can do first." Fain was certain the authorities were probably close and he privately feared for his friend's safety. "Mike," he said, "be real damn careful."

Fain's wife, who instinctively knew from the conversation that it had been Mike Wilson her husband was speaking with, watched as he slowly replaced the receiver.

"How did he sound?"

OPEN SECRETS

"Like someone who wants to come in out of the cold," her
husband replied.

On Monday, Wilson placed another fruitless call to the Town
& Country, then began driving east. By late afternoon he had
reached the lakeside community of Osoyoos, just a few miles
from the Washington border, and checked into the Safari Beach
Resort. During the five-hour drive through the Canadian countryside two goals were accomplished. He had, he felt, succeeded in putting time and distance between himself and those
searching for him. And, more significantly, he had managed to
outrun the idea of suicide.

Early on Tuesday morning Jody Culos, front-office manager
of the Town & Country Inn, spoke into the phone. "Yes, Mr.
Storms. I'm so glad you called. Yes . . . a lady telephoned just
a few minutes go. She didn't leave her name."

On the other end of the line, Mike Wilson made no effort to
disguise his excitement. "Good. If she calls back, tell her I'm
still in B.C., and ask her to call me here." With that he gave her
the number and name of the resort in Osoyoos.

"I'll see that she gets the message." Ms. Culos could not
bring herself to add her usual "Have a nice day" to the end of
the conversation.

Looking up at a note attached to the bulletin board above her
desk, she slowly dialed the number of U.S. Immigration and,
following instructions she had been given days earlier, gave
them the telephone number of the Safari Beach Resort.

"You've been a big help," the businesslike voice on the
other end of the line said.

"I hated lying to that man," Ms. Culos coldly replied.

Within an hour, eight Royal Canadian Mounties were in
place. All exits to the Osoyoos resort were sealed off, two officers crouched near the entrance to Wilson's room, and another,
armed with a high-powered rifle, was positioned on the roof.

After receiving an all-ready signal, one of the Mounties
phoned Wilson's room from the reservation desk. Mike answered on the first ring.

"Come out with your hands up," the voice instructed.

335

In the parking lot, guests of the resort had gathered, watching the flurry of activity. Howard Gruhlke, the front-desk manager, was among those looking on as Wilson was escorted to a waiting car while other Mounties entered his room.

"They don't look very happy," one of the spectators commented.

"They're not," Gruhlke said. "They were hoping to find a woman with him."

Following the arrest, the Mounties turned Wilson over to U.S. Customs officials, and he was immediately driven into the United States and placed in the Oroville, Washington, city jail. Finally, his winding journey was headed back in the direction of Dallas.

On Wednesday he was moved to Spokane, then transferred to Yakima the following day to appear at a removal hearing before a U.S. magistrate.

In Yakima he first came face-to-face with one of the men who had been pursuing him.

Ken MacKenzie had kept a packed suitcase at the Richardson Police Department for weeks in anticipation of a call from Canadian authorities notifying him that an arrest had been made. He was at the airport forty-five minutes after receiving word that Wilson was in custody.

During the flight, MacKenzie anxiously reviewed the questions he would ask the fugitive once they were face-to-face, wondering just how helpful Wilson might be. Though he'd never met Mike, he'd talked with scores of people who knew him and had come away with the image of a likable man whose weaknesses had been his downfall, another victim of Joy Aylor's manipulation.

As he neared his destination, MacKenzie felt his excitement muted by a sense of dread. In addition to interrogating Wilson and escorting him back to Dallas, he would also be the bearer of bad news he knew his prisoner would not be prepared for. Wilson's father had died just days earlier.

Once back in Dallas, Wilson contacted an old friend. Gary Noble, a former assistant district attorney, had fought his own battles with drug problems and could identify with Wilson's plight. In the late seventies Noble, too, had stepped beyond legal boundaries into a drug nightmare that led to marital problems, depression, and ultimately the loss of his law license and a five-year prison sentence. Only through a courageous and dedicated effort had Noble regained his status in the Dallas law community. Following a long, hard-fought battle to earn renewal of his license, he had eagerly accepted an invitation to join Wilson and partner John McShane in private practice.

He readily agreed to represent Wilson at his arraignment and upcoming bond hearing.

On July 21, Dr. Robert Powitzky, a big, gentle-voiced, bearded clinical psychologist, traveled from Dallas to the nearby Mansfield Correctional facility at the request of Wilson's attorney. Noble hoped that U.S. magistrate John Tolle, who had released Mike on his own recognizance following his March arrest, might allow Wilson to post bond and retain his freedom until time for his trial. Noble had requested that the doctor interview his client in hopes of proving that Mike was not, in fact, a flight risk.

Though Powitzky had agreed to do an evaluation, he knew even the most positive recommendation was likely to fall on deaf ears. Judges, once burned, were rarely generous the second time around. Thus, he approached his task with mixed feelings.

He had first met Wilson in the mid-eighties when Mike had sought his services as an expert witness in the trial of a drug dealer Wilson was defending. While he had not known Wilson well, Powitzky had been aware of the attorney's reputation as an aggressive, highly respected member of the bar. The profile he had mentally formed from brief encounters with Wilson and discussions with other lawyers was that of a friendly, highly qualified attorney whose devotion to his craft met all the qualifications of a legal workaholic. He also knew of Mike's work with fellow attorneys who suffered from alcohol problems. Mike Wilson was part of a celebrated collection of attorneys the doctor privately referred to as "the AA Lawyers," a group the doctor felt was endowed with the best of intentions but one that placed a terrible burden on itself. Recovering addicts, whether their problems were alcohol or drugs, Powitzky knew, constantly fought battles with moments of weakness that resulted in falls from grace. Those who placed themselves in positions of serving as positive examples—role models lending strength to others, traveling throughout the country speaking out about how they had defeated their addiction—were, in his opinion, among the most vulnerable. In the event of a relapse, it was all but impossible for them to admit to renewed problems. Wilson, he strongly felt, was a prime example.

Seated in a sterile medical examining room at the Mansfield facility, Dr. Powitzky tried without success to mask his shock when Wilson, wearing an orange jumpsuit and tennis shoes, was escorted in for their interview. The haggard, drawn man standing in front of him bore only a faint resemblance to the gregarious attorney with the taut athlete's build he had remembered. Wilson's eyes were sunken, looking out from above deep, dark circles. The smile Mike offered the doctor was forced, the handshake barely felt.

For the first half hour, it fell to Powitzky to keep the conversation going with a series of questions, gently probing, urging the weary prisoner to provide reasons for his recent series of unreasonable acts.

In time Wilson seemed to relax and, as the doctor had hoped, fell into a fascinating narrative of all that had happened since he had first met Joy Aylor. He spoke of the night he had accompanied her to the emergency room where her dead son had been taken, of the deepening of his feelings for her, the strange, hectic weeks spent on the run, and finally his bout with thoughts of suicide.

Wilson's voice had a genuine tone of sadness as he spoke of those last days in Canada. In retrospect, he felt Joy had simply used him, just as she had so many others.

Most impressive to the doctor was that at no time during the interview had Wilson suggested blame for anyone but himself, accepting full responsibility for his situation. There were no bitter swipes at social injustices, no claims of mistreatment or lack of understanding from friends and family, just an almost tangible sense of regret and resignation.

Dr. Powitzky had talked with few men more beaten down than the one seated across from him in the infirmary room.

As he drove away from the jail, the doctor soon found his thoughts shifting from Wilson to the mysterious woman Mike had accompanied to Canada. He would dearly like to interview Joy Aylor, a woman whose apparent charms and self-centeredness fascinated him.

He had little doubt that she had been manipulating Wilson from the beginning. Very likely she had even encouraged his continued use of cocaine, using his drug dependency as a leash to keep him close. The Joy Aylor whom Wilson had described possessed the classic personality traits of a sociopath, a charismatic but shallow, manipulative person completely lacking in conscience and concern for others.

Wilson, the doctor felt, had been teetering on the edge of a psychological cliff when he first encountered Joy. And she had wasted precious little time in pushing him over the edge.

In his business, Dr. Powitzky had seen hundreds of Mike Wilsons—men who after extended periods of drug abuse had allowed their moral values to deteriorate. Joy Aylor, he was convinced, had helped that deterioration along.

Yes, the doctor thought to himself as he eased into the flow of traffic headed toward Dallas, Mike Wilson had definitely been used.

The following afternoon, in federal court, Wilson's request for bail was quickly denied, and he was ordered to remain in custody until his trial.

In the lobby of Banco de Mexico in Mexico City, a smiling, attractive American woman, dressed casually and wearing dark glasses, identified herself as Jodi Packer and inquired about renting a safety-deposit box.

# 22

---

THE OLD RED Courthouse, an ancient sandstone and granite monument to Dallas's judicial past, remains as one of the final landmarks of another time in the city's colorful history. All but lost among the ever-growing number of multistoried steel-and-reflecting-glass structures that form the city's skyline, it was built in 1872 at a cost of less than $300,000. Once the location for the county's most celebrated trials, the stage for legendary fire-and-brimstone arguments delivered by the best attorneys in the Southwest, it has long since yielded its criminal courts to larger, more modern structures. At Old Red, as local historians now refer to the two-story building with its menacing gargoyles and majestic turrets, the justice dispensed from its small courtrooms is generally of a family and civil nature; a place where divorces are routinely granted, custody arguments heard, and litigations between angered business associates ruled on.

On the morning of Friday, August 3, 1990, Larry Aylor, accompanied by John Barr, entered the gloomy hallways of the musty old building to continue his litigious assault on his ex-wife. Undeterred by the fact that Joy's whereabouts remained unknown, Aylor was clearly pleased that the day had finally arrived.

For weeks, Kevin Chapman had tried to convince Aylor and his attorney to postpone the civil action until after Joy was captured and convicted of felony charges, even offering to help with preparation of the case when the time was right. For now, he argued, any judgment would be virtually meaningless so long as she remained a fugitive.

Too, he had pointed out, Aylor's testimony in civil court might very likely provide not only Joy's lawyer but attorneys for all those indicted with important discovery information. Dr.

Gailiunas, contemplating similar civil action, had heard the same reasoning and finally agreed, reluctantly, not to endanger the state's case by filing charges.

Chapman's plea to Aylor, however, had fallen on deaf ears. Having grown increasingly displeased with the tight-lipped policy of the assistant DA who had virtually shut him out, refusing to discuss even the smallest details of the case, Larry Aylor wanted his day in court.

Sworn in by pipe-smoking district judge Bob O'Donnell, he dispassionately talked about the murder of Rozanne Gailiunas, attempts on his own life, and the death of his son.

For over an hour, Barr addressed his client with a wide range of questions designed to outline a far-reaching plot set in motion by Joy and expanded to include a remarkable cast of characters. Several of those Aylor accused had never been considered or had long since been dismissed as suspects by the police.

Aylor recounted a confrontation with Henry Davis during the time he and Joy were separated. Davis had warned him to "get my ass back with Joy and Chris or he would have some of his henchmen take care of me."

The Davis family, Larry said, had made it increasingly difficult for him to see Chris during the months following his breakup with Joy. His son, Aylor told the judge, had been induced to live with his grandparents with the promise of a new car. That car, Aylor testified, would be taken from the youngster if he ever chose to move in with his father.

And Aylor told of how Joy and Mike Wilson had, according to a police officer at the scene of Chris's accident, spent a great deal of time searching Chris's car instead of going immediately to the hospital.

He also recalled two previous attempts on his life, the first coming when the motorcycle he was riding was forced off the road by a speeding car.

On another occasion he had seen the silhouette of a gun-wielding man outside the window of his apartment. Frightened for his life, he began sleeping on the living-room couch of his apartment to avoid being near any windows.

Additionally, he testified about a recorded conversation between Joy and Carol Garland that had supposedly occurred on the evening before the attempt on his life in Kaufman County. On the tape, which he said had been played for him by the Richardson Police Department, Carol had told his ex-wife that "it would be done this weekend."

With neither Joy nor an attorney representing her present, the strange, one-sided proceeding ended without cross-examination or demand for any documentation to back Aylor's claims.

Judge O'Donnell, citing the unavailability of testimony from Joy, was therefore legally obligated to declare Aylor's allegations true and awarded him $10 million for actual emotional stress, pain, and suffering and $20 million in punitive damages. Additionally, he ruled, Larry was owed another $200,000 for legal fees and for the loss of his home, which he claimed Joy had obtained by fraudulent means.

Legally, Joy Aylor now owed her ex-husband $31.2 million.

The courthouse gossip mill was abuzz with the amount of the judgment, but it was difficult to find anyone who believed Aylor would ever see a penny of it.

Relieved that the court proceedings were over, Larry accompanied Barr back to his office where they sat, talking of the decision that had just been handed down. There was, however, none of the exuberance, the celebratory atmosphere, that would normally accompany such a triumph. It might look good on Barr's résumé and would make interesting headlines in tomorrow's newspaper, but, as Chapman had predicted, the victory was hollow.

After a while, Aylor began reflecting on events surrounding Rozanne's death that he had not mentioned in court. "You know, as I look back on it all, Joy had probably been sending me a subtle message for quite some time. On several occasions after the murder, she told me that Rozanne would 'burn in hell.' It wasn't until years later that I learned the killer had left the message 'Burn in hell, bitch' written in blood on Rozanne's bedroom wall."

He did not say where he got this information, which was backed by nothing investigators had reported finding at the crime scene back in 1983.

Again he began strongly hinting that Henry Davis had been involved in the plot to kill him. On one of the tapes played for him by the police, he said, was a discussion of driving him to the Davis ranch where he and his pickup would be buried in a huge ditch that was part of a new lake his former father-in-law was having dug on the property.

Neither Kevin Chapman nor Morris McGowan had any knowledge of this tape.

Barr had a story of his own to recount. On the day he took Joy's deposition, he had made a morning trip with his daughter to the zoo. They had spent considerable time at the predator birds exhibit, and Barr had been impressed with the steely-eyed eagles and hawks as they stared back at him and his daughter. "Later that day, as I sat across the table from Joy Aylor, the look in her eyes reminded me of those I'd seen at the predators' cages earlier in the day."

In time, the discussion turned to speculation of how successful Joy, now apparently alone, might be at avoiding capture.

If indeed she had as much money with her as he had been led to believe, Aylor said, she could remain at large for a long time. Joy, he insisted, lent new definition to the word *frugal*. "She's the kind of woman who would rather have one five-hundred-dollar dress than five hundred-dollar dresses," he explained. "But what she'll do is shop around until she finally finds that five-hundred-dollar dress marked down to one hundred dollars."

If her ability to elude the law depended solely on careful money management, Larry suggested, it could be a long time before she was caught.

Though discouraged over the missed opportunity in Canada, McGowan felt some degree of satisfaction in the knowledge that Joy was finally in Mexico. All along he'd had a gut feeling that she had planned to go there. From the moment he'd led a search of her house after she and Mike had fled to Canada, finding Spanish-language tapes she'd left behind, he'd been reasonably certain her ultimate destination was somewhere south of the border.

And while he'd never dealt with Mexican authorities before, he had initially felt confident that given proper incentive, the *federales* would welcome the opportunity to join in the chase. In Mexico, he'd always heard, money spoke loudly. If the FBI put out the word of a reward for assistance in the capture of an American fugitive, the job was as good as done.

He quickly found out this was not the case: Mexican officials, still angered over the Guadalajara kidnapping of Dr. Humberto Alvarez-Machain, a suspect in the brutal and highly publicized torture-murder of undercover DEA agent Enrique Camarena in 1985, had made it clear to U.S. authorities they would no longer be welcomed.

Briefly, McGowan and MacKenzie had even discussed the possibility of traveling to Mexico City themselves, hopeful they might find Joy, take her into custody, and bring her back into the United States where they could formally and legally arrest her. The idea, however, was quickly dismissed when FBI agent Matt Chapman explained that Mexican authorities would immediately arrest any unauthorized U.S. law enforcement personnel found in their country.

John Barr had phoned Kevin Chapman, offering whatever help he might be able to lend to the search. He and his firm, he said, represented several large Mexican businesses, operated by influential people with friends high in the country's government. He even volunteered use of his own investigators.

Chapman quickly turned down the attorney's offer with a stern warning that he not interfere.

The hurry-up-and-wait pace of the investigation, then, was destined to continue, and McGowan found himself spending long hours contemplating what plans Joy, now on her own, might be making. He was reasonably certain that she would not try to make contact with members of her family. She was, he surmised, smart enough to realize that their phones would probably be monitored. Very likely she now knew that Wilson was in custody, making any attempt at communication with him impossible. And since she'd apparently jilted Jodi Packer, it seemed unlikely that she would attempt to reestablish her relationship with him.

Joy's plan, McGowan decided, would be to distance herself from everyone, to simply disappear. If she was as smart as he thought her to be, she would trust no one.

Jodi, in fact, had come to the Richardson Police Department shortly after Joy and Mike had left for Canada, voicing concern that he had heard nothing from her and offering to help. He still loved Joy, he told McGowan, and feared for her safety so long as she was in Wilson's company. He would rather see her arrested and returned to Dallas then continue her travels with Mike.

After reading newspaper reports that Joy was suspected to have flown to Mexico, Packer had telephoned McGowan again, talking at length of stories he'd heard about treatment of Americans arrested and imprisoned in Mexican jails. He wanted her back in the United States as badly as they did. If Joy did contact him, he promised to call immediately. "All I'm concerned about is Joy's safety."

In truth, neither the Richardson police nor anyone in the DA's office actually expected any real cooperation from Jodi Packer. For reasons no one could fully explain, they had collectively come to distrust and dislike him. Like many who spend their lives in law enforcement, they had developed what some called a built-in "bullshit detector." From that long-ago evening in Joy's house when his arrogant, abusive behavior had suddenly turned friendly after his brief private conversation with Joy, his motives had been suspect. Jodi was too friendly, too quick to drop names, too eager to volunteer help that never seemed to come.

Additionally, Chapman and McGowan had long been convinced that Packer knew far more than he was telling them.

And while they had no way of knowing it, their feelings paralleled those of Joy's friends, who had long been puzzled by her attraction to Packer. He was a greedy man whose primary interest and concern centered squarely on himself.

Officials had learned that Mike Wilson, too, held Packer in great disdain. Shortly after his arrest and return to Dallas, Mike had been visited in jail by Kevin Chapman, with whom he'd been bird hunting on numerous occasions in happier times, and

Kevin's fellow prosecutor Dan Hagood. For some time the three men had talked generally about Wilson's relationship with Joy and his own legal troubles before getting down to serious questioning.

The interview had been under way only a few minutes when Mike interrupted. "Look," he said to Chapman, "before we go any further, you guys have got to answer one question for me."

Surprised, the two prosecutors waited to hear what Wilson wanted to know.

"Tell me what you think of Jodi Packer."

Both secretive men who routinely went to unreasonable lengths to guard information, neither Chapman nor Hagood responded for several seconds as they each stared at the cement floor of the holding cell.

Finally Chapman lifted his head and looked Wilson squarely in the eye. "Mike, he's the most despicable, sleazy sonuvabitch I've ever been around."

Wilson nodded, a satisfied smile spreading across his face. He was, he said, now ready to answer their questions.


With their hands legally tied, the Richardson police could do little but await the FBI's word of any new developments. Occasionally, some new rumor would surface—Henry Davis had a friend who owned a large ranch in Mexico and Joy might be hiding out there—which they would pass on to FBI agent Matt Chapman, who, in turn, would notify his fellow agent in Mexico. But each time they were rewarded with nothing but silence.

In essence, the case had been taken from the men who had worked it for seven years, their passivity creating a new, unwelcome level of frustration.

The idea of doing nothing, of being unable to participate actively in the search, grated on McGowan and his fellow officers. Perhaps it was finally time to take the case to the media and see what new leads might result. For months, reporters from throughout the country had heard McGowan's polite refusal to discuss the case. Now, he suggested, the time might be right to tell journalists just enough to renew public interest. Someone out there just might be ready to come forward with helpful information.

MacKenzie, recently returned from a law enforcement conference, suggested contacting the television show "America's Most Wanted." A representative from the popular Fox Network program that had aided in the apprehension of almost two hundred criminals had attended the meeting and urged officers to submit any particularly interesting cases they might have for consideration.

"This one," Ken suggested, "has everything they're looking for." FBI agent Matt Chapman agreed.

"Give them a call," McGowan said.

In short order, producers of the show were making plans to send a film crew to Dallas the first week in August.

Excited about the possibilities the upcoming nationwide telecast might create, the officers were unaware that the local media had already done a story that would recharge their enthusiasm.

Upon her return from Mexico, a Dallas woman named Stephanie Grimes, reviewing back issues of the *Dallas Times Herald*, saw a photograph accompanying the paper's story on the multimillion-dollar civil judgment that had been awarded Larry Aylor.

Late in the afternoon of August 4, 1990, Ken MacKenzie received a phone call from Grimes. She explained that she had spent the previous month attending a Spanish-language school in Cuernavaca. She was certain that the woman who had lived with her in the home of an airline pilot and his wife, who served as one of the school's "host families," was the same shown in the photograph that had accompanied the *Times Herald* article.

Any skepticism MacKenzie had immediately disappeared when Grimes told him that the woman had introduced herself not as Joy Aylor but as "Jodi Packer."

"Ma'am," the officer said, "if you'll give me your address, I'd like to come by and continue this conversation in person."

An hour later he was sitting in the living room of the Grimes home, taking notes as the woman related her month-long association with Joy Aylor:

"She was very nice. She was already there when I arrived to

enroll, and we were put in the same home with one of the local families. She told me that her husband was on the coast, fishing, so she had decided to enroll in the language classes. She talked a lot about her children—all boys—back in the States.''

Only after MacKenzie began questioning her did she begin to remember what she defined as "strange behavior." The woman often went to a drugstore nearby to make calls from a pay phone. And on those days when the students would make group sight-seeing trips, she seemed always to shy from anyone taking photographs.

"The only time I ever saw her upset," she recalled, "was when I opened the door to her room one evening and found her lying in the middle of the bed, crying. I asked her what was wrong, and she began telling me about losing one of her sons in a terrible car accident.''

MacKenzie exerted great effort to control his excitement. Was she still at the school?

No, Grimes explained, she had left rather suddenly to meet her husband in Mexico City. Apparently they were having marital problems. She had, however, indicated that she planned to return for the next semester of classes. Registration was scheduled for September 17.

"One other thing," Stephanie Grimes said.

"What's that?"

"When she left, she stole my travel card. I was concerned that I might have trouble getting back home without it.''

MacKenzie drove quickly back to the office, telephoned McGowan at his home, and relayed the conversation he'd had with Grimes. Morris felt a rush of adrenaline as he listened, his mind suddenly racing again. To have found a witness who put Joy in a specific location was a giant step in the right direction. On the other hand, the fact that the sighting had occurred almost a month earlier was troubling. Joy could have put a lot of distance between her and Cuernavaca since Stephanie Grimes last saw her.

As the two officers discussed the new information, weighing its value, they focused on two things MacKenzie had been told. If Joy did, in fact, return and attempt to enroll for the fall semester—something both felt highly unlikely—the FBI could be there, waiting for her.

And even if she had fled to some other part of the country, with no thought of returning to Cuernavaca, she was probably still in touch with whomever she'd been making phone calls to from the drugstore.

"If we get the number of that damn pay phone," McGowan said, "we can trace the calls and find out who she's in contact with."

MacKenzie was willing to wager that records would show the calls had been made to the same person she'd regularly phoned while hiding out in Canada: "She's still talking to her friend Fielding."

While McGowan agreed, the dangers of confronting Lonnie Fielding directly were clear. The last thing either wanted was for him to alert Joy that they knew her whereabouts.

Their first inclination, then, was to make a fast trip to Cuernavaca, locate the drugstore, and get the phone number. But the warning against pursuing the investigation without the blessing of Mexican officials quickly cooled enthusiasm for the plan. Such a trip, both knew, would never receive authorization from their superiors.

They would have to alert Dallas FBI agent Chapman and ask that he instruct one of the Bureau agents in Mexico to locate the drugstore and the number of the pay phone Joy had used. Only after the calls were traced could they afford to contact whomever they'd been placed to.

At the time, neither knew that months would pass without so much as a cursory attempt at locating the drugstore pay phone.

In truth, the only tangible evidence that the FBI was actively working the case was its release of a wanted poster that was mailed to law enforcement agencies and federal post offices throughout the United States. Larry Aylor had discovered this one morning as he entered the tiny Culpeper, Virginia, post office to collect his mail. There on the bulletin board along with angry-faced men charged with mail fraud, robberies, and kidnappings, was Joy. "Wanted by FBI," the poster read, for capital murder and interstate flight.

For several minutes Larry read Joy's description, the list of aliases she'd been using, and the crimes she'd been charged with. As he looked at the rows of fingerprints below her photo, it occurred to him that they seemed far too large to have come from hands he remembered as small and delicate.

Near the bottom of the poster, written in capital letters, was the word "CAUTION," followed by, "She may hire individuals to protect her or be in possession of a hand weapon. She should be considered armed, dangerous, and approached with caution."

As he walked quickly from the post office into the crisp September morning, Larry Aylor felt a sudden chill that had nothing to do with the Virginia weather.

Instead of the standard seven minutes of airtime generally given each case it chronicles, the September 21, 1990, edition of "America's Most Wanted" devoted more than half its show—fifteen minutes—to the serpentine Texas crime story.

An estimated 10 million viewers sat in living rooms throughout the United States and Canada watching a reenactment of the murder of Rozanne Gailiunas and the attempt on Larry Aylor's life. A Dallas actress named Susanne Savoy, her hair lightened and styled to make her resemble Joy Aylor, played the starring role.

An interview with McGowan had been filmed at the Richardson Police Department, then one with Larry Aylor as he casually leaned against a fence near his Virginia home. "The whole thing," he told the interviewer, "has been like a bad dream."

Immediately after the segment aired, the show's Washington switchboard lit up. Within twenty-four hours, over three hundred calls related to the case were recorded. One caller was certain he'd seen Joy sleeping under a bridge in Michigan. A man in Coral Gables, Florida, had spoken with her in a shopping mall. Someone in south Texas was certain she was living on a ranch near him.

A call from a Canadian businessman, however, stirred legitimate interest. Speaking in a whispered voice, he told Mac-

Kenzie that he had been with Joy while on a summer business trip to Monterrey, Mexico.

Pressed for details, the man explained that he was calling from home and could not talk freely. His wife was in another room. He gave MacKenzie his office number and suggested he contact him there the following morning.

Ken reluctantly agreed. "One quick question. Did she give you a name?"

"Yes. She said she was Julia Packer."

The officer quickly scribbled the name on a notepad and held it up for McGowan, MacKenzie, and agent Chapman, all in the studio, to view. The men broke into wide smiles.

"We're back in the game," Morris said.

Following a late-night flight back to Dallas, MacKenzie was back on the phone to the Canadian informant early the next morning, listening as he apologized for being so secretive the night before. See, he explained, he had been mixing a little pleasure with his business in Monterrey, something his wife would not look kindly on.

At the Monterrey hotel where he'd stayed, he and a couple of American businessmen had fallen into a routine of having drinks each afternoon with some women who were also registered there. Among the group had been "Julia Packer," an attractive, friendly blonde. She said she was from Atlanta, Georgia, that her husband was in some kind of construction work, and that she had several children.

The man said he had introduced her to another woman in the group who sold real estate in Mexico, and they had developed an immediate friendship. "I got the impression that Julia was interested in buying some property."

MacKenzie asked the caller if he'd ever seen her husband with her.

"No, he wasn't there." He paused, then continued, "but there was some guy who she talked to one afternoon. We were in the bar, talking and having a drink. She was seated where she could look out at the reservation desk. This man apparently comes in—from where I was sitting I couldn't see him—and she jumps up and tells everyone that she'd just seen some old friend of hers from Atlanta. She went out and talked to some-body for quite a while. But when she came back into the bar, she didn't mention anything about it.

"The person you really need to talk with is Lydia Mon-toya," the caller said.

"Who's she?"

"The realtor lady I mentioned."

MacKenzie relayed the conversation to McGowan along with a suggestion he felt might allow them to check out the new information without having to deal with the apparent disinterest of the Mexico-based FBI.

He knew a U.S. Customs official named Larry Viejo, who was stationed in Monterrey. Since Viejo was also a federal agent, what was to prevent him from looking into the matter?

Briefed by phone, the Customs agent had immediately gone to work. First, he checked with the hotel and determined that no one using any of the aliases MacKenzie had provided him was still registered.

His next stop, however, had been more productive. Having located Lydia Montoya, he learned that she had taken Joy to a local bank where she had rented a safety-deposit box.

Additionally, the woman had given him the names of two other men she had introduced Joy to during their afternoon happy-hour meetings in the hotel bar. "They're both from Dallas," he told MacKenzie.

Viejo's information created a flurry of activity in the Rich-ardson Police Department. The Monterrey police chief was contacted and told of the safety-deposit box and the possibility that Joy would return to it. "If that's where she's stashed her money," McGowan said, "you can count on it."

The chief agreed to post one of his men in the bank for a few days. If, after a while, the woman did not return, he would arrange for bank officials to notify him immediately if and when she did show up and do whatever possible to detain her until he could get some of his men there.

MacKenzie meanwhile went in search of the two Dallas businessmen who had met Joy at the Monterrey hotel. They told much the same story Lydia Montoya had, adding one new piece of information.

"She seemed really anxious to find a ride to Nuevo Laredo," one of the men recalled. "She said something about having to meet a friend of her brother-in-law or something like that. I got the impression that it was pretty urgent. I thought it was a little strange that a woman of her apparent means was without transportation, but after a while, I decided she was just leery about making a trip like that by herself.

"She was still talking about it when we left to come back home."

Though both men told MacKenzie they had repeatedly talked of being from Dallas, the woman hadn't so much as hinted she'd ever even visited there.

Joy's urgent need to find a way to Nuevo Laredo, located on the south Texas border, puzzled McGowan and MacKenzie. If true, she was likely planning to meet someone there. But, who? And for what purpose? Was it possible she was considering risking coming back into the United States?

Each new call from Viejo, in fact, offered up a more complicated set of possibilities.

A few days after learning of the rental of the safety-deposit box, the aggressive Customs agent had located two other women who had regularly attended the afternoon hotel-bar gatherings. During his questioning, they mentioned that the American woman had developed a friendship with a wealthy Mexican land baron. The man, considerably older than Joy, had evidently been quite smitten with her and had repeatedly tried to coax her to come live with him on his sprawling ranch outside the city of Torreón.

If, indeed, Joy had found someone willing to take care of her, either by hiding her or lending her help in escaping to God knows where, the cause might well be lost, McGowan realized.

On October 9, 1990, McGowan awoke to an angry realization that the search was far from an end. A headline in the *Dallas Morning News* read, "Fugitive Joy Aylor Seen in Mexico." Quoting unnamed sources "who would discuss the case only if they were not identified," the lengthy article by court-house reporter Ann Belli detailed the sightings of Joy at the Cuernavaca language school and in Monterrey. The story even included the fact she had been using the name Jodi Packer.

While McGowan and Chapman seethed over the article, MacKenzie set about finding out who the "unnamed source" was. Since the entry of the Dallas County Sheriff's Department into the case, he had shared information on the investigation with several deputies, providing them background and keeping them updated on any progress. And while he had been assured the information would be confidentially guarded, he was now certain that someone in the sheriff's office had broken that confidence.

Though he hoped he was wrong, MacKenzie's suspicion quickly focused on a particular deputy whom he had long trusted. In speculative conversations with McGowan, in fact, Ken had initially defended the officer. In time, however, he begrudgingly came to agree with Morris's suggestion of who the "unnamed source" might be.

To find out for certain, the detective solicited the aid of a female officer, asking that she phone the deputy and identify herself as a reporter willing to keep his identity secret in exchange for information on the case. Not long after, MacKenzie walked silently into McGowan's office and tossed a tape of the dispatcher's conversation with the deputy on his desk: "You were right about the sonuvabitch."

By the end of the day the surprised deputy had been severely reprimanded and removed from the case.

In time, hopes of capturing Joy in Mexico waned. Despite repeated requests, the drugstore phone number was never located by the FBI. Joy did not return to the Monterrey bank, leading McGowan to the conclusion that she likely had not put her money there. And while Viejo sought new information on the mysterious land baron, he came up with no new leads. Border Patrol agents in Laredo, alerted that Joy might attempt a crossing into the U.S., had reported nothing.

A demoralized atmosphere swept over the offices of the

Richardson PD and the Dallas County district attorney and remained for days in the wake of the publication of the *Morning News* article.

Sitting in his office late one afternoon, Kevin Chapman idly flipped through the stacks of file folders that represented the two years of work he'd put into the case. Finally, he tossed a pencil onto the desk and looked across the room at McGowan.

"Morris, we're never going to get her back."

The new year began with a growing sense that Chapman's assessment was correct. Joy had successfully vanished.

Through the cold, raw month of January, Mike Wilson again became the focus of public attention as his month-long trial got under way in federal court. A jury of seven men and eight women, after listening to taped conversations between him and Mark Northcutt and watching videotapes of Mike taking the eleven kilos of cocaine from room 909 of the Holiday Inn, returned a guilty verdict. Although Judge A. Joe Fish announced that he would delay sentencing until April, Mike was reasonably certain of his fate as he was escorted from the courtroom. Aware of the federal guidelines the judge would doubtless follow, Wilson knew that he would serve the next fifteen years of his life in prison.

Then early in February of 1991, new life was suddenly breathed into the pursuit of Joy Aylor. Agents Mike Johnson and Barry Moore from the State Department walked into the Richardson Police Department, asking to speak with Lieutenant McGowan.

"What can you tell us about a man named Jodi Packer?" they wanted to know.

# 23

In a fluke of modern technology, a clerk in the regional passport office in Houston, doing a routine computer search on an unrelated matter, had stumbled onto an unexplained situation. Due to a program that flagged any out-of-the-ordinary passport requests, the name of Donald Averille Airhart flashed in an alerting blink when it appeared on the screen.

After lengthy cross-checking, Airhart, whose application had been processed the previous November, was found to have died in a hunting accident twenty-five years earlier. Still, the passport had been okayed and issued.

Investigators were soon convinced that some fraud had occurred after traveling to nearby Beaumont, Texas, where they located the gravesite of the man to whom the passport had been registered.

Quickly moving the investigation into high gear, officials determined that the applicant had used a birth certificate, Texas driver's license, a library card, and an international driver's license when filing for the passport.

Ultimately, the search also revealed the license plate number of the applicant's automobile.

A check with the Department of Motor Vehicles showed that the Jeep Cherokee was not registered to Donald Airhart, but to Jodi Timothy Packer, a forty-four-year-old Dallas businessman and nephew of the late Airhart. State Department investigators Johnson and Moore were assigned to learn what they could about Packer.

Initially, they had gone to the Dallas County sheriff's office. Though they found that Packer had no criminal history, a deputy, overhearing the conversation, had mentioned that Jodi was the former husband of district judge Ann Packer.

Judge Packer, upon learning the nature of their investigation, had recommended they speak immediately with the Richardson police.

Lieutenant McGowan briefly explained his long-running interest in Packer, then listened intently to the still-sketchy information collected by the State Department agents. They said that Packer, using the falsified passport as well as his real one, had been traveling extensively since the first of the year, making trips to Mexico, Spain, France, Morocco, and Saudi Arabia.

Intrigued by the story, McGowan had told of the stymied search for Joy Aylor and her link to the man they were seeking. Agent Johnson was quick to volunteer his department's help. Suddenly, what had begun as just another routine case of passport fraud sounded far more interesting.

''I'll have the DA's office get in touch with you,'' McGowan promised.

''You think your lady is with him?'' Johnson asked as he rose to leave.

McGowan only shrugged, doing his best to mask the new rush of excitement he was feeling. Privately, he was ready to bet on it.

Maybe now, McGowan thought, friendly, always eager-to-help Jodi Packer was finally going to come through, whether he liked it or not.

Dialing Kevin Chapman's office, McGowan was disappointed to learn that the prosecutor and his wife were vacationing in Cozumel, Mexico, but he had no intention of waiting until Kevin returned to share the news and called their hotel.

''You just thought you were going to get a vacation,'' Morris said when he heard Chapman's voice.

''What's happened?''

''I think we're back in the hunt.'' McGowan quickly outlined the information he'd received.

''We'll be home at the end of the week.''

Though two days remained on their vacation, Rhonda Chapman knew it was over as soon as her husband hung up the phone. His interest in scuba diving in the pristine coral reefs died abruptly, replaced by solitary walks along the beach. His mood changed from carefree to pensive. Though hundreds of miles away, Kevin Chapman had mentally returned to his office, his thoughts occupied with things to be done. Getting a warrant for Joy Aylor's arrest, if in fact she could be found, would be no small order. To secure an international warrant required the co-operative efforts of the DA's office, the FBI, and the State Department. Once prepared, it would be forwarded to Interpol, the Paris-based international clearinghouse for law enforcement agencies. Interpol would ultimately supply the warrant to whatever agency was charged with making the actual capture.

Chapman, certain that Packer had left a paper trail, was eager to see where it led. By the time he returned to Dallas, the assistant DA already had a plan of attack.

While the State Department investigators began tracking the activity of the fraudulent passport, Chapman requested a court order to look into Packer's credit-card records and any overseas bank transfers that might be originating from Jodi's business.

In short order, they discovered that money was, in fact, being regularly sent by Packer's remodeling company to various banks in Europe. Making several trips to Houston to speak with executives of Visa, Chapman learned even more about Packer's activities. However, Visa officials could verify Jodi's use of his card only after three weeks had elapsed. The computers could not speed up the process, so Chapman began phoning the reservation desks of hotels where the Visa card had been used, each time hoping that someone might remember a woman being with Packer.

The most recent receipt had come from Nice, France, but as with the other hotels contacted, no one could remember whether a man or a woman had registered.

"As long as we stay this far behind," Chapman told McGowan, "it's going to be impossible—unless they decide to settle into one place." Again the frustration was mounting. Though certain they were getting close, thousands of miles and hours of time difference still separated them from their goal.

And even at home their hands were tied. Though relatively sure that Packer was in regular contact with someone at his

Dallas business office, they could not risk contacting anyone there for fear Jodi would be alerted.

Thinking aloud, McGowan came up with a new investigative avenue. "I wonder what kind of transportation they're using?"

Chapman's eyes brightened at the question. At that moment, without a word being spoken, both men were thinking the same thing.

Later that day, McGowan assigned Richardson detective Mike Sandlin to begin a check of the rental car agencies. Remembering the car Joy had rented prior to her and Mike Wilson's flight from Dallas, the lieutenant suggested that Sandlin check first with Budget.

In a matter of hours Sandlin was back in McGowan's office. He'd just gotten off the phone with the European vice president of Budget Car Rental in London. "Jodi Packer has rented a car at the Nice, France, airport."

"When's it due to be checked in?"

"He didn't know but said he would call back."

For the first time in days a broad smile spread across Morris McGowan's face.

From her window in the small, two-room tourism office in St.-Paul de Vence, France, Dominique Margot could look out on a picturesque village square that had long been the vibrant heartbeat of her ancient home. Vendors, selling fruits and vegetables grown in mountainside gardens and orchards; couples strolling hand in hand, exchanging whispers and having picnic lunches on tree-shaded benches; old men sharing coffee and warmed-over war stories; and children crowded around the bandstand, eagerly awaiting the arrival of the next musician or a puppeteer.

Dominique, a pretty woman in her early thirties, had not realized just how much she had missed her home near the French Riviera until she had been called back from the United States a year earlier to help care for her ailing grandparents. The idea of an American education dismissed, she was at first reluctant to leave the excitement of New York, but was surprised at how quickly she had embraced her old friends and old ways in Vence. From the time she had been a small girl, the historic village had been something of a magical place with its priceless works of art and idyllic setting. Upon her return, the beauty of the tiny corner of the world in which she had spent much of her life had embraced her again, as if for the first time.

Having left once, Dominique had no plans ever to do so again. Vence was where she would remain, letting the world come to her.

This picturesque setting drew many of Europe's greatest artists—Picasso, Matisse, Chagall—lured by the remarkable light of the Mediterranean's sparkling reflection off the mountainsides. Their work remains in evidence throughout the village, adorning the walls of the Matisse Chapel and the Hotel Colombe d'Or.

As a tourism information official, Dominique Margot's job was to point out the historical landmarks to vacationers seeking a respite from the seaside bustle of nearby Nice or Cannes, people more eager to absorb the region's colorful history than battle for a place at the gambling tables just over an hour's drive away in Monaco.

Some, like the handsome American couple who had walked into her office one day in early January, became so enchanted with the area that they wished to stay.

The woman, pleasant and smiling, had introduced herself as Elizabeth. Her husband, Don, was in Europe on business that would likely take quite some time. Having lived in Geneva for the past few months, they were now hoping to spend some time in Vence if they could locate a furnished apartment to rent.

Dominique immediately liked the easy manner of the lovely American woman. Though no doubt wealthy, she was casually dressed in a jogging suit, her shining auburn hair framing a face free of makeup. There was a glowing warmth to her smile that the tourist official could only describe as "angelic."

A self-proclaimed romantic, the tourist official sensed immediately that the two people seated in her office were very much in love. They held hands, laughing easily and often. On the rebound from a stormy relationship that had recently ended, Dominique felt a twinge of envy as she talked with the couple.

Delighted at the opportunity to use her rusty English, she quickly agreed to check on rentals in the area though that went beyond her official duties. She suggested that while she made inquiries, they might like to spend a few days in the hotel just across the street.

Sensing the possibilities of a new and interesting friendship, Dominique found herself wanting badly for the American couple to remain in Vence.

In short order she had located a small villa in the mountains just north of the village. "It's a lovely place," she told the couple as they sat sharing a bottle of wine in the lobby of the Colombe d'Or, "just down the road from where Picasso once lived. The woman who owns it says it is available now. She will even provide dishes and linens."

"It sounds perfect," the woman said. Vence, then, had two new residents, and Dominique had a new friend.

"Since your husband will be away on business," she said, "come by and see me."

Over the next three months, she and Liz saw each other often, meeting for long lunches in the courtyard of the Le Pigeonnier, wandering through the boutiques, having a glass of wine in the late afternoons after the tourism office had closed for the day.

Dominique found the American woman fascinating. With Don away most of the time, she had begun taking French lessons from a woman who lived nearby and spent mornings helping a neighbor in her flower gardens or walking in the mountains. After Don rented her a car, Liz began to explore the region, taking occasional drives along the Riviera to visit museums, perfume factories, and pottery shops.

And she always seemed to look forward to their increasingly regular meetings for lunch or a drink. Occasionally, when not away in Kuwait or Morocco, Don would join them.

Soon, Dominique had introduced Liz to her mother, and an immediate invitation to join the family's weekly gathering for champagne and dinner was extended. Everyone, it seemed, was instantly charmed by her American friend.

When she learned that Liz and Don's rental agreement would

soon be ending and they had decided to remain in Vence until October, perhaps even November, Dominique's mother volunteered that she would be happy to make an apartment she owned available to them.

When Liz decided to have her hair cut short and lightened, Dominique introduced her to her hairdresser. When Don mentioned the need for a safety-deposit box, Dominique directed him to the bank where her father served on the board of directors.

Liz was eager to return the favors being showered on her. Learning that Dominique's ailing grandmother had been placed in a rest home, Liz had been quick to suggest she help tend to her. "I love elderly people," she said. "Listening to them, you can learn so much."

As their relationship grew, the women began to share personal matters. Liz had explained her Southern accent by saying she and Don had grown up in Dallas, then moved to California after they married. They had a beautiful home there, she said, and two grown sons attending college.

Dominique soon felt comfortable enough to confide in Liz about the breakup of her recent love affair. The man, she explained, had been separated from his wife yet after long months of promises had refused to get a divorce. Dominique had begun to feel like a mistress and, despite being very much in love, had decided to end it.

The conversation had eventually turned to the French tradition of men and their mistresses. "I could never stand for it." Dominique insisted. "If I learned that my boyfriend or husband was sleeping with another woman, I would throw him out of the house."

Liz smiled and shook her head. "No, you wouldn't. Not if you really loved him. What you would do is talk about it, try to understand it, and find a way to work things out. Communication is the most important thing a couple can share. Believe me, I know."

Liz confided that she and her husband had, in fact, also had a "problem" years earlier.

"And how did you handle it?"

"Rather than let things get out of hand, I decided to work it out. Now everything is fine."

Dominique, who on a recent evening had seen Liz and Don strolling through the village arm in arm, stopping occasionally to share a brief kiss, found it difficult to imagine them ever having had problems in their marriage. She was convinced that she had never seen any couple more in love. Or a woman more in control of her life.

Not only did Dominique welcome the budding new friendship, but she felt interesting and valuable lessons could be learned from it.

Therefore she became very concerned after receiving a call one morning telling her that Liz had been in an automobile accident while en route to meet her for lunch.

Dominique felt genuine relief when her friend phoned to explain that it had only been a careless fender bender. Liz had not been hurt and would be in touch as soon as the rental agency replaced the damaged car.


For several days Detective Sandlin had regularly spoken with the Budget executive in London, increasingly impressed by his eagerness to help.

"According to the records I have in front of me," he said, "the car—a Corsa—was returned on the sixteenth of January."

But even before Sandlin's disappointment could set in, the executive apologized, "No, I'm sorry, that's not correct. You see, I'm not at all accustomed to reading these printouts. The rental agreement was extended to February sixteenth."

"And was it checked in then?"

The Englishman again apologized. "I'll have to check on that and ring you back."

In less than an hour he had learned that the rental agreement had again been extended for another month. Sandlin glanced down at the desk calendar in front of him. Saturday, March 16, was but three days away.

The news set off a chain reaction of activity. McGowan phoned Chapman. Chapman contacted the FBI and the State Department. They, in turn, began making overseas calls to

Interpol and the legal attaché at the American embassy in Paris. Plans were set in motion to have people waiting at the Nice airport on Saturday.

If they were lucky, Jodi Packer just might lead them to Joy.

Early Thursday morning Sandlin received yet another call from London. "The car isn't coming in," the Budget vice president reported. "I spoke with our agent at the Nice airport and was told there was some kind of minor accident. It is my understanding that the car was picked up by a wrecker."

Sandlin exhaled heavily and rolled his eyes.

Unaware of the officer's disappointment, the caller continued, "I spoke with our agent at the airport and learned that we replaced the damaged car. As a matter of fact, she told me that the lady who phoned to tell them about her wreck was quite nice."

For a second, Sandlin said nothing. "Did you say *the lady* phoned?"

"Yes, that was my understanding."

Sandlin thanked the caller, quickly replaced the receiver, and clapped his hands together. Speaking aloud to an empty room, he said, "I think we've finally got her."

McGowan wanted badly to speak with the Nice police, to offer a warning about Joy's cunning nature and answer any questions they might have. Legal attaché Allen Ringo, however, quickly nixed the idea. International diplomacy, something the Richardson officer knew little about, would be violated if such direct contact was made. There were, Ringo insisted, channels, rules that had to be followed.

"You got very lucky," he said, trying to soothe his disgruntled caller. "They have assigned a man named Huy Decloedt to the case. He's one of the French police's very best." Ringo, sensing that McGowan's agitation had not waned, then assured him that he would monitor the investigation closely and remain in touch.

"I assure you," Ringo said, "that I'll phone you immediately with any word I receive."

For McGowan, the promise was small consolation. The idea of conducting an investigation by waiting by the telephone, hoping that a stranger with whom he was not even allowed to speak would do his work for him, caused knots to form in his stomach.

In the Richardson Police Department, time began to pass in slow motion. In France, however, things were far different.

On Friday morning, Detective Huy Decloedt woke earlier than usual, dressed quickly in jeans and tennis shoes, and left for the office without breakfast. Long before he arrived at the Nice Police Department, a mazelike compound of bleached-white stucco buildings, a familiar feeling of mounting excitement had begun to build.

He was well into his first pack of Carlton cigarettes before reaching his small office located in the center of the compound.

For Decloedt, a member of the department since 1978, it was always like that when the time neared to apprehend a fugitive. The prospect of making an arrest, of bringing an investigation to its conclusion, was what made the long hours and tedious aspects of the job worthwhile. Outwardly low-key and friendly, he lived for each new chase.

That, sometimes more than the paycheck and job security, made what he did worthwhile; it allowed him to dismiss the fact that he had been shot at on no less than four occasions during his career. The only things that rivaled the rush of arresting a criminal were mountain climbing and playing the guitar, his favorite off-duty activities.

A small man, standing barely five seven, the forty-one-year-old Decloedt hardly looked the part of his reputation as one of France's premier law enforcement officers. Son of a Belgian father and Vietnamese mother, he was an accomplished guitarist, fluent in five languages, dabbled in others, and spoke often of the day he would retire and move with his wife to Hawaii.

On this morning, however, there were no thoughts of mountain climbing or sandy beaches. For two days he had carefully planned the apprehension of an American fugitive residing in a mountainside villa just outside the tiny village of Vence. And now, with the team of fellow officers who would accompany him briefed a final time, there was little to do but watch the clock and wait.

Like most in his profession, Decloedt had often wondered at the logic of a governing body that had seen fit to make it a national law that no arrest could be made between the hours of midnight and nine in the morning unless a person was actually caught in the act of committing a crime.

Initially, he had been surprised when given the case. Assigned to head a team that devoted most of its time to the investigation of terrorist activities, he had other pressing matters cluttering his desk, yet he had been instructed to put them on hold and devote his full time and energies to a case he had only sketchy knowledge of.

When he had asked why it had been assigned to him, he was told simply that the case required someone who spoke English.

An American woman, it was explained, was wanted for involvement in a murder-for-hire in Texas. U.S. investigators, Decloedt was told, had been following the movements of the woman and her male companion by monitoring credit card and banking activities.

In truth, locating the woman had not been difficult at all. After learning that the automobile she had been driving was towed away, Decloedt had simply telephoned the wrecker service used by the rental car firm. In a matter of minutes he was given the address of the woman who had been driving the car.

The only real problem, then, had been to locate the villa, determine that the woman was there, and decide how much manpower would be required when the arrest was made. Alerted to the possibility that she might be armed and was likely to resist arrest, Decloedt had decided to take four officers with him to surround the mountainside residence.

What he and fellow detective Roland Seja encountered as the door opened at 7370 Route de St.-Jeannet was something neither had been prepared for. Dressed in jeans and a loose-fitting sweatshirt, the woman smiled as Decloedt identified himself.

"Is this about my accident?" she asked.

Decloedt avoided a direct answer. "Madame, is your name Joy Davis Aylor?"

The woman continued to smile. "No, I'm Liz Sharp."

"Your husband, is he here?"

"He's away on business. Can you please tell me what this is about?"

Nothing in her manner suggested the slightest hint of fear. Over the years, Decloedt had learned to focus his attention on the eyes of a suspect—which most often signaled a person's hidden fear—but Joy's gave away no secrets, no indication of concern. If, indeed, she was the person the Americans so badly wanted, she had to rank as one of the coolest the detective had ever encountered. And far more beautiful than she had appeared in the photograph provided him by the American authorities.

"You'll need to come to the police station with us," Decloedt said, pulling the arrest warrant from his denim jacket.

Brushing a hand through her short blond hair, Joy shrugged, smiled again, and invited Decloedt and Seja inside. "I just woke up. Would you mind if I shower and change before we go?"

The two detectives stood waiting in the living room of the tiny villa, their eyes searching the surroundings. Outside were a well-tended garden and neatly pruned fruit trees. But inside the mood was dark, almost suffocating—a dramatic contrast to the personality of the woman who had disappeared into the bathroom. Dirty dishes were stacked high in the sink and on the kitchen table. Discarded clothing was strewn over chairs and piled on the floor. In virtually every corner, trash spilled from stained paper sacks. Yellowed newspapers were taped to the windows, blocking what would have been a breathtaking mountain view.

"This place looks like a dungeon," Seja remarked.

As if ignoring the criticism, Decloedt gave voice to a thought that had lingered in his mind from the moment the woman had opened the door: "She has the face of an angel."

In the bathroom, Joy had changed into fresh jeans, a pair of white socks, and tennis shoes. Looking into the mirror, she decided against any makeup and made only a few hurried brush strokes through her hair.

Before returning to the living room, she took a small, shiny object from her purse and carefully slid it into one of her socks. That done, she opened the door and nodded to the officers.

"I'm ready." The smile had disappeared.

As she walked to the waiting police car, flanked by the two detectives, Joy touched Decloedt lightly on the arm. "My name is Elizabeth May Sharp. I have papers."

It was the last thing she said until the forty-five-minute trip into Nice was almost completed. As Decloedt entered the city and drove along the Promenade des Anglais, Joy silently looked out on the emerald-green Mediterranean as they passed fishermen, early-rising sunbathers, and people drinking coffee and reading newspapers at umbrella-covered tables.

"You know," she said in a voice suddenly flat and filled with despair, "I once had a beautiful son. But he was killed in an automobile accident." With that she again fell silent.

In the front seat, neither Decloedt nor Seja were certain if she had been speaking to them or simply making the strange observation for her own benefit. Though they sensed she was crying, neither turned to look.

At the Nice police station, after her fingerprints had been matched with those supplied Decloedt by the FBI, Joy Aylor admitted her true identity. Calmly, she told of traveling to Oklahoma City months earlier and securing a driver's license in Liz Sharp's name, then getting a passport in Houston. She had entered Europe through Frankfurt, Germany, traveled to Zurich, Switzerland, and finally to the French Riviera.

"I just don't understand how you were able to find me," she said, genuinely perplexed. "I thought it was all over. I had begun making a new life for myself."

She told the detective that Jodi Packer was away on business, probably in Morocco or Kuwait. He was, in fact, away a great deal of the time. For all practical purposes, she explained, she had been living alone in Vence for the past several months and had preferred it that way.

Only when Decloedt tried to question her about the Texas crime she was charged with did she become agitated and defensive. "I don't want to go back there ... ever. Will I have to?"

"That," Decloedt replied, "is not my decision."

Ordering that a jail matron search the prisoner and put her in a holding cell, the detective left the interview room to place a call to Paris and alert the legal attaché that the arrest had been made. He was eager to learn more about Joy Davis Aylor, but it would have to wait.

A few hours of sitting alone in a cell, he hoped, might encourage her to speak more freely.

At his home in McKinney, Morris McGowan was pacing the floor, coffee cup in hand, trying to decide whether to wait by the telephone or drive on to the office and risk missing the call he hoped would come.

The agonizing wait ended shortly after eight A.M. when he picked up the phone on its first ring and heard the voice of Richardson PD dispatcher Brenda Moreland: "Boy, have I got good news for you."

Morris didn't even have time to reply.

"They got her. Allen Ringo in Paris wants you to call him immediately."

McGowan replaced the receiver and stood motionless for several seconds, letting the news soak in. Finally, a wide smile broke across his face as he looked across the room at Sandy, waved a victorious fist in the air, and nodded: yes, yes, yes, Joy Aylor was in custody at last.

He dressed quickly for his trip to the police station, anxious to phone France for more details.

Decloedt had spent most of the afternoon at his desk, forcing himself to remain away from the jail where Joy was being held. Several times he reread the information provided him on the woman now in his custody, marveling at the fact the crime she was charged with was eight years old. By now, he thought, word had no doubt reached the United States that she had been captured, and he tried to imagine the reaction.

Late in the afternoon his patience and curiosity finally

reached their limit. Making his way across the compound toward the jail, Decloedt hoped that Joy might now be more willing to talk.

Approaching the cell where she was being held, watched over by a guard, he saw her lying beneath a blanket in a far corner.

"She's been sleeping for some time," the guard said as he inserted a key in the door.

Decloedt stepped into the dimly lit cell and spoke her name. When she did not move, he called her name a second time. When she still failed to respond, he walked to her and gently lifted the blanket from her shoulders.

Suddenly pale, his hands shaking, Decloedt turned to the guard. "Call an ambulance. Immediately."

Joy Aylor, curled in a fetal position, lay in a pool of blood, both wrists cut deeply by a razor blade she had hidden in her sock earlier in the day.

The detective knelt beside her and placed two fingers against her throat. Relieved to detect a pulse, he again yelled out orders for an ambulance.

Joy raised her head slightly then and looked up at the man leaning over her. The sparkle he had seen earlier was gone from her eyes, replaced by a haunting, pleading stare.

In a faint voice that sounded as if it belonged to a child, Joy finally spoke.

"Please let me die."

# EPILOGUE

—

# Justice

Who would bear the whips and scornes of time,
The oppressor's wrong, the proud man's contumely,
The pangs of despised love, the law's delay,
The insolence of office, and the spurns
That patient merit of the unworthy takes,
When he himself might his quietus make
With a bare bodkin?

—*Hamlet*,
Act III, Scene 1, Shakespeare

For several days Joy Aylor remained in a Nice hospital, guarded around the clock as she recuperated from her suicide attempt. U.S. authorities, at first skeptical, thinking that the wrist-slashing was little more than another of her ploys to earn sympathy, soon learned that was not the case. Aylor had severed tendons in both wrists, and had not Decloedt appeared when he did, she might well have bled to death.

Among those not at all surprised at her drastic measures was her former lover Mike Wilson. In jail awaiting sentencing for his cocaine-possession conviction, he warned that Joy, who had repeatedly voiced an extraordinary fear of being imprisoned, would continue to try to take her life unless watched constantly and carefully. "They'd better not even give her a sharp pencil," Mike said.

The arrest immediately gained the attention of the media. The Dallas papers detailed the capture in front-page articles while in France headlines labeled Joy the "Devil Woman of Dallas." The weekly newsmagazine *Paris Match* ran a lengthy story as did several of the country's lurid detective magazines. "America's Most Wanted" rushed a film crew to the French Riviera, and the tabloids were soon having a field day. Movie producers and book publishers quickly began expressing interest in the story.

In the offices of the Richardson Police Department and the Dallas County district attorney, however, the excitement over the arrest was soon tempered by the realization that a maze of legal roadblocks remained. Because of a long-standing extradition treaty between France and the United States, Joy could not be returned to American soil without promises to French authorities that prosecutors would not seek the death penalty.

Through the State Department, the Dallas County DA's office provided written assurance that it would comply with the rules of the extradition treaty. However, despite the fact that France's Prime Minister and Minister of Justice finally signed extradition papers in January of 1993, Aylor's Belgium-based attorney, Jean Bornet, continued to fight an aggressive appellate battle that would lengthen her stay in France to well over two years. Meanwhile, on the Côte d'Azur, a former cellmate of Joy's daily gathered signatures on a petition urging Aylor's release. Rumors reached the U.S. that even the wife of the French president had begun to express sympathy for the imprisoned American fugitive. There came a time, in fact, when speculation ran high that Joy might be released and, perhaps, deported to some other country that shared France's firm stance on extradition and the death penalty.

Then, in the early morning hours of November 4, 1993, Joy was quietly escorted from Marseille's Baumettes prison by U.S. marshals and returned to Dallas.

Ironically, she would travel under one last pseudonym. In an effort to keep her departure secret, the U.S. marshals booked her passage on the Delta Air Lines flight under the name Kelly Carson.

It was a different woman whom Morris McGowan greeted at the Dallas–Fort Worth International airport. The changes he saw went well beyond the forty-four-year-old woman's short auburn hair, beyond the thinner face, the body wirier from months of prison-yard bodybuilding.

"When I looked into her eyes," he said, "there was nothing there."

She appeared to be a woman aware that her last chance for freedom had disappeared. Just weeks earlier, during a brief interview with a reporter from *Paris Match* who asked her feelings on the death penalty, she had made a telling observation: "I'm already dead," she said.

Then, there was the matter of Jodi Packer. Shortly after Joy's arrest in Vence, he successfully eluded French authorities and returned to the United States. Two weeks later he was arrested by federal marshals at the Cedar Creek Lake house owned by the Davises and charged with passport fraud. At the time of his arrest, Packer had in his possession $13,000 in cash and two open-ended airline tickets, one to Costa Rica and another to Mexico City.

Freed without bail on the passport charge, Packer again fled the country. As authorities searched for him, he was indicted on additional charges of harboring and concealing a fugitive and attempting to cover up numerous financial transactions that netted thousands of dollars for Joy.

Not everyone, however, managed to continue to postpone justice.

Following one of the longest trials in Dallas County history, Andy Hopper was convicted for the murder of Rozanne Gailiunas in March of 1992 and sentenced to death. The stop-and-start jury selection, several times put off in hopes that Joy Aylor might be captured and tried first, lasted over six months. Even before the first potential juror was questioned in June of 1991, Jan Hemphill, the court-appointed lawyer originally assigned to defend Hopper, became a state district judge, and the case was handed off to Dallas attorney Larry Mitchell. Best known as an appellate specialist, Mitchell immediately sought out Peter Lesser, a friend since SMU Law School days, to serve as the first-chair point man. A New York native, the shaggy-haired, bearded Lesser had a reputation as a strong civil rights advocate who made no secret of his disdain for the judicial system in general and police in particular. Outspoken and fiery, sarcastic and fanatically dedicated, he handled the bulk of the case, giving opening and closing statements to the jury and questioning witnesses, while Mitchell stood on alert for reversible error.

A tedious proceeding resulted in which constant objections forced district judge Pat McDowell to regularly remove the jury from the courtroom while points of law were argued. Irritated jurors eventually established a betting pool on the length of time they would remain in the courtroom each time they were seated. Finally they became so frustrated with the slow progress that they volunteered to work through weekends—a gesture unheard of by the judge or attorneys—in an effort to bring the trial to an end.

# Epilogue

Kevin Chapman, meticulous and low-key, speaking in a soft, self-assured voice, served as a marked contrast to the boom and bluster of his adversary. He left the occasional verbal jousting with the defense lawyers to fellow prosecutors Dan Hagood and Jim Oatman.

In fact, during the trial Lesser and Mitchell also had a running wager. Whoever succeeded in causing a public display of anger by Chapman would buy dinner for the other. After almost six weeks, neither had eaten a free meal.

The prosecution team, most courthouse pundits agreed, was as powerful as the DA's office had to offer. And by the sheer good fortune of Judge McDowell's appointment, Andy Hopper would receive—at no cost to him—as good a defense team as money could have bought.

The defense's case, however, was lost from the moment the judge ruled that the videotaped confession Andy had given the Richardson Police could be viewed by the seven men and five women on the jury.

For all the efforts of the defense attorneys to convince the jury that Andy was a basically good person who, for a brief period of his life, had simply "lost his moral compass," and despite emotional, long-winded attempts to persuade those sitting in judgment that police had blatantly violated the Constitution in coercing a confession from their client, they could not overcome Hopper's cold, almost casual detailing of the crime before the police camera.

And there was other damaging testimony.

Michael Matthews, an inmate to whom Andy had detailed the crime while in jail, spoke of Hopper's lack of emotion or remorse while telling the story. "There was no sign, no hint of regret," Matthews testified. "When Andy talked about it, his eyes were as cold as a fish."

Also introduced into evidence was a letter written from jail to longtime friend Buddy Wright in which Hopper admitted his guilt.

Jurors were also moved by the testimony of twelve-year-old Peter Gailiunas III. Dressed in a suit and tie, he sat on the witness stand and recalled that tragic afternoon eight years earlier. He had, the youngster recalled, wakened from his nap and turned on the living-room television, planning to watch a videotaped movie. Unable to get the tape to play, he had gone to his mother for help. Several members of the jury wiped away tears as he told of attempting to comfort his injured mother by taking her a glass of milk and his teddy bear while waiting for his father to arrive.

Still, of the forty witnesses who took the stand, none affected the verdict so dramatically as did the videotaped words of the man on trial.

Forced to concede that their client had entered Rozanne's home and fired two shots into the back of her head, Lesser and Mitchell had suggested the possibility of a guilty plea in exchange for a life sentence. The prosecution showed no interest in the offer, a gesture that prompted Lesser to refer to the stance as an example of "Kevin Chapman's bloodlust."

Lesser and Mitchell therefore had to focus on protecting their client from death by lethal injection.

Lesser's defense was, to say the least, imaginative. During the trial he hammered at the all-but-dismissed fact that the autopsy report had revealed possible traces of Thorazine in Rozanne Gailiunas's system. With that as his foundation, he outlined a scenario wherein Hopper had, in fact, entered the house and assaulted the victim. But since she was still alive when authorities and medical personnel arrived, Andy Hopper was not responsible for her death. Rather, Dr. Gailiunas had arrived at the Loganwood address later to find his wife seriously wounded and assured her death with a massive injection of Thorazine. To strengthen his case, Lesser put a highly regarded forensic pathologist on the stand to swear that Rozanne might have survived the gunshot wounds and strangulation had not the Thorazine slowed the flow of oxygen to her brain.

The jury didn't buy the story.

Nor did the jurors seem at all impressed when, suddenly in mid-trial, Lesser spent most of one day trying to show that Bill Garland, not Andy, had entered the house and shot Rozanne.

The prosecution countered the Thorazine theory with expert witnesses of its own. While none was certain, the most logical assumption—since the drug had not been prescribed to Rozanne and her husband had never used it in his practice—was that the tests were faulty or had been mixed up with those of another patient. Such occurrences, they noted, were not unusual.

When all was said and done, the jury remained unconvinced that there had, in fact, actually been Thorazine in Rozanne's system.

Dr. Gailiunas, testifying that the drug was not used in his specialty and that he was not even familiar with its characteristics, labeled Lesser's speculations "ridiculous."

Seated in the courtroom, the doctor's mother agreed. "When this trial is over," Kay Gailiunas whispered in her charming old-country accent, "I'm going to tell Mr. Lesser that I wish him a lifetime of hiccups and diarrhea."

The Thorazine issue remains at best a minor mystery, yet no one in the jury box seemed to care. Throughout the trial, their attention remained focused on the fact that Andy Hopper had strangled Rozanne, then fired two point-blank shots into the back of her head.

Lesser's only other hope then shifted to his argument that Hopper had been unfairly denied counsel during his interrogation. Playing a tape of an interview McGowan conducted with Hopper two months prior to his confession, Lesser pointed out that his client had asked for an attorney no less than sixteen times and was routinely ignored on each occasion. What, he asked the jurors, was to keep the authorities, hell-bent on convicting Hopper, from refusing him counsel prior to his confession as well?

"What McGowan did," Lesser would later insist during his closing argument, "was more criminal than the crime itself."

While some on the jury shared Lesser's concerns, they were clearly not strong enough to affect the verdict. Observed one of the jurors later, "Even if the confession was improperly obtained—which we don't know for a fact—what Hopper told them was true. The bottom line is that he admitted the crime in great detail. He killed the woman."

In truth, Andy Hopper convicted himself with his graphic confession.

# Epilogue

Pacing in front of the jury box during closing argument, Hagood repeatedly raised a large photograph of the once-beautiful Rozanne Gailiunas, her black hair shining, a smile on her face. "Andy Hopper is as dangerous a human being as you are ever going to see. He had the capacity to take this . . . and turn it into this." With that the prosecutor raised a horrifying autopsy photo, showing the victim, her head shaved, her face grotesquely swollen.

Finally, the wheels of justice had begun to turn.

Buster and Gary Matthews, already serving prison terms in New Mexico for kidnapping and auto theft, were returned to Dallas to face conspiracy-to-commit-capital-murder charges in connection with their attempt on Larry Aylor's life. Following brief trials, both received life sentences. At one critical point during Buster's trial—the playing of a damaging taped phone conversation between him and his brother—the obviously bored defendant actually fell asleep while seated at the defense table.

Though jurors had no difficulty in reaching verdicts in both cases, several did express surprise that Larry Aylor, the intended victim, was not called to the stand in either case.

In February of 1993 Brad Davis pled guilty to aggravated perjury charges, admitting he had lied to the grand jury when he said he had driven Mike Wilson and Joy to a motel on the outskirts of Denver. He was sentenced to five years' probation.

And in October of that same year a motion to reduce Wilson's fifteen-year sentence was granted and he was released from federal prison on the third of December after serving less that four years behind bars.

On May 5, 1994, U.S. Customs Service agents arrested the elusive Jodi Packer as he entered the United States at a border crossing near McAllen, TX. He was carrying with him false indentification and $13,000 in cash.

In the decade that passed following Rozanne Gailunas's murder, other lives had dramatically changed. Immediately after the Hopper trial, Kevin Chapman resigned from the DA's office and moved to Austin to oversee his father's insurance business. Assistant prosecutor Jim Oatman also resigned and ran unsuccessfully for a district judge's position before entering private practice. And Morris McGowan, after twenty-four years of law enforcement service, retired from the Richardson Police Department in January of 1994 to accept a position as a senior investigator for MCI.

In time, however, Chapman and McGowan would return to the case that had consumed so much of their lives, one as a special prosecutor, the other as a key—and suddenly controversial—witness.

On the first Monday in August of 1994, the long-awaited trial of Joy Aylor got underway to the blare of headlines and the glare of Court TV cameras that would broadcast the daily proceedings live. And another surprising twist had been added.

Just days earlier, during the course of last-minute trial preparation, McGowan had informed prosecutors Chapman and Hagood that while still investigating the case, he had entered into a contract with the author of this book and a California-based television production company that later sold a miniseries based on the story to ABC ("Telling Secrets," with Cybill Shepherd as Joy Aylor and Ken Olan in the McGowan role). The author as well as the production company had financially compensated him for his exclusive cooperation.

Upon learning of the contracts, Chapman informed Judge McDowell, who was to preside over the Aylor trial, and the attorneys who had earlier defended Andy Hopper. Lesser and Mitchell immediately insisted that if they had had knowledge of McGowan's financial interest in the case at the time of the Hopper trial they could have used the information to impeach the investigator's highly damaging testimony. They promptly filed a motion with the Texas Court of Criminal Appeals, pointing to the revelation as just cause for a new trial for Andy Hopper.

Aylor's lawyers also seized on the new discovery to argue to Judge McDowell that McGowan's credibility as a witness was seriously tainted and asked that the court dismiss the indictments against Joy or, at least, declare a mistrial.

McDowell made clear his anger at the turn of events but denied the defense's motions. While noting that there was nothing illegal about the actions of the former police officer, the judge said, "I'm not at all pleased with what Mr. McGowan did as far as jeopardizing this case as well as the Hopper case. He made his own bed and he's going to have to lie in it as far as cross-examination is concerned.''

In a manner of speaking, then, Morris McGowan also went on trial. Even his testimony that it was his intention to anonymously donate his earnings from the book and miniseries to college funds for Peter Gailiunas III and the children of Steve and Paula Donahue failed to silence many of those critical of his actions.

In time, however, the furor over what defense attorneys repeatedly referred to as McGowan's ''secret book deal'' died away, supplanted by the evidence being methodically put on by the prosecution.

It was Packer, dressed in a white jail-issued jumpsuit, who dealt the first major blow. For most of a day, Aylor's attorneys argued that Joy and Jodi had long been common-law husband and wife, citing a provision in the law that statements made in confidence to a spouse cannot be used in evidence against a defendant. With the jury dismissed from the courtroom, Joy briefly took the stand to lend to the argument. Drawn and weary-looking, her ankles shackled, she insisted she had considered herself Packer's wife since the time she'd divorced Larry Aylor.

Doug Mulder read from several letters Jodi had written to Joy after her arrest in France. In one, he wrote: ''You are my friend, lover, wife and always will be.'' It was signed, ''Your loving husband.''

Packer, who had agreed to testify in hopes of leniency on the federal charges against him, said that he had written only ''what she wanted to hear.'' At no time, he said, had they ever shared a joint bank account or filed tax returns as a married couple. He had never considered himself to be the husband of the woman on trial.

The judge ruled that his testimony should be allowed. And in doing so, virtually assured the prosecution's victory.

''She told me she wanted Rozanne Gailiunas eliminated, out of the picture,'' Packer told the jury. ''If Rozanne was gone, Larry would have to move back home and put the money back in the accounts.'' Joy, he said, had shown no remorse as she detailed for him her role in Rozanne's death on the night of her initial arrest in 1988.

On several occasions, he said, he tried to persuade Joy to consider the plea bargain her attorney was attempting to arrange but she had adamantly refused. "She said there was no way she would ever go to jail," he recalled. "She mentioned all the money she had and said that with it she could live like a queen for the rest of her life."

As he spoke, Joy stared toward the witness stand expressionless.

During his day-long testimony, Packer outlined his involvement in helping her to gather money for her flight, then described how he and Joy had reunited once she had left Mike Wilson in Canada and traveled to Mexico. He told of helping her to secure a false passport that would provide her a new identity and allow her to travel to Europe in search of a new hiding place.

And, for the first time, longtime followers of the case learned what had happened to much of the money that had so long been unaccounted for.

Under cross-examination from Mulder, Packer admitted withdrawing $200,000 belonging to Aylor from banks in Zurich, Switzerland, and Mexico City after her capture in Vence. He had used the money while on the run following his own arrest. Packer described his high-living lifestyle following Joy's capture: living for a time in Mexico, where he became a regular participant in amateur tennis tournaments, then purchasing a sailboat on which he traveled up the East Coast before selling it in Annapolis, Maryland. Later, after returning to Mexico, he bought an automobile and embarked on a lengthy trip along the U.S. West Coast.

An estimated $100,000 remained in a bank in Mexico City, he said, and he admitted no plan to return it to Aylor. "Quite frankly," he said, "I think that money should be used to pay my legal fees since every problem I have is a result of trying to help Joy Aylor."

In the days that followed, jurors heard audiotapes of the conversations between Joy and Carol Garland at JoJo's and the

Continental Inn and listened as Carl Noska told of Joy contacting him and giving him money that he later turned over to Bill Garland. Brian Kreafle's appearance on the witness stand further detailed the link to the eventual murder.

And McGowan, showing no effects from the controversy that had continued over his book and movie earnings, was poised during the three days he spent on the stand recounting his role in the lengthy investigation and detailing his involvement in the book and miniseries.

The prosecution, then, put on a surprisingly brief but damaging case.

Trial followers anxiously waited the response of the celebrated Mulder. A year earlier he had earned nationwide headlines when he gained an acquittal for client Walker Railey, a former Dallas Methodist minister accused of the attempted strangulation murder of his wife. Now, questions centered on how he might mount a defense for Joy Aylor.

For days, speculation had run high that Mulder would call Joy to the stand, adhering to his long-standing "if you don't talk, you don't walk" philosophy. And, inasmuch as the defense's cross-examination, lacking Mulder's trademark thunder, had done little to discredit the state's case, it seemed likely that witnesses Chapman had opted not to call—particularly Bill and Carol Garland—would finally appear.

Thus it was that a shock ran through the courthouse when Mulder rested his case without calling a single witness. No one was more surprised by the defense's decision than Chapman, who, following a recess, posed a highly unusually request to Judge McDowell. He asked that he be allowed to reopen the state's case.

Throughout the two-week trial, it had been the plan of Chapman, Hagood and Knox Fitzpatrick (who had replaced Oatman on the prosecution team) to use Mike Wilson as a rebuttal witness, calling him only after Mulder had put on his case. Judge McDowell, making clear his displeasure at the idea of further extending the proceedings, ruled in the prosecution's favor.

If the jury had entertained any doubt of Aylor's coldhearted intent, it was swept away by Wilson's dramatic testimony.

Remarried, a new father, and working as an assistant in a Dallas law firm, Wilson recalled his troubled days of cocaine abuse and life on the run with Aylor.

And he detailed conversations about the murder of Rozanne Gailiunas. "She (Joy) said she did not feel bad about what she had done; she had done what she needed to do," he said. "She did say that if she had to do it all over again, she'd do it differently—she'd do it herself."

Guilt, Joy had repeatedly told him, was a "wasted emotion." That a four-year-old child was in the house at the time of the assault, she told him, was "not her responsibility." The child, she said, has simply been in the wrong place at the wrong time.

Thus it ended. Joy Aylor the accomplished user of others, had been betrayed by a sister and two men who had once loved her.

On the morning of August 18, 1994, members of Rozanne's family gathered in the crowded courtroom to hear the jury's decision. Seated directly behind Joy, Paula Donahue leaned toward her husband, buried her face against his chest, and began to cry as the guilty verdict was read.

Judge McDowell then sentenced Joy Aylor to life in prison. She had, just four days earlier, turned forty-five.

In February of 1995, fifty-two-year-old Bill Garland pleaded guilty to his participation in the murder plots and received a thirty-year prison sentence. The cases against Carol Garland, Joe Thomas, and Brian Kreafle have not yet been resolved. They remain free on bond. Noska, whom Joy initially approached about "scaring someone," was not charged with any crime.

Following the Aylor trial, Chapman returned to Austin and the insurance business and fellow prosecutors Hagood and Fitzpatrick resigned from the DA's office to enter private practice. No longer is there anyone involved in the long and demanding investigation and prosecution of the Aylor cases left in the district attorney's office.

McGowan has returned to his work at MCI, and Ken MacKenzie is back at his first love—auto theft investigations—and currently serves as president of the National Association of Vehicle Theft Investigators.

While Larry Mitchell continues work on Hopper's appeal, seeking a new trial for his client, Lesser says he doubts he will ever take another capital-murder case. As 1994 ended, the appellate courts had made no ruling on the motion for a new trial for Hopper.

Dr. Gailiunas rarely speaks of Rozanne's death and its traumatic aftermath. Admitting that the ambitious fires that once drove him are now gone, he has drastically cut back his workload in order to spend more time with his family. In September of 1994, state district judge David Cave awarded Gailiunas and his son a staggering $400 million civil judgment against Joy. Judge Cave ruled that Dr. Gailiunas and Peter should each receive $100 million in actual damages and $100 million each in punitive damages from Joy.

Earlier, Don Kennedy, who had filed suit against Joy for injuries he suffered in the Kaufman County ambush, had been awarded a $20 million judgment. And in yet another civil action, Rozanne's parents received a $35 million judgment.

With the $31.2 million awarded earlier to her ex-husband, the uncontested judgment total against Joy Aylor now stands at $486.2 million. It is unlikely, however, that any of the claimants will ever receive any payment.

Peter Gailiunas III, now fifteen, has developed into an outstanding student and soccer player and aspires to one day be a writer.

The Donahues and Agostinellis, who remain estranged from Dr. Gailiunas, have tried to put the case behind them. Even with Joy Aylor's conviction it is not easy: the Cape Cod cemetery where Rozanne is buried is just off the road they travel on regular visits to each other.

They are, however, not the only family affected by the tragic events of so long ago.

George and JoAnn Hopper, after sitting through every day of their son's trial, returned to Houston following the verdict and immediately began making plans to retire and move to their farm in an isolated section of Tennessee.

# Epilogue

Becky Hopper is enrolled in nursing school and contemplating remarrying.

Becky's friend Wanda Price returned home from work one day to find a strange note from her husband that abruptly ended their marriage. Pointing out only that he was frustrated with his life, Don had deeded the house to her before leaving on a bicycle tour of the United States. For a while Wanda received an occasional card postmarked in towns and cities in the Midwest, but when, after a year, he had not returned, she moved with her daughter to another state.

A month after his daughter's conviction, Henry Davis, long immobilized by his stroke, died at age seventy. Rarely does Frances get out to see the local theatrical productions and musicals she so dearly loves. Those friends who have stayed in touch are careful not to ask about Joy. Elizabeth has moved to another state.

In November of 1994, Jodi Packer was sentenced to serve forty-three months in federal prison and ordered to pay a $110,000 fine. Additionally, the judge ordered that at the end of his prison term the forty-seven-year-old Packer would remain under supervised release for an additional three years.

Larry Aylor continues to live in Virginia, where he works as a homebuilder. Occasionally he returns to Dallas to visit his father and when in town makes time to have coffee with old friend Don Kennedy.

As in any story of this nature, there are always nagging unanswered questions. One puzzle, however, was solved. During the Hopper trial, Richardson Police officer Wayne Dobbs admitted that he was the one whom Larry Aylor had heard yell out to little Peter that October day in 1983, insisting that he "hang up the goddamn phone."